SYSTEMS OF FAMILY
AND
MARITAL PSYCHOTHERAPY

SYSTEMS OF FAMILY
AND
MARITAL PSYCHOTHERAPY

by

A. C. Robin Skynner
M.B., F.R.C. Psych., D.P.M.

BRUNNER/MAZEL, *Publishers* NEW YORK

Third Printing

Library of Congress Cataloging in Publication Data
Skynner, A C Robin
  Systems of family and marital psychotherapy.
  Bibliography: p. 385
  Includes index.
  1. Family psychotherapy. 2. Marital psycho-
therapy. I. Title. [DNLM: 1. Family therapy.
2. Marital therapy. WM430 S627s]
RC488.5.S55   616.8'915   76-2577
ISBN 0-87630-117-0

Published by

BRUNNER/MAZEL, INC.
19 Union Square, New York, N.Y. 10003
Published in England with the title *One Flesh: Separate Persons*.

MANUFACTURED IN THE UNITED STATES OF AMERICA

To my family

Therefore shall a man leave his father and his mother and shall cleave unto his wife: and they shall be one flesh.

Be fruitful, and multiply, and replenish the earth.

The Bible, Genesis

CONTENTS

INTRODUCTION

The institution of the family stands in a peculiarly central, crucial position. It faces inward to the individual, outward toward society, preparing each member to take his place in the wider social group by helping him to internalize its values and traditions as part of himself. From the first cry at birth to the last words at death, the family surrounds us and finds a place for all ages, roles and relationships for both sexes. Our needs for physical, emotional and intellectual exchange, and for nurturance, control, communication and genital sexuality can all exist side by side and find satisfaction in harmonious relationship to one another. It exists to make itself unnecessary, to release its members into the wider community as separate, autonomous beings, only to recreate there images of itself anew. It has enormous creative potential, including that of life itself, and it is not surprising that, when it becomes disordered, it possesses an equal potential for terrible destruction.

Clearly, any increase in our knowledge, skills or techniques which enables us to intervene and effect beneficial change in this crucial area of human existence, whether by remedying pathology or facilitating growth, must hold unusual value for our well-being. In what follows, I hope to show that conjoint intervention in this most central, pivotal region can indeed have effects so profound and rapid, as compared with conventional forms of psychotherapy, that we are evidently harnessing an entirely different dimension in addition to those customarily tapped. Despite the ills and perils that beset our time, the burgeoning of this new field of investigation is perhaps one real ground for considerable optimism. It is as if we have suddenly discovered how to apply a lever to the point of balance of a great boulder, previously moved only with difficulty and against enormous forces that repeatedly undid our efforts and restored the previous equilibrium, as long as our leverage was applied unintelligently.

The literature on family therapy is now extensive, and a recent attempt at a comprehensive bibliography by Glick and Haley (1) listed about 2,000 books and papers. But despite a wealth of publications describing the ideas and techniques of particular schools of thought and groups of researchers there has been no satisfactory introduction to the subject for the beginner who needs both a theoretical overview and practical advice to help him begin work. Joan Stein's concise review (2) and Beels and Ferber's lucid paper (3) both give good outlines of the main theories but are not intended as practical manuals. Bloch's *Techniques of Family Therapy* (4) is, so far, probably the best practical aid to the beginner, but it represents the thought and practice of only a limited selection of the various exponents of family therapy and, even so, is a collection of disparate papers, without attempt at integration.

Moreover, existing contributions tend to focus either on therapy of the family, or on treatment of the marriage and the sexual relationship, rather than bringing together these two aspects of family life and clarifying the relationships between them.

My own involvement in teaching family and marital therapy, at the Institute of Psychiatry and the Maudsley Hospital, at the Institute of Group Analysis and in many other institutions, has made me increasingly aware of the need for an introductory text which would provide a review of the various main theories as well as attempt to relate and integrate them (insofar as this is practicable at present), with sufficient practical guidance and detailed examples to enable professionals to experiment with the method.

The present volume is an attempt to meet this need. For the reasons given, it is inevitably a compromise in relation to several possibilities. First, it was necessary to compromise between a summary of the work of others and a more detailed account of my own, sufficient to enable the reader to understand and apply it; fortunately, this has not presented a problem since my own approach has drawn so heavily on the fruit of others' work that it is natural to describe it in this broader context. Secondly, a compromise has been necessary because of the various levels of psychological understanding to be assumed in the readers, for while the need for a book of this sort is perhaps greatest among younger professionals in the various helping services, nevertheless, many more senior and experienced psychiatrists, social workers, psychoanalysts and psychologists are becoming interested in family and marital work and are seeking an exposition of the main principles, despite their considerable training and expertise in more well-established forms of treatment. Also, clergymen, teachers and marriage-guidance counsellors, whose training in some aspects of psychological principles may have been limited, are becoming increasingly aware of their need for more understanding of the psychological mechanisms underlying the ways in which families and marriages function. These individuals may need a more extensive preparation than psychiatric professionals in the meaning of certain basic concepts.

To try to deal with this difference in background and basic knowledge, I have compromised by writing as simply and clearly as possible, using ordinary language and avoiding jargon (or explaining this clearly when it is inevitable), but without oversimplifying or "writing down." Many of the ideas presented are quite demanding, but experience has shown that students usually welcome a presentation which respects their intelligence by making some demands upon it. Also, Appendix A on sources attempts to summarize some of the main ideas fundamental to psychological and psychodynamic theory for those whose training has not included these. Those with limited training in the principles of psychology and psychotherapy are advised to give this appendix particular interest and attention, either before or after reading the rest of the text; those who already possess extensive knowledge of these fields can leave much of this elementary material aside. In either case, however, I have tried throughout the rest of the book to begin from first principles and the presentations should be understandable without much preparation.

Extensive use of relatively detailed examples of treatment situations has been made. Such material usually has the advantage of revealing "between the lines" much that is not included in the concepts on which the work is explicitly based; if the examples therefore reveal aspects of my individual or family pathology or my personal bias, of which I am imperfectly aware, that is all to the good, and it will help the reader toward a more critical and objective judgment of what I have to say.

The examples have been set in a way that distinguishes them from the rest of the text, permitting readers to skip them if desired. In a busy clinical practice, the letters to referrers were often also used to record in outline form the crucial findings of the interviews, for there would often be no time to write a separate account for the notes. Where this was the case, extracts from such letters are used rather than summarizing the information in different words, largely because there seemed to be a life and vividness about the letters that disappeared when they were paraphrased, but also because it may help convey to younger colleagues the value of taking trouble over communications with referring colleagues and of bringing them in this way into the therapeutic interaction. Such care over correspondence does more than anything else to gain the cooperation of referring professionals and to ensure an effective referral procedure whereby the person requesting the interview not only ensures that the whole family understand the need to attend as a group, but also comes to know what information may be valuable in the referral letter. Needless to say, facts which might identify individuals or families have been omitted or disguised, and names have been changed.

In Chapter 1 some of the fundamental concepts of general systems theory are presented, with sufficient illustrations to make them readily understandable in terms of everyday experience. Since there is much more one would have liked to include regarding these new ideas, suggestions are given in the notes about further reading.

Chapters 2 and 3 attempt to outline in workable form a composite, simplified developmental scheme bringing together common elements in the ideas of several authors who have interested themselves in such developmental patterns. In bringing together these elements I have sought to discern similar sequences encountered in the development both of individuals and of groups.

Chapter 4 brings together "object relations theory" and other psychoanalytic constructs about the inner world with role-playing theories from sociology and modeling concepts from behavior modification techniques, using the idea of the "model"—a word which can be applied both to events in the outer world which are copied and the copies formed in the inner world through their influence—as a central, linking concept. Chapter 5 extends this to include the "unconscious"—the parts of the psyche for which the model provides no accepted pattern of expression, and which must therefore find outlets in other, usually deviant and disturbing ways. The importance of the nonverbal communication system as a channel of communication concerned with the control and restriction of some aspects of behavior, which if suppressed sufficiently strongly become "unconscious," and also as a channel permitting hidden expression of these suppressed and unconscious feelings, is also stressed.

Chapters 6 and 7 apply some of the simple principles already put forward to the institution of marriage, extending at the same time the concept of "model" from the example and influence provided by a *person* to that afforded by a *relationship* between persons, and exploring the complications and potentialities provided by the fact that the cooperation of two individuals is essential to reproduction and important for the rearing of the young. Chapter 8 examines existing knowledge in order to link marital patterns and pathology with family problems and developmental arrest in children.

Chapter 9 extends the principles already put forward from marriage and the family to the wider social network, and seeks to clarify the meaning of pathology and of motivation in this wider context as well as to examine the ideas of Laing, Szasz, and other critics who view conventional psychiatry as a form of social control.

Chapters 10 and 11 begin the second part of the book, which is concerned more with application than theory, though the two are in fact presented side by side throughout to some extent. An outline of the different schools of family therapy is followed by more detailed explanations and illustrations of my own technique, as well as practical guidance regarding interviews in the clinic, home visits and other topics frequently raised by beginners. Chapter 12 sets out principles of selection and the variations of technique required with special personalities or pathologies, particular attention being given to deprived and disadvantaged families which are of such concern to social service departments and other branches of the helping services which are open to all. Chapter 13 deals with couples' groups and multifamily therapy, two situations where the principles of natural and of artificially constituted groups operate simultaneously; they are therefore used to elucidate concepts of "small-group" theory.

The development of conjoint therapy has had profound effects on the roles and relationships of the practitioners themselves—indeed, it is the change that the practice of family therapy has brought about in the professional's self-image and mode of functioning which constitutes its revolutionary influence—so that the implications of co-therapy and of the greater frankness and mutual criticism and control common in professional teams receive special attention in Chapter 14. After a survey of the (unfortunately) still limited information regarding the results of these new techniques, and a consideration of the optimum frequency of meetings (Chapter 15), an example is given of the research application of the family approach to one type of problem (Chapter 16). Finally, in Chapter 17, a treatment case is presented in some detail. Besides showing the development of family interaction from one session to another and outlining the pattern over the whole sequence, it is hoped that this example of a longer treatment, together with the long-term work demonstrated in the account of the couples' groups, will help to compensate for the emphasis in other illustrations on very short-term work, an emphasis made necessary by the interest in brevity and clarity. However, although some psychotherapists accustomed to conventional analytic techniques who have seen the book thought at first that the cases must be atypical, it will be apparent from the chapter describing the results of family therapy that the rapid and dramatic changes noted in several of the illustrations are quite common.

ACKNOWLEDGMENTS

I would like to thank Dr. Ronald Casson, Dr. Michael Crowe, Dr. Lionel Kreeger, Dr. Malcolm Pines and my wife for reading all or part of the manuscript and for their most valuable suggestions to improve it; however, I have not always taken their advice, and responsibility for faults and errors remains wholly my own. I also acknowledge gratefully the help of my wife in the preparation of the chapter on couples' groups, with which we work as co-therapists, and in discussion of the book as a whole. Both she and our children have treated me most generously over spare time that had to be given to this project, rather than shared with them, and their patient forbearance while my function as a family member was thereby impaired is affectionately appreciated; I hope it may be repaid not only directly but also through other families becoming able to share our good fortune through application of the ideas here presented.

I also wish to thank those who cheerfully undertook the wearisome task of typing the manuscript, and rendering other assistance, including Susie Boundy, Pamela Jameson, Pamela Walton and Diana Williams. I am greatly indebted, in addition, to Susan Barrows and Elfreda Powell for their most helpful and constructive editorial criticisms and suggestions. .

For permission to quote from published works, I would like to thank the publishers, authors and others listed below (bibliographical details of all the works cited are included in the chapter notes): Basic Books for *Families of the Slums*, by S. Minuchin *et al.*; Churchill Livingstone for "Neuroendocrinological, Behavioural, and Intellectual Aspects of Sexual Differentiation in Human Development" by Corinne Hutt, in *Gender Differences: Their Ontogeny and Significance*, edited by C. Ounsted and D. C. Taylor; Brunner/Mazel Inc. for chapters by Judith Bardwick and Anne Steinmann in *Women in Therapy*, edited by V. Franks and V. Burtle; Penguin Books for *Males and Females* by Corinne Hutt; Basic Books and Routledge and Kegan Paul for *Marital Tensions* by H. V. Dicks; Tavistock Publications for "Self Reliance and Some Conditions that Promote It" by John Bowlby, in *Support, Innovation, and Autonomy*, edited by R. Gosling; Wildwood House for the poem from the *Tao Te Ching* by Lao Tsu, translated by Gia-Fu Feng and Jane English; the Editor of the *Journal of Psychosomatic Research* and M. J. Crowe for "Conjoint Marital Therapy: Advice or Interpretation?"; the Editor of *Psychiatry* and J. R. Stabenau *et al.* for "A Comparative Study of Families of Schizophrenics, Delinquents, and Normals"; and, of my own previously published work, the Editor of *Group Process* for "An Experiment in Group Consultation with the Staff of a Comprehensive School," the Editor of the *Journal of Child Psychology and Psychiatry* for "A Group-Analytic Approach to Conjoint Family Therapy," the Editor of *Social Work Today* for "Boundaries" and "The Minimum Sufficient Network," and the Editor of *The British Journal of Medical Psychology* for "School Phobia: A Reappraisal."

Part One
CONCEPTS

1 SYSTEMS, ORDER, HIERARCHY

Something mysteriously formed,
Born before heaven and earth.
In the silence and the void,
Standing alone and unchanging,
Ever present and in motion.
Perhaps it is the mother of ten thousand things.
I do not know its name.
Call it Tao,
For lack of a better word, I call it great.

Being great, it flows.
It flows far away.
Having gone far, it returns.

Therefore, "Tao is great;
Heaven is great;
Earth is great;
The king is also great."
These are the four great powers
*   of the universe,*
And the king is one of them.

Man follows the earth.
Earth follows heaven.
Heaven follows the Tao.
Tao follows what is natural.

Lao Tsu, Tao Te Ching

No man is an Iland intire of itselfe; every man is a
peece of the Continent, a part of the maine.

John Donne, Devotions

A number of basic principles underlie the functioning of natural groups and must be taken into account in order to work with them therapeutically. Much confusion and conflict among schools of psychological thought arise from a failure to formulate such underlying assumptions systematically. Concentration on detail and superficiality, whatever the subject, must always give an impression of diversity and unrelatedness; a deeper examination usually reveals common patterns and relationships invisible to a narrower focus. Further, the broadest perspective, spanning customary divisions between "subjects" and asking simple and seemingly trivial questions to which the answers seem so obvious that they hardly appear worth examining, often uncovers an increasing simplicity and elegance in the fundamental principles from whose combination the detailed diversity and complexity stem.

This viewpoint probably corresponds with the nature of the universe itself—that at all levels its diversity and complexity are the product of the interaction of a few simple laws—but such a view is not fully demonstrable by scientific means and it is in no way necessary to accept it to use the therapeutic techniques described here. For those who prefer a more pragmatic and positivistic approach these principles can be regarded merely as convenient abstractions, concepts that allow us to order and classify our experience so as to grasp and examine it more readily.

As will be seen, these ideas are so closely interrelated that they could be presented in any order; they all say something about the order and structure of the universe and the living systems it contains, but viewed from different perspectives, much as the plan, elevation and section of architectural drawings provide complementary information about a three-dimensional building.

SAMENESS AND DIFFERENCE

The universe as we know it is neither completely homogeneous nor totally discrepant, but composed of *parts* (or regions showing different characteristics) we can discriminate, between which relationships of various kinds can be observed. In other words it has a *structure*; the parts can be ordered in various ways. The relationships between the parts are not static, but change at varying rates, more rapidly in the combustion of a fire, less rapidly in the movement of a river, slower still in the erosion of a cliff by the sea. The universe not only has structure, but seen over time is a *process*, a changing structure where the changes also show relationships one to another.

Living systems are processes that maintain a persistent structure over relatively long periods despite rapid exchange of their component parts with the surrounding world—even in bone, for example, the molecules are repeatedly replaced though its form and hardness show little variation. The structure reproduces itself, the form is maintained, the difference between the inside and the outside of the living thing persists, despite the fact that it is the most vulnerable of entities, constantly threatened with destruction. It utilizes energy (or rather order—negative entropy) from its surroundings to maintain its own pattern in the face of the inevitable law of change and decay which surrounds and permeates it, and it does so by repairing and replacing its elements or by replicating its whole pattern faster than the copies can be destroyed.

At the limits of the living thing, dividing it from the surrounding world, is the *boundary*. This boundary permits, or ensures, that certain materials pass across it, entering the organism from outside or passing from it out into the surroundings, while restricting or preventing the exchange of other elements.

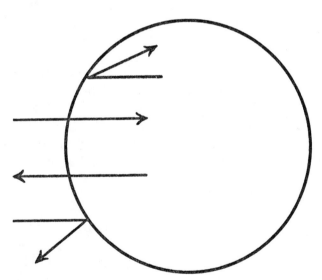

FIGURE 1.1   The semi-permeable boundary of living systems

Failure of the boundary to restrict exchange across it leads to a loss of difference between the living thing and its surroundings, of its separate identity; instead, there develops an identity of inside and outside, one meaning of death. Too impermeable a boundary, preventing any exchange, brings another form of death, the fixed and stained tissue we see beneath the microscope.

On the psychological level, the formation and preservation of individual identity similarly requires effective boundaries or defenses, ensuring sufficient communication to transmit information adequately from one generation to another, while at the same time permitting each individual to select some influences and reject others and to retain some information within a private sphere not open to the inspection of his neighbors. Differences as well as similarities in psychic function are thus assured.

On the psychological as on the physical level, living systems are made up of parts which are themselves systems on a smaller scale (*subsystems*, in systems theory language) and are related to other systems in still larger organizations (*supra-systems*) (1). Each level has its own boundary, across which the passage of information is restricted relative to that occurring beyond the boundary region, whether inside or outside.

Similarly, boundaries exist on different levels, dividing greater psychological systems from lesser ones within them, like a series of Chinese boxes. At the very least, we can recognize a boundary within the individual, separating those aspects of his psyche which are unconscious from the contents of his conscious awareness; another between him as an individual and those around him, guarding and maintaining his separate total identity; yet another around the family as a whole, governing its exchange with the wider world and both expressing and maintaining its difference from other families; perhaps a vaguer one bordering the extended family, or in other cultures the tribe; and eventually national boundaries with materials, people and information moving back and forth across the frontier in each direction in a selective way—gold, wanted criminals and atomic secrets being restricted from going out, "pot" and pornography from coming in. Not all systems show this simple arrangement whereby one is included in the other. Schools, professional organizations and international business corporations do not show a simple Chinese box arrangement but overlap in a more complicated way.

The characteristics of the boundaries between successive systems, each included in the other, will show definite relationships. Families containing schizophrenic members, for example, appear to have excessively permeable boundaries between the individuals which comprise them: Murray Bowen (2) speaks of an "undifferentiated family ego mass," while Lidz (3) and Wynne (4) have shown that schizophrenic pathology is associated with lack of clear boundaries between the generations and so anxiety over inadequately controlled incestuous, emotional

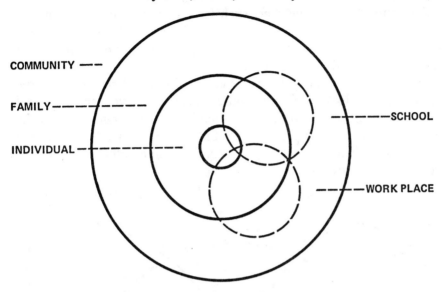

FIGURE 1.2. Systems within systems

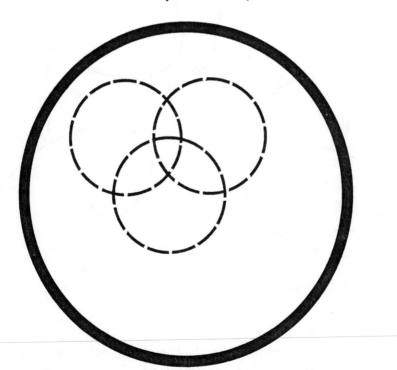

FIGURE 1.3. Diffuse over-involved intra-family relationships together with isolation of family from community

involvements. At the same time, such families appear to possess excessively rigid and impermeable boundaries between the family as a whole and the outside world, preventing the entry of information which might facilitate more healthy functioning.

Other families demonstrate excessively rigid boundaries between the members and a lack of family cohesiveness in relation to the social environment—in one such family the children were required to make appointments with their parents on a bulletin-board, while the parents spent most of their time attending committees and fulfilling important civic responsibilities.

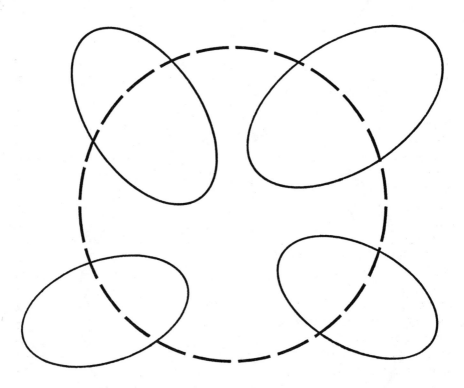

FIGURE 1.4. High involvement of individual members in community, with lack of family cohesion

At this point it may be helpful to look at the boundary characteristics in an actual family, showing how the intrapsychic and interpersonal boundaries may be connected in meaningful ways (5).

Susan, aged twelve, was referred by a pediatrician because of repeated hospitalization for abdominal pain, for which no physical cause had been found. When this case was first seen in the conventional way for diagnosis, history-taking from Susan and her mother revealed a pattern of response to distress with abdominal pain in both parents, together with a recent stress in the form of great anxiety over an elder sister who had left home and become increasingly promiscuous and finally addicted to drugs. This sister was making her living, at the time Susan was seen, as a "hostess" in a night club. The sister's place in the family's dynamics was perhaps summarized very clearly by the fact that she had apparently spoken of wanting to leave this form of life and come to live near her family again, but she had expressed fear of doing so in case she upset them once more by her "bad tempers."

A family session was subsequently arranged for the parents and both daughters, and it was no doubt significant that the sister was once again excluded because the parents "forgot" to ask her to come. Nevertheless, this family session outlined the family problems very clearly, through their behavior rather than through what was said.

Susan said, on inquiry, that her pain had been much the same. After a brief discussion of this, the mother suddenly said that father suffered pains similar to Susan's, adding that he suffered acute indigestion for two or three weeks at a time, after which the pain would cease completely for a period. The father denied that this had any significance, claiming that the pain was physical, but the mother countered by saying that it usually began the day after a severe shock, giving as examples the time when a load fell off a truck just in front of father's motorcycle, and another occasion when he had seen one of the children up on a roof and in danger when they were younger.

After this discussion had continued for about ten minutes, the father suddenly said, "Talking about this has brought my pain on." He turned to Susan and added, "What about you?" Susan answered, "Yes, my belly hurts as well." The father then pulled out a packet of indigestion tablets, took two for himself and gave two to Susan, after which they both sat leaning towards each other, their heads close, as if sharing some important experience through their pain and its relief. The mother, who had not been asked whether she felt pain or offered any tablets, sat at the other end of the table looking annoyed and very obviously excluded from this close relationship between father and daughter (which had not emerged at all in the previous history-taking). Further discussion led to the father's saying that any form of unpleasantness led to pain of this kind, such as their worry over the sister's drug addiction or Susan's anxiety over a forthcoming examination.

They went on to emphasize how they never had arguments at home, and were therefore such a happy family that only unpleasantness arising outside the family circle could affect them. Their exclusion and self-exclusion of the sister, who seemed to be containing all the family's aggression and sexuality, appeared increasingly relevant in this context.

We continued to talk about the apparent connection between supression of feeling and development of symptoms. The mother said that she tended to avoid expressing her feelings for fear of upsetting others in the family and giving them pain, though she admitted she felt much better when she could express her emotions freely. The father then went on to describe a recent disagreement with his boss, where he had stood up to him for the first time. No pain had followed on this occasion, he reported, but from past experience he thought it would have followed if he had not answered back.

Figure 1.5 illustrates in a simple way the manner in which the boundaries within the family as a whole mirror that within each individual. Certain elements of the personality, related to aggressiveness and genital sexuality, are dissociated from consciousness in mother, father and Susan. A similar boundary at the family level appears to have occurred between the three individuals and the elder sister, who shows a similar split but with the signs reversed, for she acts out the aggression and sexuality for the whole family but seems to lack the ordinary virtues or ego-strengths of the others.

Because the elder sister was admitted to an addiction-treatment center some considerable distance away, making conjoint therapy impracticable, and also because Susan was adolescent and separate treatment appeared to have a reasonable chance of success, she was invited to join a group of young adolescent girls which she attended for about six months until its termination. As she improved, the mother became increasingly depressed though she expressed pleasure that Susan was beginning to lose her temper and to reject her sometimes. At one point, the mother reported that she had been helped by taking the tonic prescribed for Susan by the general practitioner, an event which perhaps demonstrates that the medicine sometimes gets into the right person, despite all our mistakes! However, Susan's abdominal pains, though reduced in severity and frequency, still continued. A few weeks after the end of the group, she relapsed and spent two weeks out of school, when I saw her for a few individual sessions. It emerged that her relapse followed a visit to her sister's apartment, where it had been obvious to Susan that the sister was once again taking drugs and lying to her. At a session shortly after, she reported several disturbing dreams. In the first, her mother and father were going to disown the sister, who went mad and committed suicide. In previous dreams, she had several times experienced her sister coming home well, and often wept on waking that this was not true. An interpretation of her intense ambivalence toward her sister was for the first time accepted, and she began to face her depressive anxiety instead of denying it. In another dream on the same night, a man in the kitchen,

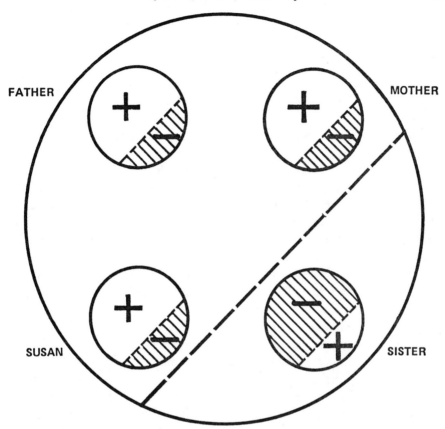

FIGURE 1.5. Isomorphy of individual (intrapersonal) and family (interpersonal) boundaries

who was being scolded by her mother, threw a knife at Susan's lower abdomen, whereupon she woke with her characteristic pain. For the first time she accepted a sexual interpretation, and confirmed that she was preoccupied with sexual thoughts. She said that she could not talk about such matters to her mother, who believed that sex was the evil at the root of all her sister's problems.

Over the next two weeks, Susan accepted her hate as well as her love for her sister and said, "You have to be cruel to be kind sometimes," and, "It has to work itself out the way it will." She began to concentrate on her own life, found a boyfriend, and started to detach herself emotionally from her family. There was no relapse over the two-year follow-up. In this case it was possible to change the intrapersonal boundary of the referred child without altering the family boundary since the child was at an age where she could move increasingly outside the latter. By withdrawing projections into herself she was able to establish a true boundary between herself and the other family members.

CONSCIOUSNESS AND SELF-ACCEPTANCE

The example just given illustrates two principles fundamental to all psychotherapeutic work: first, that nature balances automatically what we do not balance consciously, a condition clearly expressed by Jung in regard to the complementary nature of unconscious and conscious functioning; and second, that aspects of the psyche excluded from conscious awareness operate autonomously, continuing to find expression but doing so in a manner disconnected from, and often harmful to, the personality as a whole. Thus, denied and dissociated parts of the personality, like sexuality and aggression in the family just described, do not cease to exist when they are put "beyond the pale." They simply disappear from view but continue to gain expression in disguised form or appear somewhere else, or in some*one* else, instead. In the individual, or within the family system, such emotions may achieve expression as apparently meaningless symptoms in one or more members, or the emotions denied expression may burst through in one member who acts as a safety-valve for the whole group but has to be expelled from the family system, or to expel himself from it, in order to make this possible. Such dissociated psychic contents are like soldiers who, cut off from their army and isolated from control by headquarters, become marauding bandits seeking only their own satisfaction and neglecting the welfare of their comrades. A constructive solution requires the re-establishing of connections between the part and the whole, as such errant soldiers might again serve a useful function if accepted back and re-integrated under military discipline.

An interesting example of such a situation, at a level intermediate between family and society, occurred during an experiment in which four members of a child guidance unit, representing each discipline (psychiatrist, psychologist, psychiatric social worker and child analyst), visited by invitation a school in an area where children and families showed unusually high levels of social and emotional disturbance (6). The unit met with all the staff who wished to attend, once a month for one hour at lunch time over a period of about two-and-a-half years.

The group was large, rarely less than 30 and up to 60 at times. The meetings were based on a case-discussion approach, it being agreed that the children would not be seen by us so that we would, in fact, have to see them through the eyes of the staff, while they at the same time would share the understanding of members of the unit.

After a presentation of a hopeless case at the first session, already committed to an approved school, the cases discussed showed symptoms indicating increasingly primitive violence related to early emotional deprivation, with corresponding degrees of rejection by the staff based on their anxiety over the underlying infantile conflicts which they clearly recognized unconsciously, but denied through anxiety, leading to vicious circles of increasing rejection by the staff and reactive violence in the children concerned. Increasing understanding, through our discussions, that the overt violence stemmed from feelings of helplessness and unfulfilled longings for parental care led to increased acceptance of these children by the staff, so that their needs for inclusion and affection were met and the symptoms improved. The children came to be, as it were, embraced by the school as a corporate entity and fed emotionally through the real attention they began to receive when the staff's perceptions, previously blocked by anxiety, were freed and enabled to receive the information which had been there all the time.

One good illustration of this was a case considered the most difficult by the school itself, a boy whose uncontrollable screaming aroused panic and rejection in others. As it happened, this lad gave a blood-curdling demonstration, at a critical point in our discussion, outside the door of the library in which we met, whereupon I reported a spontaneous fantasy of wishing to strangle him. This remark led, after some obvious shock that a psychiatrist should express such feelings, to the acknowledgment of similarly violent but previously denied feelings in the staff, enabling everyone to accept such alarming emotions more easily and so also to accept the boy himself.

Other cases discussed were usually not mentioned again for some time, presumably indicating improvement or at least increased staff tolerance, until after some months we would often be told how much improved they were. However, the teachers said they felt this case was beyond them and the headmaster requested firmly that the boy be taken on for treatment at the clinic. The psychiatric unit had no alternative but to agree, but to let him wait for two months. As it was hoped he was no longer a serious problem by that time. My notes of the initial treatment interview state "an open, warm and friendly boy, who agreed he used to get into trouble but said he had improved because 'the teachers are different this term.'" He found it hard to explain the difference but made such comments as, "If I am asked a question and I don't know it, they will tell me now, so the work is easier for me." I have no doubt that the teachers always answered him on a factual basis but perhaps this was his way of describing a needed emotional response he was not given before. A further school report obtained just before the interview confirmed these improvements, and a few months later these were still continuing so that no further action was needed.

The principle indicated here seems applicable at all levels. Society's deviants are characteristically those denied a place within its structure, so that security and the satisfaction of ordinary needs are not available in normal ways, and demands have consequently to be made in ways which are inevitably violent and disruptive to the larger social context. On the level of the individual the emotion which is denied a place produces disruptive symptoms; on a family scale the individual carrying the rejected aspects becomes a scapegoat; on a national scale we see similar consequences in the link between childhood emotional deprivation and crime; and on an international scale the world suffers such consequences as the hijackings and killings of Black September, where the Palestinian refugees, who have no real place either in Israel or in the neighboring Arab countries in which they have taken refuge, seek increasingly desperate and violent solutions.

BOUNDARY MAINTENANCE, HIERARCHY AND CONTROL

In the example of the school just described, how was the staff enabled to tolerate the inclusion within the school group as a whole, and within their own individual psyches, of the primitive emotions these disturbed children represented? To some extent it was due, of course, to increased understanding, and even more to the example of the team. My own reaction of wanting to strangle the screaming boy, and the laughter and relief that followed after the initial shock, provided a good example; by showing I was not alarmed at containing murderous impulses I perhaps gave them permission to acknowledge similar feelings in themselves.

But, in addition, a safe situation had to be provided—a secure boundary whereby the staff could feel protected against acting out the regressive emotions which, emerging into their own consciousness, raised their anxiety and threatened their own self-control. This was well illustrated by the problems that arose in the management of this large group in the early stages:

The first session was well attended by about 30 teachers, and I led it in a rather passive and unstructured way as I might do a small analytic group (at the time of this experiment I had little knowledge of the special dynamics and management requirements of large-group situations). It may therefore have been their feeling that the large-group situation was too chaotic (7) that led the senior staff to alter the arrangements for our second visit, without prior agreement or warning. Only four teachers were present and it was explained to us that these were "the only ones concerned with the case." The meeting was inevitably more formal, and the case itself centered around anxieties about control. A twelve-year-old boy had aroused anxieties in the school staff by his violent rages, particularly as he had, during one episode, injured another child with a milk bottle. This boy lived alone with his grandfather, and in the course of our discussion the lack of a mother figure appeared increasingly relevant. The staff gradually perceived that the boy's rages were related to his deprivation and realized he was calmed by a nurturing, maternal attitude on their part. However, there was a constant demand that the clinic team should relieve the staff's anxiety by taking action or responsibility rather than by the more gradual and uncomfortable process of offering understanding and insight. They asked: Should not the boy be referred to the clinic? Should he not be sent away to a boarding-school? What would happen if he were more accurate with the next milk bottle?! These insistent demands for a practical and immediate solution made real discussion difficult and interfered with the help we could offer with our knowledge.

We emphasized the need to stick to our original plan of working with as many of the school staff as possible, but the third visit brought a crisis. We arrived on time to find the library locked, while the teachers were still eating and paying little attention to our presence in the dining-room from which the library was approached. A teacher finally saw us and fetched the key but the deputy head was five minutes late and made inadequate excuses for his colleagues, who drifted in without apology over the next fifteen minutes. The case presented was of a boy who avoided effort and difficulty and was supported in this by an overprotective mother! She sent notes claiming that he was delicate and asked that he be excused from games and exercises. The staff appeared sympathetic about the inadequacies and fears of both boy and mother and this seemed to inhibit them from acknowledging or accepting the frustration and anger they also felt. They wondered whether they should listen to his excuses. Was he really unfit for physical exercise? They appeared to seek an external authority, in the form of medical sanction, to enable them to apply the firmness that they sensed was necessary without running the risk of damaging him. The clinic team sought to help the staff see that the two needs of the child to which they were responding—to challenge the manipulation and firmly demand effort, while at the same time providing nurturance and support—were not incompatible but were in fact complementary. Throughout the discussion, the difficulty of integrating these two aspects of parental care, perhaps representing a union of paternal and maternal stereotypes, appeared again and again. Exactly as the session was due to end, a second case was raised which took up ten minutes over our time and shortened our own brief lunch period. It was no doubt significant that the problem was one of stealing!

I perceived the significance of this too late and my colleagues were annoyed, I thought, at my allowing the school staff to steal from us. Two of them confirmed this by arriving exactly ten minutes late to the staff conference which followed at the clinic, saying that they had needed extra time to finish their lunch, but they refused to accept any suggestion on my part that their lateness had any connection with their feelings over the events at the school.

This refusal of my colleagues to accept an interpretation of their behavior which was blatantly obvious led me to realize that my management of the situation, at clinic and school, was permitting anxiety to rise to excessively high levels, thereby threatening the project with breakdown and leading individuals to set up their own personal boundaries because those I was providing were inadequate. It was at this point that I became convinced that more structure was needed, for I perceived that the headmaster's authority was in fact passed to us by his sanction during the session, so that I, as leader of our group, must be prepared to take over his role to some extent, as a pilot undertakes responsibility from the captain for guiding the ship into a difficult harbor. Accordingly, I telephoned the headmaster and "carpeted" him for his staff's lateness and the disrespect this implied. At the next session, the reproof had clearly not only been registered but also been passed on down the line. The turn-out was large, everyone was on time, and the previously demoralized atmosphere was replaced by a much keener, more alert and cooperative response. From this point on the discussions went well, and though the difficulties were repeated later in various forms, we appeared to deal with them more adequately.

Such problems of boundary maintenance and control arise in all living systems at any level. The structure of the system has within it certain limits to be maintained, despite the passage of materials, energy or information across its boundary. All such exchange, whether food intake, urine output, news of a death or of winning a lottery, provokes temporary disturbance to the pattern, but homeostatic mechanisms, set in motion by feedback loops, act to restore the equilibrium. Nevertheless, there are limits beyond which the system cannot be disturbed without the change becoming irreversible—prolonged oxygen lack may lead not only to temporary confusion and unconsciousness but to permanent brain damage or even death, and there is a limit to the damage and disruption society can suffer if it is not to fall into chaos and become displaced by another stronger, more integrated social organization. One function of the boundary is to restrict the input of matter/energy/ information to an amount the system can cope with, in order to avoid such irreversible change.

At those times when the living system itself is growing and changing, the boundary characteristics may need to alter in order to provide greater protection against disturbing inputs (or outflows); this is especially necessary at times of greater vulnerability when the organization is particularly loose, or when the system variables are already close to that limit of tolerance beyond which irreversible breakdown of the sustained pattern will occur. There is a need for communication and coordination of information about the state of affairs within the boundary, and of events impinging or likely to impinge on it from outside, in order that the boundary characteristics may be varied appropriately. In the case of psychological systems it is usually arranged that input is reduced (or that external conditions are maintained steady, which is the same thing) when the system is in a particular state of instability and change—when, for example, the reorganization consequent upon a spurt in growth is taking place, or immediately after some previously disturbing upset. The bereaved or the sick traditionally have reduced demands made on them, and are shielded from normal stresses, while the pregnant mother arouses a natural protectiveness for the same reason. In all psychotherapy, where a change in growth is being facilitated, boundary conditions are given particular importance and the time, place, duration and characteristics of the situation are kept as constant as possible, except for those changes which are deliberately planned to facilitate the therapeutic movement.

In the case of the school described above, the time of beginning, the duration, the number of participants and the agreed program were all fluctuating wildly and restoration of some of these constants was necessary in order to provide sufficiently secure boundary conditions for the staff to be able to cope with the inevitable temporary disequilibrium necessary for change to occur, without suffering intolerable anxiety, which was in this case a signal of real danger. Similar principles apply in all therapy or training situations: The need for boundary constancy becomes greater as the instability of the situation increases.

We have already noted that all systems have their existence within larger ones, with a succession of boundaries like concentric or overlapping circles. The functions of these boundaries show relationships to each other, in that an increase in the permeability of one may require, in order to maintain adequate stability, greater impermeability of those interior or exterior to it. It is difficult, for example, for an individual to allow previously unconscious emotions into his awareness while he is exposed to the ordinary demands of life, and this is one reason for the couch, the quiet room, the analyst's silence and the undisturbed analytic hour. An analytic group or therapeutic community also requires some insulation from the wider social system, at least at certain periods, if the persons within it are to be able to let down the normal social barriers and communicate with each other more freely.

Boundary maintenance is a basic responsibility of therapists, caseworkers and all those in the helping services, at least where help means facilitating growth rather than simply performing tasks for those unable to fulfill them personally. The same applies to those responsible for the functioning of businesses and other organizations. For example Rice (8), writing of such organizations, states: "Because the regulation of interaction between the internal and external environments of an enterprise is a major task of leadership, the functions of leadership must be located on the boundary between the enterprise and the external environment," and "the primary task of leadership is to manage the relations between an enterprise and its environment so as to permit optimal performance of the primary task of the enterprise. For an enterprise, the environment consists of its total political, social and economic surroundings; for a part of an enterprise, the environment includes other parts and the whole."

COORDINATION AND CONTROL

The maintenance of the unity of a dynamic system, and persistence of its capacity to perform its characteristic function require not only some restriction across its boundary, but also some provision for ensuring that within the boundary the changes in the parts of the system are coordinated one with another. This maintenance of a certain degree of order despite change requires that some part of the system be concerned with obtaining information about the disposition of other parts, comparing this with information about the system's goals, and where necessary sending back commands correcting the disposition so that certain necessary relationships are preserved.

The part of the system fulfilling this coordinating function is called, in systems theory, the "decider-subsystem" (9). *To perform its function, it must be so constituted that it can overrule any other part and impose its will on the whole, if conflict harmful to the system arises.* The legs of the caterpillar must move in a certain order, must submit to a general pattern of movement, if the whole animal is to move forwards instead of falling over. A group of people who wish to pass through a revolving door have similarly to give up the right to do so in any way they wish, and must agree to go through one at a time— submitting to a certain order in which each has a place—if they are to get through as swiftly as possible with a minimum of trapped fingers.

This is not to say that the brain of a caterpillar is "better" in any absolute sense than the legs, or that the first man through the revolving door, or the man who decides what the order shall be, is necessarily "better" than the others; but in each case an inequality, predominance or hierarchy is necessary if the task is to be accomplished effectively. In living systems, the decider-subsystem itself contains a hierarchy, lower levels making simpler decisions but being overruled by higher levels if conflict at lower levels arises. However, although the function of the decider-subsystem is to overrule some part of the system when it acts in conflict with the general requirements of the whole, the function of deciding may nevertheless be more or less dispersed throughout the system.

SERVING THE WELFARE OF THE WHOLE

It will be readily apparent that, to perform its functions adequately, the decider-subsystem, like the other subsystems, must *serve* the whole. Its function in the organism, and the special characteristics which enable that function to be carried out, both derive in fact from its *capacity to be aware of the whole* in a way that other parts cannot achieve. In living systems other than man, this principle that the decider serves the total system seems generally to be the case. The nervous system of the caterpillar does not arbitrarily impose its will on the legs to their disadvantage, but enables them to perform their function effectively so that they, in turn, serve the organism by moving the animal towards a source of food. The nervous system is dominant because it knows what is good for the legs (the order of movement) in a way that the legs do not know what is good for each other or for the brain. I labor this point, perhaps, but only because the concepts of hierarchy and control are currently out of fashion and are so often viewed as involving the exploitation of one part of the system by another. Man does indeed appear to be so constituted that the individuals to whom decision-making power is delegated often tend to seek their selfish advantage at the expense of the system they are supposed to serve, unless careful safeguards are built in to restrict this tendency. But a decision-making *process*, and so a hierarchical organization of some sort, is inevitable if the individual, the family or society-as-a-whole is to work at all. Whether it is the casting vote of the chairman of a committee, the flip of a coin to decide the kick-off at a football game, or the formation of a line at a bus stop on the basis of first come-first served, some method is necessary to order and coordinate human interaction.

Further, coordination at its most effective is a *mutual* process. If the decisions are to be of maximum benefit to the whole system, then the decider-subsystem must be provided with the fullest information about the whole system, and about details of any conflicts between other subsystems, before any choice is made. Lack of such connection and concern with the whole leads eventually to harmful consequences, not only for the disconnected parts but for the remaining parts as well. A part of the body whose nerve supply is damaged may suffer injury at the expense of the rest, as when we unwittingly bite our cheek after dental anaesthesia; the scapegoated child, as we saw in the family containing the drug-addicted sister, represents a loss to the family of psychic qualities necessary to normal functioning as well as a disturbance in the individual suffering the rejection. For the most effective functioning of any system, authority and power must be related to and dependent upon *responsibility*. The most effective leader *serves* those he leads, a point clearly recognized in the army where the officer does not eat and sleep himself until he has ensured that his men are fed and housed.

In human groups, the individuals who have ultimate control of the passage of materials and information within the system, and across its boundary with the exterior, have control of the system itself. This applies whether those controlling the system are seeking their own selfish advantage or serving the general welfare. Dictators always seize control of the press, radio and TV; they jam foreign broadcasts and censor written material from abroad, forbid public gatherings and set up a network of informers, both to ensure that they receive the maximum information about the system's functioning themselves and to restrict, by intimidation, communications between others. The same principle applies to families. Malfunction will usually be associated with excessive control of communication by one member or subgroup, putting its own selfish advantage above the welfare of the family as a whole. Discussion of certain topics is characteristically discouraged, and contact with people outside the family who might stimulate interest in such topics is also restricted. Further, in disturbed families the control is usually secret, hidden. The scapegoated child does not comprehend the real reason for his rejection; there is no appeal or possible remedy, and restrictions on conversation cannot be challenged and discussed because they are not explicit but conveyed by gesture and posture, by "black looks" and tones of voice. In the healthy family, restrictions and controls on communication and outside contacts are present as well, to be sure, but these are in the open, reasons are given, the decisions are negotiable and punishment for breaking the rules is understandable and leads to reacceptance.

The analogy between totalitarian social systems and constricted families should not be taken too far, of course. Repressive social control is often conscious, deliberate, vicious and evil, while in the families I see professionally this is rare, and the constriction on the family's function is most often unconscious and no more than an automatic consequence of an equivalent split within the psyche of the most powerful member(s) (deliberately malevolent control is perhaps more common in some pathological families least likely to seek psychiatric help). The comparison is apt, however, in that in all cases an attempt to change such a rigid constricting pattern requires the application of some degree of *force*, whether physical or emotional. There is inevitably some form of confrontation or struggle, or at least the taking of a firm hold on the situation, setting up a different hierarchy serving different values. The crucial session at the school certainly involved this; not only was it necessary to insist firmly on accurate time-keeping, regular attendance, and adherence to the contract originally made, but I was also aware of a change in my whole manner in the subsequent sessions—a crisper, more forthright tone of voice, more definite gestures, a firm interruption of irrelevant material, more definite encouragement of information that was being withheld through anxiety, and an altogether tighter grasp of the situation. Family situations often require a similar temporary period in which the therapist takes charge, and frequently show a similarly positive response to firm and forceful intervention where leadership patterns in the family itself are chaotic, divisive or repressive. The following case presents an excellent example (10):

Pam, the referred patient, was a girl of almost 14 at the time of the first family session, and had a history of repeated separations from the mother, beginning at the age of ten months, which had clearly damaged the relationship between them. The original symptoms twelve years earlier included destructiveness and hostility to the mother, together with depression and separation anxiety which took the central place as she grew older, as well as difficulty in spelling. As she entered adolescence, behavior problems, including stealing, truanting and sexual acting-out, gained prominence.

The mother was a vulnerable, unstable person, with several admissions to the hospital for severe depression; during one of these, lasting almost a year, the children had been taken into foster care and had not seen her throughout this time. She felt herself to be intellectually and socially superior to the father, an aggressive, forthright "rough diamond." Just as Pam, the referred patient, had been used all her life as the container of all the family's unacceptable aspects, Sarah, three years older and 17 at the time I first saw her, was the receptacle into whom all the family's good qualities were projected for safe-keeping. Their appearance was in line with this: Pam sullen, bad-tempered, evasive, poorly controlled, sitting clumsily slumped in her chair; Sarah sitting calm, straight, with a clear level gaze, gentle yet naturally commanding respect.

At the first interview, I invited the family to put me in the picture about the current problems. The mother at once expressed intense anxiety about Pam's stealing and truanting, while the father was more concerned about Pam's failure to return home at the proper time at night, clearly fearing sexual misbehavior. Pam hung her head, looked miserable and about to cry, and angrily refused to contribute. The elder sister, Sarah, opened up the conversation several times: first by saying that father was too strict; then that Pam lost all her friends by being too possessive; and later that she felt Pam was jealous of her and that this was partly caused by the unfair treatment of the parents, who praised her (Sarah) and blamed Pam.

Most of the early part of the session was nevertheless devoted to Pam and her difficult behavior, and attempts to clarify this led us to focus on the way Pam always felt herself to be deprived and left out. Here it was possible to confront Pam with the fact that she was in fact depriving herself by the way she was refusing to participate in the interview, despite our attempts to include her.

The conversation then moved on to criticism by the children, and later mother, of father for being rigid and restrictive, particularly in his refusal to allow his daughters to have boyfriends. This was then partly explained by the way he expressed unhappiness at losing his former close relationship with Pam as she entered adolescence and made more contacts outside the home. Next, as the girls described their enjoyment at fooling about with father, tickling and teasing him, the first criticism of mother, until then carefully avoided, began to appear as they complained that she would "moan" and sulk when father and daughters behaved in this way. The mother now became increasingly tense and uncomfortable, as if angry, yet ashamed, and attempted to conceal her annoyance. The rest of the family, suddenly realizing this, became silent and behaved as if paralyzed. I pointed this out, and the mother encouraged them to speak freely, but they clearly felt she could not tolerate criticism. I tried to bring the situation more into the open, pointing out how mother had seemed to opt out of a rivalry situation with the two daughters. Father's next statement, that he treated wife and daughters "just the same," did nothing to improve matters and I questioned whether this was appropriate!

At this point the interview suddenly turned into a discussion of a marital problem, the mother complaining that father was unsympathetic and did not try to understand her disability, the father countering by saying the mother spent all her time talking to doctors and social workers instead of asking for help from him.

One of the functions Pam served in the family was clearly demonstrated when on several occasions they escaped from the marital conflict by uniting to attack Pam again, but this ceased and the marital conflict resumed each time I pointed out this defense. When it was time to stop, the father and daughters appeared involved and interested, and keenly accepted the offer of a further joint interview, but the mother appeared angry and upset that I was proposing no special treatment for Pam.

Because of the mother's history and her agitation at the end of the first session, she was offered appointments as she needed them with the psychiatric social worker who had been treating her for some years (later the mother gradually gave these up). Seen individually in this way a week later, the mother was still angry that I was "not going to do anything for Pam." I had been "casual," had not seemed worried about the extent of her anxiety. She had felt "utterly defeated." Yet she admitted she was pleased, nevertheless, that the focus had not been on Pam, and she was preoccupied with my remark that she (mother) had appeared not to be emotionally involved in the discussion, despite her attempts to appear so. Pam, it seemed, had left the interview "on top of the world" and had stayed home for two evenings after it.

The interval between the first and second interviews, due to pressure on evening appointments, was two months and this was too long. Nevertheless, the pattern had changed and even though the parents began by accusing and blaming Pam as if nothing had altered, Pam was, in fact, strikingly more open, cooperative and appreciative. She participated more helpfully in the interview and this greater responsiveness contrasted sharply with the rejecting behavior of the parents, who seemed to refuse to see the improvement demonstrated before them; I felt angered by the way they seemed determined to destroy any progress we made. Sarah hesitantly supported Pam, and the argument gradually developed from a focus on Pam's behavior to the familiar quarrel of adolescence with adulthood, especially over symbols of sexual freedom, an important change in the family structuring.

The third interview was arranged after only a month's interval, a spacing which was subsequently adhered to, and progress was more satisfactory. The session began with the usual attack by the parents on Pam, but the realignment reached at the previous session had persisted and the girls were now united in criticism of both parents, while the parental coalition, though partly defensive against the marital conflict, was also more secure and healthy as compared with the previous pairing of each parent with one of the children. Indeed, it was Sarah, the "good" one, who this time received the main attack from father. Nevertheless, movement was blocked by the parents' refusal to acknowledge any share in the difficulty and every approach to understanding would be negated by subtly destructive maneuvers.

At some point in the interview I realized that I was failing to deal with this straightforwardly in response to my fear that to pursue the truth might risk the mother's sanity, and decided that the danger must be risked and, if necessary, coped with. I then confronted the parents with what I saw as their failure to involve themselves honestly in the transactions, and, as if released by my more active control of the situation, the parents at once began to speak of their feelings of failure and inadequacy. This led, in turn, to a sharing of feelings of concern and responsibility by the children, and painful recollections of the early separations and the mother's illnesses appeared.

At the fourth interview, a dramatic change was evident in the entire family, dating from the previous session. Both parents were now showing warmth and almost weeping with relief as if they had passed through a depression too deep to risk acknowledging at the time of its greatest intensity. The children both expressed very positive feelings in return and, since the previous interview, all the initial complaints had been in abeyance. Pam was cooperative and helpful, and they were getting on well.

In the rest of this fourth session we focused on the family problem of envy which, by making the parents deny their contribution to the solution of the problem, led them to feel they had no persisting control of the situation and so to fear a relapse. The fifth session, to which father was obliged to come late, revealed the parents' diffuse ego boundaries and the mutual projection which constantly occurred between them; this was an object lesson in the dangers of treating one parent alone. Also, at this session the mother's need to keep Pam ill, or to keep her own illness in Pam, was pointed out by Sarah in relation to the intense separation fears of mother and, indeed, of both parents.

The sixth session was the last of the treatment series (though follow-ups continued for two years) and all improvements persisted in general although Pam became a problem for a time again in school when mother was admitted to the hospital for a hysterectomy early in the year. Pam had a good report from school later, had been helpful and friendly about the house, and had become a comfort and support to mother, who almost wept at the warmth of Pam's response and now seemed able to reveal and let the children satisfy her own needs in a way she had not been able to do before.

The original paper contains a verbatim transcript of the crucial (third) session in which a clear boundary was finally established and the parents ceased scapegoating the referred patient.

I would like to emphasize once again that authority and control, as described here, are to be regarded simply as tools providing sufficient order and coordination in a system to enable its task to be accomplished. I do not wish to suggest that authority has any value in itself, for if it is there to serve the total process this can never be the case. Indeed, there seems little doubt that the most happy, productive and creative organizations are those in which deciding functions are dispersed widely throughout the system; or, to put it another way, where *responsibility* for the welfare of the group is most fully shared and accepted by all its members. The degree of formal organization required to maintain the necessary level of communication will of course depend on many factors, including the size of the organization.

Though the development of the commune is seen by many today as a possible substitute for the conventional family, the study by Speck and his colleagues (11) indicates that the rapid disintegration of most communes, within a few months of their formation, is due to a lack of such differentiation and structure in the service of maintaining the organization, although a hierarchy of *privilege* was found often enough. Some politically oriented communes, with the external discipline provided by a common goal, survived longer.

2 DEVELOPMENTAL SEQUENCES: CONCEPTS

To every thing there is a season, and a time to every purpose under heaven.

The Bible, Ecclesiastes

And one man in his time plays many parts His acts being seven ages. At first the infant...

Shakespeare, As You Like It

We are all born mad. Some remain so.

Samuel Beckett, Waiting for Godot

Not only is the universe a constantly changing process which maintains, nevertheless, certain enduring relationships between its elements, but the changes are also in their nature *cyclic*, repetitive in varying degree. This principle is inherent in religious ideas even on the scale of cosmic events, but if this is true it is certainly as yet unknown to science. On smaller scales, cyclic, repetitive patterns are obvious enough, and no more so than in the case of living organisms which retain their patterns of organization over time. This "life" comprises a developing sequence of events, an unfolding of a pattern characteristic of the species, yet also individual and unique, which is ended, if not by some earlier disruptive event from the environment, by a progressive disintegration of the pattern partly programmed, like the rest of the sequence, from the beginning. All individuals die, but a part or parts of them survive to repeat the pattern again from the beginning, maintaining a form characteristic of their species or group at least over long periods compared with the duration of its individual members.

This pattern is to a large degree predetermined, programmed into the genetic template or charter, embodied in the structure of the DNA of the chromosomes, but its fulfillment requires a sequence of inputs of matter/energy and information from the surroundings, both physical and social. On a psychological level, psychiatry has become increasingly concerned about defects arising from failure of the environment to meet these needs (1). Inadequate protein in the early months, for example, leads to a failure of development of brain cells that can never be made up, however adequate subsequent nourishment may be. Spitz, Goldfarb, Bowlby, the Robertsons, Mahler, Harlow, and others (2) have demonstrated how lack of opportunity for a rich one-to-one relationship with a mothering figure in infancy impairs the capacity for subsequent relationships. Many other studies have demonstrated the intellectual deficit produced by lack of sensory stimulation and opportunity to move and play, or of possibilities for communication, at the time when the foundations of the child's capacity to perceive and conceive the world are being laid down. In his review of 25 years of child psychiatry, Eisenberg has demonstrated an increasing recognition of the importance of such phase-specific provision, if growth is to be facilitated and defects minimized; this contrasts with the earlier emphasis on treatment that seeks, inevitably often unsuccessfully, to repair damaged individuals through substitute caretaking figures who attempt to provide what was missing originally.

In work with families, we need to be aware of this developmental sequence and alert to those needs of the child that the parents and the social environment may be failing to meet altogether, or may in other cases be seeking to meet at an inappropriate time. Pressure for self-control and conformity before the genetic pattern has unfolded to a point where this is appropriate, or encouragement of self-indulgence at an age where self-control should be developing, can be as harmful as failure of the parents to respond at all. Probably no response is wrong in itself and perhaps every experience can be potentially harmful or helpful, depending upon the time at which it occurs. One child, for example, was almost destroyed by an admission to the hospital without his mother at the age of ten months, and thought to be autistic when first seen for psychiatric examination at the age of three. He was subsequently helped more than anything else by a well-handled admission for another physical complaint at the age of six, during which warm and well-organized interaction with the nurses provided the crucial stimulation his depressed and apathetic mother had never been able to give.

A THREE-STAGE DEVELOPMENTAL MODEL

Much information is available about the sequences of events in child development, a great deal of it unintegrated and of variable relevance to therapy. A generally useful classification is based on a combination of Freudian and Kleinian developmental concepts, modified in the light of elaborations by other individual-centered therapists such as H. S. Sullivan and E. Erikson, and also by researchers in group dynamics and development, including Bion, Bennis, Schutz and Durkin. Followers of any one of these schools of thought may feel, justifiably, that I have done some violence to the ideas of their mentors, particularly perhaps the Kleinians whose "positions" are regarded as very different from the Freudian "stages" or "phases." I readily acknowledge such criticisms, but have sought a common pattern underlying these various theories, all of which, if they contain some truth (as they all undoubtedly do), must eventually be reconcilable. There can be only one reality, even though there may be innumerable perspectives of it or abstractions from it.

As Table 2.1 shows, many contributors have arrived at a basic three-

TABLE 2.1
Developmental Stages as Proposed by Different Authors

Level	1	2	3
Freud	Oral	Anal	Genital (Oedipal)
Erikson	Oral/Sensory	Muscular/Anal	Locomotor/Genital
Bion	Dependency	Fight/Flight	Pairing
Bennis	Submissiveness	Independence/ Rebellion	Interdependence/ Intimacy
Schutz	Inclusion	Control	Affection
Foulkes & Anthony	— Leader-centered —		Group-centered
Challenge in group terms	Mother	Father	Couple

stage model of the developmental sequence, whether they are describing the growth of children or the successive stages of groups of various kinds (3). Though the frames of reference are different, so that the various concepts are not interchangeable or commensurate, one can see at once that these theorists seem to be describing the same pattern from different points of view.

In order to present the concepts outlined above in a coherent concise way, the examples illustrating them will be deferred until the presentation is complete and then given together in the following chapter.

The First or Oral-Dependent Stage

In the first year the infant is predominantly passive, receptive, dependent. Its main task is the taking in of food (matter/energy) for the growth of its body and of sense impressions (information) with which it constructs an inner world, mirroring in ever greater degree the real world outside. As yet it has little capacity for independent action, and it must rely totally upon the adult for all its needs.

The developmental task at this stage is, in Erikson's terms, the development of trust, the capacity to recognize the care-giving figure, to accept the nurture provided and, as we shall see when we amplify this stage along Kleinian lines, to begin to feel concern and care in return. On the part of the care-giving figure, essentially the mother at this point, reliable, consistent presence and succor are the main requirements, so that the infant can internalize steadily the physical and psychic nourishment she provides.

In groups we see a tendency to recapitulate this type of relationship in the initial stages with attitudes of passivity, dependency, idealization of the leader. This uncritical acceptance is combined, of course (since the individuals are in fact not infants but the products of later developmental stages too), with defenses against these tendencies, expressed particularly by members who had particular difficulties with this stage originally and so have reason to fear the dependent, passive position. Bion speaks of dependency, an expectation that solutions will be found by reliance on the leader; Schutz speaks of inclusion, a willingness to be absorbed as part of the larger organization. Bennis' submissiveness clearly describes a similar relationship.

The Second or Anal-Resistant Stage

The second stage, extending in the normal infant from about fifteen months to three years or later, is made possible through the increasing maturation of neural connections linking the brain and musculature, permitting the child to become more active in relation to its surroundings, to act as well as to be acted upon. Though the outward expression of choice was already present in rudimentary form in the ability to take or refuse food, to bite or to suck, the child now begins to walk and so to run away as well as to come when called; to talk and so to say "No" as well as "Yes"; to achieve control over its sphincters and so to release its excreta deliberately at the wrong time or place as well as in the manner demanded by the parents.

This is the reason, as Freud demonstrated, for the curious importance of attitudes centering around the excretory functions—though not, as was earlier thought, because toilet training itself determines social attitudes, but because this function is a battle-ground on which the first conflicts between social demands and desires for personal gratification are inevitably fought, and in which parental attitudes inevitably reflect their general view of the proper balance between self-will and conformity. This stage is characterized more by activity than passivity, by emphasis on movement rather than sensation, by a release of energy outwards rather than a taking-in. Tempers, stubbornness, resistance and rebellion are normal and desirable and their absence is a cause for concern, often indicating that energy and drive needed later for initiative and independent functioning have become blocked.

From the parent, the child at this stage needs clear and definite limits, both adequately wide (to allow him to experiment and learn how to control these new powers) and sufficiently firm (to provide a safe container within which the new energies can be released without too much fear). If these are provided, in a degree graduated to the child's developing confidence and self-control, a satisfactory compromise is reached whereby the child becomes socialized enough to consider others and fit into the social group of the family (and later the school and work situation) while retaining a sufficient sense of independence, difference and autonomy to allow him both to enjoy himself and to be interesting to others. Excessively strict control, providing rigid and narrow limits, leads at best to a timid, conforming personality, unable to take risks or use his potentialities fully, at worst, if the control is really persecuting, to a reversal and rebellion against all social constraints, leading to delinquency and other antisocial behavior. Control which is too permissive or inconsistent paradoxically can have similar harmful effects, leading either to a self-centered, uncompromising attitude which makes the individual unable to cope with the give-and-take required in a social group, or to fearful, obsessional restrictions of activity because the early environment did not feel safe enough for experiment and exploration. In this case, a rigid, primitive form of self-control is developed by the child himself because of the lack of opportunity to internalize something more flexible, mature and compassionate from the parents.

Students of group development have noted very similar issues arising when the group emerges from its initial dependent stage. Resistance, rebellion and opposition make their appearance, all of which need to be seen as precursors of independent, autonomous functioning, even though they may at first appear entirely negative, based on obstinacy, unconstructive argument, lateness, absence, or failure to pay fees. At this point the group is still leader-centered, the group behavior showing a reaction against the leader's wishes in place of the earlier wish to please him; members are not yet striving towards their own goal in a truly autonomous fashion.

At this stage the leader, like the parent of the toddler, needs to stand his ground without being provoked, to give the group members something to bite on or struggle with, so that they come gradually to work through this phase of opposition and detach themselves from him. The anger and criticism the group members express at this stage are like the rocket fuel which overcomes the gravitational force of the earlier wish to possess the leader, eventually enabling the previously dependent, earthbound members to go into orbit at an appropriate distance.

Just as the first stage shows predominantly oral activity in the infant, and oral associations in the group interaction with much talk of eating, food, the breast, or being absorbed or immersed in maternal images like the sea, so the second stage usually contains more references to anal associations and a good deal of "shitty" behavior (teasing, spitefulness, sadism, dirty tricks, and destructive attacks).

The Third or Genital-Cooperative Stage

The third stage, beginning in the fourth year and lasting until about the age of six, is accompanied by evidence of excitement in the genitals, and emotional arousal with many features similar to that seen in adult sexuality. There is an interest in, and exploration of, bodily sexual differences, as well as curiosity about the origin of babies, and about adult sexual activity, concerning which there appears to be some intuitive awareness. The Oedipus complex makes its appearance at this point (4), whereby the child demonstrates unmistakeable signs of a love affair with the parent of the opposite sex, together with jealousy towards the parent of the same sex who is now perceived as a rival. Confusing its own wishes with the thoughts of those towards whom they are directed, the child fears an equivalent jealousy from the rival, same-sex parent, and corresponding punishment to fit the crime—castration. Bodily differences between the sexes may reinforce this fantasy, the little girl perhaps feeling she once possessed a penis but lost it, the boy that he may suffer the same fate.

The resolution of this conflict occurs, if it is successfully surmounted, by the child deciding, in effect, that if you can't beat them you might as well join them, whereupon the primary allegiance is swung to the parent of the same sex and the opposite-sex parent is both given up in a real sense and still loved and vicariously possessed through identification with the former rival. The boy turns to his father, and through identification with him hopes both to secure the mother's regard and to win a girl of his own, like her, one day. The girl similarly identifies with her mother and both sexes draw apart, showing some hostility to each other, until the fuller emergence of sexual drives in adolescence brings them into relationship again. This stage thus has as one of its consequences the working out of the implications of *sexual* identity (established much earlier), the development of the attitudes, roles, and interests appropriate in the given society to the child's physical form, male or female, and the renunciation of those allocated to the opposite gender. The situation is, however, usually somewhat more complicated, with some residue of wishes to enjoy the advantages of both sexual roles (and so to possess both parents as fully as they do each other), and to some measure a reversed oedipal conflict appropriate to the opposite sex also is present in varying degrees, especially where the parental roles and expectations are confused.

To transcend this challenge the child needs to suffer a clear defeat of his rivalrous hopes, yet at the same time to do so at the hands of a loving and generous victor. The parents' sexual relationship needs to be satisfying and uninhibited, free of guilt or other complications which might make the child feel that he has won the battle either because he is actually preferred to the rival parent, or because the parents' embarrassment makes them limit their pleasure in each other and so prevents the child gaining a clear awareness that he is not sexually preferred. In other words, there must be no doubt left in the child's mind that the most fundamental loyalty and attraction in the family are between the parents and that he is excluded where this is concerned—that his domain stops at their bedroom door. If he can cope with this exclusion and the pain and jealousy it arouses, the stage is set for the next challenge, his need to cope with the jealousies and exclusions of the peer group.

The third stage may be widened helpfully to include the further achievement of peer group membership. Stages one and two are both leader-centered, non-mutual, based, as Foulkes and Anthony (3) have pointed out, on an authoritarian model. With the beginning of stage three we see the origins of sharing, of mutuality, of reciprocity, whether it is the mutual giving and taking of the sexual act or of a group of individuals interacting on the same level.

The child shows this by becoming more helpful, more responsible, more able to share and take part in the family decisions and activities. The group demonstrates the same process by becoming less leader-centered, more responsible for its own management, more able to share and help itself. If, in the first stage, the leader was idealized, and in the second opposed with irrational criticism, in the third there is constructive exchange and discussion where the leader receives something as well, provided he can give up his former pre-eminence and accept a less dominant position in a more democratic arrangement, functioning now more as a resource person with special knowledge and skills whom others will call upon when they wish to do so.

Mother/Father/Couple

I have related the first stage primarily to the mother, the second to the father and the third to the couple. This is not to suggest, of course, that the father should not feed the child, change the diapers or get up to comfort it when it cries in the night; the father who refuses all these functions will lose the possibility of experiences which will enrich him personally and deepen his relationship with the child later. Nor is it desirable that no discipline should come from the mother; both parents need to share this responsibility. As I am using the words here, mothering and fathering refer more to *functions* which are always mediated to *some* degree by both sexes, and often enough, as Rutter (5) has demonstrated in his review of the evidence, by the parent of opposite gender to the usual one, or even by a number of caring figures. The fact that we have no adequate terminology to discriminate those human functions more commonly found in one sex than another from the fact of biological gender itself, but have to use masculine and feminine or mothering and fathering for both function and physical form, is a source of great difficulty and confusion.

Nevertheless, there seems little doubt that the mother has a special capacity to respond empathically to the requirements of the first stage, both constitutionally and because of the special bond formed by the earlier development of the child within her body. At the same time, this special relationship of closeness, trust and comfort makes it difficult for the mother to bear unaided the next task of introducing the demands of a wider social reality, with the inevitable but necessary pain of frustration, delay and separation this brings with it. This is so not only because the child at first may find it difficult to accept and integrate these two functions from the same person, but also because it is difficult for the mother herself to withdraw and accept separation unless the father intrudes to disrupt the original symbiotic relationship, hauling in the life-line and pulling the mother back from her necessary regression to what Winnicott called her "primary maternal preoccupation" (6) as she identifies with her infant during its first year or so. The study of the dynamics of school phobia in Chapter 16 deals with this point more fully.

That the third stage is related to the couple, to a *relationship* rather than to a person, and therefore to a capacity to deal with *triangles* or more complex relationships, needs no stressing.

This process of development has been worked out in great detail, particularly in psychoanalytic theory, but for ordinary purposes it is convenient to sub-divide each of the three stages described once again.

KLEINIAN CONCEPTS REGARDING THE EARLY MONTHS

The first stage often appeared vague and hard to grasp, particularly in American publications, and the events of the first year of life tended to remain, in William James' words, a "booming, buzzing confusion" until they were clarified by the work of Melanie Klein (7) and her followers, who constitute the so-called "British school of psychoanalysis." Of course, this stage is by its very nature confused, chaotic, bewildering, "insane," and any theory must to some extent reflect this character of early experience if it is to be accurate. But Klein provides us with a map with which to orient ourselves if we can accept its inevitable strangeness and "madness." Before going further, I should make it clear that Klein's followers would almost certainly object to my presenting the two Kleinian "positions" as subphases of the Freudian developmental sequence, for they view their concepts as belonging to a different conceptual framework, a different dimension. Nevertheless, what I shall suggest does provide some framework for integrating Freudian and Kleinian ideas sufficiently for beginners to be able to use them, and Klein's clearest expositor, Hanna Segal (8), accepts such a rough correspondence.

The Paranoid/Schizoid Position

Klein's theories center on the notion that the child, in early infancy, normally progresses from one manner of organizing its experience to a strikingly different one. The earliest months—roughly the first three—are characterized by modes of psychic function where the perceptions of the mother or primary care-giving figure are not yet integrated to form the image of a whole person, so that the child is relating to *part* of her—to her breast, hand, face, etc. Even insofar as there is perception of continuity in space, the capacity to integrate experience over time is also limited and the emotional life so fragmented that there is restricted ability to synthesize and balance emotional responses. Hunger is pure pain and rage, unrelieved by a memory or expectation of the pleasure of feeding, which in turn is unmitigated orgiastic bliss. Even when the mother begins to be perceived physically as a whole person, the loved one who feeds and the hated one who deprives and leaves to cry are still two people, angel and devil, or fairy godmother and witch. Moreover, the diffuseness of boundary between self and outside world is such that, to begin with, the two are not discriminated and the child feels he *is* the world, that he is omnipotent or omnipresent. And even when some discrimination begins, it is so permeable or fluctuating that painful experiences are projected out and attributed to the external world, so keeping "bad" qualities outside and enabling the self to be experienced as positive and pleasurable. Thus this stage, called by Klein the "paranoid-schizoid position" (and the fragmentation of schizophrenic functioning to which Klein related it), is characterized by *part-object relationships*, *splitting* and *projection*, together with *confusion* over the boundaries of the self.

The Depressive Position

Provided maternal care is adequate and reliable, this gives way from about three months onwards to the "depressive" position. The maturation of the nervous system brings about an increasing capacity to integrate experience. Perceptions of the mother's presence come together to form a whole, a person, while the mother who feeds and the mother who leaves the infant to cry become connected, are seen as the same. The fairy godmother and witch begin to be fused, together with the hate and love felt towards them, bringing *ambivalence*, the capacity to hold two contradictory attitudes towards the same external object or person in awareness simultaneously.

The pain of recognizing that there is a desire to harm and destroy that which is most loved brings with it as reward what Klein called (perhaps unfortunately) "depressive anxiety" and what Winnicott called the "stage of concern." This is the beginning of a feeling of responsibility, of desire to protect and help, the origin of the urge towards *reparation*. The ego boundaries are also clearer; the pain is no longer projected out and loaded on to others but contained and coped with despite suffering. Thus, the "depressive position" starts to be achieved, characterized by *whole object* instead of part-object relationships, *containment of ambivalence* instead of splitting and projection, and by increasing *differentiation of the self* from its surroundings instead of the former confusion.

The achievement of this position is at first precarious, never final, and until about the age of two at least, and to a lesser extent thereafter, even a well-mothered child is vulnerable to loss or separation, as may occur in bereavement or badly managed hospitalization. The consequent decrease in gratification and love, and increase in rage and pain lead the child to regress to the "paranoid/schizoid" position, splitting off the painful affect and projecting it outside the self again. Or, if the integration is better established, the child may protect itself by *depression*, which, almost the opposite of Klein's "depressive anxiety," turns all ambivalence, love and concern as well as hate, away from the outer world on to the self, manipulating, coercing and exploiting the caring figures by subtle means. Alternatively, the individual may escape the pain of a continued integrated relationship by *manic defense*, a more sophisticated development of the paranoid/schizoid mechanisms characterized by *denial of dependence* and attitudes of *control, triumph* and *contempt* towards the needed supportive figure. Such denials of reality are features of all the more primitive ways of relating, as are *greed* and *envy*, both of which lack concern for the care-giving figure and lead to a ruthless exploitation. The capacity for *gratitude*, like concern, by contrast is another consequence of the achievement of the depressive position.

Passive and Active Rebellion

The anal stage can similarly be divided into two parts: the first passive, characterized more by resistance, stubbornness and a generally constipated attitude; the second more actively rebellious and outgoing. It is often helpful, in the earlier subphase, which, in groups, frequently shows itself in silence, lateness, absence and not being able to think of anything to say, for the therapist to be somewhat provocative, stimulating and giving of permission for more open aggressiveness by manifesting a little of this himself, perhaps in the form of a good-humored challenge or teasing.

The second part of this subphase requires on the part of the parent or therapist a firm standing of ground, without being provoked, so that the new-found assertiveness can be tested out in a situation which feels safe and contained. If the parent or therapist is too passive, permissive, or eager to adapt at this stage, the aggressive and destructive impulses felt towards him are inhibited through fear of going too far and destroying the situation altogether; this may lead to rigid, premature self-control and obsessional or phobic attitudes, with a block in the development of individuality and autonomy. The parent or therapist must hold his position so that others can work out their own identities in relation to him.

Phallic and Genital Subphases

The third, truly sexual phase can be subdivided also. In the earlier part (the beginning of the oedipal conflict) the new interest in genital differences and sensations is focused more upon the organs themselves, which are viewed as proud possessions by those who have them (or have them to observe, as external appendages) and objects of envy to those who do not. The keynote of this stage is competitiveness, not cooperation, and Freud's concept of penis envy, whereby women are supposed to be envious of male superiority in possessing a penis and thereby become castrating females, or Adler's corresponding concept of masculine protest, refers to attitudes developed at this level. In fact, the emphasis on female envy of the male sexual apparatus in early analytic theory seems to be a consequence of the fact that the main leaders in the field of dynamic psychiatry were men, but their female colleagues have since made us aware of the similar envy felt by males for female creativity.

The final genital subphase, beginning with the conclusion of the oedipal conflict and extending (in the simplification I am presenting here) through latency into adolescence and adulthood, includes a gradual integration of sexual feelings and functioning within the whole personality, so that eventually sexual desires and the sexual act come under the natural control of feelings of respect, tenderness, responsibility and loving care. They thereby become included in the wider context of loving relationships where sharing, mutual regard and consideration, and a general capacity for peer relationships are well developed.

The phallic subphase, like the second anal subphase, requires a sense of just and fair control and containment by authority figures if the child is not to fear the destruction of his security that real triumph over his same-sex rival would bring. Fear or embarrassment by the parents over their own sexual relationship will make it difficult for them to provide this benevolent, facilitating sense of control and safety, within which the child can experiment with his new powers. Where this is the case inhibition of sexual expansiveness and of normal competitiveness will result. Fears of success, generally as well as sexually, are a frequent consequence, sometimes overlaid by the compensatory striving one sees in the Don Juan, the femme fatale or other forms of compulsive self-proving.

The second genital subphase requires for its achievement models provided by mutual, reciprocal, complementary relationships, both of a sexual nature (ideally of course by the parents though other models may be found if they are lacking) and in relationships with peers. The first friend is a vital step here, as Sullivan (9) emphasized, leading to all the experimentation with relationships characteristic of adolescence.

Table 2.2 summarizes the developmental model presented here. It

TABLE 2.2
Sub-division of Three-phase Developmental Scheme, to Give Six Subphases

Oral		Anal		Oedipal	
1a	1b	2a	2b	3a	3b
Paranoid/ Schizoid	Depressive	Resistant	Assertive	Phallic	Genital

should, as I have said, be regarded merely as a provisional scheme, a basic structure which can be modified and developed in detail. If the diagram is regarded as representing a series of stages, a sequence in time (which is one way of viewing it), it can of course be extended to cover the whole life of an individual, as Erikson (10) has done. I have kept to the present three-stage model because it seems to offer something else as well, a series of *phases* which can be seen to occur in any process of learning, growth and development, no matter what the age of the individual, and which also applies to the development of groups. The three phases represent a kind of dialectical process—thesis, antithesis and synthesis—which is repeated over and over, the final phase of one sequence becoming the first of the next. This is particularly clear in adolescence, which is in so many ways a recapitulation of the early years, with its renewed strivings to master problems of attachment, autonomy and sexual identity.

CONTINUED AVAILABILITY OF RESPONSE PATTERNS

Progression through the phases described is not irreversible, but neither is it desirable that the patterns of relationship characteristic of any one phase should be left entirely behind. No matter how capable an individual, couple or family may become of mutual, cooperative interaction, there will always be times when they will need to compete, to fight for what they believe in, to stand their ground, to accept dependency, and to trust others to look after them. The need to be totally independent can be as much a weakness as an inability to fight when threatened. Normality, then, is measured not only by the extent to which the individual or family has met the sequence of challenges described, but also by the degree to which these patterns characteristic of each level remain available for use in a flexible manner appropriate to each external situation.

USE OF SOME STAGES AS A DEFENSE AGAINST OTHERS

A further complication needs to be mentioned, for unless it is borne in mind errors will often be made as to the level on which the essential failure has occurred. Frequently, the pattern characteristic of one level is emphasized in response to a fear of inadequacy or danger related to another. Freud's concept of regression emphasizes this adequately when an earlier level is clung to in response to difficulties experienced in coping with a later one, as where aggression is emphasized to avoid sexuality, or excessive dependency protects against conflict. But the reverse pattern occurs also. Compulsively aggressive, challenging behavior often has its origin in fears of tenderness, intimacy and trust, and a surprising proportion of cases of marital conflict can be helped by recognition of this pattern alone, with a focus not on the conflictual issues, which are largely irrelevant, but on helping the partners to express the profound needs for nurturance and fears of disappointment that they are constantly hiding from themselves and each other by their warfare. Similarly, compulsive sexual behavior often defends against fears of conflict or dependency.

RELEVANCE TO FAMILY MALFUNCTIONING

Freud's ideas about *fixation* and *regression* (respectively the failure to progress beyond the attitudes and relationships characteristic of a given stage, or a tendency to return to an earlier stage because of some particular difficulty in coping with a later one) seem to be valuable in relation to families as well as to individuals. Severely disturbed families, including multi-problem families and those producing schizophrenic members, seem unable as a group to progress beyond the use of predominantly paranoid/schizoid mechanisms, so that one sees marked use of scapegoating and other forms of splitting and projection of painful affects. Seen alone, father blames mother and vice-versa. Together they blame one of the children, or with the children present they may project responsibility outside the family altogether and blame the school, the neighbors, blacks (if they are not blacks themselves) or whites (if they are).

Similarly, families may be capable of a fuller relationship but be unable to get beyond a precarious mutual clinging, feeling threatened by any suggestion of separation, disagreement or even of any real individuality. Other families may be more independent but only at the cost of maintaining their independence by constant fighting, manipulation and "shitty" behavior. Some parents are endlessly competitive with one another, each striving for sexual dominance and constantly fearful of being the loser. And, it is hoped, some families can share with each other, showing real cooperation and creativity at least for part of the time. The position of a family on this developmental scale affects profoundly the type of intervention required of the family therapist, as we shall see in the next chapter.

3 DEVELOPMENTAL SEQUENCES: EXAMPLES

All happy families resemble one another,
each unhappy family is unhappy in its own way.

Leo Tolstoy, Anna Karenina

Without contraries there is no progression.

William Blake,
The Marriage of Heaven and Hell

The refined punishments of the spiritual mode are usually
much more indecent and dangerous than a good smack.

D. H. Lawrence, Fantasia of the Unconscious

In order to clarify further the developmental pattern proposed it may be helpful to examine some real families in terms of structure. It will readily be seen that the actual details are, in fact, quite complex. Not only is one stage used to defend against another in which greater difficulties are experienced, but since each stage underpins the following ones defects involving one level have consequences at all later stages too. For example, lack of satisfying care and comfort from the mothering figure at the oral-dependent level may later lead to attempts to gain substitute attention in a masochistic way by provoking care-taking figures and inviting punishment; in addition, the unfulfilled primitive desire for attachment may become fused with genital sexual desires so that sexual intercourse is seen as a fearful engulfment and loss of autonomy, while orgasm is resisted since the loss of control it represents is associated with loss of identity. Nevertheless, the scheme proposed enables one to dissect and understand these complications more easily and so to find appropriate measures to remedy them.

ORAL LEVEL PROBLEMS

Paranoid-schizoid mechanisms are seen most clearly and fully in the functioning of schizophrenic individuals and their families (we shall look at these more closely in Chapter 12), but the *mechanisms* of splitting, of projection, of part-object relationships and of confusion between what is actually inside or outside the personal boundary manifest themselves in varying degrees in any family. In the following example the family was functioning reasonably effectively but borderline psychotic aspects are clearly evident, with an actual schizophrenic disorder in a close relative. Inability to tolerate certain psychic contents—probably powerful emotions of both love and hate, though fear of the latter is more obvious—leads to projection of these outside the individual and family boundaries into external danger, in this case fire.

Stephen, aged nine, was referred with the following note from the pediatrician: "For about three months Stephen has had an overpowering fear of fire—all books and events seem to relate themselves to fire in some way. At school he is withdrawn and feels the other boys are getting at him. Mother's brother is schizophrenic and mother just wondered about Stephen and so do I—we would be grateful for some advice."

During the family interview it emerged that the fear of fire had developed while the boy was helping an electrician to re-wire the house and he learned that overloaded wires could overheat and burst into flames. The psychological significance of this was suggested both by the fact that he was not at all bothered by real fires—he had been unperturbed to see a school on fire shortly before the interview—and by curious questions he would ask his parents: For example, when the mother let herself into the house with a key instead of ringing for his father to answer the door, he had asked her, "Did you use the key because you thought father might have died or that the house had caught fire?"

During the interview these various connections were pointed out and the meaning of the symptom interpreted in terms of fears of emotional "overheating" through intense feelings, especially hostility. His father understood this well, but his mother blocked out such understanding and returned constantly to a literal interpretation of the symptoms in a way which overtly denied but covertly confirmed the interpretation. Father's association to the word fire was "insecurity" while mother said she did not connect anything with it but continued, "Of course, I am always careful of fires, so there is no danger." At one point a marital problem began to emerge, as father said that they always avoided arguments, and that this tended to produce atmospheres instead. Mother again denied that there were any arguments or atmospheres, and went on to say that because her parents fought she liked to avoid arguments because she knew they had a bad effect on children, as in the case of her schizophrenic brother.

During all this Stephen took little part, looking miserably and passively at the mother, but he became lively and cheerful once we pointed out the interest and pleasure he showed at any mention of aggressiveness. His younger brother, aged six, also said little. The focus of the interview was on helping the boy and the father to accept the idea that some measure of hostility and aggression was acceptable, without pushing this so strongly that the mother might be made too anxious. It was considered too threatening to explore the marital situation further, at least at this stage, in view of the mother's brittle defenses.

At the next session six weeks later the whole family was more relaxed. Stephen's fear of fire had faded considerably. ("I haven't thought about it. I can't think what the reason is but I just feel different.") He had become more confident and assertive and enjoyed sparring with his father as soon as he came home from school. ("I've got the bruises to prove it.") The teachers had reported that he was less sensitive and could cope with criticism. Tentative exploration of the marital relationship was again resisted and not pursued, but it was clear that the father had understood well the interpretations of the previous session and had been able to support the boy in accepting his aggressive feelings and to diminish the effects on him of the mother's anxious rigidity. It was clear that this male assertiveness also had a fearful sexual meaning to the mother, but again it was not judged viable or necessary to pursue this more explicitly.

Four months later the fears had disappeared, the paranoid attitudes towards other children had been replaced by further confidence, assertiveness and enjoyment of games and sport, and the case was closed on the understanding that they would return if further problems developed. We learned that asthmatic attacks present since infancy, which had been mentioned but not much discussed in our previous interview, had improved over this period to a point where the pediatrician had also discharged him. The younger brother manifested a similar improvement in confidence and liveliness.

I hope it will be clear from this and from many other examples in this book that profound changes can come about in family systems without the therapist needing to make his own understanding of the problem fully explicit. Understanding the significance of symptoms and the underlying pathology is the lesser part of therapeutic skill; the greater part, as wiser therapists have made clear to us, consists in judging how much a family is able to accept as well as how much they wish to change. The family just described was handled with great gentleness, and the results justified the caution exercised. In other cases, where persecutory attitudes are manifesting themselves openly in violent attacks on others, and other methods fail, vigorous and forceful control may sometimes be called for, as in the following example:

Susan, aged 14, was referred by the pediatrician for long-standing enuresis and encopresis as well as behavior disorders. There was a history of severe deprivation in her early childhood.

The mother, who arrived with her 25 minutes late for the half-hour interview, appeared borderline-psychotic and presented as a hard-faced, angry, witch-like figure who blamed and scolded Susan while the child sat silent and sullenly depressed. As she heaped abuse on Susan, who was clearly being used as a scapegoat figure, the mother violently rejected any suggestion on my part, however mild or carefully phrased, that she might be partly responsible for a continuation of the child's resistance; instead she shouted, interrupted me, refused to listen when I asked her to do so, kept getting up and threatening to leave and then sitting down again. After a short time I decided I should meet her on the same terms, and shouting louder than she had done said that I would be behaving as badly as Susan, and soiling and wetting myself as well, if I had to put up all the time with the sort of treatment I was receiving from her. I rebuked her forcefully for failing to treat me with proper respect and ordered her to leave the hospital premises and not to return unless she was prepared to behave more appropriately.

The mother stalked out in a fury, and a gentle social work student sitting in for her first interview with me was deeply shocked until she perceived that I had not lost my temper but had been acting a part; even then she was still critical and doubtful that my action could have anything but a bad effect. This student agreed to visit the home at my request and reported, after doing so a few days later, that the mother had felt deeply remorseful after the interview, had realized that all I had said was true and had dramatically changed her whole attitude towards Susan, trying now to repair the relationship.

When I saw the mother and Susan for a second interview a few weeks later, the mother apologized for her previous behavior, was quietly spoken, cooperative and clearly eager to make a good relationship with Susan. However, though the mother was much more patient and understanding, within her limits, Susan was refusing to cooperate in improving the relationship and instead was behaving in a way which was calculated to make the mother feel useless and bad. I was now able to rebuke Susan sternly for her continued contribution to this unhappy relationship and she accepted this and wept. It was then possible to deal more directly with the deprivation in each of them and to offer warmth, support and sympathy, now that they were open to such emotions.

Though the mother made a disastrous second marriage several months later which necessitated further treatment for depression, the relationship between herself and Susan continued to be constructive and steadily improved. Both remained able to offer support and affection to each other in a way they had not been able to do before.

Both these families were of working-class origin, the second one on welfare, but similar splitting and projection of painful aspects of the self, with consequent scapegoating of others, can occur at any social level. The following excerpt from a transcript of the last session of successful marital therapy with a middle-class couple, first referred because of a scapegoated child, where the problems had improved to a point where family interviews had been discontinued, expresses these dynamics in a more explicit way than one can usually hope for with those less educated. It will be evident that the couple have a background in the theater.

Father: How long is it that we have been coming?
Psychiatric Social Worker: We started to meet regularly in March this year. We met first when the psychologist first referred you a year ago, then there was a short truce and we met again.
Mother: That's right, we brought Max then. Crazy that we used Max the whole time as the key to oursleves.
Father: We did use the children!
Psychiatrist: Why did you need to use the children? What were you using them for?
Mother: Well, we did not realize there was anything wrong with us.
Psychiatrist: What was it that you could not face?
Father: It was to create the illusion that we were all right, we were not failures, we were successes, but the children were failures instead. We did not want you to discover that we were failures as human beings. We wanted to dazzle you with our credits and that's how we went through life, trying to dazzle people with our dance routines.
Psychiatrist: You talk as though it was an individual thing. You do not talk as though it was a threat to your relationship together as well.
Mother: That is very interesting. I never believed or accepted until very late in the day that we could split. We were two halves of one person. How could we ever separate? It was not until the witch came on the scene, that I thought "you had better believe it is possible to lose him."

The "witch" refers to the taking back by the parents of the negative aspect they had projected out into the children; in the case of the mother she referred to this disturbing and frightening side of herself as the "witch," perceiving this destructive aspect as threatening the marriage itself.

The following case, a boy of five referred by a pediatrician because he had suffered eight hospital admissions, four for investigation of coughing and vomiting, which appeared to have more basis in the mother's anxiety than in actual medical disorder, shows a family which has suffered much loss, and where achievement of the depressive position is precarious.

The letter to the family doctor after the first interview, which summarizes the events concisely, states, "I saw John today at the request of the pediatrician, since during his last admission here it once again appeared that the child was responding to his mother's excessive anxiety and protectiveness, and he was in fact free of all complaints and difficulties while away from her in the hospital situation. The father was fortunately able to attend the family interview as well, and I saw them all together.

"The boy's difficulties were certainly very much heightened by a partial separation which occurred at a crucial age—he was in a day nursery for almost a month at the age of 21 months during a complication arising from the mother's second pregnancy. He was disturbed while away and after he returned could not bear separation, was unable to sleep on his own and extremely nervous. Symptoms have persisted since that time.

"However, the mother makes it clear that she has been frantic with anxiety about his health since his birth, when his prematurity and all the anxieties arising from this made her hover over him and guard him 'like a cat watching a mouse.' She has never felt this anxiety with the second child, and has been able to let her go her own way.

"Further, this difficult start occurred against a background which made trouble likely. Both parents had suffered the loss of mother figures in their own early lives, the mother losing her mother when she was seven, the father losing his at the age of six, both in situations which would be likely to exaggerate the development of later fears of loss or harm to loved ones. Because of this the parents appear to deal with anxiety over aggressive or destructive impulses by intense protectiveness and hypochondriacal anxieties, though the father's anxiety is directed mainly towards his own health, the mother's towards this male child. The mother also had a fierce temper when she was small, which no one helped her to control, and this is another important factor since she has never been able to feel safe in the face of her hostile feelings."

The fears of the parents for John's health, which proved to be related much more to the serious illnesses which had preceded their parents' deaths than to reality, were very fully ventilated in this first family session and their fears that their ambivalent feelings had contributed to their parents' deaths, and so now threatened John, were made explicit and discussed with them. However, the security provided by relaxed discussion of the subject by my co-therapist and myself, together with the accepting and supportive attitude we were manifesting towards them, probably was more relevant to the subsequent change than any intellectual insight.

One month later the mother reported that, though the boy was still coughing, she was less prone to anxiety about him and she was now sending him to school and "letting him get on with it." He had begun to stand up for himself and by the third interview, after another month, he had turned on a former bully and had given him a bloody nose. At the fourth interview, three months from the first session, the coughing was not mentioned at all. The boy was lively, cheerful and mixing well with others while the mother was letting him grow away from her.

In such cases it is very likely that it is the reliable, secure mothering provided by the therapist's warmth and acceptance to all the family which facilitates the beneficial change and brings about the more adequate mastering of the depressive anxiety centering around ambivalence to loved ones. The next example shows this very clearly, in the case of a child of 15 months who was admitted to the hospital for severe feeding difficulties.

The notes state: "I saw Michael with his mother on the ward, and the nurse arranged for him to be fed while I was present. There was no difficulty over his feeding himself, or the mother feeding him, until she suddenly misinterpreted something I said as indicating that she would be asked to have him home very soon. The mother became agitated and her excited emotional state immediately affected the boy, who began to turn his head away and refuse the food when the mother presented it to him, or to throw it about. As soon as I was able to calm the mother by explaining her misunderstanding, the child began to feed normally again. The nurse had also noticed this interaction, and commented that the mother's emotional attitude had gradually improved as she had been supported and helped by the nursing staff to remain calm when feeding the child."

Regression to paranoid-schizoid mechanisms at a point where the parents feel threatened with loss is also well illustrated in the following case. Splitting and scapegoating in the parents' relationship with the children were obvious from the beginning.

Connie, aged ten, was described as stubborn, provocative, willful and jealous towards her brother, driving her mother into feeling murderous towards her. It was relevant that the maternal grandmother had died when the mother was five and she had subsequently suffered at the hands of an unkind stepmother. The school reported that Connie was "perfectly normal, confident, happy and well-adjusted." The notes from the first interview state: "There was some hesitation before anyone began as if there was uncertainty about the authority structure, but finally the mother said, 'Connie is the problem.' She then described the difficulties listed above, while Connie sat and grinned defiantly. The father agreed with mother's judgment, and also with the fact that the boy was as good as Connie was bad. Father queried whether the fault might lie to some extent in the parents, and said that he had been spending too much time away from home and giving too little attention to the family, at which mother agreed and said that she missed him. Father appeared to be moving towards discussing difficulties in the marriage, but the mother steered the conversation away from this repeatedly and papered over the cracks.

"It became clear that the problems with Connie had developed as she was beginning to break away from an excessively close attachment to her mother. Mother seemed to find it difficult to cope with this separation. Father then brought in information about the mother's deprivation, and was able to reveal the fact that the mother had not been able to deal with ambivalent feelings and feel safe with them in her own early relationships, and also could not cope with similar feelings with Connie. Because of her anxieties that anger might destroy loving feelings, the mother was unable to be firm or to discipline Connie, who would scream loudly before she was touched, making mother fearful of what the neighbors would think.

"Connie, who had said almost nothing throughout the interview but had wept for a period earlier, had by now recovered her spirits and said, 'Yes, if you didn't worry so much about the neighbors and what they think you wouldn't need to see a psychiatrist.' At this point there was a sudden change and the mother began using a paranoid defense claiming that everyone was against her, including myself and my co-therapist, and that we and the father were all siding with Connie against her. It was not possible to change the mother's attitude in the limited time left in the interview, and she left still absolutely furious. The children followed her out, but the father turned around and shook hands warmly at the door as if he felt grateful that some insoluble problem had at last been aired."

The mother was already involved in individual psychotherapy with a psychiatrist and the family interview proved ultimately constructive when the events of the interview were reported to this colleague, who was able to help the mother, in the more supportive individual situation, to accept her own part in the problem. As Connie was continuing to show no problem at school and the difficulties at home were obviously in relation to the mother's own disturbance, further interviews were not arranged at the clinic.

In some of the above cases the fathers were able to take a more supportive role and to act as allies in the therapeutic intervention, but often they have equal or greater difficulties in coming to terms with ambivalence and achieving the depressive position securely. In another case, where both mother and adolescent daughter were receiving psycho-analysis, I was asked to see the family together since it was felt that the father's difficulties in facing his own aspect of the family problem was impeding progress of these separate treatments. It will be seen that fears of ambivalence in this family restrict the exchange of positive, supportive feelings as well as negative ones, until a secure and reliable therapeutic situation is provided within which such expression can be encouraged. The following extract was taken from the second family session of this professional family, which included both parents and four children.

The whole family said that everyone was angry with father. The word "battle" was used, and the youngest boy talked of castles and forts, but I said that this seemed to be a battle of a different kind. The younger adolescent daughter was unable to say why she got so angry with father except that she wanted something from him that she never received and could not describe even to herself. The mother mentioned that things were at present much worse because she had been away to a health farm for a rest, but instead of coming back refreshed and more able to look after everybody else she had suffered an accident and injured her spine, so that on returning she had to be looked after by the others. The children then said how angry they were about this and the father said that he became resentful when the mother was unable to mother him. The whole family went on from this to talk about accidents, saying how they all frequently suffered accidents of one kind or another—cutting themselves, scalding themselves and so on—which they somehow recognized as claims for attention. However, this never worked because other members of the family resented the demand for attention and didn't give it anyway. I focused on the fact that they could not communicate about their needs directly and had to send these messages in disguised form. They continued to talk of their resentment at mother's not being able to look after them all the time. Father said how he had been obliged to mother his own mother and indeed all his family, so that he felt fed up with this and wanted some of it himself. He felt he expected this particularly from one of his adolescent daughters who was now the same age as when he had felt required to perform this function in his own family. The mother then took up the thread, and talked about her own lack of mothering and her need for it. What came across to me was everyone's fear of being given attention and indulgence as well as each individual's desire for it. . . .

Later in this second interview the father was able to weep and express for the first time, before the family, his own distress and need. Both parents were subsequently involved in a combination of group and individual therapy in their own right, combined with marital interviews. It was felt that the individual sessions were a vital provision for these people who had never received a secure individual relationship in their own early lives, which they could therefore naturally not supply to their children.

At this level something rather different is required of the therapist(s). Instead of the supportive, totally accepting containment required in the oral-dependent level, a more active, controlling, authoritative and demanding relationship is needed, which seems particularly related to the role of the *father* at this stage (1).

Glen, aged ten, was sent for an opinion by the pediatrician after the general practitioner had requested assessment because of a persistent learning difficulty, distractibility and inability to concentrate, for which a physical cause was wrongly suspected. It was almost certainly relevant that the father failed to attend, an event rarely met with at this children's hospital.

When the mother and Glen were first seen together, both seemed remarkable for their miserable, apathetic expressions. The father was said to be even less sociable than either of them. The mother felt that there was no difficulty apart from the reading problem.

At a full family interview, including the father and Glen's baby brother, all seemed to show the same depressed, guilt-stricken facial expression noted on the first occasion. They gave an impression of profound envy and incapacity to deal with it, so that no one enjoyed life. The parents scarcely ever went out and even though father had bought a car they said it was too much trouble to use it by the time they had dressed the children and got them ready. However, some benefit seemed to derive from the family interview and it was arranged for Glen to be transferred to a day school for maladjusted children. Here he continued to receive adverse reports regarding his learning difficulty and reading-block and the teachers appeared increasingly frustrated with him, demanding that something be done. A psychiatric social worker and I therefore arranged to see him at the school with both parents and the head and class teachers. At this joint interview the teachers complained that it was impossible to get through to Glen and consequently difficult to help him. In the interview he behaved in a manner which confirmed this, looking unconcerned, comfortable and withdrawn and answering all my questions with "I dunno." Both mother and father described, on inquiry, how they hesitated to confront Glen when he showed difficult behavior; instead, they would both withdraw into themselves, to which Glen would respond with an attitude of "not caring." At this interview, as in the previous ones, he had shown no animation except on occasions when we talked about aggression or violence, when his face would light up and he would come alive briefly.

After he had successfully frustrated me, as he had done to his parents and teachers, I finally expressed the anger which had been rising in me and confronted him with the way in which he was trying to defeat me and make a fool of me as he did with everyone else; I told him forcefully that I was not prepared to tolerate this and that I wanted more from him. At this his behavior changed. He not only made an effort to answer the questions and contribute usefully from this point on, but his face became alive and warm and he showed a positive, smiling response towards me, as if we were now in good contact. My own anger had disappeared immediately with this change in him, and I realized that it had been an appropriate response he needed.

Glen was able to agree that he could not bear to give in, and later made some aggressive comments about his brothers and his father. This was in response to a discussion about the film *Kes* to which his teacher had taken him, and where Glen had shown great pleasure when the boy had sworn at and hit his brother in a drunken stupor. He agreed he felt like this towards his brothers and father sometimes himself. He also told us that he succeeded in defeating everybody by ensuring that, even if he didn't win, they didn't win either.

We went on to talk about school work and about Glen's failure to learn, where the same principle seemed to be operative. Glen felt discouraged at his lack of progress, but also was able to say that he didn't work because he didn't care. He agreed that it would help him to be made to care, as I had made him care in the interview through my angry demand on him. This demonstration that it was possible to get through to Glen by confronting him and responding warmly, even if only with warm anger at first, made sense to the school representatives who felt that some new possibilities had emerged in the interview as to how they might proceed.

Unfortunately, routine follow-up was not carried out in this case, but it is hoped that the fact that school officials did not refer him again, despite the fact that they had been so concerned and made so many demands previously, meant that some progress had been made.

Another case demonstrates clearly the active encouragement that may be needed with children whose assertiveness is inhibited, as well as the more profound and rapid effect when sanctions for more aggressive behavior can be given indirectly to the parents, as well as the child, in the course of the family interview.

Paul, a boy of three-and-a-half, was referred by the family doctor for nervousness and stuttering. The father also stuttered and both parents were inhibited people who insisted that they never had disagreements or expressed anger, though they could express affection and the sexual relationship was said to be normal. The mother felt ambivalent towards the maternal grandmother, who was always dropping in and interfering, though she did not dare to complain about it.

In the family consultation, the fears of aggressiveness and violence were brought into the open, and the parents were helped to examine their fantasy that expression of anger would lead to the break-up of the marriage. At first, Paul showed a great fear of spontaneity and kept saying, "I can't do nothing," and "I can't think," finally bursting into tears of distress. However, as the problem was opened up and the parents began to relax, Paul began to play more freely in the sand tray, scattering some sand on the floor. At this the parents became tense and anxious, whereupon he froze, so I encouraged him vigorously to fling some sand at the wall. Paul hesitated, and the parents became extremely apprehensive, but all three relaxed and looked relieved and happy when he followed my suggestion and let fly.

At the second interview four months later, a dramatic improvement was reported following immediately on the initial consultation. The mother had begun to release her feelings more freely and was able to shout at Paul when she felt like it, while Paul in turn had become much more outspoken and even cheeky at times. The stutter had cleared up completely, he no longer clung to his mother, and he had begun to mix easily with other children.

Sometimes the needed containment and firmness can be directed towards the children, and the parents succeed in identifying with the therapists and become able to take a more authoritative role. Often, however, it is necessary to take a tough and controlling position in regard to parents as well as children, particularly when the former use the interview in a manipulative way. The following example, of an 18-year-old boy who had received ten years of various different types of conventional treatment, without any success, is a good example. The problem was of facial tics (grimaces) and grunting noises, apparently worse on frustration. The following letter to the referring general practitioner summarizes the interview:

"I saw this patient and both parents as well as his sister yesterday. My experience is that tics always represent a problem of control and limits in the family as a whole, and this is certainly the case here. The mother has always given in to Matthew from his babyhood, particularly after he was hospitalized twice about the age of three, and he has really had his own way and lacked any adequate discipline and control throughout. The father was even more reluctant to control him than the mother, for the father was brought up very strictly and wants to do everything by kindness and reasoning. In the interview, Matthew's behavior was consistent with this picture, and his noises and grimacing appeared attention-seeking and provocative throughout. He looked perfectly cheerful and happy with no sign whatever of anxiety or depression, while the mother, who appears a miserable, negative woman in any case, seemed quite depressed. The father seemed a much more sensible and straightforward, warm person and I felt he understood better what I was trying to communicate. The sister had little to contribute on this occasion but agreed that her brother gets away with everything.

"Although this issue of discipline and control was presented over and over again in almost everything they said, the parents, and the mother in particular, repeatedly tried to change the subject back to the grimaces and the grunting, treating them as if they were a meaningless medical symptom and asking for a diagnosis. The object of all this seemed to be to manipulate me into taking responsibility for the problem, which they have successfully done with others over the past ten years. I refused to play this role and instead told them that the whole problem was one of control and limits and that I could not take over the parental role for them. The father seemed to grasp the point, however feebly, but the mother went on trying to misunderstand me, asking how long the treatment would take. I told her it would take just as long as it took her to carry it out, since she and the father would be giving the treatment, not me. Matthew complained feebly about his various difficulties and problems in getting to the family interview but I also told him that these were his problems, not mine. I have given them another appointment in a month's time to report on their progress. I find it better not to see people like this too often, or they simply wait for the next session instead of getting on with the job."

The second letter, a month later, stated: "I saw this young man, together with his sister and both parents, for a second family interview yesterday, several weeks after the first. I am glad to say that the situation is vastly improved, to a point where everyone seems to be satisfied and they feel no further need to attend. The parents appear to feel that the problem had been understood at the first interview, and though they described it as 'shock therapy,' they felt they now knew what to do and were able to apply this knowledge at home. The mother has withdrawn from her over-involvement with Matthew, and also made it clear that she is not prepared to tolerate his continued disturbance of the family. The father was also able to use the support to be much firmer and to take a more active part in Matthew's management. Matthew was not only improved to a point where they no longer feel a particular worry about him, but he has also withdrawn from his own over-close attachment to the parents and is spending much more time away from home. In particular, he said that he now spends four evenings a week acting as leader at a youth club, and when he spoke of this he showed quite an astonishingly mature and responsible attitude, compared with the helpless and infantile behavior he demonstrated earlier with the family, and still does to some extent now. Matthew made very few noises during the interview, and when he did so it was in obvious response to feeling left out and a demand for attention; he stopped at once as soon as this was pointed out.

"I was surprised to find how much the mother had changed. She expressed herself as being at breakdown point when she came last, but since the interview she has seen the whole problem in a different way, has considered herself more, and now feels happier and more settled. The father shows no serious problem though I think he needs to have, through his children, the happy childhood he missed himself through his evacuations and boarding school experiences, and I think he finds it harder to let the boy go. However, the parents seemed quite happy with their own relationship, and the sister confirmed the improvement."

Though such rapid changes are commonplace using the family approach, in this case more was needed. The parents sought a further appointment six months later, and the family interview which was then arranged revealed that the boy had regained control of the family and that the parents had been unable to sustain their previous independence of him. Nevertheless, the previous diagnosis and recommendations still appeared appropriate and worked effectively when applied again, but a few interviews with the parents separately were necessary to enable them to repair their own relationship and to deal with some of the anxieties and deprivations stemming from their own early experiences. A more permanent solution appears to have resulted.

As will be apparent from some of these examples, parental difficulty in setting adequate limits and providing sufficient control often stems from difficulties of the mother in detaching herself from the previous close involvement with the child, particularly where the father has been unable to assist in this process. In another family where a male child was showing much difficult behavior, his sister expressed the problem very clearly in the following transcript:

Sister: I don't understand really. If he has done something wrong, she doesn't want Dad to tell him off. She does, you know, she'll go on about it, but when he is about to do something about it. . . .
Psychiatric Social Worker: She interferes?
Sister: Exactly! She nags and nags and nags about it, but when he is going to do something she doesn't like it.

Psychiatrist: So he doesn't take any notice, he knows he has got the government divided, really?

The importance of the father at this stage is illustrated well in the next example, where a boy of seven had suffered from difficulties in self-control including encopresis and enuresis since the mother's admission to the hospital three years previously. Once again, it was unusual and significant that the father failed to attend the first interview. My letter to the referring surgeon said:

"Thank you for referring this little boy, whom I saw today in company with his mother and three siblings. Though the psychiatric social worker had emphasized the need for the father to attend when she took the social history, he failed to do so. It is so rare for fathers not to attend the family interview these days that we have come to regard his absence as very significant, and so it was here. The mother presented the father as passive, inadequate, frightened of attending, and sees herself as the more mature and responsible parent that the children respect. She was surprised to find the children giving an exactly opposite picture when I asked for their viewpoint, for they all said unanimously that they all respect and listen to their father because he means what he says, but that they all feel that they can get around their mother and admit they have a battle of wills with her which they are sure they can win. This seems, in turn, to be related to the mother's own persisting resentment of authority, derived from the difficulties in her own childhood...."

It was left that we would be pleased to see them again, but that we would require the whole family to come. Four months later, another appointment was requested and all the family attended, including the father. They reported that the encopresis had stopped completely following the first interview, for a month, but this had then resumed. The father seemed unconcerned about the symptoms, saying it was all just laziness, and that the boy would grow out of it. In response to this the referred patient grinned. In discussion it emerged that the older sibling, aged ten, had also suffered from encopresis at the age of six while the father was away from home; this had cleared up on his return. The interview concluded with more focus on the marital relationship, where both parents seemed to be fighting a stubborn battle with each other which the children were understandably copying. It was left for the family to get in touch with us again if they wanted further help, but they did not do so and it seems unlikely that the interviews were beneficial, except in clarifying the nature of the problem.

The next example also illustrates problems related to this level of development, similarly connected with the failure of the father to pay an active and responsible role in the boy's management, but in this case the family responded extremely well when the father took a more active part. It will be seen that I had to model the more active and controlling function I considered necessary, not only towards the boy but towards the mother as well. In this case the problems were closer to a delinquent pattern, with less conflict and more uninhibited acting-out of antisocial tendencies.

Michael, aged 14, was referred for persistent truancy and wandering; he was due to appear before the juvenile court, charged with breaking and entering. Both parents appeared immature and inadequate, the father opting out of family responsibilities. The mother seemed a hard woman, constantly critical of Michael, showing little warmth or affection and preoccupied with her own problems and nervous troubles.

Michael was placed in a boys' group and his behavior improved during the six months he attended. When the group was terminated Michael was referred again by the school because of deterioration "beginning the day he stopped coming to the group."

At the first family interview the parents had both appeared to me so hopeless than I had not considered further work with them, but in view of the relapse this was now attempted. My report on the second family interview states, "The pattern was much the same as on the first occasion, the father rather wet and apathetic, the mother strident, hard and critical in a nagging way. I thought we would get nowhere but surprising progress was made. This was accomplished by a much more direct interaction than I had attempted before. It was possible to show how Michael does in fact respect his father and would really like more guidance from him, but that the father dislikes having to be strict and lets Michael get away with things. It was also possible to bring out openly how Michael resents and resists his mother's irritable criticism, and this could be linked with her identification with her own mother. To my surprise, she responded favorably to very direct confrontation over the way she was behaving, seemed to swallow my adverse comments and appeared almost grateful for the interest. It had emerged clearly that she undermined the father's authority, and she agreed that she would allow him to take more charge of the situation. All this was said with Michael present. Altogether the interview seemed surprisingly positive and might well produce sufficient limited change in the pattern."

The report on the next family interview, almost two months later, states: "The whole family looked remarkably different, all relaxed and cheerful and relating favorably towards each other. The mother in particular looked glowing and pretty, and I felt astonished at the difference in her whole manner throughout the interview. Michael has been in no further trouble, is attending school regularly, making efforts with his work and generally doing well.

"The whole family pattern changed after the last interview. The mother went away upset and remained so for days, but accepted the criticism and made efforts to change. During this period Michael became very protective towards her, and the relationship improved steadily. Both parents had accepted that the father should take over Michael's control and discipline, and this has worked very much better. They have also been able to sort things out in a calm fashion with the paternal grandmother, who used to spoil Michael and undermine the mother's authority; because of the different way the mother was able to approach things, this grandmother accepted criticism in turn. The mother said that the criticism I had made of her was true, but that she had never realized it before and she said she was glad I had pointed it out. They all agreed that the family was getting on extremely well and that relationships were good, but that they would nevertheless like to come and report on their progress occasionally."

Michael's improvement continued for a further six months, when there was a relapse and he appeared again before the court for breaking and entering. He left school shortly after and appeared to settle down after he began work on a building site. The reason for the deterioration was not clarified.

OEDIPAL LEVEL PROBLEMS

Although problems at an oedipal level are obviously best dealt with by seeing the whole family, since the conflicts center around the relationship of the parental couple, the following case illustrates that work can nevertheless be done with one parent only. Mother and child were seen at a time when I was interested in working with mother-child couples, before I had begun to use family interviews routinely.

The mother complained that four-and-a-half-year-old Brenda was a rebel, always provocative and defiant towards her and constantly trying to separate the parents and come into the parental bed. My immediate impression of two very strong-willed and determined personalities was confirmed in the subsequent interaction. When together in the play room, the mother kept focusing her attention on the child and away from herself, demanding help and understanding from me but becoming defensive and resistant and contradicting everything I said when I tried to help her. No progress was made until I pointed out how the mother was fighting me exactly as Brenda fought her, producing a stalemate. At this the mother wept, admitted it was true, and began to speak for the first time of her timidity and shyness during her childhood. She said, "If my father had not been so strict, I would have been exactly like Brenda," suggesting that the child was acting out her own secret wishes. I gave Brenda some puppets with which she expressed her problems very clearly, making a little girl fight with a mother whereupon the mother-doll would smack the girl-puppet. When I set up a bedroom scene with the parents in bed together and invited Brenda to continue, she put the girl between the parents.

The couple was seen for monthly interviews. At the second interview, Brenda looked much happier and separated easily from her mother instead of clinging in a resentful way. Brenda again acted a puppet scene in which the girl came between the parents in their bed. I pointed out how sexually provocative Brenda was and how she flirted with me the whole time, asking if she acted in the same way with her father and, if so, how the mother felt about it. The mother was reluctant to allow herself to express any jealousy over this, but admitted such behavior did occur and that it made her furious both with her husband and with Brenda.

At the third interview a further improvement had occurred and at the fourth the mother said that "the penny had dropped" and that all the problems had disappeared both in herself and the child. She was "really living for the first time," and realized that though she was not the sweet and reasonable person she had always tried to be, everyone seemed to enjoy much more the "spitfire" that she had become. All improvements persisted a year later.

The next case illustrates a situation of severe persisting phallic rivalry between parents and its effect on a child, together with striking change when this is brought into the open. It will be seen that the change takes place by a simple confrontation of the more powerful parent (in this case the mother), whose controlling and competitive attitude is highlighted by my spontaneous response to her nonverbal expression of it. The parents were separated, but agreed to come together for the sake of the child.

Graham, aged ten, was referred by the general practitioner. The complaint was that he was passive and effeminate, and had become enuretic in the previous year after being dry for three years previous to this. The parents had separated five years before this interview, and Graham was living with his mother. There seemed to be little male influence in his life.

Both parents were invited and agreed to come together with Graham. We learned, among other things, that the father had wet the bed until sixteen, and Graham himself said that he was having dreams of floods in which the people of the world drowned and the world itself got increasingly muddy and fell in half!

However, the crucial incident seemed to be a comment I made, based on my curiosity about the meaning of the mother's facial expression and gaze, which I could not understand at first and explored by reporting the feelings these observations induced in me. I said I had the feeling that she was a very controlling person, as if she felt that men were dangerous creatures who had to be watched carefully in case they got out of hand and did something unexpected.

The father seemed freed by my comment, and said that this was just how he felt the mother had treated him throughout the marriage, though he had never been able to recognize it clearly or put it into words. The boy also appeared to cheer up at this time and the whole family interaction appeared altered, the males becoming more active as the mother's controlling and perhaps castrating attitude was brought into the open.

When seen again three months later it was learned that the wetting had ceased since the day of the interview. Graham appeared happier and was reported to be changing, growing up, playing war games and giving up his previous quiet timid friends in favor of rougher and more boisterous boys. Six months later the improvement was still continuing.

In the next case, oedipal rivalry between a mother and her adolescent daughter is brought out very fully and openly. Joan, aged 18, referred for an opinion after being seen by a psychiatrist at her local hospital, was suffering from depression which had culminated in a suicide attempt. She had shown a school-phobic and work-phobic pattern, clinging to her parents in an immature way and feeling unable to cope with the responsibilities of life. The three were seen together, and the following letter to the referring physician outlines the sequence of the first discussion.

"Many thanks for asking me to see this girl with her parents. You were quite right that this would prove worthwhile and I hope that some progress has been made. Seen with the family, Joan looked strikingly hopeless, withdrawn, and angry with herself, while the mother looked quite astonishingly cheerful, bright, vivacious, and almost triumphant by contrast. The father tended to sit outside, gazing in a rather abstracted way out of the window and leaving things to others, though he also contributed.

"It was very striking how the parents, particularly the mother, spoke for Joan, as if she could not speak for herself. When I finally got Joan to tell me about the problem it actually began to happen in the room, whereby she went to pieces, wept, and told me she felt the same way in any new situation, wanting to escape and wishing she had never come. I nevertheless pursued my inquiries gently but firmly, and she then recovered and was able to get through the block which obstructs her thoughts at such times. I explored what everyone felt about this situation and it seems that the family have now become very frightened of pursuing and pressing her in this way, in case she makes a suicidal attempt. They therefore fall between two stools, realizing that they would be more help if they were firmer, yet feeling unable to do this.

"The other striking feature was the way in which both parents focused visually and emotionally upon Joan, forming a kind of V. I pointed out how the third side of the triangle seemed to be missing, and that I learned nothing of the relationship between the parents though I saw a lot of what they both felt about Joan. At this a very clear oedipal problem emerged. Joan had already been able to speak of the competitive attitude she feels towards the mother at home, over the placing of the furniture, etc., which she loses when she goes to pieces and needs mother's support outside. The father was able to say how deeply and painfully he had missed Joan when she went on holiday and how happy he feels in her presence. He obviously enjoys her company enormously, can talk to her, but feels that his wife is bossy and intrusive. By this time mother looked very excluded, and when I pointed this out she agreed that she always felt the odd one out. I remarked on how she made the best of herself, in contrast to Joan's complete lack of interest in her appearance, and told her that I thought she was attractive and that I noted that she was aware of me as a man; by contrast, her husband did not seem to notice her or to respond at all, and I wondered how she felt about this? This produced quite a lot of feeling, whereby she said that her husband had never taken her out during their marriage, had always been content to stay at home, in Joan's company, while she would have enjoyed parties and social life. She had hoped that she and her husband would have more of a marriage as the children grew up, but he had maintained his deep attachment to them, especially Joan, instead of turning his attention more to her.

"All this had great meaning for Joan and she was able to say how she did in fact feel extremely guilty over this situation, often wanting to tell her father to pay less attention to her, and more to her mother, though she obviously realized that this would put her even more in the position of the victor and wife.

"I said that the father really needed to decide which of them he was married to, and left it to them to think it over. Now that the oedipal rivalry, previously denied on all sides, is out in the open I think that the mother may fight for her place a bit more, while Joan may see what strings are holding her in this situation and be able to pull out a bit. The father will, I hope, not be able to go on having the best of both worlds, with two women fighting over him, as at present.

"I find that an interval of three weeks is just about right to give the consequences of the session time to percolate, and we will see what has transpired by the time of the next interview. It may be that Joan will need to be in some kind of therapeutic community situation where she can get the kind of help she needs from a peer group to emancipate herself from the parental attachment, particularly in the way of normal heterosexual relationships, but I will wait to see if this is necessary."

At the second interview, two weeks later, the parents reported that Joan seemed much happier, that they were less worried about her depressions and their former fears that she might make further suicide attempts, and that they had been able to stand aside and leave her to find her own solutions more than they had been able to in the past. Joan's former collapsed posture, apathetic appearance and almost inaudible voice were replaced by a more upright bearing, the beginning of a more resilient attitude and a firmer tone to her speech. She confirmed that she felt less depressed, but was unable to explain why this had happened. The discoveries of the first session had shocked her but she had later seen that they were true. She felt more able to go her own way and the parents confirmed that instead of the profuse apologies and self-accusations Joan formerly expressed over any family disharmony, she and her parents were now able to have arguments, a change which pleased them all. She now saw her main task as escaping from her dependency on her parents, for she realized that she always ran back to them when she faced difficulty, and that they took responsibility for her problems.

It seemed that we had done as much as was appropriate in the family situation, and that keeping them together as a family was now working against the need for emancipation that Joan was experiencing. Accordingly, individual psychotherapy was arranged for her, with a therapist who might be able to take her into group therapy when she was ready, and further family sessions were not arranged. This was a serious error since continued work with the marital couple might well have avoided some of the subsequent difficulties.

Unfortunately, there was some delay before Joan's individual therapy could commence, and in the interval she was admitted to hospital by the general practitioner for investigation of one of the main remaining symptoms —her "nervous sickness"—on the assumption that this was a separate, physical disorder (this symptom may have the psychological meaning in such cases of wishing to expel projections received from the parents). After three further family interviews over a period of time when mother lost her vivacity and retired to bed, leaving Joan in command of the field (at which point Joan turned up looking flushed, attractive, wearing make-up and dressed for the first time in bright colors), admission to a therapeutic community was arranged for her. She ran out of the first situation (operated on rather rigid psychoanalytic lines) but was able to remain for a longer period in a second hospital which was operated on more flexible and eclectic principles. She appeared more confident and emancipated on discharge but the future remains in doubt.

Though many therapists have anxieties about bringing out sexual material in the presence of both parents and their children (an anxiety which may have its origin in the misconception that enabling parents and children to *talk* about sex together is identical with actual incestuous behavior), it will be evident that quite open discussion is possible. However, I believe at present that the discussion of details of intercourse, like sexual intercourse itself, is best carried out in private with the children excluded.

The working out of the oedipal challenge does not require the presence of both parents, or even of one, provided those dealing with the child can be helped to understand the significance of events at this stage:

Stephen, aged 13, was an illegitimate child, father unknown, who was placed in a children's home at the age of ten months after his mother was evicted from welfare accommodation. The mother visited him only once subsequently, after which she disappeared, and Stephen had spent his whole life in various children's homes. Up to the age of twelve he had lived in a small children's home under the care of an unmarried woman who had been particularly possessive towards the children and had discouraged any form of masculine assertiveness. For two years before I saw him he had been living in a home run by a married couple. He was said to be "extremely immature and far too gentle" and there were various difficulties including persistent enuresis. He was showing various problems in his sexual development, kissing and caressing the younger boys in his group and demanding to wear white gloves and to play with a tea-set and dolls. He would often wander around naked and exhibit himself from the window. On some occasions he had been observed prostrating himself across some of the larger dolls in the house, trying to imitate the motions of sexual intercourse. It is reported that for several hours at a time he appeared incapable of understanding or even hearing any conversation made to him and seemed to have to fight his way back to reality.

When he was seen in a joint interview together with the director of the children's home (whose wife was not present) clear oedipal rivalry and castration fear emerged on suggestive questioning. He agreed that he wanted all the girls, that he would like to cut the director's head off, that he would take his wife and marry her and give her babies. The significance of this material was explained to the director, a perceptive and thoughtful man, who was encouraged to confront the boy over this oedipal rivalry in a firm and friendly way.

Six months later a vast improvement was reported. The enuresis had ceased, and he no longer exhibited himself. He had spoken at one point of killing everyone in the children's home, and then bringing back his former house-mother, but after this he had changed his mind about cutting off the director's head. He was subsequently seen with the former house-mother and the present director for a family interview and the oedipal conflict was discussed in terms of them both. Though he remained an odd, schizoid child his behavior continued to improve and he did not present further serious problems over a two-year follow-up.

4 INNER AND OUTER WORLDS: MODELS

Example is always more efficacious than precept.

Samuel Johnson, Rasselas

Considering the prevailing influence of example in the development and regulation of human behavior, it is surprising that traditional accounts of learning contain little or no mention of modeling processes.

Albert Bandura,
Psychological Modeling: Conflicting Theories

A particular clinical and research problem is that disturbed individuals seem often to maintain within themselves more than one working model both of the world and of the self in it. Such multiple models, moreover, are frequently incompatible with each other and can be more or less unconscious... the concept of working models is central to the schema proposed.

John Bowlby, Support, Innovation and Autonomy

In Chapter 1, where we looked at the world in terms of systems theory, living organisms were seen as part of larger organizations—the supra-systems which include, at different levels, the group to which a given individual belonged, its species, animal life, living beings generally and so on; at the same time the parts of a given organism were seen as subsystems which could be further divided into smaller and smaller meaningful assemblies, the whole being interrelated in a hierarchy whereby the greater dominated and controlled the lesser, within certain degrees of freedom.

But with living organisms we find a seeming contradiction, for the lesser is not only contained within the greater, but in some degree the lesser also contains the greater as part of its own structure. The organism includes within itself a model, map or representation, however abstract, incomplete or distorted, of its environment and also of itself. Not only is the system part of the supra-system; in a certain sense the supra-system is also part of the system.

MODELS

The word model means here simply a correspondence in relationship between two structures, one more abstract than the other; thus the picture on the TV screen and the pattern of electrical impulses in the aerial are both models, at the same level of abstraction, of the scene depicted in the studios.

Such models may, of course, be inborn or built up through experience. Certain birds appear to possess from early in their life a reaction of fear and avoidance towards hawk-like objects in the sky, indicating a model of the external world programmed into the genetic material, independent of learning, which would currently be explained in terms of natural selection. At all levels, and especially in simpler forms of life, much information about the supra-system is transmitted by inheritance in this way, but as we examine more complex living organisms, particularly man, we note an increasing plasticity of the neural apparatus and increasing reliance on learning—that is, upon progressive modification of the structure of the living material itself in response to events impinging on it, leading to responses to future similar events which are more closely tailored to promote the organism's well-being in that particular set of circumstances. This plasticity and capacity for progressive adaptation to experience reach their most remarkable development, of course, in man, increased immeasurably by the further possibility, combining the advantages of inheritance with those of learning, of transmission of learning from generation to generation by the use of language, whereby inner models can be passed from one individual to another.

In simpler animals, the process of learning seems slow and laborious—one hundred trials being the order of time for a worm to learn to turn at a T-junction away from a painful stimulus. Such learning also plays a part in humans, but more rapid processes of change also occur, variously described as imitation, identification, incorporation and introjection. Though these words refer to different types of response, all of these processes appear to operate by the taking in of a coherent, total perception of the behavior of another individual, whereby that behavior becomes available to the person receiving it. And the new possibility often seems to be available immediately, without need for repetition, though repeated similar experiences may be necessary to get the details right. It is as if a model of that piece of behavior has been internalized, which can subsequently be used as a program to reproduce it within certain limits, as well as to respond appropriately to it in others. In the field of psychology and learning theory, Bandura (1) has paid particular attention to this kind of learning or "psychological modeling."

Psychoanalysis also bases its ideas primarily on this type of learning, and object relations theory is concerned with the study of the way in which children internalize the behavior of their parents and other significant figures, thereby populating their inner world with images which are models or abstractions of the people concerned, corresponding to the reality more (in later life and in mental health) or less (in earlier development or mental disorder). These images, objects (in the current psychoanalytic terminology) or models are subsequently a source of information providing programs for dealing with the significant person concerned or with others requiring similar responses (e.g., of coping with father and with authority figures encountered later in life), as well as enabling the individual to play such roles himself when necessary (e.g., becoming a father, or accepting responsibility and a position of authority).

In the field of psychoanalysis, no less an authority than John Bowlby (2) has proposed that the concept of model should replace that of inner object:

> Also much influenced by the special role given to feeding and orality in psychoanalytic theorizing is the concept of "internal object," a concept that is in many ways ambiguous. . . . In its place can be put the concept, derived from cognitive psychology and control theory, of an individual developing within himself one or more working models representing principal features of the world about him and of himself as an agent in it. Such working models determine his expectations and forecasts and provide him with tools for constructing plans of action. What in traditional theory is termed a "good object" can be reformulated within this framework as a working model of an attachment figure who is conceived as accessible, trustworthy and ready to help when called upon. Similarly, what in traditional theory is termed a "bad object" can be reformulated as a working model of an attachment figure to whom are attributed such characteristics as uncertain accessibility, unwillingness to respond helpfully, or perhaps the likelihood of responding hostilely. In an analogous way an individual is thought to construct a working model of himself towards whom others will respond in certain predictable ways (pp. 37–38).

Bowlby's use of the phrase "working model" is intended to remind us that such images, models or objects are not to be thought of as static, like pictures in a photograph album. Studies of an individual's inner life, under psychoanalysis, show that the models are dynamic, interacting, changing, more like a family movie. Yet even this dynamic image is not fluid and creative enough, for an actual family movie merely reproduces events from some of the limited behavior and interaction which were actually witnessed. The inner models do more than this: They appear to be made up not only of a set of perceptions but also of associated attitudes, beliefs, tendencies and types of relationships which are recombined into new syntheses all the time.

The models are alive in the sense that they continue to form new combinations and to have a life of their own in this inner world, within the limited scope of the original information absorbed about them. By experimenting or playing with the models internally (a process expressed in actual play in the case of children, and made use of in play therapy), patterns of behavior appropriate to different situations are worked out. The subject identifies with one inner figure and casts a real person he has to deal with in the role of another, subsequently reproducing in his behavior actions which have their roots in past experiences. The source may be relationships he has witnessed, in which case he will be playing a role learned from another person, or he may reproduce a relationship in which he was actually one of the participants. In the latter case, it is important to remember that he may identify with, and play or enact, not only his own previous part, but also that of the person who interacted with him in the first place, casting his present companion in the role that he himself played earlier. Thus a person who has suffered persecution as a child at the hands of a parental figure may protect himself in later life from a repetition of this intolerable situation by taking the persecuting role himself, taking care that it is always someone else who plays the part of victim.

Such patterns do not necessarily have their origins in childhood, of course, even though the basic patterns are likely to be laid down early on. In concentration camps a similar defense to that just described was common among the prisoners, who would often begin to identify with the Nazi guards and act cruelly towards weaker prisoners in imitation of their captors; indeed, this was one of the aims of the camps—to re-educate or brainwash the prisoners and turn them, through such mechanisms, into brutal supporters of the régime.

A characteristic of this form of learning is that it seems to occur wholly or largely below the threshold of consciousness, in ways that are not yet clear. Indeed, making the process conscious seems to interfere with it, just as thinking about one's movements interferes with the process of walking downstairs. All therapists have noticed the tendency of patients to copy their mannerisms unwittingly, but pointing this out usually brings conscious mechanisms into play which disturb this automatic identification process.

Provided a child grows up in an environment where those around him are reasonably healthy and well-adjusted, and provided also that the figures influencing him are open and honest, neither concealing important aspects of themselves nor confusing him about their motives, the models the child internalizes will be a reliable guide to the world in general and he may be expected to be healthy and well-adjusted in later life. What idiosyncrasies and wide deviations from the norm occur in parental figures or in the family as a whole will be corrected by later experience with siblings, teachers, other adults and the peer group generally.

This process of correction is experienced subjectively (when we are made aware of it at all) as something unexpected or startling happening to us. The model is experienced *as if* it were outside of us, just as our visual image is perceived *as if* it were external rather than an image on the retina of our eye or a pattern on the visual cortex of our brain. The model is *projected* on to the real figure before us. Or, to put it another way, we experience the real figure *as if* it were the projected model; we discover this is not the case only when the model fails adequately to predict the actual behavior of the person before us. There is then a sense of shock or surprise, and the projected model may subsequently be re-internalized in a corrected form whereby its prediction is likely to be more accurate on the next occasion. Unless something interferes with this corrective process, the models are normally subject to continuous revision, so that adaptation and reality sense should, other things being equal, steadily improve with widening experience.

Defective adjustment, when it occurs, can result from two main sources, one more serious than the other. If the parents or other adults who have a formative influence on the child are themselves maladapted, the child will necessarily internalize their examples and suffer from similar or related problems, at least in the earlier stages before correction of the model is possible from interaction with other, less deviant examples. But as the child grows older, moving increasingly outside the family circle and coming under the influence of other adults or children, the values and attitudes implicit in his early models will be more and more questioned, and the models corrected steadily to approximate gradually the norms of the wider society. This process is, of course, especially striking on those occasions where an individual, formerly closely tied within a family system, is seen by others to change rapidly for the better (or by his family for the worse!) when he moves suddenly into a wider network. Moves into boarding school, the first summer camp, army service or a relationship with the first boyfriend or girlfriend are all well-known examples producing such changes. One sees this phenomenon particularly in immigrant families, embodying the values of an older, more authoritarian culture, when children become adolescent and begin to demand the freedom and independence customary at that age in the host country.

The second, more serious set of problems occurs where the child is not only presented with models which are maladaptive (or even where he is given models that were once adequate but are unsuited to changed cultural conditions), but is also led by his early experience to avoid testing, correcting and changing them. He may be discouraged from mixing with others who might challenge the family attitudes ("You don't want to play with the rough boys, they are not our sort." "She is common." "We don't like people who try to be better than others."), or punished for expressing views he hears contrary to those his parents hold ("Don't let me hear you say that again." "How can you criticize our ways after all we have done for you?").

But even such barriers to the development of new models are relatively easy to overcome, precisely because they are open and recognizable. More difficult are the innumerable habits of evasion, avoidance and subtle distortion of the truth that the child incorporates as part of his own inner models, since they are the only way of relating to reality he knows. If the parents preserve fantasies about themselves to hide painful deficiencies, or perpetuate grandiose family myths to distract attention from the skeletons in the family closet, the child will learn to misperceive reality in similar fashion. Once his perception and judgment are distorted, exposure to a more healthy environment is not by itself an adequate remedy. Painful truths are simply denied; feelings are kept apart to avoid awareness of contradictions; or faults are blamed on others (paranoid/schizoid level). Alternatively, more sophisticated avoidance may occur at subsequent developmental levels, such as avoidance of an honest relationship of dependency by a depressive rejection of others as untrustworthy or unable to provide adequate care ("I am

so awful that nobody can love me"), or by contemptuous manic superiority and manipulative control ("I am so marvelous that people cannot help loving me") (depressive level). Thought may become divorced
from feeling, attitudes kept compartmentalized (anal level), or a massive
but organized dissociation may take place to enable the person to play
a convincing but false role throughout his life, for the deception of
himself as well as others (oedipal level). Hanna Segal (3) and Anna
Freud (4) have described such mechanisms with great clarity.

Once such defensive mechanisms are established, ordinary experiences
are no longer enough to enable the inner models to be progressively
corrected and mental health increased. For though the necessary events
may occur repeatedly in a person's external life, the corresponding inner
experience may be prevented from occurring in response to these. For
an external event to bring about a corresponding inner experience, the
connecting link of *attention* must be maintained, and it is precisely this
which is lost, or, rather, deflected by habit, at the crucial moment. Sullivan (5) expresses this more clearly than many others in his idea of
"selective inattention," whereby the unconscious is regarded more as
the sum total of the experiences (inner and outer) we habitually avoid
perceiving, than as a box in the attic or basement in which secrets are
locked away.

Such avoidance mechanisms are well known in experimental psychology. For example, if a succession of words, some neutral and some
emotionally loaded, are flashed on a screen for such brief periods that
they are hardly recognized, the neutral words are correctly recognized
more often than the loaded ones. Yet, for such differential recognition
to occur, the words must have been perceived accurately at some lower
level of the nervous system, which instructs a higher level (connected
with consciousness) not to recognize them. Once such mechanisms have
developed, we are in the position of the rat on the electrifiable grid,
who is repeatedly shocked just after hearing a buzzer or seeing a light.
At first he leaps off when the painful shock is applied, but soon he
learns to jump when the neutral stimulus occurs just before it. By doing
so he automatically avoids a painful experience, but he also automatically prevents himself from discovering whether the shock is still actually being applied, and continues to jump off even if the experimenter
disconnects the electrical current.

Though all other forms of learning of this type (instrumental learning) gradually fade or extinguish if not reinforced by repetition of
the punishment or reward (reinforcement), the type of learning just

described, called a traumatic avoidance response, is extremely enduring and resistant to change, for the obvious reason that the model (grid electrified) itself prevents the corrective experience which would change the model (grid not electrified) from taking place. The *connection* is lacking between event and experience. Exactly the same principles appear to apply to human learning, except that the relative complexity of human functioning allows correspondingly subtle and sophisticated forms of evasion. Unlike animals, man is able to lie, and above all to lie to himself.

To cure the rat in the above example, the animal must somehow be held on the grid long enough to discover that it is no longer electrified. This may be done either by force or by some form of reward sufficient to counterbalance the fear, but as soon as the way is found to enable the animal to experience the changed conditions the habit will begin to dissipate. The problem with humans is the same in principle but different in degree.

CORRECTIVE PROCESSES

Ordinary life provides in varying degree for correction of inadequate models, and it also provides some possibility for correction of the avoidance mechanisms which prevent improvement of the models themselves. Deprived children who have learned not to trust may gradually begin to expose themselves to the risk of hurt in the stable, loving and patient environment provided by a good substitute home, until they can once again put themselves in the hands of others and accept love. The persistently rebellious child of an unloving father may be fortunate in finding a kindly, interested teacher or employer, from whom he can discover that authority, properly understood, is a manifestation of love, care and respect. The child traumatized by exposure to premature or excessive sexual experience or emotion, who flees from sexual involvement thereafter, may encounter a tender and patient lover with whom sexual desire may gradually appear and unfold.

Such individuals are, nevertheless, fortunate. For many, particularly those whose defense mechanisms are complex and powerful, life if anything continues to reinforce a tendency towards avoidance, and here the various forms of psychotherapy have their special place. All seek to supply a special form of learning situation where, in a basic atmosphere of security and trust provided by the support of a professionally trained person, the avoided experience is approached and re-experienced at a pace adjusted to the particular requirements of the subject.

Psychoanalytic Methods

Psychoanalysis and its derivatives are still perhaps the best known methods of attempting this. In a secure, relaxed situation the patient is encouraged to associate freely. The sudden blocks, jumps or "knight's moves" in the stream of thought and feeling are noted by the analyst and the underlying fears causing the obstructions or diversions are explored and clarified. A gentle pressure is thereby applied to hold the patient "on the grid," to enable the more mature aspect of the patient to see his evasion and to exert pressure on himself to face his avoiding.

The most powerful aspect of such work seems, however, to be the relearning that occurs through the transference—the projection onto the analyst of the patient's inner models. The analyst notes the distorted ways in which he is being perceived and points this out, perhaps connecting such distortions with the parental or other significant figures with whom the models were first developed. At first, this is just information as far as the patient is concerned, something he knows in his head but which has little effect on his feelings or on his actual control of his behavior. A long process of repetition or working through is usually necessary for the relearning to alter the subject's whole being rather than his intellect alone. The painfully slow effect of this approach is a cause for concern by analysts and non-analysts alike.

Action Learning

Psychoanalytic methods developed in the context of a two-person relationship, particularly in a situation where (in the influential Freudian school) nonverbal observation and communication were actually limited by the prone posture of the patient and the position of the analyst behind him, on the whole listening carefully but not looking with the same attention or able to perceive clearly even if he did. The technique was also developed in an era characterized by great valuation for intellect, which had been responsible for the development of scientific knowledge and the powers this made available. This overvaluation was, paradoxically, implicitly retained in the form of psychoanalytic treatment even though the rationale of the treatment developed from a distrust in intellect and a new respect for the emotional forces which had, until then, been denigrated.

The development of group psychotherapy, however, put people face to face, and inevitably focused more attention on nonverbal exchanges and the helpful ways in which people became models for one another by direct observation. With the development of conjoint family methods, many practitioners recognized rapidly that this nonverbal interaction was even more important than the verbal communication in determining the changes that occurred, and one sees a focus on this aspect in most of the work of the pioneers, even where they developed their methods quite independently. As the technique evolved one sees an increasing awareness that what the therapist *does* is much more important than what he says, that the model he provides is rapidly, often immediately, internalized and effective, in contrast to the slow process of change accompanying verbal interpretation and transmission by symbolic means through the intellect.

The mechanisms by which this process of change occurs are still obscure, and their clarification may perhaps be the next major breakthrough in family therapy (and, indeed, in psychotherapy generally, since these mechanisms are clearly operative also in group therapy with strangers and individual work, though less obvious). At this stage we can only look at what evidence is available from clinical experience, and speculate about possible explanations.

The first mechanism is perhaps obvious enough, and has already been touched on. The original models were internalized by the child not through hearing verbal descriptions of parental figures but by seeing them behave, experiencing them directly. The models were internalized as wholes, as total images, not built up bit by bit as must happen through hearing verbal descriptions. It would seem more natural to correct such images or models by a similar process, by exposing the individual to a different corrective experience rather than to a description of one. At the same time, the new experience must occur in relation to the old model if correction is to occur, since not every present good experience changes the effect of a past unpleasant one; this condition is perhaps fulfilled when transference has developed, for then the program of expectations or predictions is arising from a particular model, or, to put it another way, the model is projected onto the real present figure. In such a case one might expect correction of the model to occur where it is discrepant with the actual experience, leading subsequently to the internalization of an altered model and to a different program or set of expectations in reaction to similar future experiences.

The second condition is akin to that of holding the rat on the grid. The new event must actually be experienced, and the therapist must provide conditions in which the patient does not use avoidance behavior and "switch off" at a crucial stage when anxiety mounts, leaving the expectations uncorrected. This can be provided by a secure situation in which other anxieties have been minimized by establishing a safe boundary. The therapist provides support and encouragement, in order that trust in the helper developed by previous experience may enable the healthy part of the patient to join him in the treatment alliance and maintain the thread of his attention despite the fear evoked by the disturbing fantasies the model arouses.

This correction of the inner world of models or object-relations may occur in fact much more by role-playing than by interpretation, provided role-playing is understood here not as acting a false or invented part but responding naturally (with a real response already formed and available in the therapist from his own models) in a manner which is called out spontaneously by the situation itself. The therapist does not act in the sense of pretending to be someone he is not; he simply reacts in distinction to not-reacting, releasing a response already present in the form of a preparatory postural set which he might, however, choose to inhibit if he feels such an experience would be premature for the patient, or if he wishes to remain more of a "blank screen" to encourage the development of a richer transference fantasy first (projection of the model on to himself).

In trying to communicate *in words* about this aspect of psychotherapy I have encountered great difficulty. When watching videotape recordings the modeling influence is always obvious, often deeply meaningful, even moving. But when one attempts to *describe* it, tries to communicate it in a mode suited to the conveying of verbal, conceptual information or interpretation, it appears either banal, or too obvious to speak about, or unconvincing. Even where it does carry conviction, it comes across with quite different emphases from the interaction witnessed on video. Descriptions of modeling of nurturance and supportiveness can sound maudlin; controlling interventions can carry the impression of violence or brutality; actions which have the intention of releasing sexual feelings all too often seem to be coarse and to discourage tenderness and sensitivity. Perhaps this is inevitable, for only video recording of this nonverbal aspect can convey *simultaneously* all the nuances of expression, posture and tone of voice, the warmth as well as the abrasiveness, the smile which accompanies the sharp provocation, the quiet receptiveness as well as the lusty sexuality. An artist could perhaps convey all this adequately on paper; I cannot, and am obliged therefore simply to warn the reader of the inadequacy of the verbal mode to communicate nonverbal events, at least as I employ them.

In simpler, more straightforward instances these methods are nevertheless easier to describe, at least in general terms. Deprived, inadequate parents who respond to a frustrated, hyperactive child by indulging or ignoring it, alternating with violent rejection and punitiveness, are sometimes astonished as the child becomes quiet, responsive and controlled when the therapist gives it his full attention together with patient, firm containment. At a following session, the parents' management has often changed dramatically for the better as if they had "imprinted" the therapist's behavior. Similarly, anxious, hesitant parents may gain confidence and authority rapidly if the therapist sharply rebukes a provocative, misbehaving child.

In a marriage where spouses shrink from conflict and pull their punches, the occasional use of forceful, direct criticism by the therapist, if carefully measured and not overdone, will often lead to more honest and meaningful exchanges between the partners.

In the therapy of one couple, the wife shrewishly attacked while the husband encouraged her by suffering passively, his eyes moist and mournful like Tenniel's carpenter in *Alice Through the Looking Glass*. Instead of supporting him, I good-humoredly "sent up" what he was doing by imitating his responses in an exaggerated way, adding deliberately to his persecution and saying I was not surprised that she was the biggest shrew I had ever met, and that she might as well finish him off. "I'm amazed at you," he said, "Surely one doesn't kick a man when he's down!" "Why not?" I replied, "If you kick him hard enough he might get up!"

This so provoked him that he did in fact "get up" and berated me for my callous attitude, saying he thought it disgraceful for a doctor, who should be kind and sympathetic, to have such views. Having taken me on in this way he became less masochistic and was subsequently more active and forceful, not only with me but also with his wife, which she welcomed. Her shrewishness had been an automatic and healthy, if unsuccessful, response to his passivity.

Similarly, the capacity of the therapist to feel relaxed and at ease discussing sexual matters, and to make it clear by his manner that he has an attitude of acceptance and enjoyment towards his own sexuality, is quickly absorbed by patients; even blunt, coarse language, if carefully adjusted to the patient's responses, may diminish inhibition in the behavior of spouses towards each other.

In one videotape of a complete marital treatment, I say in the first interview to a passive, mother-dominated husband whose wife complains that he prefers to masturbate instead of making love to her: "You can't have a *really good fuck* on that basis; it has to be forceful, and spontaneous...." (meanwhile thrusting my fist in the air, like a cheerleader). On the video one sees him stop in his tracks and change the subject (and her eyes light up!) before he says: "I would prefer you had not said a word like that...I feel a little bit ashamed of...." I make it clear that I have used it deliberately. This leads on to a discussion of her relative relaxation in relation to sex and words describing it (her own frigidity emerges later), his prudishness and over-control, and her desire for him to be more "randy" and passionate (which such interventions facilitated).

While writing this, I have become aware that such descriptions seem most convincing when the process is witnessed and reported by a third party. This occurs in the following illustration, where modeling influence was taking place quite unconsciously until the observer spotted it. Though a trivial example in one way, it was at the same time quite awesome to realize how much the behavior even of sophisticated psychoanalysts could be influenced, without our or their knowledge, and that such unintended nonverbal interaction, taking place below the threshold of awareness, might leave its traces when the symbolic communication which was the conscious purpose of the meeting had long been forgotten.

The occasion was a seminar that my wife and I were leading with a group of psychoanalysts in a foreign country, whose leaders, a psychiatrist and a psychologist, were themselves also married. Towards the end, various manifestations of oedipal rivalry and desires "to split the parents" led one of the participants to make an interpretation pointing out that this was occurring. He emphasized in particular the mutual admiration and rivalry between the two leading couples and clinched his argument by saying "Normally, Dr. and Mrs. X, as our leaders, behave before us in a correct and formal manner. I have never seen them touch each other while they work with us. But I have noticed that Dr. Skynner, as he speaks, quite often touches his wife, and as he does so I have observed that Dr. X touches *his* wife!" In fact, neither of the couples had noticed these events at all.

Encounter methods make extensive use of this type of interaction, and in my experience, both personal and professional, they do so very productively where avoidance reactions are not too severe and where there is a sufficient degree of stability in the personality as a whole (it has been demonstrated that the methods can be dangerous in some more unstable individuals, leading to breakdown). Many forms of behavior therapy use this technique even more explicitly and according to carefully planned programs whereby the patient is brought to face the type of experience which makes him anxious by a carefully graded sequence of experiences, each closer to the dreaded happening than the one before. Both encounter and behavior therapy however tend (except in the case of some practitioners well versed in analytic principles as well) to ignore another important aspect of the interaction, and its neglect must always lead to rather naïve and limited techniques. This complicating aspect is that the *projected model can actually affect the internal experience and behavior of the therapist himself* in such a way that he is manipulated into enacting the behavior pattern predicted by the model and so verifying its correctness once again. Thus, patients who fear rejection manage to get themselves rejected repeatedly; patients with harsh parents manipulate their doctors into scolding them; the woman who fears sexual assault often provokes it; and people who prefer drugs to psychotherapy often succeed in getting their physicians to prescribe them.

It is not clear how this comes about. Nonverbal communication certainly seems to account for much of it, as when someone who projects an unaccepted, sadistic or bullying aspect of himself into others then adopts the corresponding postures, gestures and facial expressions of the victim, provoking others to bully him. But some manifestations of counter-transference, as this is usually called, are hard to explain on this basis if only because of the detailed nature of the response, as in the following example:

A physician and his wife had been referred by two psychoanalyst colleagues for conjoint therapy because of a vicious and intractable marital conflict which had persisted despite separate psychoanalytic treatment extending over nine years and four years respectively.

After about four months of four-way conjoint interviews with my wife and myself, and following a confrontation between myself and the wife over her destructive bitchiness, the wife appeared more integrated and contained, and the husband's confusion, dependency and lack of identity showed clearly for the first time. His wife for the first time was also able to avoid seeking to rescue him and to give more care and interest to herself. At a certain point in the interview I noticed I was having a fantasy of taking him off to the pub for a drink, and found myself thinking, "It's hopeless staying here with these women; what he needs is a man to talk to him and help him, away from them." I could have reported this fantasy and this would have opened up the problem in a different way, but I decided to wait and the outcome was more interesting.

A little later, my wife began to talk to him in a rather lecturing, scolding tone, upbraiding him for his passivity. I found myself increasingly irritated by this, and finally decided to report my responses. I told my wife that it was unhelpful to lecture him in this way, saying that such behavior on her part never helped me if I was the recipient, and that it certainly was not helping our patient either. I said the women must leave him alone, and let him find his own way.

The husband responded dramatically to this intervention. He said he could accept the kind of criticism my wife was making of him from a man, and could feel that this could help and strengthen him. But to accept it from a woman somehow diminished him; it was like hearing his mother keeping on endlessly at him or at his father. By contrast, my telling my wife to stop was what he had always wanted his father to do for him, to support him and strengthen him against the powerful females in the family. Instead, his father had always wanted to take him off to the pub, where he and his male friends would drink and complain about the wives they did not dare to challenge at home! He had always resisted these invitations, fearing that there was something homosexual about these relations into which his father sought to draw him, and that they took him even further from being a man. This interchange seemed to be a turning point in his therapy, which was relatively successful by the conjoint method and terminated after 15 months with a reasonably satisfactory marital relationship established. Although I reported my fantasy to them later during the interview, it is clear that the crucial interaction was on a modeling, action basis rather than as a result of intellectual understanding alone.

In this example, both my wife and I were clearly responding to some projections of the husband's models. While my wife's behavior could well have been accounted for on the basis of postural cues in the husband, my fantasy about going off to the pub with him cannot readily be fitted into this type of explanation, and this type of tuning in to a patient's fantasies, which all experienced group therapists will recognize, is best left open until further knowledge is available. A physical or physiological explanation is fortunately not necessary in order to make use of this type of communication.

This phenomenon enables us to clarify further the manner in which change in the internal models occurs, particularly in certain forms of analytic work. The prime necessity is for the therapist to receive the projection without being taken over by it and acting it out, so that he can maintain his own identity and respond in a way which is related to the expectations inherent in the model projected, but which is different and, hopefully (if the therapist is more mature or healthy than the person on whom the original model was based), a more accurate and effective guide to dealing with the world. Sometimes the therapist is aware of such a projection as an alien force with which he has to struggle, while in other cases the struggle and choice may be less conscious and determined more by the discipline of good technique.

The example just cited was less conscious, for at first I believed my fantasy of taking the husband to the pub was a purely personal feeling based on my mood. My inhibition of the impulse was of course based on technique—the principle that one should not change the rules or the limits of the treatment situation on impulse, in case the decision should be determined unconsciously by the pathology one is trying to understand (as in fact would have been the case in the example given). It would, of course, have been appropriate within the rules of the situation to *report* the fantasy, but instead I *did* something, also within the established rules, by criticizing and checking my wife. This was, in fact, a different response to the same set of conditions, which gave the husband an experience he had always needed from his father, and which subsequently seemed to alter profoundly his relationship to his wife and to women generally.

There are times when the therapist may feel himself to be possessed, indeed, even overwhelmed or threatened with the loss of his identity and sanity, and he may carry around such disturbing projections within himself for quite long periods before they suddenly disappear and return to the patient. Klein calls this massive involuntary transfer of psychological functions "projective identification" and Jung has also described clearly this type of experience, whereby the therapist seems to internalize the patient's problem for a time and work on it himself, handing it back in altered form. At a recent conference at the Department of Children and Parents at the Tavistock Clinic Dr. Hyatt Williams and Miss Elizabeth Henderson presented a fascinating experience of this kind where, during conjoint therapy of a family, the co-therapists seemed to internalize and work on a terrifying mother-image responsible for the family's many difficulties (6).

My personal experience suggests that the more disturbing encounters of this kind occur in relation to one's own unresolved problems based on primitive, uncorrected models. Though frightening and at times quite disturbing, the therapist, as well as the family, often derives great rewards from a successful outcome of such a struggle because he has been obliged to tackle a personal unresolved difficulty in the process. A team at the Eastern Pennsylvania Institute (7) has developed a highly sophisticated and effective technique of this kind, whereby one co-therapist allows himself to be "sucked in" to the family pathology, and is then rescued by his colleague who has remained more detached. The family is thereby confronted with the destructive aspects of its interaction through the therapists' accepting the experience of suffering from it themselves.

In such circumstances the therapist needs to remind himself of the danger that his responses will in fact be self-protective, but that he will deceive himself by justifying them in therapeutic terms. I am sure that many interpretations, particularly in work with groups, really serve this protective purpose. Two incidents come to mind in this connection. The first occurred in a supervision group composed of house-parents of children's homes, with whom I met over several years. Towards the end of the group's existence, one member said to me hesitantly, as if I might be offended, "I often wonder if you know how we use you to solve our problems?" I replied that I knew from the way I had used my own group analyst, during my personal group analysis, how little a group leader ever learned of the ways in which the individuals were each using him differently as a transference figure on whom to project their feelings. But I had also understood from this that the group leader did not need to know these details, provided he could trust the healing powers inherent in the group and its members, could see when the group process as a whole was blocked and could understand how to free it.

The second incident occurred at the end of a session of a therapy group I was conducting, which had been quite the most complex and interesting I had ever experienced. I had been used as a transference figure on many levels simultaneously—parent, sibling, spouse and child —and felt a desire at the end to point this out. I realized in time that I felt myself to be confused and fragmented by the conflicting projections that had assailed me, and that the real object of the long interpretation I had in mind was to put myself together again. When I reported these thoughts to the group, the members confirmed that the interpretation I had proposed would almost certainly have been more in my interest than theirs, for they had already found the session rewarding and complete. I realized that my comments would be an unnecessary imposition and that I could equally well recollect myself on the way home.

What is necessary, I believe, is for the therapist to keep still, to keep his balance, to maintain his own identity in the face of the multiple projections that bombard him. In a recent paper Cooklin (8) has expressed a similar view:

> It also seems to me that much of the therapist's activity, interpretation or whatever, can be seen as work in the service of keeping his role alive and defined. Bowen stresses that continuously *"defining his self to the families"* is "one of the most important processes in this method of psychotherapy." This part of the work may be in order to stay still, in the face of whirling family communications.

In association with my own experience of such situations, the phrase "the eye of the storm" seems appropriate. The eye of the storm in a family interview is the still center, reached by allowing oneself to move willingly into the middle of the emotional cyclone, through the region of greatest turbulence and danger to one's own stability, into the "I" where one is most truly oneself and, since it is one's own center and point of balance, the point where one is most free and most in control of oneself.

If one can reach this point, probably any response one makes will be valuable, whether interpretation, action, or simply waiting in order to allow others to interpret or act instead, as they usually do if the therapist can inhibit himself. When a decision is difficult, the best advice is that of my friend and colleague Malcolm Pines, regarding a difficult countertransference problem I was encountering.

He suggested, "When in doubt, shut up."

5 CONSCIOUSNESS, COMMUNICATION AND CONTROL

Alas, after a certain age every man is responsible for his face.

Albert Camus, The Fall

It takes two to make a murder. There are born victims, born to have their throats cut, as the cutthroats are born to be hanged. You can see it in their faces.

Aldous Huxley, Point Counter Point

The study of Expression is difficult, owing to the movements being often extremely slight, and of a fleeting nature. A difference may be clearly perceived, and yet it may be impossible, at least I have found it so, to state in what the difference consists. When we witness any deep emotion, our sympathy is so strongly excited, that close observation is forgotten or rendered almost impossible; of which fact I have had many curious proofs. Our imagination is another and still more serious source of error; for if from the nature of the circumstances we expect to see any expression, we readily imagine its presence.

Charles Darwin, The Expression of
the Emotions in Man and Animals

ORGANIZATION OF PSYCHIC MATERIAL

In the previous chapter, the emphasis was on the role of learning and the readiness with which models of human functioning are transmitted from one generation to another as if man were clay on a potter's wheel, waiting to receive whatever shape the potter's hands imposed and having no inherent form of his own. However, the model seems rather to determine the organization of psychic material which is already to some extent given, selecting some types of emotion for inclusion and providing patterns of behavior for expressing them, while rejecting and

82

suppressing alternative possibilities. The basic material itself seems remarkably similar in all individuals; the deeper one goes in the exploration of oneself or of others the more one finds, despite differences of sex, class, ethnic group and creed, that human nature is remarkably consistent even though what is done with it produces an astonishing variety of human beings.

In human development an initial undifferentiated unity, wholeness, completeness or balance is divided and arranged according to a pattern provided by the parental and other models, producing a particular personality or identity—a unique combination of some of the common material. These included aspects of an individual's psychic life will feel to him familiar, acceptable and good, while excluded aspects will be rejected and condemned (if they are perceived as part of the self at all), or they will be denied altogether and experienced only insofar as they occur outside the boundaries of the self. The components sanctioned by the model become "what I am," while the rejected aspects, though inevitably still within us even if not acknowledged, become "what I am not."

Freud's theories contain this concept clearly, though in practice the issue is dealt with in a rather piecemeal manner as if such one-sided and partial manifestations were an inevitable consequence of civilization and maturity. Jung's system expresses the same idea in a more comprehensive and systematic fashion: the "shadow" containing all that is not accepted within us; the "persona" including all that is presented to others; the "anima" and "animus" standing for all that is denied and rejected in the original taking of male and female positions, respectively. By Jung, all these splits were seen as temporary solutions, stages in a developmental process in which the most satisfactory solution is a reintegration of the denied or neglected aspects of the self, whereby the opposites are transcended in a new synthesis. Such an idea is to be found, of course, in all religious and mystical sources. It is not the "good" man, identified with and even excelling in those aspects of himself he accepts, who proves the most fertile ground for the seed of knowledge, but rather the man who acknowledges his "sins," who begins to re-admit to awareness his rejected aspects and to realize, in doing so, that he is like all other men who have ever lived.

Whether the ultimate goal is seen as an adequate adjustment to the ordinary demands of life (as the Freudians and behaviorists tend to view it) or as a synthesis of psychic functions going beyond this and giving a new understanding and unity with the world in general (as

Jung and the more mystical and religious writers would have us believe) there seems no doubt that the original infantile state of wholeness and unity has first to be lost and inner divisions of some sort imposed. In mythical terms, man is cast out of the Garden of Eden with a fall into duality, the knowledge of good and evil; he descends, in other words, to a lower level of organization lacking that third principle which can reconcile the opposites and enable them to coexist. Many, perhaps most, individuals appear satisfied to live in this state of division, adhering to a clear concept of themselves at the expense of losing all they have rejected. Only a small proportion of people feel the need to return to the source, to regain the original unity, and even these do so in varying degree and always at great cost in terms of temporary confusion, loss of identity and of sureness of purpose.

However, though the unity from which we fall and to which we may find our way back appears to be the same for all men, the divisions which split this original unity into fragments, into conscious and unconscious, into "me" and "not me," are different; on the scale of whole cultures, different solutions are found.

While no absolute preference can be justified for any one solution, a particular type of organization may facilitate certain necessary aspects of human life more than another. For example, the harshness of Spartan child-rearing practices, or of the traditional British boarding-school system, may have been good for producing obedient and resilient warriors or diligent and self-sacrificing administrators, but at the same time they may have limited the capacity for warm and tender relationships.

On the level of the family, too, solutions to this problem of what is to be selected and rejected, out of the original pool of possibilities, may make possible a greater or lesser degree of self-fulfillment. Some solutions may permit the satisfaction and expression of a wide range of human needs and tendencies, so that the necessity for repression or denial is minimal and easily coped with. Other solutions may be highly taxing, obliging the individuals concerned to spend much energy containing a great deal of their natural tendencies, with much conflict, exhaustion and perhaps explosive and destructive eruptions of affect when the defenses are overwhelmed and inner pressures become acute.

Most restrictive of all are those solutions where the models contain inherent contradictions and inconsistencies, whereby the individuals bearing them are confronted with almost impossible tasks and doomed to lives of insoluble conflict and inevitable failure, unless they are rescued through the entry of more accurate information into the system.

Thus a boy may be told at some moments that he must be brave, strong, confident and successful, yet scolded at other times for manifesting these very qualities and punished for attracting attention or being assertive. In the middle fifties, a multidisciplinary team of behavioral scientists, psychiatrists, mathematicians, anthropologists and communication engineers attributed the severely disordered mental functioning of schizophrenia to such logical inconsistency in the original programming of the child by its parents. These double-binds, as the incompatible instructions were called by the Palo Alto Group (1), might lead to breakdown and withdrawal from reality into an inner world of fantasy, with its inevitable crippling personality restriction, as the only escape. British writers such as R. D. Laing, A. Esterson and D. Cooper (2) have since expressed similar views, though in a rather polemical fashion attributing a conscious intention to mystify to the families of such patients. In my experience this is usually not present; rather, all seem to be joint victims of a pathological family process, though it is true that the diagnosed patient is often more open and vulnerable to the contradictions, and so also more accessible to treatment and the truth it conveys, than the more heavily defended family members who thereby escape mental breakdown themselves. Studies of this kind, which have looked at individual psychopathology and family processes side by side, have over the past 25 years developed increasingly sophisticated ideas relating the individual and group aspects and bringing them together in unified concepts of family psychopathology.

Fundamental to those theories which have their roots in dynamic, analytic principles (as opposed to behavioral ones) is the notion, summarized above, that those aspects of the human psyche denied legitimate expression in the value system of a particular family will manifest themselves in other ways. Their expression can take many forms and may appear to involve individuals, or the family group, or perhaps the wider social context without seeming to affect the family group itself, though in all cases only a study of the whole situation will provide a satisfactory explanation.

Denied or restricted emotions may result in the children displaying symptoms, either physical, like recurrent infections or accidents, or psychological, such as nervous fears or nightmares. Alternatively, one or more children may be scapegoated, seen as manifesting characteristics alien to the family values and so labelled "the jealous one," "the greedy one," and so on. Another possibility is that the parents may manifest open conflict, each projecting unacceptable aspects into the partner who is then attacked for possessing them; this in turn may be dealt with by one partner completely capitulating and becoming an extension of the other's personality, losing his own identity. Or the family may not complain at all of problems within itself, because all members project them onto neighbors or the social agencies dealing with them, producing problems outside themselves or conflict between the family and the surrounding social matrix. The latter possibilities will be explored in later chapters, when we come to study marital interaction and the relevance of social networks.

Of course, the denied aspects are still present, finding outlets in alternative ways which are disguised and hidden by complex systems of attitude and thought, like the expression of impulses in dreams. Ferriera (3) has described the family myths which are passed from one generation to another, disguising and rationalizing the aspects of the family pathology which cannot be hidden or displaced entirely. Byng-Hall (4), extending this concept in an attempt to widen individual-based psychoanalytic ideas to comprehend family dynamics, has pointed out how philosophical and ethical systems are created not only to disguise denied needs and impulses, but also to create defensive attitudes and reaction formations against them. Jealousy and competitiveness thus become ambition and team spirit, to be used only against out-groups, while group solidarity and the sacrifice of personal needs—justified in terms of family loyalty, brotherly love, and consideration of others—may be emphasized within the family system to a point where it is harmful to the development of its individual members and their ultimate independence.

If this view is correct, an approach to family therapy which recognizes it will not expect radical, beneficial and lasting change in family functioning unless these denied and disruptive factors are given expression in a more acceptable and integrated way. This is true whether the actual techniques of treatment are based on analytic methods and the fostering of insight in the family members, or on behavioral principles where retraining takes place according to insight and understanding which the therapist may keep to himself. Either way, an expansion of consciousness whereby the hidden determinants of the family's functioning become meaningful is an inescapable condition of any real change, even if this understanding is largely confined to the therapist.

What *is* made conscious, in practical terms? More detailed principles about the conduct of family interviewing will be set out in a later chapter, but here we can state in general terms that what usually needs to be made more explicit is the family communication system. After this is achieved, other changes, often including insight, will follow, both during the formal interviews and in family interaction among family members. In particular, the nonverbal components of the interaction need to be recognized and translated by the therapist into the verbal mode, at least for himself and possibly for the family too.

NONVERBAL COMMUNICATION

As a child develops towards maturity, the means by which the parents communicate with him, in order to influence his behavior, change according to the degree of autonomy the child has developed. A toddler wandering near the fire will be picked up and removed if he is still at the stage where little cooperation can be expected. When he is a bit more responsible he may be slapped, scolded, or spoken to sharply, in which case the posture, expression and tone of voice—the nonverbal components—are the important factors. A still older child can be ordered or instructed, using a more emotionally neutral mode. And, as the child becomes more autonomous, mature parents will make a greater use of reasoning and explanation, until in adolescence the information relevant to a suggestion or request is increasingly given and the individual is left to make up his own mind and to be responsible for his own actions. As we know, it is useless and indeed harmful for adults to give children more choice than they are able to manage, but a steady increase in freedom and personal responsibility, according to developmental level, is also necessary if independence is ultimately to be attained.

This increase in responsibility and autonomy is accompanied by a progressive substitution of verbal and symbolic communication for the phylogenetically and ontogenetically earlier nonverbal mode, until verbal communication is, in educated members of a civilized community, the dominant form of interaction. However, the more primitive, uneducated and stimulus-bound the culture, the more the nonverbal mode will prevail. And in families showing pathology, from the point of view we are taking here, an inability to translate the nonverbal mode into the verbal is usually a crucial contributing factor. Once substitution of the verbal for the nonverbal is made more possible, an entirely new range of possibilities for change is usually opened up.

John E. Bell (5), among family therapists, has perhaps expressed this fundamental principle most clearly, in a way that is in accordance with both psychoanalytic and group-analytic ideas:

> The symptom may be thought of as an attempted communication expressed in such a manner and intensity as to effect disturbance in the group. Often signs learned in early life are used because of their simplicity, even though they may have lost their historical sign value and be now less efficient in most situations than more complicated symbolic language. The use of a more primitive sign-language suggests the breakdown of more complex communication, and ineffectiveness in more mature language.... Sometimes the nonverbal represents a breakdown of the verbal method of communication. The latter may then be restored only when there is a special support and sanction for expressing content verbally (p. 7).

Charles Darwin, in *The Expression of Emotion in Man and Animals* (6), pointed out the remarkable similarity of animal and human nonverbal communication and concluded:

> The movements of expression in the face and body, whatever their origin may have been, are in themselves of much importance for our welfare. They serve as the first means of communication between the mother and her infant; she smiles approval, and thus encourages her child on the right path, or frowns disapproval. We readily perceive sympathy in others by their expression; our sufferings are thus mitigated and our pleasures increased; and mutual good feeling is thus strengthened. The movements of expression give vividness and energy to our spoken words. They reveal the thoughts and intentions of others more truly than do words, which may be falsified.... He who gives way to violent gestures will increase his rage; he who does not control the signs of fear will experience fear in a greater degree; and he who remains passive when overwhelmed with grief loses his best chance of recovering elasticity of mind. These results follow partly from the intimate relation which exists between almost all the emotions and their outward manifestations; and partly from the direct influence of exertion on the heart, and consequently on the brain. Even the simulation of an emotion tends to arouse it in our minds (pp. 365–366).

So little further interest was shown in the subject, perhaps because of the nineteenth century Western preoccupation with reason and with verbal, logical expression, that Darwin's book could have been written yesterday; indeed, if written tomorrow one cannot help feeling that it would be a bestseller, so great is the current interest in ethology and so limited the progress made in this area until the past few decades. When I wrote a dissertation (7) partly concerned with this subject as part of my psychiatric training 19 years ago, a search of the literature revealed very little of interest regarding human ethology, most of it poor stuff compared with Darwin's contributions; today, as the sale of books by ethologists like Lorenz, Tinbergen, Morris and Ardrey (8) has shown, interest in the field has mushroomed among the general public as well as within science itself.

What was only suggested a decade or two ago, but now seems clearly established, is the fact that nonverbal communication is mainly composed of fragments of different types of action which are used to signal the individual's attitudes and intentions and to affect, through these, the behavior of others. Nina Bull (9) pointed out that nonverbal communication appeared to consist of what were really postural "sets," "preparednesses for action," and that these physical attitudes correlated so closely in humans with emotional attitudes that it was found impossible for experimental subjects to feel depressed when maintaining a buoyant, elated posture, or vice-versa. The nonverbal mode is thus composed of actions frozen in their first unfolding into movement or manifestation, like the preparatory posture of a runner as he crouches waiting for the starter's pistol, though such communication is in general based on minimal, subtle postural clues, often unnoticed without careful and repeated study (10).

These postural sets or attitudes convey to others that a particular action is likely or unlikely to take place. Thus frowning, while leaning forward, with tight lips and staring eyes, fists clenched, is a step towards overt aggressive behavior. Translated into verbal form it says, "I am ready to fight you, but whether I do so or not is conditional on *your* behavior." The condition required to release the action may be apparent from the context (a dog growling over a bone, a man scowling as another flirts with his wife) or, in humans, it may be conveyed in the verbal mode ("You have insulted my name"). Smiling is based on another type of attitude (similar to the bared-teeth response in some animals), which indicates that there is no intention to attack, that the individual wants to avoid provoking others or being molested. The second type of response described might be a reply to the first, when the threatening attitude of the first individual might be more likely to dissipate in the face of a conciliatory response from the second.

The nonverbal signaling system is thus mainly concerned with social control, the attempt to influence the behavior of others. It has, as the Palo Alto team (11) put it, command functions, and its importance in families lies in the fact that it is the main means by which the system of family rules is conveyed, including rules about what may or may not be communicated in the verbal mode. Little Johnny reacts to mother's frown as a slap-coming-if-you-don't-change-your-behavior signal, and he takes avoiding action. Similarly, the fact that Aunt Agatha drops the tea tray with a look of horror when they repeat a four-letter word has some permanent influence on the way in which the children use language within the family system.

Verbal communication, on the other hand, is based on a totally different principle. While nonverbal communication uses an actual part of an action to signal something about the whole, verbal communication utilizes symbols, whereby one thing (usually a sound, shape, or in deaf and dumb language a movement) is *agreed* by a group of individuals to stand for an object or relationship which may in no way resemble it or be connected with it.

Being arbitrary and inexhaustible, words and symbols can be used to label not only objects and events but also, on the basis of noting similarities and neglecting differences, groups and classes of objects and events. We can continue if necessary to abstract fewer and fewer characteristics of the raw sense data, thereby achieving increasingly general categories—Fido, Pekinese, dog, mammal, vertebrate, animal, living organism, etc. (12). Relationships can be subjected to the same process, so that we can label a spatial relationship between two objects and two others (distance), a relationship between the change in this distance and a change in the movement of hands about a clock-face (speed), the rate of change of this change in turn (acceleration), and so on.

Symbols also enable us to represent a much greater range of possibilities. The negative can be expressed, whereas with nonverbal communication this expression of the negative can only be achieved by beginning to do something and then not carrying the act to completion. A threat-posture, for example, is in effect saying, "I'm going to hit you" passing into "I have stopped short of hitting you," with the implication, not possible to formulate in nonverbal fashion, "I would hit you *if . . .*" with the "if" left open to conjecture. The danger of misinterpretation with nonverbal communication is very great, with destructive potential for all involved.

Various other logical connections in relationships can be expressed only in symbolic form, such as the non-exclusive "or" which means "either one or both" of two alternatives. Watzlawick, Beavin and Jackson (13) have pointed out how these key logical concepts underlie others, so that nonverbal, analogic communication does not confer the advantages of logical thought and reasoning.

A further feature of symbolic communication is the possibility it gives of representing, and communicating about, the process of communication itself. When workmen are demolishing, constructing or repairing a building, the first step is often to put up a small temporary building alongside it to accommodate them while the work is in progress. On a big project one can sometimes even see a hut provided for a night-watchman to watch over the temporary building until it, in turn, is ready for occupation. A similar principle applies to verbal communication. The same raw material of symbols can be used to study symbols, and this communication-about-communication can in turn be communicated. One can also study *this* process itself (linguistics, semantics, etc.) and communicate-about-communicating-about-communicating, and so on indefinitely. Just as the temporary building or the watchman's hut enables the workmen to have some quarters to use while they are demolishing, constructing or altering the main building, the possibility of communicating-about-communication makes it feasible for us to stand back from, observe problems in, and improve our ordinary communication processes.

This, it will be evident, is exactly what psychotherapy is all about. The family is occupying the system, is subject to its faults and is so much a part of it that its members cannot see them. The therapist can help because he stands outside the system (and, indeed, only as long as he can do so), having his base not in the family conflicts but in theories about family conflicts generally. His communications are taking place on a different level from those of the family, on a *meta-level*, though of course he may aim to get the family to join him outside the system as part of the therapeutic alliance, to spend part of their time outside their "house," which he is helping to rebuild, in his temporary "workman's hut." To achieve this, he helps the family to translate its private, unconscious, nonverbal interaction into the verbal mode where it can not only be *said* but also *talked about*.

The point needs emphasizing because there are important philosophical implications. Bertrand Russell solved many apparent logical contradictions with his "Theory of Types" (14), where he demonstrated that many seeming paradoxes arose from the simple failure to distinguish between these meta-levels, rather in the same way as there would be difficulties if the workmen forgot the nature and purpose of their temporary hut and regarded it, and the scaffolding, as part of the house they were building.

For the therapist the implication is that he must avoid being drawn too fully into the family system, because if he allows this to occur he will become confused and ultimately controlled by that system—he will become another member of the family, as powerless to help them as they are to help themselves. Though he goes into the system and works on it, he does so from a base outside it, a base which is temporary for each particular family even though the therapist moves this base from one site to another.

A further important difference between the verbal and nonverbal communication systems is the extent to which we are normally aware of the signals we send by means of them. Nonverbal communication takes place mainly below the threshold of awareness, and though we may subsequently become conscious of changes in our mood, consequent on nonverbal signals from others, we are often ignorant of the signals themselves. Similarly, we have little awareness, until we see ourselves on movie film or television, or hear our voices on tape recordings, of the signals we are sending to others through our expressions and postures, as is evident from the surprise and embarrassment most people experience when they hear and see themselves.

It is too much to say that we are always more aware of our verbal communications than the nonverbal, for a moment's reflection shows that this is not the case, and that there is considerable overlap. In social intercourse we learn from an early age to smile and to conceal any expression of negative feelings, while at a cocktail party we are usually more concerned with manifesting an agreeable facial expression and tone of voice than with the content of the verbal small-talk which is often largely irrelevant. At the same time, one does not begin to realize what a vast amount of information is transmitted nonverbally, below the threshold of awareness, until one starts to be alert to this aspect of family interviewing. Even then it is difficult to register most of what passes unless one can watch a videotape of the same interview several times.

One striking example of a nonverbal signal which we all send, and to which we all respond constantly, is the eyebrow flash. This is a brief raising and lowering of the eyebrows and opening of the eyes, usually accompanying a bob (brief backward movement of the head) and a smile. We are all aware of the significance of a smile and not only learn to feign it when we are not feeling friendly but also receive it from others, in consequence, with caution and reserve. But the eyebrow flash is usually performed unconsciously, and the response to it is equally automatic and outside awareness unless it is caricatured grossly, as by Groucho Marx. When it occurs, we simply come to regard someone as friendly and feel warm to them in return, without knowing how these feelings were engendered. The reader can soon become convinced of the importance of nonverbal communication by paying attention to the effect of this signal alone, both when he makes it himself and when he sees others doing so.

Because the nonverbal system is usually below the threshold of awareness, it expresses clearly and constantly, for those who pay attention to it, that aspect of psychic functioning we call the unconscious, as well as that other hidden area which is conscious but secret. Those who take the trouble to learn this language will find that it is frequently possible to cut straight through to the essence of a patient's problems simply by being visually attentive to him, literally *seeing* in the first interview, sometimes as he comes through the door, a crucial attitude or conflict which might be difficult to find even with hours of verbal inquiry or months of attention to verbal associative patterns alone. It takes much time, of course, to develop sensitivity to this kind of information, but patience and persistence are amply rewarded. Becoming interested in this neglected subject while doing my psychiatric training, I sat and unobtrusively sketched patients at conferences where I was not personally involved in the interviewing, trying to link the expressions I discerned with the history being reported by the examining doctor, or being elicited from the patient. Gradually my perceptiveness benefited from this exercise, and though I still take histories from patients partly for record purposes, and partly also because they expect this, my diagnoses are based largely on nonverbal information.

While engaged in this exercise of sketching patients, I noticed that I was casting my own features and posture in a form similar to their own, in an attempt to draw them. In the course of this, I became aware that this was perhaps the basis of empathy since if one feels one's way into someone else's posture and expression one soon finds that one has felt one's way into his emotional attitudes as well. As Bull (15) demonstrated, physical and emotional attitudes are two aspects of the same thing. I came to the conclusion that this mimicking of other people's attitudes and movements, taking place at a subliminal level imperceptible to them and, indeed, usually below the threshold of awareness of the person in which it is occurring, is probably the basis by which we usually understand how others are feeling (16).

In this way, one can gradually become sensitive to fine gradations of expression, and see layer upon layer of attitude and counter-attitude, like a series of onion skins, in physical form. The voice may be soft, but too gentle to be true and with a hard quality concealed within it, accompanied by a similar over-sweetness in the smile in an attempt to conceal a harshness in the facial expression. Beneath that one may discern a deeper fear of rejection, and below that again an unsatisfied longing for affection and recognition. At first only the more gross, obvious attitudes may be apparent. Then, as one becomes accustomed to these, something behind them becomes perceptible, first faintly and then more clearly, just as the details of a landscape are picked out after the first fleeting impression (17).

If, therefore, the therapist becomes aware of the family's nonverbal expression and interactions, and makes the experience available to them by formulating these observations in the verbal mode, he gives them the possibility of making what is unconscious conscious, at least to some degree. The verbal mode brings about the possibility of objectivity, of criticism, of standing outside what is happening and correcting it— something akin to scientific method, however rudimentary. A distillation of the accumulated knowledge of others, past and present, can be brought to bear on the situation, giving the opportunity of modifying the pattern and developing a more subtle, intelligent and adaptive reaction to the same stimulus. Because history can then be learned from, history can stop repeating itself, whether it is the history of the individual (Freud's repetition compulsion) or of the family (the condemnation of children to reproduce the parent's neuroses).

The following examples illustrate well the fashion in which inner objects or models of past relationships, projected on to current figures, can produce profound difficulties of the kind frequently seen in psychiatric referrals. The first is of a mother-child couple, in which the father was not seen though the younger sister was also present at the interview:

David, a lively and sturdy boy, aged three, was referred because of uncontrollable temper tantrums over the previous two years which appeared to have the effect of capturing all mother's attention in a negative way. The sister, aged one, was developing a similar problem and would scream if the mother cuddled David. The mother, a simple woman, seemed kind and well intentioned but hearing her story one obtained the impression of intense jealousy throughout her family of origin which had never really been acknowledged or resolved. Her statement that she "had not a single feeling of jealousy in her anywhere" strengthened rather than diminished this suspicion. At first she presented her family of origin as happy and united except for one brother, the next following her in the sibling order, who was said to be always jealous, difficult and disruptive. It seemed all negative feelings were either projected into, or directed towards him, and how intense such feelings were can be judged by dreams the mother reported of this brother strangling her and stubbing out cigarette ends on her hands. While the mother was speaking of this brother, David played quietly beside us, a change often noted when a projection is withdrawn from a child and its origin is being discussed.

My surmise that this brother was scapegoated because mother's family of origin could not cope with jealousy, that she had joined in this defensive process by projecting all her jealousy into him too, and that the present problems with her son were connected with her own unadmitted jealousy and hostility towards him as a new rival, were all put straightforwardly to her. She was incredulous but nevertheless left this first interview saying, "You have certainly given me something to think about," and appeared to feel that some light had been thrown on the mystery.

When seen with the boy a second time a month later, she reported, "We are better. I am a lot better, we are all a lot better and he is a lot better too." It seemed significant that she began with herself, then spoke of the family as a whole and mentioned the boy last. She said that she had been mystified and intrigued by the unresolved problems revealed by our discussion, but two weeks later, while in church, she had suddenly become intensely aware of her jealousy towards this black sheep brother, realizing that she had always resented him because her own mother had given him more attention since he was sickly. She also recalled that about the time of his death everyone had seemed to be rejecting him; she had suddenly felt responsible for his death and guilty that she had hurt him during his life; in consequence she had broken down and wept quietly during the service. (The associations in the service itself which may have linked with the events of the first interview to bring this about were not elucidated.)

Since this time, in fact for the previous two weeks, her relationship with David had changed greatly and she was able to give him more affection and play with him, and had managed to avoid being upset and provoked by him. She had realized that she had identified David with her brother, and because she had always felt left out and rejected by her own mother, who favored the boys in the family and particularly this brother, she had never been able to love her son and had wanted to hurt him. David's behavior had also changed completely for the better.

The second example was also first seen as a mother-child couple, progressing later to a family interview:

Steven, aged just under two at the time of referral, had suffered repeatedly from severe status asthmaticus and had been referred by the pediatrician because the severity of these attacks gave reason to fear for his life; he was no longer responding even to steroid therapy. There were various indications of associated emotional disturbance, including severe tempers in which he would bang his head and pull his hair out if frustrated, and he would frequently hit other children and be sorry afterwards. He had not been a troublesome child, and there had been no problem complained of until he suffered from pneumonia at the age of 18 months, when he was hospitalized for six weeks. During this hospitalization, mother visited him daily and was with him most of the time.

On inquiry, it appeared that the asthmatic attacks tended to follow excitement and over-activity. Mother said he appeared better when he was able to be sick and "get it off his chest." At the time I saw him, Steven had once again been admitted following severe status asthmaticus and the situation was worsening as the mother's anxious and rejecting attitude towards Steven was exciting anxiety and rejection towards her in the nursing staff, leading to a vicious circle which was not helping the situation. I therefore saw mother and boy in the outpatient clinic first of all, when my report to the pediatrician stated:

"I had quite a fruitful interview with them. Curiously, Steven sat quietly on her lap throughout and they displayed a pleasant and easy relationship. As this contrasts so much with the mother's behavior as seen on the ward, I think it may indicate that she is able to show warmth and affection when her need for security is met in an individual situation. Though physical precipitants are prominent, there are certainly severe anxiety and several related psychological factors, as follows:

"1. Mother's mother, who was a severe asthmatic, died during what is believed to have been an asthmatic attack when mother was seven. It was the mother who found her and she has never been able to forget this experience. When she sees Steven becoming asthmatic an image of her own mother, dead, appears before her, the two become confused and she fears Steven will die as well. I believe her anger and punitive behavior towards him are defenses against intolerable feelings of panic, i.e., she attacks an intolerable experience rather than the boy himself.

"2. She has always been frightened of her temper, and so fears in these circumstances that she may harm him, becoming increasingly guilty and anxious in consequence.

"3. Since the onset of Steven's asthma she has been frigid and the marital relationship has become increasingly strained, the husband resenting the child and saying she prefers him. No doubt this is connected with the maternal grandmother's death, which mother could perhaps have interpreted as punishment for her normal oedipal incestuous wishes, so that the child's illness now invokes similar anxieties in turn.

"I will write to the GP to suggest that he puts the mother on some Librium which will diminish her fear of her hostile impulses. As regards the general management of the case, the behavior I witnessed during the interview with me suggests that support and contact to the mother herself by all those dealing with her would relieve her own anxiety and panic, and indirectly help the boy."

This intervention sufficed to break the previous vicious circle of increasing anxiety and rejection, bringing about a more positive interaction between mother, child and medical staff. Shortly after, a family interview was arranged at which father, mother and child were seen together. The following point-by-point summary of the tape recording of this session demonstrates the complex relationship between the experiences of both parents in their families of origin and the family relationships which developed after this child was born. The nonverbal component in the interaction is also interesting:

I inquire about the associations of the asthmatic attacks, and the mother links them with excitement. For example, when she plays with the boy she becomes excited herself and realizes that he gets excited in response. She can recall that this kind of excitement was something of which her own mother was very critical. At this point, even though the parents are talking to me and not offering any stimulation to Steven, he stands up and begins to pull mother's hair.

The father now says that Steven is highly strung, like the mother, and that his (father's) sister is also excitable in a similar way. He goes on to say that the child's asthma does seem to follow excitement, for example being tickled, though since Steven was given medication to counter the asthma he would often get "heated" instead.

I ask if the excitement leads to attacks of asthma or to the behavior problems, or both, and the parents agree that it may lead to either result. At this point the boy again grabs the mother's hair and begins pulling it in a violent, excited way, at the same time making pelvic thrusts towards her body as if attempting intercourse. The possible sexual significance of the boy's behavior is not pointed out but some confirmation of my impression is given when the father immediately begins speaking about the way Steven comes into the parents' bed at night, and both parents talk about how they lose their tempers when the boy interrupts their sleep.

They go on to talk about exchanges of anger, in which mother says that she gets "heated up" when she becomes excited, throwing things at father or walking out and slamming the door. The father says that he remains calm and always avoids a fight though both feel like being aggressive to each other and would welcome a more open display of anger.

I ask about expression of positive feeling, at which the mother reports that their sexual life is bad. The father confirms this, saying that sex has been very unsatisfactory since Steven was born, mother agreeing that she cannot bear to have her husband touch her. She has been unwilling to acknowledge the problem or do anything about it, refusing to take the medicine prescribed by her GP or to see a specialist about her frigidity. The father continues by saying that their lack of sexual intercourse is what makes them both irritable. The mother says that she wants to make love to him but can't get any pleasure out of sex.

The father next says that he became very jealous of the boy after he was born, since all the mother's affection seemed to be transferred to him. He accepted the fact that she needed to look after the child to begin with, but became more upset when she did not transfer her affection back to him as the boy became older. He began to go out with friends and get drunk, which caused fights between his wife and himself.

The mother at this point agrees that sex was "lovely" before Steven was born, and admits that she put the boy first in her affections after his birth. She suddenly changes the subject to talk about her father, and how she was his favorite. When her mother died she recalls feeling bitterly jealous of her stepmother and almost succeeded in breaking up the marriage. At this point the father cuts in to describe how he had an almost exactly similar relationship in his childhood, being very close to his mother, losing his father and bitterly resenting his stepfather.

At the end of the interview the mother returns to speak of how she can't forget seeing her mother dead, being reminded of this whenever she feels Steven may have an attack.

It will be apparent why, in all such situations, traumatic experiences need to be examined in the context of the complex relationships of the family of origin and the effects on the developmental sequence of the individual concerned. In the second case, we see that the mother's loss of her own mother through an illness similar to that displayed by her child had a particularly threatening significance since it occurred in the context of an ambivalent relationship between them. This was complicated by the fact that she was her father's favorite and therefore likely to have been exposed to greater conflict and fears of success in the oedipal relationship. The mother's recollection that her own mother disapproved of excitement, with associations in the interview suggesting that it was sexual excitement which was forbidden, could have been an important factor in the failure to resolve the oedipal situation, since it is likely that mother's father turned more to her and burdened her with adult emotions she could not cope with. When mother had a male child the exciting, incestuous relationship is once again made possible from one point of view, but the negative, prohibited aspect of it now seems to be turned towards her husband. She becomes frigid and frustrates him, while the boy appears to be over-stimulated, from all the evidence presented in the interview, by a relationship which is excessively sexual. Present knowledge of the nature of asthma does not enable us to decide whether the origin of the disorder in this child is wholly constitutional, producing terrifying associations for the mother, or whether it arose in some more psychologically meaningful fashion.

The parents in this case were both very limited, primitive personalities and after the considerable improvement in the boy's condition which followed this limited intervention they did not persist with marital or family interviews, though these were offered. It was left to the pediatrician to refer the child again, should there be further cause for anxiety, and though, unfortunately, the case was not followed up routinely by the psychiatric department, the fact that further requests for intervention were not made suggests, on the basis of previous experience, that an adequate degree of improvement in the presenting problem was maintained.

The mirror-image family constellations in the families of origin of this couple are also interesting, and a common finding if one looks below the surface when examining marriages. Such shared experiences in early life will be linked, according to the principles outlined in this chapter and the previous one, with similarities in the models internalized by the marital partners and with similar patterns in the nonverbal communication systems, whereby the marital partner can be relied upon to respond to nonverbal signals in similar fashion to members of the family of origin.

6 MARRIAGE: GENDER AND ROLE

*The value of marriage is not that adults produce children
but that children produce adults.*

Peter de Vries, Tunnel of Love

*There isn't any formula or method. You learn to love
by loving—by paying attention and doing what one
thereby discovers has to be done.*

Aldous Huxley, Time Must Have a Stop

*I have found that women and men are so different in
their approach and concept and in their way of working
that the mere fact of a woman taking part in a meeting
can change the solution of problems in an important
way. If women take part in all fields of our social and
economic life, and not just in family questions, this will
to my mind produce important changes. This must be
wholly beneficial, and need not apply specifically to
political life.*

Simone Veil (French Minister of Health), quoted in
The Guardian, *6th August 1975*

In all that has been said in the preceding chapters no mention has
been made (except by implication and in the case illustrations) of the
additional complications which follow from the fact that humans reproduce sexually rather than asexually. But this division of our species into
two different forms of organism which must cooperate to reproduce
(an arrangement which it is believed first began with the blue-green
algae about one thousand million years ago) introduces a further and
altogether different dimension. No aspect of human experience preoc-
cupies us more, in the sense of drawing towards itself our interest, time
and energy, mostly in the form of passive fantasy which may be more
or less disguised. Yet, despite this (or because of it?), few subjects
have received less real interest and concern in the sense of systematic
and objective study and experiment. The scientific exploration of gender

100

differences and their social significance has, in fact, grown up only recently, over the past 25 years or so, and is still rudimentary. It is almost as if a temporary madness or hypnosis were programed into our species, to protect the reproductive process from examination and so ensure that it will not be affected by man's intelligence and the control that his mind gives him in other activities.

GENETIC VARIABILITY

The main advantage of sexual reproduction for the species is the great variability it ensures. Provided too much inbreeding is avoided —no doubt one reason for the incest taboo—a suitable balance is maintained between the reliable transmission of stable qualities from one generation to another on the one hand, and their constant combination into a rich variety of patterns and possibilities on the other. Organisms which reproduce asexually simply "bud off" a part of themselves till it separates and becomes a new individual; the bud is a copy of the parents, organized according to the same genetic instructions. In sexual reproduction, half the genetic instructions come from the male parent, half from the female, the chromosomes which carry the information being "shuffled" and reduced in number to form the specialized sex cells in each individual, then recombined as sperm and egg meet following the act of intercourse to make up a complete and, except in the case of one-egg multiple pregnancies, unique blueprint for a new individual.

DETERMINATION OF GENDER

In human cells 22 pairs of chromosomes are similar in size to each other, but the twenty-third pair can be similar or different in size and has a special function in the determination of gender. All females have two longer X chromosomes, while males have, replacing one of these, a shorter Y chromosome. This Y chromosome appears to have as its only function (apart from one gene producing hairy ears!) the development of part of the primitive sexual tissue in the organism into testes producing male sex hormones, and the suppression of the development of female sex glands and hormones; the opposite takes place automatically in the absence of the Y chromosome.

Once the sex glands are differentiated in a given direction under the influence of these chromosomes, the hormones they produce determine further changes; the male hormones inhibit the growth of the rudimentary female genitals (Mullerian ducts), stimulate male genital development and later, when the developing blood supply carries the hormones to all parts of the body, determines its evolution to a masculine pattern, including the structure and function of the brain. Female sex glands, triggered by the double-X chromosomal combination and producing female sex hormones, similarly suppress the development of the rudimentary male genital apparatus (Wolffian ducts), stimulate development of the female sexual organs and modify the body and brain to a feminine pattern (actually, it seems to be the absence of male hormones, rather than the presence of female ones, which results in this).

Once the hormones have influenced the body and brain towards a male or female pattern, which in humans takes place before birth, the change is largely irreversible. It is this early influence on the structure of the body and the nervous system which accounts for many differences between the sexes in aptitudes and interests, even though the level of hormones also has a *direct* influence on their later manifestations too.

Corrine Hutt (1), in a concise and clear review of the evidence on gender differences, summarizes the difference between male and female developmental patterns in the following way:

> ... from the very early weeks of uterine life, males and females develop in characteristically different ways. Not only do the respective genetic complements confer especial properties on the course of development, but the gonadal hormones, and the testicular hormone in particular, have important formative and organizational functions. Even intra-uterine factors affect male and female fetuses differently.... From the moment of birth onwards differences in structure, in metabolism, in physiological and psychological functions characterize the development of the two sexes. Many of these non-cognitive differences are shared not only with other societies which manifest very different culture patterns but with other primates as well. The similarity in many attentive, exploratory and social behaviors between monkeys, chimpanzees and children is remarkable, and this fact alone makes a purely environmental interpretation of sex differences difficult to countenance. In addition, the demonstration that hormones can, directly or indirectly, exert an influence on reproductive structures and sexual behavior as well as nonsexual behavior implies that the endocrinological experience in early development can determine a number of sex-dependent features and behavior patterns (p. 112).

Summarizing the main differences, she concludes in another review (2):

> It must be emphasized once again that we have been describing and discussing males and females *in general*, not any particular man or woman, and the degree of overlap on any performance or function is appreciable. Nevertheless, the *patterning* of abilities is characteristically different in many women.... The male is physically stronger but less resilient, he is more independent, adventurous and aggressive, he is more ambitious and competitive, he has greater spatial, numerical and mechanical ability, he is more likely to construe the world in terms of objects, ideas and theories. The female at the outset possesses those sensory capacities which facilitate interpersonal communion; physically and psychologically she matures more rapidly, her verbal skills are more precocious and proficient, she is more nurturant, affiliative, more consistent and is likely to construe the world in more personal, moral and aesthetic terms (p. 133).

In the volume first quoted (3), Hutt comments upon the significance of these different developmental patterns:

> The characteristic patterns of behavior and styles of development are particularly well suited to the roles that males and females fulfill. The conformity and the consistency of the female's behavior, in fulfilling a predominently nurturant role, make her a stable and reliable figure for the dependent infant. For more effective communication, increasing reliance is placed on the linguistic skills and it is noteworthy that in verbal functions, as in nonverbal ones, it is in *execution* that the female excels. The male on the other hand excels in spatial and numerical abilities, is divergent in action and thought, and is generally superior in *conceptualization*. There can be little doubt that these sex-typical patterns of abilities and behaviors are adaptive and, in evolutionary terms, have conferred distinct advantages (p. 113).

Furthermore, such sexual differences have been demonstrated clearly among other primates and mammals, and across widely different cultures. The Whitings (4) found consistent differences between the behavior of male and female children across cultures as varied as India, Kenya, Mexico, Okinawa, the Philippines and the U.S.A.—for example, between the ages of three and five "boys engage in more horseplay, rough and tumble physical contact; girls seek help or touch others more frequently ... Boys remain more aggressive in the older age group, insulting and continuing horseplay, and they increase in seeking attention and dominance" (p. 182). They conclude however "that none of the traditional theories alone can account for the social behavior of children. That boys are more aggressive and less nurturant than girls cannot be completely explained by either a biological or a cultural model" (p. 184).

This complex interaction of nature and nurture has received attention from other researchers, particularly in the United States, where the degree of malleability of human nature under social conditioning has been a question with special relevance to the formation of the nation itself from a mixture of different ethnic and cultural backgrounds. Thus, while Hutt tends to emphasize general, statistical differences between males and females as a whole, and the importance of genetic and hormonal determinants, Money and Ehrhardt (5), like Stoller (6) earlier, focus more upon the great variability within each gender and the overlap between them, especially in the hermaphrodites—rare aberrations where clear, full physical expression of one gender, and suppression of the other, has not occurred. There may be difficulty in deciding which gender such individuals should be assigned to, for they may be genetically male, hormonally female, and so on. What has been clearly demonstrated is the great and overriding importance of psychological and environmental factors (attitudes of parents, playmates, etc.) in determining gender identity in humans, as compared with the greater influence of physical factors in animals. A careful study of a pair of male twins, for example, where one was brought up as a boy while the other was raised as a girl (because the penis of the latter had been accidentally destroyed during circumcision) revealed a successful outcome and the development of healthy, unconflicted male and female personalities and attitudes in the boy and "girl" respectively.

Nevertheless, despite differences in emphasis and interpretation, there is much agreement about the importance of physical, hormonal influences in the development of differences of attitude and behavior between males and females. For example, summarizing the results of various studies of aggressiveness in rats produced by isolation or by electric shock, Hutt (7) concludes:

> Males exhibit aggression under both these conditions far more frequently than females.... Not only is the frequency of fighting greater but the males also maintain the fighting stance for longer.... Ovariectomy of the adult female has no effect on the amount of fighting she displays, but castration of the adult male does depress the level of aggression slightly. Castration of the young male, how-

ever, considerably reduces the amount of aggression. Since in the rat sexual differentiation of the brain takes place soon after birth, the younger the rats are when castrated the less "male" the brains will be. Accordingly, if rats are castrated at weaning (about three weeks of age) their level of aggression in adulthood is considerably lower than that of intact males, but that of males castrated at birth is lower still and indistinguishable from the female level of aggression.... Conversely, if females are exposed to androgens in infancy, and their brain is thereby masculinized, they show levels of fighting and aggression as adults comparable with those of normal males. In monkeys, too, we saw earlier that females virilized by androgens before birth show more threat, attack, chasing and rough-and-tumble play than normal females. Males castrated at birth show no appreciable decrement in these behaviors, since at birth differentiation of the brain has already taken place (pp. 110–111).

Money and Ehrhardt (8), reporting on studies by their group on genetic females (XX chromosomes) who had been affected by male hormones before birth either through abnormal growth of a gland (adrenogenital syndrome) or by side-effects of drugs given to their mothers in pregnancy (progestin), but who had all been brought up as females with early correction of any anatomical abnormality, found many statistically significant differences from matched controls. They tended to be tomboys, highly active physically, showing a lack of satisfaction with the female role, choosing male rather than female playmates, preferring slacks to skirts and rejecting jewelry, perfume and hair-styling, choosing toy cars and guns as toys rather than dolls, demonstrating a lack of interest in looking after babies and an absence of fantasies and dreams of marriage, pregnancy and motherhood, being more interested in a career instead.

Exact counterparts to these syndromes do not exist, for though male hormones produce a masculine pattern, the female pattern does not need the presence of female hormones but occurs in the absence of male hormonal influence. However, genetic males (XY chromosomes) suffering from a disorder in which the effects of their existing male hormones are prevented from occurring by an inborn defect (androgen insensitivity syndrome) show many physical and psychological features more usual in females. Besides the physical feminization, they were found to show a high incidence of: preference for marriage and homecraft, putting these before a career; fantasies and dreams of raising a family (though they were sterile and needed to adopt when they actually did so); play with

dolls and other toys usually associated with girls; strong interest in infant care; and contentment with the female role, preferring female
clothing and enjoying a strong interest in personal adornment.

Attempts to change gender patterns in general by altering the social
environment alone have so far had limited success, if success is judged
by the criterion of making women more like men rather than facilitating
their fullest individual development within the possibilities of their
natural, biologically determined role. Writing of the kibbutzim, a disappointed feminist (9), states: "Young women, rejoining the kibbutz
after army service, wish to begin as early as possible to build their
family nest. . . . Job involvement seems to be weaker among young
women in the kibbutz than are family considerations; when job and
family conflict, preference is given to the latter, as indicated by the trend
to early marriage. Thus, with all of the achievements of the kibbutz,
two basic problems of women remain: dissatisfaction in the sphere of
work, and comparatively little participation in civic activities and the
management of the society" (p. 569).

This followed upon a period when "the concept of women's equality
was greatly distorted. Women's striving was towards an identification
with men, toward an equality that disregarded sex differences and it set
forth male qualities and activities as a model for both sexes. This distortion of the concept of sex equality has occurred in the early stages
of other women's emancipation movements" (pp. 571–572). This period
was followed, with the easing of the economic situation and increase
in the numbers of children, by an increasing regard for the family as the
"corner-stone of stable kibbutz life," when the "former male-oriented
and mechanical interpretation of women's equality gave way to a recognition of differences in the interests and capacities of men and women—
differences that in no way render women inferior to men" (p. 571).

However, the interaction of genetic, hormonal and environmental
factors, and the interrelationship of all these with social learning are
extremely complex and only beginning to be glimpsed. In a fascinating
recent experiment Joslyn (10) gave male hormones to the three females
in a group of six young rhesus monkeys. The masculinizing effect of
male hormone on the brain takes place in monkeys before birth, and the
sexual and playful behavior of the females retained the usual female
pattern. However, though the three males were all dominant to the females before the experiment, the females gradually became dominant to
the males and their aggressiveness became so marked that the males
largely ceased making sexual advances to them.

There were also two points of special interest. First, the dominance of the females remained stable after the administration of male sex hormones to them was stopped, though it is at present not established whether this was due to a permanent physical change brought about by the hormone or to some form of social learning made possible by its influence. The second observation sounds all too human and demonstrates how, even in monkeys, the issues of dominance and leadership between the sexes are not always what they seem! "An exception to the female usurpation of dominance was a male, originally third in rank, which became the top monkey of the group and increased his frequency of aggression.... This male's enhanced status depended on the support of the second-ranking monkey, a female. When this female was removed from the group, the otherwise dominant male screeched, fear-grimaced, withdrew from social contact and was often attacked and beaten by the other monkeys. During the third trial, however, this male was able to retain his dominant status as long as he had the support of the second-ranking female at the beginning of the test session or as long as he could see or hear her" (p. 140). It seems that with monkeys, as with humans, it is difficult to discern who really runs the company, the boss or the boss's wife!

From all the evidence there seems no doubt, then, that unisex, which would be such a loss to both sexes, is a fantasy and that in general males and females show marked differences in psychological as well as physical structure and function which seem meaningful and adaptive in terms of the reproductive process and the needs of children. But these are *statistical* differences, abstractions, and the degree of overlap is so far much less carefully studied and documented. We all have indisputable experience that *some* men are less strong, less adventurous, less aggressive, less independent, less ambitious and competitive, worse at logical thought and conceptualization, more nurturant, affiliative and consistent, and more interested in children than *some* women, and so on. Though a woman can never be more than a second-class man, if she chooses to be a man at all, she may be better than a third-class man nevertheless, and vice-versa.

Whether these different variations around the general rule are best considered equally valid, or whether some, approximating more closely what seems to be the general biological pattern, provide a richer, potentially more harmonious and effective base for the rearing of children is difficult to decide. There seems at least to be general agreement that clear and unambiguous differentiation of the two gender roles within a marriage is necessary if the children are to develop without a harmful degree of confusion and conflict. This is true even of those authors most aware of the flexibility of early gender assignment. Money and Ehrhardt (11), for example, conclude that:

> despite great variability between cultures in the prescription of gender-dimorphic behavior in childhood, adolescence and adulthood, the existence of gender-dimorphism of behavior is itself invariant. The options are not limitless. In the final analysis, culturally prescribed (or prohibited) gender-dimorphic behavior stems from the phyletic verities of menstruation, impregnation, gestation and lactation. These verities are procreative imperatives, so to speak, in the design of any culture's definition of male and female roles, if that culture is to maintain its membership and survive. They specify that, regardless of peripheral options and alternatives, a well-designed, gender-dimorphic complementarity constitutes the nucleus—the procreative nucleus—of any system of behavior between the sexes. Children growing up in a culture differentiate a gender identity free from ambiguity if the adults of that culture, especially those closest to them, transmit clear and unambiguous signals with respect to the procreative nucleus of gender-dimorphic behavior, no matter what the signals with respect to peripheral options may be (p. 145).

What *essential* differences in gender role are required for mental health, as contrasted with non-essential cultural variants, is simply not firmly established by any scientific research to date, whatever answers clinical experience or traditional wisdom may suggest. Money and Ehrhardt (12) suggest that "cultural and historical variations of the masculine and feminine social and vocational roles are acceptable so long as there are clear boundaries delineating, at a minimum, the reproductive and erotic roles of the sexes. The traditional content of the masculine and feminine roles is of less importance than the clarity and lack of ambiguity with which the tradition is transmitted to a child" (p. 164).

Dicks, speaking as a clinician of vast experience, in his classic work on marital problems (13), goes further though his own conclusions still rest on the biological basis of marriage and the family:

> For success in marriage there must be present in each partner a clear and definite sense of *sexual identification*.... The male parent is typically equipped to fight, hunt, build, manipulate, roaming outside the home *for* the home. The female parent gives expression,

more typically than her man, to tender and protective emotions, and responds to those of her offspring, staying close to them.... The woman's identity is typically linked with cherishing, nourishing, maternal functions toward *his* children *for* him. Few marriages can endure when these primary biological tasks are completely denied, or even if some of the secondary roles deriving from them are too flagrantly reversed.

However, Dicks makes it clear that

brittle and anxiety-laden overcompensations to mask an uncertain sexual alignment make for very insecure human relations. The secure male does not have to trumpet his virility and toughness, nor a secure female proclaim her femininity. It is the doubting, insecure man that is more likely to make aggressive sexual demands, to refuse "demeaning" chores, such as helping with the baby, and to act in defensive derogation against women. Similarly, it is the Amazon who puts on the "war-paint of sex appeal," ... or exploits the power of hysterical feminine weakness. At best, such exaggeration belongs to adolescent courtship behavior, when adult identity has not yet been achieved (pp. 34–35).

Many authors today would take issue with Dicks' image of woman's identity as based so completely on the function of motherhood, and performance of this *for* her man. In present circumstances, we can only acknowledge our ignorance, rejecting the extreme and partisan views of "sexists" of both sexes, and awaiting further scientific evidence and the fruit of more careful clinical investigation, both of which can develop only in an atmosphere of calm, patient and questioning openness. Some authors have already provided models of how this much-needed inquiry should be pursued.

Dana Breen (14), in a beautiful study of psychological changes in women accompanying the birth of a first child, using objective measures (repertory grid) informed by psychoanalytic concepts, has effectively dispelled the myth of female "passivity" as a core role-characteristic, even in relation to motherhood. Anne Steinmann (15), in a cross-cultural study of attitudes towards the female role, found that women not only desired a balance between activity and passivity, between the satisfactions of marriage and motherhood and of achievement and self-actualization, but regarded themselves as having attained it. And even though they felt that men desired a woman who fitted the dependent, passive, home-oriented stereotype, similar studies of men revealed that they also preferred the more balanced, autonomous females the women desired to be.

Suzanne Keller (16) has provided a superb overview of the female role and its assets and liabilities, which attains a rare objectivity and detachment. Reading it, one realizes that our difficulties in this area stem not so much from prejudice as from the fact that the experience of gender is so close to us, so much a part of us, that like our noses we cannot see it, cannot stand back and examine it.

The question of the relationship between the form or level of the marital relationship, and the development of the children growing within its influence, will be considered a little later. Meanwhile, we may find it illuminating to look at the institution of marriage from the viewpoint of the main dimensions we have already sketched out in previous chapters, that is: boundaries; hierarchy; developmental sequence; models; and communication. I shall, however, take them in a different order.

DEVELOPMENTAL LEVELS AND SEXUAL ROLES

Normal, healthy development is characterized, as we have seen, by a progressive capacity to relinquish the original relationship of egocentricity, total dependency and expectation of gratification without return, in favor of a more equal, mutual relationship where the needs of others and of the group as a whole are increasingly considered and respected, at the cost of greater self-discipline and restraint or delay in personal gratification. The three stages, or six sub-stages, set out earlier may be seen as bringing us to the point of genital primacy and of the mutual interdependence of the peer group characteristic of adolescence.

At this point the emergence of sexuality and the impulse to pair and procreate which then arises, consequent upon both the sudden rise in the level of circulating sex hormones and social pressures, bring new challenges. The adolescent or young adult is now obliged to integrate the various levels he has earlier passed through, in such a way that they can all coexist in one relationship. Having achieved his independence, he now finds himself impelled to fuse and blend more completely with another individual, in the relationship and act of love, than he has ever done since he left his mother's breast. And he must be able, between such moments of intimacy, to separate and become an autonomous individual again. For a full relationship to develop, each partner must be able to be totally dependent and trusting, yet able also to resume an attitude of independence upon resuming ordinary tasks, on rejoining the peer group, or when the partner needs support or cooperative endeavor is required.

There must also be, as Charny (17) has so clearly expressed, a capacity of the partners to fight and struggle with each other, or to hold to a position despite opposition, if the individuals comprising the relationship are to grow and retain their separate identities. And there is a place sometimes for healthy competition as well as for mutual, cooperative and complementary activities and interaction, both in the sexual relationship and other joint pursuits. A relationship or marriage in which these different forms of interaction can be fruitfully blended, and in which the partners can move from one to another with grace and ease, will be rich, rewarding and constantly renewed.

Problems arise when the participants have not successfully mastered a particular developmental level. Paranoid/schizoid functioning is characterized by the projection of unacceptable aspects of the self into the partner (who has been unconsciously selected to fit the projection satisfactorily) or by projecting it outside the marital dyad into a scapegoated child, or outside the family altogether into some agreed persecutor. Fixation at a later stage of the oral level, where the integration of perception and feeling characteristic of the depressive position had been to some extent attained, may lead to the mutual clinging of a "babes-in-the-wood" marriage, or to the kind of relationship which is exemplified in the "doll's-house marriage" (18), where a competent, powerful (but actually dependent) male is both mother and father to a helpless, childlike wife.

An anal-level fixation may be revealed in a relationship characterized by endless stubborn obstructiveness, an incessant struggle for power together with resistance to anyone being granted it, overlying a deep fear of loss of identity if there is any compromise or giving in. Such a constant state of hot or cold war (open attack or stone-wall obstinacy) which may be a defense against fears of the boundary-blurring intensity either of the earlier oral or the later genital levels, is essentially a nonsexual form of competitiveness.

Phallic rivalry, by contrast, is manifested in conflict which clearly has its origin in envy of each other's sexual roles, and so leads to impaired ability to use the other's sexuality for mutual pleasure. This may lead to militant sexual chauvinism, male or female, or to a "Don Juan" or "femme fatale" exploitation of the opposite sex. Genital level cooperativeness and acceptance of complementarity and mutuality (instead of excessive demands for infantile gratification, for power and total independence, or for equality in the sense of sameness) is required to integrate and give harmonious expression to manifestations of the other levels.

It should be added, of course, that one of the great benefits of marriage and the family is the opportunity they give the couple to re-experience and deal more effectively with the unsurmounted challenges of childhood. Only psychotherapy can offer a similar degree of freedom and opportunity to express difficult and unacceptable aspects of the self; indeed, a good marital relationship can provide care, tenderness and real gratification at a level and intensity that is seldom possible even in the psychotherapeutic relationship. But for repair to be possible, the regression still has to take place within the context of a more mature overall relationship, whereby the regressing partner can feel safe to trust the other, and the mate can know that the regressive demands are temporary and can possess a sufficient store, or continuing supply, of pleasure and gratification to enable him to tolerate them willingly. If this condition is lacking regressive demands have a destructive effect, bringing into play protective defenses or similar demands in the partner, with the possibility of a vicious spiral of escalating demand and deteriorating interaction. Thus, marriage can be hell or heaven, kill or cure, destroyer or curative agent, depending upon the degree to which the more mature levels have been securely reached.

Assortative mating appears to occur whereby spouses choose each other because of similarities or complementarities in developmental level. The choice is, of course, unconscious, and each partner may be consciously seeking the opposite of the feature on which the attraction is really based. The insecure female in the "doll's-house marriage" consciously chooses a competent, assertive male, but automatically selects the man in whom these attributes are a form of pseudo-maturity, covering and keeping at bay infantile longings very like her own. The man's underlying weakness, successfully hidden as long as he can project this into his wife, often emerges in the form of a breakdown when the wife receives successful psychotherapy and develops confidence and independence in her own right. Similarly, a man, thinking to escape from a possessive, controlling mother (though actually fleeing from the *wish* to be possessed and controlled) is consciously attracted to a girl who heightens his self-esteem and sense of independence by idealizing him as the strong father she never had, but she later becomes disappointed in him and dominates and controls him in a way he has become used to and which makes him feel secure.

Again, such similarities can be fruitful if the couple also have enough maturity and insight to work constructively on their shared developmental arrest, for then they will be ideally suited to cooperate in solving it. But if this is not possible, they find that they could hardly be more ill-matched, and will be more rejecting and attacking towards each other than if they selected partners at random. It should be added, finally, that though couples are usually attracted by shared developmental failures, the degree to which they operate at common regressed levels may be very different. Where this is the case, the partner who is in other ways functioning at more mature stages may be expected to outgrow the other, and the union may be likely to break up unless growth and change are avoided altogether. In the psychotherapy of such couples separation or divorce may often be a healthy and desirable outcome.

SYSTEMS, HIERARCHY AND MARRIAGE

The developmental advances required by marriage and the creation of a new family may usefully be looked at also from the perspective of systems theory and boundaries. From infancy to adolescence, the individual becomes increasingly free from external constraints and controls until, in early adulthood, he is very much his own master however much he may be unable, through personal limitations or ignorance, to exercise that freedom. He is concerned particularly with the idea of independence, often to the point of provoking conflict with the authorities he has until then had to submit to, and he is also preoccupied with finding his own identity, following the line of his own particular interests and desires. He is engaged, in particular, in seeking sexual freedom and opportunity.

It is ironic that it should be the sexual drive itself that confronts him with a new yoke. Love requires a partial giving up of personal, selfish demands in order to be able to consider and respect the needs of the loved one; though the sacrifice is voluntary, performed gladly and out of delight when it actually takes place, it is nevertheless a real loss of the freedom that has been so hardly fought for. However light the new burden of responsibility may prove to be, once it is actually assumed, it will always seem in advance a submission to a new slavery. Thus love and sexuality draw the young adult, who has struggled so hard against "the system," into a new and wider system where he is again a part of something larger than himself (as if he had ever really been anything else!).

The arrival of the first baby takes the process further (19). To the woman in particular (since she cannot so easily escape, like the man, to avoid the responsibility of a helpless, living being who needs constant care and attention if it is to survive at all—though the change is ultimately the same for him), there is a dramatic alteration overnight in her whole life-style. She is now more bound than she has ever been, obliged to serve and wait upon another individual when she may, 24 hours earlier, have been more spoiled, cherished and independent than she had ever been in her life. Both partners now discover that to control, to be responsible for, is to serve, to give up one's own desires and put the needs of others first. For those with good early experiences and loving parents who provided satisfactory models of generous care this may be a source of pride and satisfaction, though it will still entail inner struggle and increasing self-discipline nevertheless. But for others, who have lacked warmth and love in their own infancy, or who have been spoiled and encouraged to see themselves as the center of the universe, the spouse or the new baby will be seen much of the time as disturbing competitors or persecutors, and therefore resented and rejected.

Here, as elsewhere, the issue of authority and control is only another consequence of the position of one system within a greater one, expressions of the fact that the whole is more than the part. For a family to function, the parents must be responsible for, and so must be in charge of and dominant to, the children, even though the power is used for their benefit. While this may seem too absurdly obvious to need stating, a large proportion of family problems arise because the opposite situation prevails, and they are resolved satisfactorily when the therapist's authority is used to put the parents firmly in charge. Such unhappy relationships usually develop where the parents are themselves deprived or over-indulged, and need the children's approval and affection more than the children need theirs, for whoever needs support and approval least always has the power, at least potentially. Problems of this sort are often iatrogenic, a consequence of popularized and distorted child psychology and, alas, bad child guidance. Freud himself was eminently practical about matters of discipline and control, as can be seen from his views on soiling (20). Klein also makes it quite clear that children need structure and limits if they are not to become anxious at the possibility of losing control of their impulses (21).

The optimal power relations between husband and wife are less easily agreed upon, particularly in a time of change like the present. As we have seen in Chapter 1, some decision-making process is required which will permit *both* mutual consultation and discussion to find compromises most satisfactory to all, *and* an agreed procedure whereby controversies not resolvable by such discussion are settled one way or the other. Someone must carry this ultimate responsibility and accept the arousal of ambivalence and the position of loneliness that it entails.

The combination of autonomy and assertiveness required for this function to be exercised may be present in greater degree in the wife than the husband, in which case she will more often play this role and be the effective "head of the family" whether or not the husband is allowed to appear to have the final say because of social convention. Where this situation exists and is acceptable to both parties, and where there are no children, it is difficult to see what possible objection could be made to it.

It is possible that this question of who is to make the final decisions cannot receive a generally acceptable answer unless the *phase* of a relationship is defined, for the pattern surely changes with time. In courtship the woman may like the man to take certain initiatives towards her, but a little reflection reveals that those she desires are directed towards her own gratification. Even where partners enjoy periods in which he acts the dominating male who sweeps her off her feet, the knight in shining armor who rescues her, this is scarcely simple dominance of her by him—rather he is also submitting voluntarily to her pleasurable domination, putting himself into *her* service. In courtship and early marriage, too, there is a great deal of mutual gratification and "mothering"—baby talk, "billing and cooing," cosseting and nurturing of a pregenital kind in addition to genital intimacy—where each recaptures the warmth and tenderness of childhood or makes good what was lacking there. "Dominance" here is usually reciprocal or alternating, in the sense that each takes turns at being a gratifying parent to the other.

Only when children arrive does the issue of responsibility and control inevitably become more asymmetrical, for at this point the roles diverge by the very nature of their different anatomies and the biological functions these serve. The child grows within the mother, not the father, requiring him to give a greater share of attention to the family boundary and the supra-system beyond it while her physical and emotional responses are devoted to the child within her, and later at her breast. In our work with couples' groups, my wife and I have both been struck by a characteristic change which occurs in women who become pregnant in the course of therapy, when they become abruptly intolerant of the shy, boyish quality they previously found attractive in their husbands and begin to demand a more tough and manly attitude. Many men, at least in the beginning of marriage, want a mother rather than a wife, someone to look after them rather than someone to look after, but at this point their new role demands that they begin to accept a lonely position where others can lean on them while their own needs for comfort and support become more restricted (22).

As the child grows older, the father appears to have a key role in assisting the separation of child and mother, which seems difficult for her to bring about alone by virtue of the earlier physical and intense emotional bonds, a function which will receive more attention in Chapter 16. Perhaps this is also the main reason for the apparent importance of the father in matters of discipline and control, which has already been demonstrated.

I have the impression, from discussions with many mothers, that this issue may extend a little further. In expressing their desire for their husbands to take a more controlling position when children are behaving in a difficult way, they have repeatedly expressed *the wish that the husbands would control them as well*. They speak, in other words, as if they were one of the children, needing the same imposition of limits, and I wonder whether this is in a sense true? For when the mother has the main caretaking function she needs in some measure to be in touch with the more child-like parts of herself in order to understand and respond to her children's needs, and therefore stands in danger of being overwhelmed and losing her more adult, mature functions at times. When children are particularly provocative and succeed in reducing her completely to their level in this way, the father, if he has been in adult company all day and consequently has the more adult and disciplined aspect of himself activated, may provide exactly what the mother needs to restore her own adult functioning if he does indeed sometimes "treat her as one of the children" when he demands more order and control. Indeed, if this is the case, she cannot herself regain control of the children until he does so. Needless to say, the situation could equally well be reversed, between father and mother, if the former regresses too far through prolonged contact with the children and the mother returns from the outside world to bring order to the situation.

It is also my impression that, later in life, such "dominance" or responsibility patterns often change again, sometimes profoundly. In traditional family situations at least, when the children finally leave home the mother is free to develop her own personality and interests. She may become more of an individual, find a new confidence, and begin to share, or compete in, her husband's more externally based life, rather than to complement him by activities within a separate territory. Insecure males are often threatened by such alterations in the assurance and involvements of their wives, expecially if the latter are successful and popular, and marital problems in later life can stem from this. This situation seems today to be occurring more frequently and earlier in the life cycle, perhaps because the Women's Movement is encouraging females towards greater personal autonomy, growth and achievement even while child-rearing is in progress. But where both partners are more flexible, a new richness may be added to their relationship by this development.

Although there must be some machinery in any family for resolving otherwise insoluble conflicts, like the casting vote of a chairman in a tied committee, in a loving and generous relationship the need to resolve such conflicts is rare. Most of the time marital partners will divide responsibility according to their aptitudes and interests, often based on their gender; they will share decisions after discussion, and enjoy giving way and gratifying each other. Also, where the man takes final responsibility by the woman's wish and with her support, having proved himself a trustworthy leader and protector, she will be willing to take over the main responsibility by turns and allow him the relief and gratification of leaning on her and indulging his more dependent and childish side as well. Ultimately, effective responsibility or "dominance" patterns in families are always by *agreement*, and can never be imposed or arbitrary if they are to be beneficial. It is the man who can control *himself* and accept the more lonely and isolated position that responsibility brings, who gains real authority and this is not taken but given to him by the woman, willingly and from love and respect. Chaucer's "Tale of the Wife of Bath" where the ugly old woman the Knight has been forced to marry becomes both beautiful and obedient to him the moment he accepts *her* unconditionally and serves her willingly, is a very beautiful example of this truth.

The following example demonstrates one kind of developmental arrest—in this case at a phallic level where both parents were competing for the sexual role of the other and producing, among other results, divided and conflicting control of the children. It will be seen that the intervention attempted combines interpretation with modeling influence:

Judy, aged two and a half, was referred because it was thought that her squint might have a psychological basis. This had been present from the early months of her life but had worsened three months earlier when the *au-pair* girl looking after her had left and her care had been taken over completely by her mother, while she had also been moved into the same room as her younger brother, then aged six months. The referral was made on the suggestion of a psychotherapist colleague who had been treating the father for attitudes of hypochondriasis and chronic dependency on his wife, with panics when she left him. I saw the two children and both parents without any previous knowledge apart from this.

The wife appeared as a beautiful but rather cool, detached woman with a disdainful manner. The husband did not seem correspondingly attractive physically, but was nevertheless quite secure in his possession of her (an impression later explained by the mother's negative image of herself). When I asked them both to tell me about the problem, the main point to emerge was the way in which they appeared to be disagreeing on some fundamental issue, at first presented in terms of the wife's supporting a physical cause for the squint, the husband an emotional one. They disagreed when I suggested they were in conflict with each other, insisting that they were simply having a rational discussion about the matter. Eventually they did agree that their interaction with each other was tangential, whereby the response of one never quite seemed to meet directly the statements of the other. Gradually they began to acknowledge that there was some conflict and friction between them which they could not understand.

During this discussion Judy was picking up some family dolls that I had placed on the table and putting them on father's leg, ignoring her mother who was meanwhile hugging the baby at the other end of the sofa. I pointed out how both parents appeared to be pairing with the children but not with each other except by muted conflict.

At this the wife said the baby was restless and asked if she could stand up. I agreed, but pointed out how she seemed to be restless herself, and how this appeared to be occurring in relation to her husband's play with Judy. She confirmed this by complaining that he gave far too much attention to Judy during weekends and therefore spoiled her. The wife continued to make cutting remarks about the husband in a rather indirect way, but he never answered by standing up to her, countering only by reasonable argument which seemed designed to frustrate her. In the course of this discussion I learned that the wife had been involved in two groups led by colleagues, having been a patient in one and invited to visit the other in which her husband was receiving treatment. She still felt she had destroyed both these groups, implying that she had somehow rendered the members impotent so that they left in dissatisfaction. (The two groups concerned had broken up not long after her involvement, for whatever reason.)

I focused on the wife's constant attacks and frustrating comments towards the husband as well as upon his inability or unwillingness to defend himself. At this point it occurred to me that her insistence on a physical cause and his preoccupation with a psychological one might relate to their different approaches to relationships. The wife seemed to be wanting a physical, totally involving relationship with him, to be loved or struck physically and intensely, whereas he seemed able to relate and give only with his head.

They both avoided this kind of interpretation at first, until the wife admitted that the sexual relationship was good at times, but that the husband would then work late at the office or get a liver attack and lose interest for a week or two. Though she obviously found this frustration of her sexual needs distressing she seemed unable to acknowledge this, but the husband confirmed that she usually attacked him as she was doing in the interview when he was not keen on having sexual intercourse with her. I pointed out that my impression had for some time been that she had to castrate him and cut off his penis because he would not make it available to her either sexually, or symbolically by being assertive. This caused them to pause and become very thoughtful and the interview seemed to finish appropriately at this point, some constructive work having been achieved.

I learned little from Judy, except that she appeared a normal, lively and somewhat self-willed child, whose squint was present when one was not demanding her attention. When I had captured her attention in any way the squint disappeared, suggesting a link with the divided control in this family due to parental rivalry.

The whole family was seen for a second interview three months later. The notes state: "This was the second interview with this family.... As soon as they entered the room and sat down (all together on the couch) one sensed immediately a quite different atmosphere. The tension between the parents, the withdrawal in Judy and indeed the isolation of all the members no longer seemed to be present. Judy herself was much more lively, open, gay and communicative, playing with the dolls throughout and once again putting them on her father's lap. She did various things with them which I could not interpret in any useful way, but she looked directly at me and I thought the squint was quite considerably reduced. The husband said he had noticed the same and that the eye surgeon, who had seen her recently, said there was definite improvement in her sight generally as well as in the squint, although this improvement was small.

"The husband reported that Judy had been 'on top of the world' after she left the interview and had been very 'bouncy' afterwards for several days. She had continued to be much more confident, extroverted and gay since that time, and her behavior in the interview is apparently typical of her now. This is a striking personality change in her which pleases them.

"They went on to comment about their own reaction to the previous interview. The husband said that he had gone home feeling very resentful at his wife's 'castrating attitude.' He felt that what I had said had somehow crystallized and put into words something he had been aware of for years but could never quite understand or deal with. The wife said that she had not been upset by the interview, and had indeed been quite pleased by it. It then emerged that since the interview they had been speaking to each other much more forthrightly and although the husband had felt depressed, useless and increasingly hopeless for a week or more afterwards, one last straw had pushed him to a point where he fought back against his wife. He had been thinking of leaving his business because of a conflict with a colleague there, and his wife had said to him that he just did not want to be a success. He had exploded for the first time during their marriage and told her that what she had said was 'just a lot of Freudian crap'; he carried on attacking her verbally for some time afterwards. As he said all this the wife was smiling quietly and when I questioned her about her response she said that she was quite pleased that he had stood up for himself for the first time. Although when it happened she had been very angry and refused to go out to lunch with him, she had changed her mind when he did not give in and had accompanied him anyway.

"I reminded her that it seemed last time that she was attacking him and in effect castrating him partly in the desire to stimulate him to be more potent and to get a rise out of him. She agreed with this, describing how throughout her life, if she had become involved with weak men, she had felt compelled to humiliate and crush them until they were 'just a dot on the floor,' after which she would reject them and leave. She could only respect and love a man who could control her, like her father who was very strict. However, she said that she had got rather more than she had bargained for when her husband finally came to life, and though she really wanted to be controlled by him she resented this very much when it first happened.

"During this discussion the outward appearance and manner of the couple showed that the relationship was clearly changed. The husband was much more forceful and masterful, though open and affectionate at the same time, while the wife sat smiling quietly and contentedly, close beside him and leaning toward him, clearly enjoying this new relationship in which she could feel contained and looked after.

"I asked about the sexual relationship and they both said that it had not altered. The husband said that he had been satisfied with it all along, and the wife admitted that though she had expressed herself as not being satisfied at the last interview and had attacked her husband for not being ardent enough, after the interview she had realized that she was being unfair and that it was just as much her fault as his. At the moment, she felt that the sexual relationship was satisfactory even though no particular alteration had taken place in the frequency of intercourse."

Though there appeared to be some variable improvement in the squint of the referred child, this was not sufficient to avert the need for surgery. However, the child maintained the increase in confidence and the improved changes in the marital relationship were sustained over the following year during which the family was seen occasionally for further exploration.

7 MARRIAGE: RELATIONSHIP AND SEXUALITY

Hanging and wiving goes by destiny

Shakespeare, The Merchant of Venice

The lunatic, the lover and the poet
Are of imagination all compact . . .

Shakespeare, A Midsummer Night's Dream

The finding of greatest interest is the demonstration
that patient couples differed from controls in that they
were more likely to see the relationship with the partner
as resembling their relationship with their parents, and
that when the relationship was going badly they per-
ceived their own role as more child-like while that of
their partner became less parent-like.

A. Ryle and D. Breen, A Comparison of Adjusted and
Maladjusted Couples Using the Double Dyad Grid

The biological value of reproduction by pairs rather than individuals, through the way in which it ensures continuous mixing of the gene-pool and so wide variability among individuals, is generally recognized. Less often remarked upon, though equally obvious once stated, are the similar blending and diversity which occur from the fact that sexual reproduction makes it likely that each individual will be programmed by at least two models, one from each parent, these in turn being derived from four, those from eight and so on (provided, of course, as with genetic mixing, that too much inbreeding is avoided and heterogamy ensured).

RELATIONSHIP-MODELS AND INTERACTIONS IN MARRIAGE

Marriages can also be examined helpfully by considering the way in which these internalized models affect interaction between spouses. Children absorb not just models of the behavior of people in isolation, but also of their relationship to one another. In particular, the internalized model of the parents *as a couple*, rather than as separate individuals alone, will have a deep influence on the quality of the marriages of their children, a sad and unfair truth that accounts for the fact, demonstrated by many objective studies, that the best way to ensure a happy marriage and family life is to arrange to be born from a happy marriage and into a happy family yourself. Luckily, it is possible, nevertheless, to achieve a happy marriage despite adverse experiences, and though this is not easy the struggle involved can be rewarded by a fuller and deeper relationship than anything that can be given by good fortune alone.

The Tavistock Clinic and the Institute of Human Relations, as well as bodies associated with them, such as the Institute of Marital Studies, have all been strongly influenced by psychoanalytic object-relations theory developed from the ideas of Klein, Fairbairn and others. The seminal work of H. Dicks (1) and the various publications of the Institute of Marital Studies (2), together with a recent paper by John Byng-Hall (3), have attempted to extend these concepts to encompass both marital and family interaction.

These relationship-models will vary in quality, from the primitive part-object relationships of the Kleinian paranoid/schizoid position (where other people are seen literally as objects in the ordinary sense, which one can exploit without concern and from whom one extracts what one needs, like drinking from a bottle of milk or alcohol) to whole-object relationships at a genital, mutual level (where others are seen as persons and where their needs, rights and gender differences are fully accepted and responded to). Some aspects of the internalized models will be consciously accepted; others will be consciously rejected, and there will then be an attempt to act differently from the parental example, to find other models and build a marriage different from the parental one. Alternatively, parts of the relationship-models will be internalized but unconscious, perhaps because they have been denied and excluded from discussion in childhood, for example by powerful non-verbal signals discouraging the recognition of the parents' periodic hostility to each other despite its manifestation in tense emotional atmospheres, or discouraging recognition of the fact that the parents have a continuing sexual relationship. In other cases, some aspects of the parental relationship-model may have undergone repression because these were too frightening at the time—a violent, sadistic fight, for example, or the witnessing of sexual intercourse in circumstances which made this alarming.

In such cases, where denial or repression is prominent, the unconscious aspects of the model will have a powerful influence on the choice of marital partner and on the subsequent interaction. Such split-off aspects of relationship-models may be enacted only in the intimacy of the marital situation, so that a person behaves with the spouse in a way which seems out of character to those who know him outside, who may be unable to believe that someone so kindly and sensible can be the irrational tyrant his wife describes. Alternatively, the partners may choose each other on a defensive basis, reinforcing each other in trying to keep the split-off parts at bay, and where this occurs the denied aspects are, as we have seen, likely to appear in the children or in some aspect of the outside world. Such situations, based on conflict and an attempt to escape from the truth, are inherently precarious and lead either to increasing emotional dullness, deadness and the boredom of stereotyped interaction or, if they are more unstable and external changes or temptations disturb the equilibrium, may progress to eruptions of the denied and split-off aspects in love affairs, quarrels or breakdown of the relationship altogether.

In attempting to understand the operation of the relationship-models in a marriage, it is important to remember that each partner may at times play either role in an early relationship he has witnessed. The husband may on occasions take his father's role, casting his wife as his mother, but this may alternate with periods where he plays his mother and casts her as the father. As the wife's choice of roles may be varying in a similar way, the therapist may expect to become confused, and will need the help of the patients themselves to identify the positions they are taking at any one time, even more than in individual therapy.

This situation is usually less difficult than it at first appears because one soon perceives that the husband and wife have chosen each other on a highly perceptive intuitive basis (presumably based on nonverbal information), so that the role-relationships they habitually adopt, or cast each other in, are closely related. At a more superficial level, they may have chosen each other on the basis of similarity to, or contrast to, parental figures, but as one goes deeper into the dynamics one usually finds increasing similarity in fundamental but denied aspects of the background patterns, and the inner worlds of the couple prove, under closer examination, more and more to be shared. Teruel (4), has written an interesting paper demonstrating how the relationships of couples often become understandable in terms of what he calls the "dominant internal object." This is the internal representation of one of the four parents of the couple who presented a particular difficulty in the development of the spouse concerned, and where the partner has encountered rather similar problems with his equivalent parent which are more denied.

Dr. and Mrs. A., respectively trained as a physician and a nurse, were referred by another consultant for an opinion regarding the possibility of treating the marriage as well as the separate pathologies. Dr. A. suffered from depressions, characterized by paranoid fantasies and homosexual fears, for which he had been treated with antidepressant medication. His wife had suffered throughout from frigidity, associated with general emotional inhibition and fears of losing control. Previous treatment of the wife by behavior modification techniques had been ineffective, and the sexual relationship had steadily deteriorated as the emotional problems in the marriage had grown.

The letter from the referring consultant described a background characterized by demanding, controlling and strict mothers on both sides, so that I anticipated that these relationships might be an important factor in the marital relationship. This was indeed the case, and the husband spoke of his mother, his maternal grandmother and his maternal aunt as "hateful bitches" who had manifested an evil influence. My letter to the referring consultant stated:

"Many thanks for referring this couple. . . . I felt very despondent about them in the early part of the interview. He seemed so paranoid, rigid and full of violence that I did not feel hopeful that he could be flexible about his position or accept insight, while she sat just holding herself together and blocking out the rage which he poured over her. However, there were momentary flashes of humor and relaxation in him while she smiled and relaxed when I suggested she needed to have some privacy and to feel that she was not obliged to reveal everything to him.

"From your history, which showed that they both shared the experience of strict, dominating and difficult mothers, I felt that these might well form an essential part of their reason for marrying and for the marital interaction. This proved to be the case for he becomes his own strict, controlling mother in relation to her and punishes her for not being the loving, accepting and indulgent mother he wanted. On her side, she used to block off her mother's criticisms and attacks in much the same way as she now blocks off his, and I think she keeps the more hostile and resentful part of herself projected into him, thereby rendering herself weak and useless and also giving him a double burden of hostility and paranoia to cope with.

"This was confirmed when I commented on their interaction in this light. As they began to talk about their mothers and so made them for the moment external to themselves and objective, the marital interaction changed profoundly. He relaxed and showed a very nice, amusing, light-hearted side, which I would never have guessed existed in the first half-hour or so, while she also lost her rigid defensiveness and displayed a warmth and humor she had not shown before. Instead of the former behavior in which she silently resisted his waves of hate and violence, they both began to talk together and share the conversation in a more natural way. It was possible as the interview progressed to show them once or twice how they again became 'possessed' by these inner objects and reverted to the previous pattern."

The referring consultant had suggested that the husband's demands for separate individual psychotherapy should be taken seriously, and after a further interview I agreed with this because of the way in which their curious capacity for depressive position functioning was constantly threatened by any feeling of rejection, leading to regression to paranoid/schizoid functioning and consequent mutual attack. It was arranged that two young colleagues would provide combined individual and four-way sessions but they disagreed with my assessment and felt that four-way sessions alone would be adequate.

After some therapeutic movement the husband suffered another psychotic breakdown, associated with fears of killing his children, for which he was admitted to another hospital and the marriage subsequently broke up. It was not possible to decide whether this could have been averted by the treatment recommended, or whether matters had deteriorated too far. (The wife had from the start been ambivalent about attempting to sustain the relationship.)

Though some relationships are not redeemable we may also find, as with everything else, that each problem can be seen as having a constructive potential if the right approach to it can be found. Dicks, for example, states (5): "The partner attracts because he or she represents or promises a rediscovery of an important lost aspect of the subject's own personality, which, owing to earlier conditioning, had been recast as an object for attack or denial" (p. 30). He considers that there is a

> need for unconscious *complementariness*, the kind of division or function by which each partner supplied part of a set of qualities, the sum of which created a complete dyadic unit. This joint personality or integrate enabled each half to discover the lost aspects of their primary object-relations, which they had split-off or repressed, and which they were, in their involvement with the spouse, re-experiencing by projective identification. The sense of

belonging can be understood on the hypothesis that at deeper levels there are perceptions of the partner and consequent attitudes towards him or her *as if* the other was part of oneself. The partner is then treated according to how this aspect of oneself was valued: spoiled and cherished, or denigrated and persecuted (p. 69).

Dicks suggests that the outcome of such unions would depend very much on the positive qualities in the families of origin:

> . . . There is also a great similarity between . . . "all-in-all" cat-and-dog marriages and the "happy" deep union which we do not see clinically, but know of, and regard as the theoretical model of the complete marriage. This would seem to lie in the capacity of the partners to express and to live out in their relationships many phases and object-relations potentials from the past. In the "happy" marriage, unfolding into an ever richer and more satisfying secure mutual affirmation, one presumes the dyad's inner "contents" to be of predominantly good objects or part-objects (p. 119).

Marriage is always an attempt at growth, at healing oneself and finding oneself again, however disastrously any particular attempt may fail for lack of sufficient understanding or external help. It is this which makes marital therapy at once so rewarding and often so much more effective than either individual or group therapy outside an ongoing real relationship.

In focusing on the unconscious aspects of the inner relationship-models, I have neglected the influence of more conscious values or choices, as well as of more general cultural factors. Dicks (6) has offered a simple but elegant and valuable way of conceptualizing the interaction of these different forces. He suggests a classification of bonds according to three levels: The first or "public" level or subsystem is that of sociocultural values and norms—the influence of family, neighborhood, social class, church and so on. This subsystem may attempt to influence a choice based on social homogeneity—the girl or boy next door, representing similarity of class and religion, etc.

The second subsystem is that of "personal norms"—"conscious judgments and expectations also derived from the developmental background of object-relations and social learning preceding the marriage (p. 130)," but in which conscious differentiation from the parental models, physical attraction, individual attitudes and so on are likely to lead to more heterogeneity in choice.

The third subsystem is the area of "unconscious forces," forming bonds of a positive or negative kind influenced by the repressed or split-off internalized relationship-models, which explain the mysterious chemistry that binds people in ways that seem inexplicable to others, blind to the hidden internal programming.

It will be apparent that Dicks' scheme is based on the tripartite Freudian structural model: supergo—ego—id. He concludes (7):

> It is the "mix" of the more or less unconscious interaction of object-relations in this third subsystem which governs the longer-term quality of marriages. . . .
>
> Marriages may prove unviable at any of the three subsystem levels. It would seem necessary for at least two of the three sub-systems postulated to function with credit-balances of satisfaction and dissatisfaction to both partners. Social affinity plus congruence of deep object-relations can withstand strong divergencies of personal norms and taste. Strong agreements over personal norms and values, plus deeper object-relations can override large cultural and social distances and incongruities. Even social homogeneity and good overlap of personal norms and values can endure, provided their defensive efficacy against unwelcome confrontation at deeper object levels holds. But if reality testing proves to one or both partners that the relationship was based on nothing but a social affinity or meeting ground; or nothing but some shared personal interests; or nothing but seeing a potential parent-figure or an exciting libidinal object as a guarantee against essentially infantile loneliness; then it is only a question of time before the need for a broader-based merging of lives will become felt, and, in due course, acted upon in one way or another. It is usually the case that, at this stage, the emotional content of the relationship is one of boredom, indifference and withdrawal of investment. Nothing of the self is any longer projected into the other. The institutional aspects of the cohabitation may be continued for rational or social advantages, but the marriage as interpersonal relation will be dead. The opposite to love is not hate. These two always coexist as long as there is a live relationship. The opposite to love is indifference. (pp. 131–133).

Leaving on one side those malevolent relationships which have their *raison d'être* in the infliction of pain and suffering, marriage can, it will be clear, be either a process facilitating growth (when the partners cherish and respect each other as individuals and have no desire to possess or restrict one another), a substitute for personal growth (when the partner is used to contain the lost aspects of the self, without attempt at reintegration), or a defense against growth (where they rely on each other's defenses to maintain the *status quo* and seek comfort and security only).

SEXUALITY

If, as has been suggested, each individual's capacity for relationships, including love, marriage and parenthood, is determined by the repertoire laid down or programed in the internalized relationship-models or object-relationships, and if these are derived from early experience in the family of origin, the attitude of the parents to each other, as experienced in childhood, will be of vital importance. In particular, the parent's sexual relationship will be crucial, for this interaction, which involves the most total and profound relating—intellectually, emotionally and bodily, integrating what is most animal, earthy and lusty with the most tender, spiritual and altruistic of human qualities—can be viewed as a paradigm for all other fruitful and creative human interactions. Though, like all things that are fully formed and perfected, it is not easily won and demands effort and work before it can become effortless and spontaneous, sexuality should reach an expression where it can be a model for, and illuminate and transform all other aspects of the family relationships.

In a fulfilling sexual act, the two opposite genders, at their most different and separate, simultaneously become one totality, merging with one another in an experience going beyond the capacity of either. Each is most centered in, and aware of, himself or herself, yet also wholly open and responsive to the other. Each temporarily loses his boundary, surrenders to a greater unity. Both are as spontaneous as they could ever be, yet this spontaneity is possible because of a fundamental self-discipline, an ability to deny oneself, to wait, to adapt and adjust to the other as in the unfolding of a dance. It is non-manipulative, non-controlling; the self is offered freely, from generosity and trust, and since there is no demand the return comes equally freely and fully, each emotionally responding and keeping time with the other. Each gives most generously, yet takes most uninhibitedly too, without hedging or bargaining. For a moment, both partners are fully in the present, letting the process unfold in its own form and pace, no longer lost in the concerns of the future or memories of the past. And the climax, when it "comes" in its own time, is productive, creative, sometimes through the beginning of a separate new life but always in a renewal of the separate lives of the partners and the joint life of their relationship, so that the wild, tender, simple act of affirmation is never tired of, never loses its fullness or the refreshing quality of a draught of spring water or mountain air.

Sex is not everything, of course, but it is a catalyst for many other things and, since so many other things must be right for it to function well, also a touchstone for the quality of the total relationship. When it is good people look different. The emotional atmosphere one senses in a house where it is right is one of calm and peace, yet also of lightness, fun and humor, and everything moves easily. Above all the children sense it and are happy for it, though they do not necessarily know what they sense, any more than they know, or care, about the cost of the good food that nourishes them.

I recall one family where the children showed various problems, stemming from the parents' increasing sexual unhappiness over the previous five years. The basic relationship was good, the problem a simple one of ignorance and prudishness in the parents' families of origin. It was only necessary to negotiate a fresh contract and to provide some very definite support, in the form of "doctor's orders" that they should lose control and enjoy themselves as fully as possible in bed, to improve the situation. At the second interview, the parents reported a new sexual happiness, and it radiated from them. The children reflected this also, and the adolescent girl said, "I don't know what has happened, but it's completely different at home. Mom and Dad seem happy together again, and I feel happy too."

Sexual Dysfunctioning

If we study the ways in which the impulse to sexual union can become distorted, we see that the developmental classification again assists us. At a paranoid/schizoid level there often seems to be a capacity for unusually intense, even symbiotic physical union, giving an initial impression of unusually rewarding intercourse, but this is often experienced as stultifying because the capacity for periods of detachment and recollection is lacking, and sexuality is therefore accompanied at some level by fears of loss of identity and boundaries and so of complete fusion, frequently combined with massive projection of negative feelings into the partner so that the blissful but engulfing state of being "all-in-all to each other" in the sexual relationship is periodically escaped from by explosive, paranoid hostility and fighting. Couples who have attained a more mature position within the oral stage of development may cope more successfully in some ways with a close relationship, but fear the possibility of loss so greatly that they often cannot give themselves fully in the sexual encounter.

Failure to have coped with anal-level challenges may lead to preoccupation with dominance and mastery, either in the obvious form of preoccupation with power and submission, as in bondage and flagellation, or with an emphasis on the defensive aspects, where surrender of the body to the other, or lustful possession, is both feared and avoided. Phallic fixations result in a failure to relinquish the gender characteristics of the opposite sex, or to gain a clear sexual identity, so that instead of delight in difference and complementarity there is resentful, disparaging competition or envious refusal to enjoy the partner. If, on the other hand, defenses are prominent against this latter tendency a rigid adherence to stereotyped sexual roles and forms of intercourse may result, with inability to abandon constraints and consequent increasing boredom. Developmental failures at an earlier level weaken the capacity to surmount challenges later, of course, so that in fact one often sees many such problems together, sometimes without any one level being obviously prominent.

The severity of sexual disturbances may range at one extreme from a reversal of gender identity—transsexualism, where the individual desires a bodily change to that of the opposite sex—on to transvestism where there is no desire for anatomical change but an impulse to cross-dress, to *play* at being the opposite sex, with accompanying excitement—on through homosexuality where there is acceptance of one's own gender but rejection of the opposite one—and on through impotence and frigidity to inability to combine sensual love and tenderness, or preoccupation with fantasy and lack of full enjoyment of the partner.

Generally speaking, the more profound disorders involve confusion or even reversal of gender identity, laid down within the first two years or so, and are more likely to be accompanied by wider, more all-encompassing limitations in personality development. The desire for change or capacity to respond to any form of therapy is more limited, and treatment, if it is possible at all, needs to be prolonged, to include exploration in depth, and to be started early, before the pattern is too firmly set. The less profound sexual disorders appear to have their origin later in childhood, after gender identity is more clearly established, and involve more limited personality disturbance; therapeutic change is more likely to be desired, to be successful, and to be accomplished by more brief and superficial techniques, because the difficulty usually arises from anxieties and inhibitions in utilizing responses and roles which are developed and potentially available, rather than absent or laid down according to inappropriate patterns.

If one examines the family constellations accompanying the more severe sexual deviations and dysfunctions (8), one finds that the parents have either not established clear and definite gender identities on the lines outlined in the previous chapter, or, if they have, that they are unable to relate to each other in a sexually satisfying way, or that there is a mixture of gender role confusion and inhibition of sexual function. A finding common to transsexualism, transvestism, homosexuality (in both sexes), exhibitionism, indecent exposure, impotence and many other sexual disorders is the over-possessive, engulfing mother, together with a weak or absent, or sometimes harsh and distant (but in either case unloving and unavailable) father, both of whom have a bad relationship as a couple and with one of whom the child is encouraged to side. Stoller (9) has demonstrated, in the case of transsexuals, that the mothers have prolonged intense physical and emotional intimacies long past the age when some degree of separation is normally expected, while the fathers appear to collude in this, almost to encourage it. The mothers of transvestites displayed more hostility, less attachment and identification, and at least created some distance between themselves and their male children.

Where the parents' behavior is less abnormal, but there are anxieties and inhibitions standing in the way of sexual enjoyment with each other, one sees, if one looks at the family as a whole, that sexual impulses that should be directed towards the spouse color the relationship to the children. The mother makes "a little husband" of the son, confides in him among other things about her unhappiness with his father, alienating the boy from him and binding him more tightly to her. The boy naturally enjoys his privileged position but pays for it in losing his father as a loved figure on which to model himself and, lacking his support, finds himself unable to escape the attachment to his mother; he is obliged, by default, to use her as a role-model. Moreover, he fears retaliation from his father for his competitive position and assumes that the punishment will fit the crime—the Freudian castration-fear. As independence and masculinity are increasingly expected by the social context, the tie to the mother and to her values becomes increasingly resented by the child, leading later to ambivalence towards women generally, while the failure to incorporate a good male model, or to accept a benevolent defeat from the father as an authority and sexual rival, leads to deep feelings of inadequacy in relation to other men and problems in engaging in robust and enjoyable competition. Sexuality comes to be seen as fraught with dangers and sexual dysfunctions of one sort or another follow, perhaps generalized to fears of potency and success in a more general sense.

Corresponding problems arise for the girl whose mother cannot provide an example of loving and accepting sexuality, and whose father's feelings for her become tinged with frustrated eroticism even though this may appear overtly only as a special tenderness and mutual understanding. In latency the relationship may be close and satisfying, but as the girl's own sexual drive waxes in adolescence the father's excessive attention will feel increasingly wrong, and will make her awkward and embarrassed. Since he cannot be trusted to maintain a proper barrier, within which she can feel her developing sexuality admired and enjoyed by him without prejudicing her need for her mother's love as well, she has to erect defenses herself and begins to isolate herself from the sexual emotions which feel ever more dangerous. Later, when she wants to give herself to a man, she finds she has lost contact with her sexual wishes, or cannot let go, discovering herself to be frigid or inorgastic.

Mary, aged 12, was referred because of abdominal pain, vomiting, headaches and dizzy spells, over several years. On inquiry, it was learned that the mother had suffered a history of illness and hospitalization, mainly related to the alimentary tract and the pelvic organs, from the time she began menstruating. Since a hysterectomy five years earlier all the illnesses had stopped but the mother had become completely frigid; she also suffered from depressions and headaches and was obliged to wear a wig because her hair had been falling out. Mary's father, a passive, weak-looking man, seemed excessively involved with Mary even during the discussion. He admitted that if the children got ill he became ill as well.

My impression that the father's sexual needs were being satisfied (on an emotional level) with Mary because of the mother's frigidity was completely confirmed when, leaving my room in the outpatient clinic, I saw the family collecting some medication I had prescribed from the dispensary. Father and daughter were in each other's arms, gazing sadly into each other's eyes and embracing like two lovers, while the mother was some distance away collecting the tablets. It proved impossible to alter this incestuous emotional involvement by psychotherapeutic means and Mary was eventually placed in a residential school where she did well and lost her symptoms. She continued to find holidays disturbing because her parents would not allow her to go out with boys, so that she lost her girlfriends because she could not share in their activities. However, at the time of a family interview two years after the first she had matured, felt independent of her family and had a good relationship with a boyfriend. The notes on the interview state that "father said he was delighted with Mary's progress, though he also expressed sadness about losing the satisfactions of their close relationship."

In a family where the parents are sexually harmonious the attraction between parent and child has, of course, an altogether different significance. The son learns from his mother's response to him that he is physically attractive to women, and a daughter discovers the power of her sexuality from her father's enjoyment of it. This early experience can lay deep foundations of sexual confidence when it occurs in a context which does not threaten the child's security from both parents, and is not felt to be harming or stealing from either of them.

Treatment of Sexual Problems in Marital Therapy

The types of psychoanalytic approach associated with the Tavistock Center, requiring a careful dissection and intellectual formulation of the dynamics of the inner models, is necessarily slow and laborious but may be essential in the more severe but treatable disorders, especially where countertransference complications are prominent. For the less complex problems an alternative is an approach based more on modeling and identification processes, where the model provided is a *relationship between therapists* rather than the behavior of an individual therapist. If this can be offered, I believe that the analysis of the old model is largely unnecessary, for either the correction will be automatic, through re-projection and re-absorption of the model, or some relevant insight will occur without any need for the therapist to stimulate it verbally. However, a good relationship-model must actually be provided—one that can safely be exposed to, but is proof against, the inevitable disruptive projection onto it of the original relationship-model internalized during the patient's childhood. It is here that some examination may be necessary of the patient's inner models, when they impinge on the cotherapists' blind spots and block progress by threatening the more precarious aspects of their own relationship. Examples of this will be given in Chapter 14.

In the simpler problems, where improvement is required in a sexual dysfunction, this type of complication is less likely to arise and the main requirement is that the therapist(s) be able to set an example of relaxation and ease when dealing with sexual issues.

I recall a case presentation at my seminar at the Maudsley Hospital by two trainee doctors, male and female though not married to each other, where they described their treatment of a couple mainly by behavioral methods, supervising the pair in the use of the Masters and Johnson "squeeze" technique (10) for the man's premature ejaculation (a highly effective approach in which the woman masterbates the man repeatedly almost to orgasm and then diminishes his excitement by applying strong pressure across the base of the glans of his penis, until he learns increased control). This had been very successful, but it was clear (as I think Masters and Johnson would be the first to acknowledge) that the warm, relaxed way in which this attractive pair of young doctors could speak about sex together was a key factor, providing the vital model absent in the marital couple's parental backgrounds.

Though co-therapy, preferably by opposite sex therapists, obviously has its advantages, it is not essential and much can be done in more straightforward cases by one therapist who can facilitate communication between the couple over sexual matters, setting an example of frankness and ease himself. I have found that good results are often achieved swiftly by insisting on a very detailed description of the couple's actual sexual activity, but treating this in a matter-of-fact, light way, even with the careful use of a little humor. A model is thereby provided which gives them permission to be frank, direct and "comfortably naked" with each other.

A late adolescent with schizoid traits, after some years of successful individual psychotherapy by a colleague to whom I referred him, married a lively and attractive girl. I was asked to see him again because of difficulty in the marriage, and a joint interview revealed that neither could take the initiative sexually and that both, because of their backgrounds, were too shy to speak about the problem to each other. A "play-by-play" account of their interaction and sexual relationship revealed, among other things, that the wife's clitoral sensation was too intense and sensitive to permit direct pleasurable stimulation, though she could be excited by stroking of her pubis and other areas near the genitals.

At the second joint interview they reported that they were enjoying sex more frequently and fully, and by the third session were able to discontinue treatment. The wife said that she had felt "dreadfully embarrassed" at the first interview by my insistence on such detailed descriptions, but had begun to feel relaxed by the end of the first session and since then had been able to talk and act with her husband sexually with a freedom she had never thought she could attain.

This approach in fact developed from my original misunderstanding of the techniques used by Masters and Johnson. Since they had witnessed the intercourse of their research couples I at first assumed that they did the same in the supervision of treatment couples too. Believing this, I had thought that perhaps getting couples to describe the sexual act in sufficient detail would have a similar if lesser effect in diminishing shyness and reticence over sexuality, and found that this was indeed the case. In fact, Masters and Johnson use verbal communication during ordinary interviews to supervise the sexual interaction, which takes place separately and in private, but they are well aware that the model provided by the therapists' attitudes during the discussions is as important as the practical techniques communicated.

A similar use of modeling, this time in combination with physical touching, is employed in a form of psychotherapy developed by groups of general practitioners associated with the psychoanalysts Tom Main and the late Michael Balint (11). In this technique short-term psychotherapy for female sexual difficulties is combined with physical examination of the genitals, both being carried out by the same doctor. The physical examination is intended to exclude organic disease, but it also has the deliberate aim of manifesting acceptance of the patient's genitals, at the most direct level, by the professional who is cast in the transference in a parental role. This combination of modeling and analytic approaches seems to show considerable promise.

Similarly, I find the use of a few jokes, four-letter words, and other rather coarse forms of expression by the therapist can also help the deconditioning process, though this naturally must be done with great care and sensitivity since to go too far would have the opposite effect.

My own acquaintance with more formal behavioral techniques is limited, though there is no doubt that these have great value, particularly in the simpler and more straightforward problems where education or re-education is the main necessity and inner conflicts or defenses are not serious obstacles. I am indebted to M. Crowe, an expert in this field, for permission to quote at length from one of his reviews of this branch of marital therapy (12).*

---

* The references to notes within the quote have been altered to fit the sequence of notes for this chapter.

In the behavioral field, perhaps the clearest formulation of marital disturbance is that of Stuart (13). He makes three assumptions: (i) that, of all the possible alternatives for interaction, the existing one is the most rewarding and least costly in terms of effort. Thus, if a man prefers drinking with friends to staying home with his wife, the former activity must be more rewarding than the latter; (ii) that most married people expect a fairly equal sharing of rewards and duties between the partners, and (iii) that in order to improve an unsuccessful marriage, it is essential to develop the power of each partner to reward the other. He postulates that in unsuccessful marriages this power to reward the partner has reached such a low level on both sides that the only way to get the partner to do what one wants is to use negative means (nagging, violence, threats, punishment, withdrawal of sex, etc.). This is a self-defeating process, in that the partner using the threats etc. becomes unattractive to his spouse, the desired behavior is carried out grudgingly, and such behavior is unlikely to be repeated spontaneously (cf. Skinnerian operant-conditioning principles). Other forms of coercion include withdrawal, silences, etc., and these are all the more ineffective for being passive.

Stuart's remedy for this state of affairs amounts to an indirect form of Skinnerian conditioning, in which the partners are asked to specify behavior that they want to encourage in their spouse, and to increase the frequency of it by (a) monitoring it on a chart and (b) rewarding it by some reciprocal behavior desired by the spouse. These behaviors must be described in everyday, specific terms—thus "showing more affection" might be specified as "kissing me before going out in the morning" and "being more sociable" as "talking pleasantly with me each evening for half an hour." Stuart reports four uncontrolled cases, in which desired behavior increased considerably, while marital satisfaction also showed a significant increase. In very difficult cases, he advocates a kind of "token economy," and in all cases, he explores new behaviors in subsequent sessions, setting new behavioral targets according to the partner's wishes. Any behavior is capable of being used in the exchange system, provided it is positive and specific. Thus, gardening, cooking meals at a certain time, house decorating, sexual intercourse, informing each other of plans, discussing holidays or the children, could all be used. However, "nagging less often," "not drinking," or "not criticizing" would not be suitable, as being negative goals: In practice, negative behavioral goals are much harder to achieve than positive ones.

Stuart does not state clearly whether in the sessions themselves he uses behavioral or other techniques, or whether he acts purely as an educator for the couple. However, Liberman (14), while advocating a similar approach to both couples and families, recommends the therapist to maintain a good "supportive relationship" or "treatment alliance," and suggests that the therapist express himself in a "comfortable, human style developed during his clinical training." Liberman's examples of therapy are amplified by case reports, and it is clear that at times he uses modeling to encourage parents to reinforce appropriate behavior in children, and also reinforces appropriate behavior in the session by praising it. In most other ways, his approach is very similar to Stuart's, with the added feature that, instead of tacitly disregarding negative behavior, he specifically instructs the other members of the family to ignore it, while paying attention to desirable behavior, as a form of reinforcement. His results, in the few cases he has reported, are impressive but uncontrolled.

Other workers have also used this form of behavior modification in marital conflict. Goldstein and Francis (15), in a preliminary report, show that by contact only with one partner (usually the wife) who is prepared to come for treatment, a therapist can help that partner to modify the spouse's behavior in the desired direction: Again, convincing case reports are presented, but no controlled data. Weiss et al. (16) use specific written contracts, in addition to the behavior checklists employed by Stuart and Liberman, in order to get couples to employ reward rather than aversive control of each other's behavior. They also use a videotaped feedback method of behavior modification during the treatment session, in which the couple's problem solving behavior is analyzed in their presence by the therapists, and approval or disapproval for individual behaviors is followed by a "re-run" with instructions to the couple to correct their mistakes. Videotape feedback, however, in an experiment by Eisler et al. (17), did not add significantly to the effect of simple instructions, in increasing the nonverbal interaction (smiles, eye contact etc.) between married couples.

Thomas et al. (18) use a complicated feedback system involving colored lights (green for approval, red for disapproval), used by either member of the couple or by the experimenter during conversation between the partners. They have shown, at a high level of reliability, increase in positive talk and decrease in "faulting" in couples using the apparatus. Preliminary reports have been published of a group approach to behavioral marriage counselling, used as part of a controlled experiment by Turner (19). He uses the group sessions to inculcate behavioral methodology, and then instructs the couples to practice positive reinforcement techniques on each other both during and between sessions; he also gets them to read a book by Knox (20) entitled *Marriage Happiness*.

Masters and Johnson (21) have reported an apparently highly successful method for dealing with sexual inadequacy. This method includes some general behavioral techniques, such as the "give to get" principle, similar to that advocated by Stuart, and they give a wide variety of instructions for specific sexual techniques to deal with such problems as impotence, frigidity, premature ejaculation and vaginismus. They seem to use a more supportive/interpretative approach for marital problems as such.

Crowe's own comparative study of different forms of marital therapy (22) (to be described more fully in Chapter 15) suggests that the use of the conjoint method, where the partners can be helped to perceive each other more objectively, to communicate more effectively and to negotiate more satisfying forms of interaction, is probably more important than the particular theory employed. Nevertheless, his results also indicate that simple behavioral techniques (for example, negotiation of simple contracts regarding mutually rewarding behaviors after each partner's likes and dislikes have first been made explicit, guidance regarding sexual techniques, etc.) are quite adequate for the majority of couples seeking marital counselling and also prove acceptable to practically all. Interpretive, analytic methods sometimes achieved more rapid or far-reaching changes, and were necessary where problems were more complex and motivation more conflicted, but they produced a higher rate of drop-out than the behavioral techniques when used indiscriminately. This is in line with my own experience of family therapy, where modeling and interpretive approaches need to be used selectively if one is to avoid being selective in accepting referrals (see Chapter 12). Apart from facilitating honest communication, assisting the couple towards an attitude of greater mutual generosity—giving each other room to move, change and grow—appears more important than any other single quality to be aimed at.

In recent years, rapid advances have been made in brief, active methods of treating sexual dysfunction. Masters and Johnson, referred to here by Crowe, have been leaders in this new approach, but as it has gained in acceptance it has begun to be integrated with more traditional concepts and techniques. Space does not permit a detailed account of these methods, but Helen Singer Kaplan has recently provided a clear exposition which at the same time brings together psychoanalytic "insight" methods with *The New Sex Therapy* (23); it can be wholeheartedly recommended as an introduction to this new field.

Finally, one implication of all that has been said about the internalization in each individual of models of behavior derived from each parent, as well as the relationship the two parents exemplify, is so obvious that once recognized it hardly seems worth stating. Nevertheless, it is often neglected or unrecognized despite its profound importance. The implication is this: Integration of the two parental models in each psyche, which must take place if personal integration is to occur, always has the *meaning* of allowing the parents to have intercourse together. To "get it together" in one's own inner world is to overcome one's jealousy and allow them to love and become one physically. Until one gives them this permission, one is not free to love either, but is bound by the same restricting law one imposed upon them; until this permission is given, one is not free to become a whole person.

8 THE RELATIONSHIP BETWEEN MARITAL AND FAMILY INTERACTION

The fathers have eaten sour grapes, and the children's teeth are set on edge.

The Bible, Ancient Hebrew Proverb quoted by Ezekiel

A thing which has not been understood inevitably re-appears; like an unlaid ghost, it cannot rest until the mystery has been solved and the spell broken.

Sigmund Freud, Analysis of a Phobia in a Five-Year-Old Boy

Every parting gives a foretaste of death; every coming together again a foretaste of the resurrection.

Schopenhauer

If the marital relationship is the primary model influencing all other interactions within the family, and subsequently the kind of relationship its members will form with outsiders, and if, in turn, the general marital relationship is reflected in the sexual encounter, we would expect to find a clear correspondence between sexual, marital and family patterns. This is a basic principle underlying my own techniques of family therapy so that, confronted with a presenting symptom, I expect to work back from the initial problem, usually a complaint by or about one member, to a more general emotional disturbance in the family as a whole, and then to the original pathology in the marital interaction and its expression in the sexual relationship. This principle, which is exemplified to some extent in the case illustrations already given, will be expressed more clearly in Chapter 10.

Though the connections among parental pathology, marital and sexual difficulties, and problems in the children and the family as a whole form the main substance of the entire book, it may be useful at this stage to pull some of the strands together in a more systematic, explicit way, particularly as regards the links between the marital relationship and child development.

The detailed working out of specific patterns and their clear formulation remain tasks for the future and this will probably be the next phase of development in family therapy itself. Some patterns have been clarified at least by examination of a series of cases, based on ordinary clinical experience, and in Chapter 16 (1) I have attempted this type of clinical examination of a series of cases of school phobia. However, exploration of this field, even on a clinical basis, has scarcely begun and more objective studies are very limited.

A most interesting attempt to correlate marital and family pathology in a therapeutic context was undertaken by the Galveston group (2). Working with adolescent referrals and using a highly concentrated approach whereby team and family interact together in various combinations for two full days (understandably called multiple impact therapy!), they found correspondences between the level of developmental arrest in the children referred and the degree of pathology in the parental relationship, along the lines one would expect from the general principles I have already outlined. The way in which their results are set out in their book does not make the overall pattern explicit but when I summarized these in tabular form I found that the pattern which emerged was surprisingly clear and suggestive, as will be seen from an examination of Table 8.1. Nevertheless, it must be emphasized that this is my own summary and the reader is advised to study the book itself to form his own opinion.

SYSTEMS, HIERARCHY AND FAMILY PATHOLOGY

Whatever their orientation, most psychiatrists would accept that the level of pathology, or the severity of the developmental arrest involved, or the gloominess of the prognosis, or the difficulty of inducing change by any form of psychotherapy, is greatest in the category described in the first column of Table 8.1 and becomes less as we move across the table. And we see that this maturation is associated with quite definite and progressive differences in the relationship of the parents to each other, to their children, and to the wider world.

Where the degree of developmental arrest is most severe in the child, the marital relationship is almost non-existent and mother and child are bound together in a symbiotic engulfment from which the father is totally excluded. All three are isolated in terms of the wider world, incapable of accepting a place in the larger social group and so cut off from the help the supra-system could provide. Moving across the table we note that the parents become more interested in, able to cope with, and influenced by the external world, while the child's own capacity for group membership follows theirs. And the marital relationship itself shows a progressive change, the parents becoming more involved with each other and moving towards a position of greater attribution of responsibility, and corresponding respect and authority, to the role of the father. This increasing capacity of the parents to accept a hierarchy of authority is paralleled by similar developments in the children.

Admittedly, an additional column describing the pattern of the "normal" family is missing, and one would be reluctant to believe that the fourth column, where the mother, feeling inadequate as a woman, bolsters an insecure father in the role of "head of the family," is the best solution that can be attained. But the direction in which the pattern is moving in the table, as the children begin to cope more adequately with life, is clear enough.

Another interesting study (3) of the relation between process and outcome in family therapy, based on a statistical examination of objective evidence, lends further support to these conclusions regarding the optimum marital relationship. One of the clearest findings was that outcome, in terms of therapeutic change, was generally unfavorable where the mothers talked most (and so were presumably dominant), but favorable where the fathers did most of the talking. Unfortunately a passive, clarifying technique was used by the (relatively inexperienced) therapists, and attempts to change the initial dominance pattern one way or the other, which would have given more conclusive information, were not made.

Implications drawn from this study may once again be criticized because it was based on disturbed families only, but similar conclusions emerged in another investigation where a variety of measures of marital and family interaction were applied to families where there was a schizophrenic or a delinquent child, and to others where the children appeared to have developed relatively normally. (These data are summarized at the end of Chapter 12 where the material has a more general relevance.) It was found that in the "normal" families the father was most active in initiating discussion, the mother next and the children least, despite a general atmosphere of encouragement of autonomy, of mutual understanding and of complementary interaction between the parents. This contrasted with an absence of clear hierarchy and a confusion of roles in the families containing delinquent children, and a

TABLE 8.1.

Relationship of Child and Marital Pathology in Galveston Multiple Impact Therapy Study.

	SCHIZOID Infantile functioning (Schizophrenic reaction)	AUTOCRATS Childish functioning (Near-psychopathic or near-psychotic reaction)	INTIMIDATED YOUTH Juvenile functioning (Neurotic reaction)	REBELS Pre-adolescent functioning (Personality disorder)
Classification of children in four groups on basis of degree of arrest				
Degree of arrest in development (author's classification—Erikson's concepts)	Basic trust	Autonomy	Initiative versus guilt	Fear of intimacy and of establishing own identity
Developmental task failed (present classification)	?Oral (depressive position) (1b)	?Anal (2) Acceptance of authority	?Phallic (3a) Acceptance of sexual role	?Genital (3b) Pairing, sexual intimacy
Reason for referral	Bizarre, deviant behavior	Aggressive, destructive, manipulative; refusal to accept limits	Neurotic traits, phobic symptoms, anxiety, psychosomatic symptoms	Rebellious and delinquent behavior; demand for "freedom" without responsibility
Group competence of referred patient	No group life	Demands own way, so plays with younger children or acts out destructive impulses for older groups	Desire to be one of group, but cannot fight, hold own; remains on periphery, propitiates others	Seeks to diffuse identity in group; still at gang stage when others are pairing and forming intimate ties to friends of opposite sex
Relation to authority	Authority problems with parents only; leadership and responsibility avoided by all family	Resistance to all authority; all frustration leads to uncontrolled rage	Fear of authority; "born loser," rebellion expressed only by unconscious passive resistance—learning block	Preoccupied with authority; behavior designed to provoke firm control from society
Sexual adjustment of referred patient	Autistic response—uninterested in peers	Little differentiation on sexual basis—interaction with others generally exploitative	Fair identification with parent of same sex but generally feels inadequate, fears competition	Ostentatious, bragging over relationships with opposite sex but fears intimacy; still seeks security of same-sex group
Marital relationship	Both spouses unhappy, mistrustful, soon disillusioned and disappointed in each other; father turns outward for satisfaction, mother to child; pattern resembles "autocrat" but more intense, sicker	Mother dominant, attached to child, excluding father; father accepts exclusion but preserves adequate role in outside world	Both parents intensely competitive for authority and status, jealous of each other's sexual role and consequent mutual undermining and quarrels over child-rearing	Incapacity for real intimacy and fearful of sexuality; incestuous competition with the children; father's role idealized in unrealistic way

TABLE 8.1 (*continued*)

Classification of children in four groups on basis of degree of arrest	SCHIZOID Infantile functioning (Schizophrenic reaction)	AUTOCRATS Childish functioning (Near-psychopathic or near-psychotic reaction)	INTIMIDATED YOUTH Juvenile functioning (Neurotic reaction)	REBELS Pre-adolescent functioning (Personality disorder)
Fathers	Schizoid, inadequate both in home and in outside world, avoiding involvement generally; colludes in exclusion by wife, relieved that her attention switched to child; unstable, unreliable	Detached and colludes in his exclusion like fathers of schizophrenics, but often respected and adequate outside the home, and perceptive and objective about family situation, so able to play more positive role if helped through therapy	Dominant façade with underlying feelings of impotence and inadequacy; competitive with wife for maternal role, undermining her	Successful, aggressive leaders outside home; placed by wives in superior, idealized position at home yet also undermined, excluded as if regarded as really inadequate; "good provider"
Mothers	Lonely, narcissistic, seeking recompense for unhappy childhood in marriage and then, when disappointed, by absorption in child; turn away from husbands	Dominant, competitive, denial of dependency; cannot tolerate frustration and treats child as greedy, domineering part of herself; husbands regarded as beneath them, actively excluded; disenchanted when child becomes tyrant.	Really need and desire male acceptance because of feelings of inadequacy as women, but defend themselves by aggression, like husbands; resent husband's devaluation and undermine husband's sexual role in return	Capable and competent but needy, feel inferior as women; put husbands on pedestal and seek status for themselves through husband's achievement; compete for husband with children
Parental role-balance	Father's role completely denied in relation to child; father not even potential significant figure	Power struggle with mother left in control of field, father opting out of conflict but potentially adequate if balance changed by therapy	Both parents fighting for supremacy, neither conceding leadership	Father accorded leadership position, even though on "false" basis, protected against real challenge
Relation to community	Isolated	Mother isolated, father more adequate outside home	Both parents more adequate socially as separate individuals, despite limited ability to function as marital unit	Involved socially, successful in community where there is often considerable investment compared with family interaction
Family response to crisis	First response to exclude child or have him labelled "hopeless"	Help sought in controlling unmanageable child without other changes in family being necessary	Seek relief of child's symptoms and preservation of marriage	Seek help to contain and cope with problem, without exclusion

rigid, inflexible and authoritarian pattern in those producing schizophrenics, though even in the latter the fathers were less active than in
the "normal" families.

All my own clinical experience, extending now over more than 20
years, has certainly convinced me that, other things being equal, the
optimal pattern for family functioning is one in which the *father* in general accepts the ultimate responsibility and the authority which goes
with this. That is, in seeking ways to improve the functioning of
families, in order to relieve distresses complained of or achieve satisfactions desired, I have found that problems have been regularly associated
with a relative inadequacy of the father to exercise leadership or management functions, and a corresponding overactivity of the mother in
the parental "decider subsystem." A change in the relative activity
or ultimate responsibility towards the father's side has been an essential
component in attaining the family's stated goals, including the mother's.
I have also been struck by the way this view is so widely shared
throughout the literature on family therapy, sometimes explicitly (some
examples have already been given in this chapter, and under note 1,
Chapter 3), more often implicitly in the case examples (some North
American family therapists have told me they avoid expressing such
views openly in the present climate of opinion).

How are we to understand this? I have personally found it more difficult to explain these observations to my own satisfaction—let alone that
of others—than any other aspect of family work, particularly the apparent contradiction it offers to the desirability, advocated in the previous two chapters, for cooperation, sharing, and mutual agreement and
respect. Intuitively, I can see there is no contradiction, but intellectually,
I have been unable to conceptualize it.

Recently, three ideas have seemed to offer possible explanations, all
based, like the idea of hierarchy outlined in Chapter 1, on fundamental
concepts of systems, together with the physical and physiological facts
of gender.

The first has already been noted, but it may be useful to express it
in diagrammatic form in Figure 8.1.

By virtue of the fact that the child grows within her body and is
nourished initially by her blood and milk, and also through her special
psychological aptitudes for empathic response to her infant and for its
sustained nurturance and support, a woman *in general* will be more concerned with the formation of her child's personal, individual boundary,

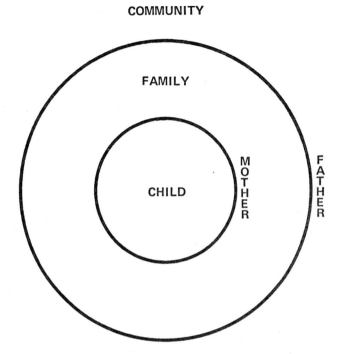

FIGURE 8.1.   Parental boundary-maintaining functions

at least in the early years. This requires the father to give more attention to the family boundary, the relation of the family as a whole to the
world external to it. Insofar as the father is the boundary-maintainer
of the larger system, its welfare will require that his decisions (in his
exercise of this function only, of course) shall take precedence over considerations affecting the individuals within it.

The second reason can be expressed by a simple addition to the same
diagram, adding the facts of *change and growth* to that of a hierarchy
of systems (Figure 8.2). The child's life begins within the mother, but,
if society is to continue, needs to end outside the family of origin altogether, as a member of the community and originator of a new family.
The child has to move away from its initial attachment to the mother
towards a greater involvement with the outside world, and in this the
father is situated in an intermediate position, a bridge between the two
worlds. Clearly, if he is to be effective in this role, then what he stands
for, in the child's eyes, must in the long run take precedence over the

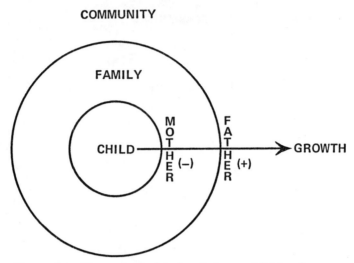

FIGURE 8.2.   Parental polarities in relation to child development

mother's initial provision of gratification and comfort. Both poles are equally necessary, but the movement must be in his direction even if, in the end, he is left behind as well.

Thirdly, some recent research has demonstrated that the sex hormones influence the level of certain enzymes which control the balance of excitatory and inhibitory functions in the nervous system, in such a way that the excitatory, adrenergic, sympathetic nervous system functions are more prominent in females, and the inhibitory, cholinergic, parasympathetic nervous system functions more prominent in males. This has been put forward as an explanation of the well-established "female tendency to excel in over-learned repetitive tasks..." and "the male tendency to excel in problem-solving and analytic behavior, which requires a suppression of the immediate response..." Thus, it is believed that "... men can do tasks which require the inhibition of impulses better than women can because parasympathetic system activity is greater in males or, alternatively, is more constant in males" (4).

Such research does offer for the first time a simple and elegant explanation of many findings in family and marital work which have before appeared puzzling and contradictory—the need for the father to be appointed chairman, and accorded the deciding vote in case of disagreement; the fact that women, even before they have children, so frequently express in therapy a desire for a man who will be a match for them; the persistent provocation they so frequently offer when this is not the case, and their pleasure and relaxation when the provocation succeeds and "the worm turns" to bring about a system of checks and balances in place of one-sided domination; and, in reverse direction, the capacity of women to activate men and to sustain a supportive, enabling force which motivates and harmonizes the whole family.

At the same time, we see that what at first appeared to be an element of "male dominance" is, if looked at in terms of the *system* of the couple or family, simply a manifestation of complementarity, a balance of "yin and yang," yes and no, in which each polarity is different but meaningless without the other, where each equally needs the other in order to be most fully itself. The resemblance of this to the paradigm of sexual intercourse is obvious enough.

Of course, either male or female *can* manage both boundaries, guide the children towards participation in the wider world, manifest both excitatory and inhibitory functions, say yes *and* no. In single-parent families this has to be accomplished, with whatever help is available from others. But it is inevitably more difficult and, other things being equal, two parents who can represent these tendencies in a collaborative, complementary way will obviously have advantages. In therapy, as those who saw the film *Family Session* (5) on BBC television will be aware, I try to strengthen the mother's position and encourage her in the use of her more assertive and "paternal" qualities if there is no hope of helping the father to take this role with the children himself; the reverse is encouraged with families where the mother cannot perform her maternal role.

DEVELOPMENTAL CHALLENGES, BOUNDARIES

I am sure that little more need be said about the impossibility of parents' assisting their children to fulfill developmental tasks that they themselves have not had opportunities to master, either at the usual time or through some fortunate later experience that made good the early deficiency. Many examples have already been given where failures of early nurture prevented the development of loving and trusting attachments at a whole-object level, or where lack of parental control and limits prevented the growth of self-discipline and capacity to tolerate the inevitable frustrations that reality imposes, or where avoidance of sexuality and the oedipal challenge led to inhibitions and confusions over gender role.

One cannot give what one does not possess, and at best parents lacking these experiences will try to provide their children with these educative experiences by words rather than example ("Don't do as I do, do as I say"), or by doing the best they can by asking advice or reading books on child psychology, often acting correctly from their intellectual understanding but missing the essence of what is needed in an emotional sense. Such unsurmounted tasks will naturally show effects both at the marital and the family level, though not necessarily in the same form. Some couples who have suffered deprivation can overgratify their children but deprive each other; others do the reverse, or establish a defensive distance in all family relationships, or exhibit a smothering intensity of attachment throughout, or show alternations between these different patterns. The details will depend on many factors, but what all variants will have in common is a difficulty in striking a comfortable, harmonious and easy balance in the handling of attachment behavior, as well as an excessive preoccupation and anxiety concerning it.

The effects of specifically sexual difficulties between the parents upon the children's development need amplification, for sexual problems are not offered for examination in ordinary life and often not inquired about in sufficient detail in the course of family interviewing to enable one to perceive the patterns clearly. Chapter 17 describes in considerable detail a longer treatment where problems in the sexual relationship and the effects of the marital disturbance on the children were both explored and changed by family and marital therapy in a satisfactory way. The following example shows by contrast that much benefit can come from a frank confrontation of the connection between parental sexuality and children's difficulties, even when there is little hope of improving the former.

The following case is one in which I went about as far as I have ever gone in the way of openly bringing out incestuous attachments during a family interview.

I will not detail the very complex background, as it is not highly relevant to the issue of technique and it would in any case risk the possibility of identification. Suffice it to say that there were four daughters between the ages of 16 and 22 at the time of the interview, all of whom had shown some difficulty in emancipating themselves from the parent-child ties, consequent on the parents' tendency to deny, split-off and project into their children their own most infantile aspects consequent upon borderline-psychotic aspects of their personalities. The present family interview was brought about when the third daughter gave up her college education and insisted on living at home and following her mother about, becoming increasingly depressed and overeating. As the parental home was distant from the clinic, and two other daughters also lived far from home in different directions, the family interview was arranged with some difficulty. The father was late, because his train was delayed, though we did not know the reason when the interview began because a telegram sent to warn us of this did not arrive until after the interview was over. My notes state:

"We began without the father and there was speculation as to the reason for his absence. When it was suggested that he was frightened of coming everyone agreed, saying how shy and nervous he was with any members of the family. The referred patient said how awkward she felt with him, how she hated him and felt she had to suffer his presence when he wished to talk with her. At this the three other girls all defended their father and it was agreed that the referred patient felt allied with the mother while the other girls tended to take the father's side.

"During this discussion one of the two older girls suggested that the problem lay very much more with the parents than with them. They rapidly agreed when I asked if they were suggesting that the parents' sexual relationship might be important, since they were all talking as if they found the father's presence embarrassing, especially when he boasted to them about his sexual exploits. The two older girls went on to discuss their slowness in maturing sexually, in getting boyfriends and having sexual experiences themselves, as if they felt some inhibition holding them back due to this relationship.

"The mother said that there had been no sexual intercourse with her husband for a long period, but added that for the first eleven years, until the youngest child was born, their life had been happy and they had been close and sexually fulfilled as far as she was concerned. After this, when the father had become more successful and widened his circle of friends in a way that the mother had resented, things had become more difficult. I had the impression at this point that the relationship might have been an unhealthy symbiotic one in the early years, even though the mother saw it as happy and fulfilling, and that loss of this marital symbiosis might have been an important factor in the intense mother/child attachments the children had found so hard to break.

"During this discussion a good deal of ambivalence flared up occasionally between the girls and the mother. They complained that she was never open and straightforward in her responses to them, and that in particular she never got angry or stood up for herself so that they felt they could not fight her or express their feelings openly. They implied that this was one reason why they found it so difficult to escape from their dependency upon her and to leave the family; the two older girls thought that now they had succeeded in doing so the referred patient was receiving the full blast of mother's overprotectiveness.

"The mother acknowledged that she could not express anger, just as she could not show sexual feeling either. Her behavior appeared stilted and artificial throughout the interview, to a point where it was difficult to assess the validity of any of her responses. I also pointed out that the mother's attitude to her husband, as on previous occasions when I had seen her (alone), was to paint a picture of him in a totally negative fashion. The mother then emphasized her alienation from her husband as a result of his frequent affairs, but presented herself as perfect and made no mention of any fault on her side.

"About 45 minutes after the beginning of the interview the father arrived, explaining that his train had broken down and that he had telegraphed to warn us of the delay. I filled him in on the substance of our discussion, and put to him very frankly the feeling the girls had expressed that the sexual relationship between him and his wife was unsatisfactory, so that they felt uncomfortable at receiving a strength of interest and affection from him that they felt to be inappropriate, or at hearing him discuss sexual matters which embarrassed them. (In saying this I emphasized the incestuous significance it would hold for them.) He accepted this, and we went on to explore his view of the early history of the marriage, which the mother had seen as so ideal. His account was very different, for he said that though he had been happy with his wife earlier he had been alienated by her affairs with other men (something the mother had never mentioned in previous meetings with me), feeling himself to be sexually rejected and humiliated by her. Mother made no attempt to deny this. He then hesitated and said he did not know whether he should discuss the main event that had come between them, looking at his wife as if this was a secret between them which could not be disclosed without her permission. When I asked her if he could continue she reluctantly agreed and he then said that she had had an affair which had "gone a long way," which had deeply distressed him and from which he had never recovered.

The mother began to cry at this point, and two of the children wept in sympathy with her. However, one of the two older girls responded in a warm and supportive fashion to the mother, saying that it "made mother feel human to her" and that it was "wonderful not to have to feel that she was so impossibly perfect." All the girls agreed that they had had no idea about this aspect of their parents' marriage, that it was a relief to know there was a good reason for the difficulties, and to realize that the mother had feelings too and needed any understanding that they could give her. This exchange was very moving and positive and the girls and the mother seemed to have established a much more real and affectionate relationship with each other."

After arrangements were made for a further interview (difficult because of the distances members had to come from different directions) the interview was terminated and everyone seemed to feel that it had been worthwhile.

A month after the interview, the referred patient wrote:

"Heaven knows what it is that has clicked into place in my mind, but it has and I am happy. So, thank you, for it was definitely through our *one* family meeting that something happened. Perhaps even the rest of the day helped, as it reached a climax, ending with Daddy crushing a glass in his hand in a restaurant and Mommy being typical. I think also having the whole family there was marvelous as it brought everything into the open.

"We all seem much more relaxed together now, especially myself. And so, once again, thank you greatly for whatever atmosphere you produced. . . .

"P.S. I still have trouble over food and find it difficult to stop eating once I've started! But probably this is just from habit and I must control it?"

The day before the above letter was written I had a further interview with the mother and father. They reported that the referred patient had secured a place in a college, had taken up many activities and that her depression had seemed to dissipate at once after the interview. However, on her own decision she had immediately given up the antidepressant medication prescribed months earlier and made a suicidal gesture two weeks after the interview, taking 25 antidepressant tablets, after which she slept for a day and then recovered, saying she "wanted a good sleep." The youngest daughter, who had for a long time shown a delinquent tendency, had been cautioned for shoplifting, but no one thought that this confrontation with the law had done anything but good in the long run. The older girl who was still unmarried had just become engaged.

The marital discussion revealed that the mother was quite frigid and that both partners suffered from profound sexual inhibitions, derived from unresolved incestuous attachments to their own parents. At first some reconciliation appeared possible and they agreed to come again two months later, but this further interview did not materialize and instead they separated on a more amicable basis than might perhaps have been possible otherwise.

Following this the referred patient suffered a relapse and wrote to say that this had coincided with her mother's returning home after visiting the father and burdening her once again with the marital problems. At this point a plan to admit the referred patient to a therapeutic community, which had been held in reserve, was put into action. She made extremely good use of this experience and appeared subsequently to have weaned herself more effectively from the family involvement, though this was clearly still incomplete and further work may be needed. There seems no doubt, however, that the family interview produced results which, though startling in some ways, nevertheless opened up a new set of possibilities and unlocked various blocked developmental sequences.

In the example above the parents were able to tolerate, with encouragement, an open admission of the fact that they had sexual problems, which made it easy for the therapist to define for the children a clear boundary between their sexuality and that of their parents, even though the latter was likely to continue spilling outside the boundary of the marital relationship in other directions. But even where such explicit discussion is not acceptable to the parents, a necessary sense of boundaries and limits can be introduced by the therapist in a different way, as in the next example where the father was unable to cope with any discussion of sexual matters. It should be explained that the phrase "three weeks in the glass-house" refers to a very determined, insistent attitude I sometimes advise over-indulgent parents to adopt with children who have gotten completely out of hand. As the words imply, there is for a period an unrelenting demand that the children should learn to do as they are told, until some adequate control has been established again.

Ruth, aged eight, was referred by her GP because of uncontrollable hysterical behavior in relation to her mother's attempts to control her. There were two younger children, aged seven and five, with constant jealousy and quarreling among them all. Advice from a child psychiatrist who had been seeing Ruth and mother over the previous year had not led to any improvement (in general, he had advised the parents to be more indulgent and to avoid making the children jealous). The GP also reported at the time of referral that there was an associated marital problem, in that the father appeared to derive his main sexual gratification from masturbation and that the mother was sexually frustrated in consequence.

All three children were seen with both parents, and the main impression was of a profound lack of inner controls in the children, consequent upon parental over-indulgence. The family was seen twice with an interval of three weeks, following which I wrote to the GP:

"I have now seen this family twice. At the first interview, it was obvious that the main problem lay in the lack of proper control and limits in the family as a whole, compounded by bad psychiatric advice. Accordingly, I prescribed what I call my 'three weeks in the glass-house' treatment for all the children. When I saw them for a second time yesterday the situation was very much improved, both by the accounts of the parents and by the children's behavior during the session. However, the parents have felt very hesitant about following my advice and told me they had not liked to switch from the previous psychiatrist's principles to my diametrically opposite ones immediately, in case it 'proved too much of shock.' Since they have been rather cautious in carrying out my suggestions, it is not surprising that the improvement is more limited than should have been possible, but both parents have got the message and have been encouraged to continue along the same lines.

"During the second interview the parental relationship came more into the foreground, particularly the mother's wish for the father to take a firmer stand and to control her as well as the children when she feels she cannot cope and becomes difficult herself. The husband's reluctance to do so also became more obvious, but I tried to support him in what she is requesting.

"The other issue which once again appeared was Ruth's regular use of the word 'fuck' in her conversation. This did not upset mother too much but it really floors father! Father said in the interview that she was never again to say that word to anybody, even to me, and Ruth then asked whether, if I was a doctor she could *not* say that word to, she would need to see *another* doctor who was allowed to understand her problem of using that word?! I pointed out how Ruth was not only beginning to understand and integrate her sexual interests but that she was also saying something about the parental sexual relationship. Although I often discuss the parental sexual problems to some extent in front of the children, in this case I felt that this was too difficult for them, particularly father, and I thought the next step should be to see the parents alone."

After another interview, six weeks later, I wrote again to the GP as follows:

"I saw the parents without the children yesterday. They say there has been a vast improvement in all the children, a fact apparently confirmed by the grandfather who does not know they have been in treatment, and they all say that Ruth is 'a different child.' The parents themselves are getting on better. Ruth's provocative use of swear words has also ceased and the parents began to talk about their own sexual relationship. The serious difficulties which they discussed earlier no longer seem to be present, and they said the sexual relationship was satisfactory. However, both of them repeatedly complain that it lacks excitement and spontaneity particularly on the husband's side. As we explored the matter, it seemed as if his feeling of dullness and lethargy when he gets home (though he finds his work exciting) is related to his feeling that his wife is very possessive and jealous, so that he feels he is controlled by her and so gives up his freedom. It is this resentful compliance that seems to cause the chronic feeling of lifelessness. We ended with the wife expressing strong views about the undesirability of men 'going out with the boys' since this might lead to infidelity, but in the end she seemed to accept that her rigid attitudes might be part of the problem. . . ."

It was arranged that the parents should attend a married couples' group, but before they were due to start the wife telephoned to say her husband had decided against it because "it would be too much like group sex." A further interview was offered to the wife, who reported that the problems with the children were completely over and that she had come to terms

with the limited sexual aspects of their marriage. It seemed she was less satisfied than she claimed but it was left for them to get in touch again if the
situation changed.

The mechanisms by which models of relationships are internalized
and transmitted have been adequately outlined already. There is, however, one important complication of this process, which has, so far, been
left on one side for the sake of simplicity of presentation. The idea of
internalized models has been presented up to this point in a largely two-
generational way, whereby one needs to take into account only the
interaction of parents and children to effect change. Such two-genera-
tional viewpoints do suffice for the bulk of family and marital psychotherapy, and the introduction of more complicated concepts only
increases the efforts required of the therapist without improving the
result, perhaps merely delaying it by using a sledge-hammer to crack a
nut.

But many cases, particularly those more intractable problems that resist all other efforts—especially where psychotic features are prominent
and where the therapist's own objectivity is threatened by countertransference distortions—can be understood and managed only by use
of a three-generational approach. Though such a conceptual scheme is
implicit in much that has already been presented, this section attempts
to formulate a more systematic presentation. It draws heavily on the
work of colleagues in Britain, where the long-standing development of
object-relations theories in the psychoanalytic field has led to particular
interest in this type of approach, particularly in the last few years, and
represents a tentative attempt to put some of these ideas together. This
is admittedly rather premature and I offer my apologies to any authors
who feel that I have not done justice to their theories.

Bowlby (6) sees attachment behavior in the infant and child as a
biologically-determined response ensuring that individuals not yet able
to protect and care for themselves remain in close proximity to more
mature members of the species who can provide for their needs. As
competence in coping with the external world increases, such attachment
behavior gradually lessens and its decrease is a sign of successful maturation. In moments of crisis and stress (e.g., bereavement, childbirth, injury, etc.) the attachment behavior recurs and evokes needed supportive

responses in others until the crisis is surmounted and relative autonomy is regained. But where there is failure to master developmental tasks, such attachment behavior persists during stages where it is normally outgrown (e.g., school phobia, the agoraphobic housebound housewife, etc.), leading among other things to spouses who are overdependent on each other or on their children.

If we add to these ideas the following further principles postulating a series of stages by which models are internalized, perhaps other concepts using three-generational theories of family pathology can be reconciled and integrated in a satisfactory way. It will be apparent that the stages proposed for the internalization of models bear a relation to the developmental phases presented in Chapter 2; in fact, they describe the same process from a different point of view.

In normal development, the internalization of a model provided by another person follows a number of stages. Initially there is a high valuation of the other—admiration, idealization—a wish to be like them, to merge with them, in effect to *be* them. This is followed after a certain period by a phase of withdrawal, of separation, of more realistic perception of the other who appears to have lost the previous enviable advantages precisely *because* they have to some degree been obtained and a greater objectivity is therefore possible because the relationship is more equal, more on a level. One sees this process at all stages of life, in varying degree: the early idealization and later necessary criticism of parents by young children; the selection of heroes and idols, or idealistic causes, in adolescence, outgrown in adulthood; more mature admiration, emulation and respect for older, more experienced colleagues and superiors, for spiritual advisers and others who can offer real moral examples to us, and so on.

The point emphasized here is the phasic nature of the process. The first phase is marked by admiration, enthusiasm, a sense of fulfillment, of belonging, of losing oneself as a part of something greater, of problems having finally been solved. But although one may have acquired new strengths at this stage they are not yet one's own; they are borrowed; in a sense, insofar as they are regarded as one's own at this point they have been stolen.

The second stage is marked by disappointment, perhaps a feeling of being let down, and certainly a feeling of needing to rely on one's own resources and of being on one's own to some degree. This feeling of separation, of loss of the previous idealized attachment, is accompanied by some depression in contrast to the previous enthusiasm and excitement, and the pleasurable experience of the first stage may even be regretted and devalued.

Both stages of the process are of equal value, both absolutely necessary to real learning and growth. The first brings us new confidence and abilities, but the second makes them our own, and is a necessary, indispensable prelude to the third stage, of real autonomy, like the moment of terror when one first begins to ride a bicycle unaided, after the previous security provided by one's father's hand on one's shoulder, but before the later different assurance and delight of feeling in control oneself. Even in the moment of disillusion which characterizes the second stage, the promise of this later pleasure and confidence is often felt as a kind of exhilaration and feeling of freedom. In diagrammatic form the process can be demonstrated as in Figure 8.3. On the left an individual who wishes to get something from another merges with him, and then on the right separates again.

A number of obstacles can prevent the effective operation of this identification process, apart from those already mentioned. One difficulty which can interfere with the first stage occurs where positive or constructive envy (a desire to emulate and to possess the other's qualities), probably the most positive force for growth that exists, becomes instead negative and destructive (a desire to spoil and destroy the object of the envy). This usually happens when the desired object or quality is seen as unattainable, the gap between being a "have-not" and a "have" appearing unbridgeable.

The other main obstacle affects the second phase, and is due to difficulties in coping with the pain and depression that loss and separation necessarily entail. Here the good qualities desired are obtained from the person providing the external model and are available as long as the dependent attachment persists, but the model is not successfully internalized, autonomy is not achieved and loss of the object of attachment is experienced as a catastrophe to be avoided at all costs. The first obstacle occurs more frequently in families characterized by a great deal of hostility, rejection and envy, where the gap is indeed unbridgeable; the second obstacle is more characteristic of the warm and loving, but overclose, over-idealized, "too nice" family.

Where separation is so painful it is understandably avoided in one way or another. When a couple marry, they may continue to live as near as possible to the parents of one or the other spouse, and the dependent attachment of childhood is maintained through constant contact. If physical separation is enforced by death or by other circumstances, the models of the parental figures are still not internalized (which would mean a final acceptance of the loss of the real external figures) but kept projected into alternative containers—the spouse, or the children, to whom the attachment is transferred. The lost grandparents are, as it were, kept hidden in the other parent or in the children.

Cooklin (7) has expressed this in terms of what he calls the Central Shared Family Group Preoccupation, which he connects with a "shared avoidance of the mourning that is required before separation can occur," a "shared avoidance of true internalization and separation." Instead, "the sense of identity of the family group is . . . based on binding around the shared preoccupation, rather than the sharing of life tasks."

Instead of following the normal process of identification with the parents, followed by internalization of the models they provide as in Figure 8.3, this family is perceived by Cooklin diagrammatically in Figure 8.4, where ". . . fixed intra-family roles interact via a centrifugal communication pattern, which maintains, and yet avoids acknowledge-

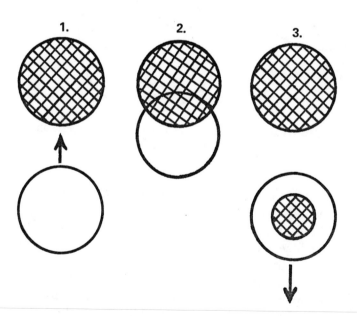

FIGURE 8.3. Process of identification, internalization of model, and subsequent separation

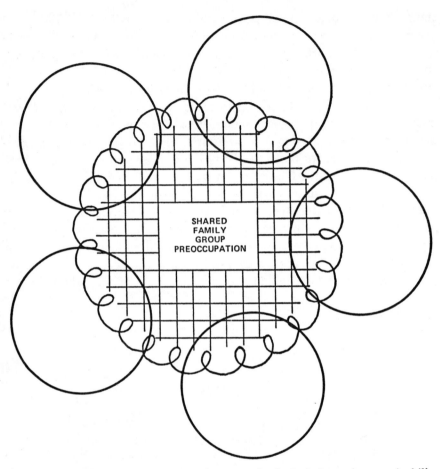

FIGURE 8.4.   Family members bound by unresolved, denied attachment—inability
to separate

ment of, a central shared family group preoccupation." Like the "skele-
ton in the cupboard" (an expression for which this may provide one
meaning), the central space provides somewhere not only to *keep* the
figures of attachment which have not been internalized, but also to *hide*
them at the same time.

Among a number of fascinating examples, Cooklin gives one where
the grandparents contained within the children (and also the children
who were free of such projections) could be clearly defined by the fact
that the death of each grandparent was associated closely with the birth
of each child, in whom they became "resurrected" by parental projec-

tion. Such projections defined for the children roles which were alien to their true selves, which were thereby denied space to develop freely and so inhibited or displaced, rather as the true chicks are displaced from a nest in which a cuckoo's egg has been introduced. Working with these concepts Cooklin sees the therapist's role as ". . . temporarily replacing the Family Group Preoccupation as a shared object—but also remaining outside, alive, functional, and free. In that sense the position is akin to a group version of a transitional object (in Winnicott's sense) . . . he then becomes an object of attachment in the process of differentiation."

R. D. Scott (8), another British author, has proposed essentially similar concepts, particularly in relation to schizophrenia. A high proportion of patients he studied with this diagnosis appeared to have suffered from the fact that one parent had identified them with a mentally ill relative with whom the parent had been in contact earlier in life, so that the referred patients were burdened with projections based on this disturbing experience, called by Scott the "shadow of the ancestor," which led to constant negative expectations all too likely to become reality on the "give-a-dog-a-bad-name" principle. Scott also speaks of a "pool of unrelatedness," perceived as "madness" by the family, which like Cooklin's Central Shared Family Group Preoccupation seems to contain intense unrelinquished but also unacknowledged attachments (which in the terminology being used here could perhaps be described as models, with the associated attachments, which are floating in limbo, ready to find a place in any family member or perhaps moving from one to another). The family members meanwhile are playing a kind of psychological musical chairs trying to avoid being the odd one out.

Stabenau (9) has recently shown, in a study of one-egg (so-called identical) twins in which one had developed schizophrenia and the other had escaped the disorder, how certain weaknesses or adverse experiences, either physical or mental, appeared to lead to the selection of one child rather than the other to receive the negative parental projections and expectancies. Stabenau concludes that "certain physical, temperamental or developmental attributes serve as a focal point for the projection of part of the parent's negative self-image on to the child. The projected features appear to be dissociated, repudiated, negative elements from the parent's personality or representative portions of repudiated, introjected objects from the parent's own life" (p. 23).

The work of Byng-Hall (10), already mentioned in another context, has helped us to understand how "family myths" are produced to rationalize the hidden pathology not only to satisfy the outside world but, more importantly, to enable the family to avoid recognizing it. Like Cooklin and Scott, Byng-Hall suggests that "family myths may originate in an unresolved crisis such as a failed mourning, a desertion or an abortion; the image of the lost person may become resurrected in a remaining member of the family" (p. 240).

In the United States Norman Paul (11) has made similar concepts a central part of his own theories and techniques, whereby the family has to be helped to bring to life the "ghosts from the past"—lost attachment-figures that have not been mourned adequately, given up and truly internalized, around which the family members are bound in a regressive way, preventing growth and renewal of life.

The relevance of such ideas to the present discussion lies in the obvious links that such situations reveal between marital and child disorder. Marriages that function adequately until a child is born and then encounter severe difficulties, or others that function well only when there are children but break down when they leave or become independent, or others that function better where a child is ill, often become explicable when the disturbing, denied models—the skeletons in the cupboard—can be located and their movement within the family projections traced.

9 THE ETHICS OF CHANGE

*There's only one corner of the universe you can be
certain of improving, and that's your own self.*

Aldous Huxley, Time Must Have a Stop

*A good deal of confusion could be avoided, if we re-
frained from setting before the group, what can be the
aim only of the individual; and before society as a whole,
what can be the aim only of the group.*

T. S. Eliot, Mass Civilization and Minority Culture

WHAT RIGHT DO WE HAVE TO CHANGE OTHERS?

In recent years, it has come to be questioned whether members of the
helping professions, or those in other positions of responsibility in society, have any right to seek change in others, particularly where the
request to bring it about comes from relatives or others affected, or
even where the wish for change is expressed, but the consequences cannot be fully appreciated, by the patient or client. Criticism of the traditional medical model, where a disease or disorder is regarded as within
the patient and a professional does something to him "for his own good"
or for the welfare of others, with or without the sanction of the person
concerned, has been most intense from some representatives of the
medical profession itself.

In Britain, Laing (1) and Cooper (2) have been particularly vehement
in their opposition to those colleagues who regard schizophrenia as a
disease of the individual, since they believe that this view results in sufferers being exposed to harmful incarceration in mental hospitals or
administration of stupefying drugs, at the request of relatives. Since
these authors regard the schizophrenic as a scapegoat, and schizophrenia
as no more than a symptom of a malady in the family as a whole, indeed
a consequence of fundamental contradictions and dishonesties in our
entire civilization, they naturally conclude that the traditional medical
approach must lead professionals to collude with a persecuting family

against its victimized and rejected member. In the United States, Thomas Szasz (3) has expressed even more radical views, implying that even the prevention of suicide in a case of psychotic depression is an unwarrantable interference with personal liberty.

It is unfortunate that these objections have been put forward in such extreme form, for this has permitted the medical profession as a whole to discount the need for careful and serious re-examination of the issues involved. The situation has not been helped by the fact that Laing, Cooper and Szasz have found a ready response in many younger members of the public and of the helping professions who seek a rationalization for their unwillingness to accept any restriction on their wish to do as they please, or the discipline of learning their profession properly. As I have already shown, studies of family interaction unfortunately show all too clearly that there is a real justification for these objections to the uncritical use of the traditional medical model, when it is extended to *social* behavior.

The common and often unquestioned assumption among doctors that it is right to prevent death, cure disease and relieve suffering (whether or not the patient agrees) is easier to justify in conditions traditionally within the province of medicine such as fractures, pneumonia or cancer. But even infectious disease may serve a positive purpose, striking down as it often does those individuals who are unable to recognize the warning signs of excessive psychological or physical strain, and obliging the body to receive the rest that the mind does not have the perceptiveness or strength to arrange. One also often encounters clear physical ill-health where an individual needs to have a period of emotional cossetting to gratify unsatisfied dependency needs which he cannot permit himself to receive unless it is given medical sanction and disguised in the acceptable, grown-up form of bed rest, special diets, convalescent holidays and so on. Indeed, it has always appeared to me that this is one of the vital functions all hospitals serve in society, and all the more effectively because it is not made explicit.

Where the emotional origin of physical disorders has been more clearly established, as with asthma, ulcerative colitis or duodenal ulcer, treatment which aims at the removal of symptoms and signs alone, without looking into the emotional significance of the whole disorder in the individual's psychology and in his social network, may actively prevent a more fundamental readjustment from taking place. Instead, with each new prescription it may preserve an immature approach to life, a persistent tendency to escape difficulty and stress, or a miserable, mutually destructive marital relationship.

The traditional medical model, where a "patient" containing a "disease" is brought to a practitioner by "healthy relatives" on the advice of "disinterested professionals," to have the disorder "removed" or "put right," is even more misleading when it is extended to problems such as delinquency or political dissent which express, in undisguised form, conflicts within a social network rather than an individual alone.

The reaction against the medical model has, however, led to equally unrealistic and unhelpful attitudes, usually claiming a base in sociological ideas. The establishment of the links between delinquency and deprivation, or between poverty and educational failure, for example, has led to the simplistic expectation that antisocial behavior or retardation can be removed merely by manipulating the social or economic structure. Envy is seen, correctly, as a potent consequence of deprivation, but the effect of that envy in generating self-destructive attitudes which perpetuate the deprivation, either directly (as in failure to learn or other refusal to take what *is* available) or indirectly (through generating destructive social conflict which ultimately harms everybody and the weakest most of all), is neglected.

The laws regarding problems of truancy, delinquency, violence, etc., and the structure of the social services set up to deal with them have been extensively altered according to the assumption that the social context, not the individual, is responsible for these consequences. Yet this new attitude is as inadequate as the previous, individual-centered one. Remedies based on social action merely turn a half-truth (remedies based on casework or psychotherapy alone) upside-down. Only an examination of the total hierarchy of *systems* and their reciprocal relationships can lead to more effective understanding and intervention. This approach has already been expressed to some extent in the chapter on systems theory, but those with some awareness of psychoanalytic ideas may find it helpful to extend the psychoanalytic structural model, developed by Freud to describe the psychology of the individual, to social networks. It is, however, simply another way of looking at the same thing.

The Freudian structural theory divides the mind into three main parts —superego, ego and id (4). The id represents the sum total of impulses and instinctual drives, the animal heritage present from the beginning in the human personality, by itself anarchic and amoral. The ego represents all the mechanisms of self-control, gradually developed through social learning, by which these drives and impulses are organized and reconciled. And the superego represents the values and principles, originally derived from those of the parents, which provide guidelines within which the ego will attempt to channel the energies of the id. These concepts could, of course, be equally well expressed in different terms such as conscience, self-control and desires. My reason for using psychoanalytic terms is only that they are already familiar to me and to many people working in the helping professions, while a formulation in these terms at once suggests a wealth of implications when extended to networks.

Related to social systems, these concepts can be helpfully expressed in terms of Figure 9.1.

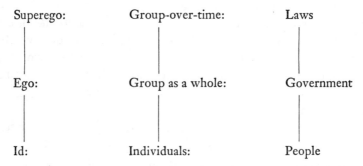

FIGURE 9.1   Correspondence of social and intrapersonal hierarchies

The conflicting impulses of the id can be regarded as equivalent to the members of a therapeutic group, or the population of a country, each member having aims which are to some extent different and conflicting. The ego is the government or therapist, which must reconcile these contradictions and conflicts. To be effective it must represent the group as a whole and find compromises which ensure the maximum common benefit and, in particular, survival of the group itself. The superego is equivalent to the laws of a country, or the ethos or matrix of a therapeutic group, developed by the group over past time and adapted, it is hoped, to ensure its welfare in the future; it thus stands in a position of authority to the group at any particular moment.

Without desires and motives, there is nothing for the ego to organize and no need for rules, just as governments and laws have no meaning except to serve the common long-term interests of the people they regulate. There must also be a mutual, continuous relationship between the two structures, so that even though the government is dominant to the people in the short term, the people determine the government in the long term. Similarly, though the government regards the law as guiding its own actions in general, it slowly modifies existing legislation according to the changing needs and demands of the people. In the same way, the ego mediates between the superego and id, reconciling the two, yet also able to change the superego itself in the light of experience and the needs of the id. This it can do insofar as consciousness, which represents another dimension, provides a connecting force linking the various structures, and permits interaction between them. In a therapeutic group, similar relationships apply. The leader at first, and then increasingly the group-as-a-whole (at least in the group-analytic method) mediate and find new compromises between the individuals composing the group on the one hand, and the demands and challenges of the outside world on the other.

Lack of balance between the structures, and failure of reciprocal communication among them are in the end always harmful to the whole system. Excessive control and rigidity of values lead to a loss of spontaneity and creativity, whether in a repressive dictatorship, a psychotherapy group with an over-controlling leader, or an obsessional individual. Inadequate control and coordination, on the other hand, can lead to a "freedom" or discoordination of the elements which ultimately leads to disintegration of the whole, as when brain damage leads to disruptive "release" phenomena, or a spoiled, undisciplined child is unable to achieve those satisfactions that require some patience, discomfort and self-restraint, or a therapy group, a therapeutic community or a country under too passive a leader becomes increasingly demoralized. Freedom and order are two ends of the same stick, and what matters is the right measure and mixture of each. No doubt the appropriate measure is different at different times—more order in times of stress (as in wartime) and less in times of growth and change, with a constant oscillation between the two.

These three functions are applicable, then, to systems at different levels—individual, family and community. With each new generation the body of information forming the ego and superego, by which the impulses of the id are organized, is internalized by the individual from society, both past and present. At first this occurs through the family, later through the school and, by contact with other individuals and groups, through the intermediary of other families as well. Where this process is successfully achieved and boundaries are clearly defined, the self is well-differentiated from other family members and ego and superego formation may be adequate.

Therapy consists largely of improving communication among these components and achieving a more harmonious balance among them. Increased consciousness of their nature (they may all be unconscious in varying degree) and the establishment of more adequate connections may facilitate adaptive modifications of the structures themselves through their more complete interaction, as well as by enhanced exposure to life experience.

This state of affairs was typical of the middle-class, neurotic patients with whom psychoanalysis was first developed, and with whom the individual approach and the study of intrapsychic processes are more likely to provide an adequate solution. In other cases, however, the situation is quite different. Where the socializing experiences which enable an individual to differentiate himself and internalize these structures are grossly lacking or distorted, he may continue to depend on others to provide these functions for him, as parents do for a young child. Different members of the family may then play roles corresponding to these functions, one child perhaps expressing aggressive impulses (the "bad" one), another child loving and caring feelings (the "good" one), the mother fulfilling superego functions (the "responsible" or "respectable" one), and the father controlling the children according to the mother's dictates (the "strong but unreliable" one). Roles may also be exchanged so that different members perform each function for the family group at different times.

In families and systems in which the three functions are dispersed among members, treatment confined to any one individual is clearly not likely to be effective. Once the individuals in a family are brought into relationship, either in an actual group or even separately through the mediation of the therapist, change may become possible.

MINIMUM SUFFICIENT NETWORK

To express this principle briefly, it is useful to introduce the concept of the Minimum Sufficient Network (5); in any situation this is the psychological or social structure containing enough of the three subsystems—superego, ego and id—for autonomous function to be possible. In cases which respond well to individual psychotherapy or casework, the three subsystems are adequately developed within the individual to permit communication within the intrapsychic network to a sufficient degree, without much need to involve others. But where developmental arrest, due to deprivation or trauma, has led to these structures remaining dispersed among a number of people, the only autonomous system will be the group containing those individuals, and treatment must go beyond intrapsychic exploration and interpretation to facilitate communication between the persons involved.

The words "minimum" and "sufficient" are used to indicate that though we wish to include as much of the network as is necessary to achieve our aim, we do not want to make the task more complex than is absolutely necessary and so intend to exclude from consideration any parts of the network whose influence is sufficiently small to permit them to be safely ignored.

WIDER NETWORKS

The minimum sufficient network may, then, be confined within the boundaries of an individual or dispersed throughout a nuclear or extended family. It may also spread wider and involve other significant figures or organizations within a community. Some families are unable to provide basic care and nurturance for the children, in that the mothers cannot cook, cannot budget, or feel such needs for support and comfort themselves that they have little to give the children. Where this is so, and the father is unable to supplement the mother's nurturing capacities sufficiently, the family's ability to function may depend upon long-term supportive contact with a social work agency. In Britain, Family Service Units have developed particular abilities to intervene effectively at this level.

In other cases, nurturance may be adequately provided, by one parent or both, but neither father nor mother may be able to provide the structure and limits within which the children can develop sufficient inner controls to cope with the world outside. Here ongoing contact with figures in the community who can supply the required ego and superego functions like persistence, firmness and consistency—perhaps the teacher, school psychologist or guidance counsellor, the father's employer, or sometimes the policeman, probation officer or court—may enable the family to operate successfully and prevent disturbances which might lead to the removal of the children and consequent deprivation of the real love the home has to give. Families which need to draw in this way upon the surrounding social networks for functions they lack usually require long-term, though intermittent, support. It is this not perceived and offered by the caring services, recurrent crises may occur to bring the needed intervention about.

REFERRAL NETWORKS

If we begin to think in this way of a network of functions each time a case is referred to us, several questions at once present themselves. Who is disturbed? Who is disturbing? Who has the motivation to alter the situation? Who has the capacity to alter it? Four different people may be involved here, or one. If the former, we are in for trouble and disappointment if we follow our usual individual-centered procedure. Within each network we must locate the main need or motivation if we are not to waste our time intervening in the wrong part of the network or ignoring some crucial aspect of it.

If we approach the problem of intervention by considering first of all the question of motivation, at least three categories of motivation can be distinguished:

1. To express impulses and gain instinctual satisfaction.
2. To control the impulses because of their harmful consequences, actual or supposed.
3. To find a compromise and resolve a conflict between instinctual drives and social controls.

The third category involves, in psychoanalytic terms, motivation to find a better solution to a conflict between superego and id, and it includes the cases for which our usual techniques are well suited. However, the first category—people who are seeking instinctual satisfaction, without personal conflict—never come to us except when we have something they want us to give them, when they are experiencing something painful they want us to help them escape from, or (a special case of the latter) when they are under pressure from the second category—people who are suffering from their behavior and who wish to see them controlled. However, if we keep the first two categories in contact (the antisocial family and the socializing forces of society, equivalent to id and superego) and help them to communicate by ourselves' acting rather as the ego does in intrapsychic dynamics, we have then converted the situation into something resembling the third category of motivation, where existing psychotherapeutic and casework principles may hope to facilitate a better compromise.

It is sometimes objected that this connecting or integrating role may be adequate for psychiatrists and voluntary social work agencies, but that statutory agencies, charged by society with implementing its laws, are obliged also to take action. This is of course correct: The social services department may be obliged to recommend to a court that a suffering child be removed from its parents and taken into a foster home; a probation officer may have no alternative but to bring an individual before the court for breach of probation. But the psychiatrist is in exactly the same position when he makes a compulsory order for admission to a hospital or deems a child maladjusted and in need of special education in a residential school. Nevertheless, in all these cases each professional or agency is still linking parts of the network, communicating information which leads to certain actions or consequences between its elements. Difficulties arise, in my experience, only when those concerned in the network forget that they have this mediating or connecting function and, by exaggerating their own responsibility in the matter, experience it as a personal failure if some of these consequences are not avoided.

NETWORKS INVOLVING THE SCHOOL

An example frequently encountered in child guidance clinics takes the form of a child who is said to present a behavior problem at school while his parents claim that he is normal at home. On investigation, it usually proves that the mother is herself immature and unable to tolerate frustration or rejection. In her attempt to avoid conflict with the child and perpetuate the original attachment, she projects all controlling functions on to the father, from whom she then shields the child. In some families, this produces a permanent conflict between father and mother about the child's upbringing, usually with behavior problems in the home due to their confused and competing management. In other families, the parents may avoid conflict through the father's joining the mother in this indulgent, nurturing role, while both combine to project all controlling and frustrating functions on to the school. The school then becomes the target of the parent's joint hostility and the child, too, is encouraged to displace his own dissatisfaction and rebellion away from the home towards the teachers. The whole procedure has the purpose of maintaining some unity within the family, and the situation is not usually changeable by work with the parents or child unless the function of the school within the network is also considered.

In such situations, we have found that a therapeutic focus on facilitating communications between the school and the family, as well as between the two parents, has the best hope of success. If the father is confronted with, and accepts, the school's authority he is supported in fulfilling his paternal role in the family, and the mother in turn, with the father's support, can begin to accept her authority over the child.

To do this, the clinic or agency seeking to assist must accept its own authority and responsibility in the situation, which is to confront the various contestants with their true positions in the conflict, despite the fact that this will arouse resistance and strong pressure to treat the child (by the parents) or the family (by the school). However, a firm but supportive and conciliatory approach usually wins trust and respect, and once the greater success of this approach is experienced by the school further similar interventions are usually welcomed.

This connecting role can be carried out by communicating with the school after a family interview at the clinic, so that the school staff appreciate the nature of the difficulty and try to establish a relationship with the parents, particularly the father. Lately, however, we have found it both more effective and time-saving to meet such families at the school, together with the head teacher (who has the ultimate authority in the school situation) and the class teacher (who possesses the detailed information about the problem). It is left to the school, which is the part of the network desiring change, to secure the family's attendance.

The following case illustrates the connecting role of the psychiatrist between the parents and the school.

Kingston, aged 11, had been left behind in the West Indies when his parents came to England nine years previously. He had joined them a year ago to find a number of younger siblings born since the parents arrived in Britain. Discipline at home was extremely strict and he was said to be no problem there, but at school he was reported to be extremely aggressive. He had struck other children over the head with chairs and at times had been completely unmanageable.

Kingston was seen at school with both parents, the class teacher and the principal. At first the parents were suspicious and aggressive, anticipating racial prejudice and accusing the teachers and other children of discriminating against Kingston on grounds of race. The teachers, already exasperated by Kingston's provocative behavior, seemed only too likely to confirm the parents' paranoid fears. However, my colleague and I insisted on a careful and thorough exploration of Kingston's behavior both at home and at school, focusing particularly on what the parents and teachers had discovered about the best way to manage him. Gradually the parents acknowledged that he often showed similar difficulties at home to those manifested at school, while the teachers reported many endearing sides to his personality. As the view of Kingston became more objective the parents began to respond positively to the sympathy, interest and knowledge of the boy shown by the school staff, which came as a surprise to them, while the teachers became more sympathetic to the parents as they became more aware of their many hardships and desire to do their best for the children. Both parents expressed their willingness to cooperate with the school to improve the situation, and the father agreed to visit the principal periodically to discuss progress.

This improvement in the relationships among the adults obviously did not meet with Kingston's approval, and it was possible to point out on several occasions how he attempted to provoke conflict between his parents, seeking his mother's support against his father, as well as to provoke his parents into opposition to the school by implying unfair treatment. At one point attention was drawn to his smile of pleasure when he had succeeded in provoking such an argument between his parents and the principal, which convinced the parents that they were being manipulated.

At the end of the initial interview, the relationship between the parents and the school, particularly between the father and the principal, appeared to have been firmly cemented. Follow-up disclosed that the boy continued often to be aggressive and uncontrolled, but the school felt able to cope with him. Further appointments were not requested.

Where the school staff are really concerned with the needs of the child or family and put these first, subject to the welfare of other children, the task of reconciliation is easier and the school staff become allies in the therapeutic endeavor. Usually this is the case, and I have been repeatedly impressed by the amount of knowledge and the quality of concern and interest shown by teachers in the children we have discussed on such visits. But there is inevitably a small proportion of schools where the personal ambitions of the principal, or the desire of the staff generally to impose middle-class standards in a working-class area, lead to referrals which have the aim of enforcing inappropriate values or, if that is not possible, getting rid of a child without the removal being recognized as an exclusion. Here the family therapist may have to take the family's side and argue its case, or at least try to manipulate the situation to the family's advantage, using the values of the school as a lever.

A request was made by a school, through the care committee, that a child be seen at the clinic for treatment, the complaint being disruptive behavior and resistance to learning though the details were vague. It was clear from the information that the family would be unlikely to cooperate in such separate treatment and also that the school was trying to transfer responsibility for the boy's problems to us. A school visit was offered but this met with some opposition. There was considerable delay, and a good deal more unsuccessful pressure on us to deal with the case in the way the school wanted, before it was finally agreed to see the family at the school in the company of the principal and the housemaster.

The parents and the boy arrived outside the school gates at the same time as the psychiatric social worker and myself and we had the opportunity to introduce ourselves and to make some contact. We met the vice-principal shortly after and were not encouraged when, in response to some positive remarks by the psychiatric social worker about the architecture, the vice-principal answered "More like Belsen, I'd say." We realized that our negative first impressions had been correct when the principal, despite absolutely clear arrangements that he would attend the interview, pleaded much more important business and excused himself, disappearing rapidly before I realized what was happening. The right action, from one point of view, would have been to point out politely that the contract had been broken, and to leave after agreeing to pay another visit if the arrangements could be adhered to. I feared that if we did so the school might not visit their annoyance upon us but upon the family, and we therefore proceeded with the interview.

The housemaster clearly had a good relationship with the boy and the family, and the parents were increasingly willing to acknowledge that the boy had not received as much interest and supervision from them as he needed, that he had been trying to play them off against the school, and that they would be glad to cooperate in any way they could and to visit the housemaster regularly to this end.

From our point of view the interview was going unusually well, and there was every reason to hope that the difficulty previously encountered by the school would be greatly improved. However, it became increasingly evident that this was not at all what the vice-principal, and presumably the principal, were hoping for, as we had suspected from the previous correspondence. The vice-principal repeatedly interrupted to steer the discussion towards the question of treatment at the clinic and the possibility of transferring the boy to a school for maladjusted children on the basis of our medical recommendation. Eventually, to block this disruption it was necessary for me to pretend to lose my temper with the vice-principal and to stimulate fear in him of what I might later say to the principal or to the education officer.

Also, knowing that it was the last thing this particular principal would agree to (because of his need to see himself as far superior in skill to his colleagues in neighboring schools), I said that if they failed (the word was deliberately used several times) in their attempt to consolidate the better relationship with the family that had been achieved in the interview, we at the clinic would be very pleased to do all we could to recommend transfer of the boy to another normal school.

By the end of the interview the relationship between the parents and the housemaster had been securely established, and we asked the educational psychologist visiting the school (who was attached to a different clinic) to keep an eye on the situation. Fortunately, such unpleasant experiences with schools are rare.

MOTIVATION OF REFERRING AGENTS

Networks producing similarly insistent but inappropriate demands can sometimes be very complex. In one family which functioned in many ways at a borderline-psychotic level, psychotherapy enabled the mother to refuse to carry a depression for the rest of the family which she had previously done to shield the father from an awareness of his own inadequacy. The father, too fearful to hit back at the mother as she became more assertive and faced him with increasing awareness of his impotence and inadequacy, turned his anger towards the daughter (who was the referred patient) instead. However, he lacked the capacity even to vent his rage on her and instead repeatedly aroused the anxiety of the physician at a neighboring hospital who was treating this girl for a recurrent urinary infection, so that the physician kept demanding psychotherapy for her even though this had been repeatedly offered and sabotaged by the parents. In this case the fact that the hospital had been unable to save the life of an elder sister, who eventually died of a kidney infection, was highly relevant.

A rather similar situation occurred with a child referred by a child care agency. I found myself unable to understand their insistent demand for psychotherapy, which appeared inappropriate, until it emerged that this was a second generation deprivation case, where the children's officer felt guilty because of her belief that the present problem might have been averted if the department had handled the mother better when she herself was in care during her own childhood.

Some problems of this kind might occur in relation to any referrer lacking sophistication in psychiatric knowledge. Other referrals may have more to do with the psychopathology of the referrer, or perhaps even of society itself. One school sent us a succession of cases of behavior problems in children who had suffered deprivation, even where this was clearly being remedied very effectively, if gradually, by the foster home and school, because the principal had suffered deprivation herself in childhood. Another school showed exceptional intolerance at being made into a "bad object" as the solution to a family's difficulties, and reacted to this by simultaneously excluding children and referring them to our clinic, which they, in turn, used as a "bad object." (I first realized this when trying to understand the seemingly irrational fury of other colleagues whenever this particular school was mentioned.) In another situation a large series of patients was referred by a general practitioner for psychotherapy. These referred patients were often unsuitable because they lacked motivation and came at his persuasion. These referrals ceased when he began his own psychoanalysis, no doubt because he was at last able to refer himself directly instead of vicariously.

We can now see, perhaps, the real objection to the views of Laing, Cooper and Szasz. Their emphasis on the individual's rights and freedom is based upon a misconception. The mature and autonomous individual, who has adequately completed his developmental tasks, can indeed be relied upon to cope independently, for he has the equipment to do so effectively in order both to achieve his own interests and to take account of his relationship to the larger system of the family or society. Society is already inside him, influencing and guiding him, but without overwhelming him or threatening his secure separate identity.

For others freedom has less meaning, for it may mean not freedom to live and grow but condemnation to fail, to remain isolated, to remain hopelessly at the bottom of the pile or even to become insane. Babies cannot be "free," for if they are left to look after themselves they die. In varying degree, those who are intermediate in autonomy between the infant and the true adult also need others to help them operate effectively. To fail to recognize this and respond to the need can therefore be a form of irresponsibility rather than a respect for the individuality of others.

IS CHANGE POSSIBLE?

If we can accept *in principle* that facilitating or even coercing change in others can be ethically acceptable, at least in certain cases and where we know what we are doing and why we are doing it, the next question in any given case must be: Is change possible? Where it is not, even a rapid screening out of such cases (which is often possible in one or two family sessions) will pay large dividends in avoiding further time wasted on fruitless effort.

Some individuals, for example, demand relief of their symptoms without any change in the rest of their personality, terminating psychotherapy when they find they cannot hope to lose their anxiety as long as they nourish their hostility, or cannot overcome their sense of inferiority unless they strive to become more responsible and independent. Such people, who tend to deny real deficiencies in themselves and either express these in somatic form or project them on to others, will usually shop around until they find a professional who will agree with their views and prescribe drugs or other physical treatments. It seems to me best either to offer these oneself in the first place or to refer them to others who will do so, rather than refusing help to those who do not share one's own philosophy.

In other cases the family expects a child to be changed without being willing to alter its own part in the problem. Gratitude and successful achievement may be sought from the child, who is at the same time scapegoated and refused the love and interest which might encourage positive behavior. Where this is so, substitute interest and concern must be provided. In less rejecting family situations this may be achieved sometimes through the ordinary school, tutorial class, special day school, youth club, or other outside contact; but in the most intractable cases boarding school placement or reception into care may be the only solution, enabling the child to receive what little love the parents have to give during holiday periods and supplementing this with affection and interest from professional care-giving figures.

When the referred patient is a child, much of course depends upon its age. The capacity of younger children to function outside the family system is very limited, and a "holding" operation, preserving what is valuable in the family and compensating for what is lacking in it, may be the only practicable response. But as the child moves into adolescence, and is biologically ready to escape from the family system, one can be more ambitious and facilitate differentiation by family, small group or individual psychotherapy.

Even if change is possible in a given system, it still remains to decide whether it is *desirable* for the therapist to attempt it. Here the value systems of the parties concerned need to be brought into relationship if the therapist is not, unwittingly and with the best of intentions, to impose his own needs and standards on a patient or family for whom quite different ambitions and requirements may already exist. The therapist may feel that a marriage he encounters would be unendurable for him, but it is not *his* marriage; he did not choose to begin or continue it, and if it breaks up as a result of his efforts he is not usually in a position to offer the spouses anything better. A child's life may seem insufferable in terms of the therapist's own childhood and the life he seeks to offer to his own children, but unless he is going to adopt the child himself or arrange other alternative care he may do nothing but harm if he arouses even greater dissatisfaction in the child, or jealousy and rejection in the parents, by giving too much himself.

The therapist may set a high value on insight, especially if his life has been enriched through his own therapy, but only some people want this; insight can also prove intolerable, shattering, even lethal, to those who live on illusions and lack ego-strength to face the deeper truth, so that the therapist does well to remember that there is no known cure or antidote for it once it is attained. For one person a breakdown may be an opportunity, a fresh start, a demolition essential to permit a rebuilding of the personality; for another it can be a meaningless disaster, or even a nightmare from which there is no waking. All experience is potentially valuable or destructive, depending on the capacity to use it. Even affluence, as we see today, can be a mixed blessing when it leads to obesity, heart disease, pollution and alienation from the self.

What is the solution to this dilemma? I believe there is no easy answer, and, indeed, that the only answer is to keep the question constantly before one. If one tries to become more aware of one's own values, instead of taking them for granted, and remains open to and interested in those of the individuals and families encountered, an exchange is possible which can benefit both parties and lead to an attitude of mutual respect, ongoing adjustment and increasing understanding.

When I first went to work in the East End of London, where much of my own early experimentation with family therapy was done, I found myself at first depressed by the weight of social and emotional problems there. Family after family seemed borderline, without insight or motivation as I understood it, and the situation often seemed hopeless, beyond any remedy that I could imagine.

Gradually I came to see that, even if I was depressed by their lives, they on the whole were not; and it also became clear that, though my middle-class valuation of forethought and tolerance of present suffering for the sake of future gain (whether for accumulating money or psychotherapeutic insight) might sometimes have relevance for them, they could teach me a great deal about living spontaneously in the moment and enjoying life as it came. As this occurred, I came to enjoy and respect them, and to see how I could be useful to them by working in a different fashion in which I was less judgmental and acknowledged that they might help me too. Becoming more realistic, I was also able to work for some amelioration of their social conditions and services in a practical way.

Sometimes this questioning of one's own values can be explicit, forming a subject for discussion in the interview itself. But more often it is for me now an inner dialogue, a question to which I expect no final solution but from which I can learn something all the time, which will benefit me personally and, by sharpening my professional technique and clarifying my aim in each new situation, enable me to meet the family's needs more objectively.

Part Two
APPLICATION

10 TECHNIQUES: GENERAL APPROACHES

"Begin at the beginning," the King said, "and go on till you come to the end; then stop."

Lewis Carroll, Alice in Wonderland

The best way out is always through.

Robert Frost, Servant to Servants

Like the empty space in a Chinese painting, the time in which nothing happens has its purpose.

Edward de Bono, The Five-Day Course in Thinking

Family therapists probably show more similarities than differences in their techniques, when contrasted with individual or stranger-group therapists, but there are nevertheless varieties of emphasis which it is valuable to mention in order that the reader may use the different studies to best advantage. To this end, the work of others will first be related to the main principles already outlined. Next, the matter will be approached from a different angle, looking at the similarities in technique but trying to see how these are altered or emphasized in the light of the background or theoretical assumptions of the therapists concerned. Finally, my own approach will be outlined, and some of the practical questions which are raised frequently when therapists begin to work in this field will be answered.

SCHOOLS OF FAMILY THERAPY

Boundaries

Not surprisingly, many therapists who have worked intensively with schizophrenic patients have been particularly interested in problems of *boundaries*. The work of Murray Bowen (1), already mentioned in Chapter 1, is particularly interesting in this regard. He sees the main therapeutic need as the "differentiation of a self" by each family member out of the "undifferentiated family ego mass" that such families often demonstrate.

Since the definition of the boundary of one member automatically defines that of others, provided they remain in contact (as the clear marking of a country's frontier automatically defines that of its neighbor as well) much of Bowen's work is done with one family member (usually the healthier parent) and with the parental couple, even though it is aimed at promoting the differentiation of the whole group. In one paper (2), written in 1966, he stated that 30 to 40 percent of his time was spent in this way, although now he appears to make more use of couples' groups (3). Following the same principle, Bowen promotes the formation of the boundaries of key individuals by clearly defining his own, through indicating what he will do and not do and by avoiding manipulative attempts to seduce him or coerce him into taking responsibility for patient or family pathology. By not *functioning* for the patient, he sets an example from which family members may ultimately learn to function for themselves and to contain their own assets and liabilities.

Bowen has also pointed out that the primitive infantile relationship of *ego-fusion* between family members is accompanied by *emotional divorce* at the more differentiated, mature level demanded in true marital and sexual interaction. This would be revealed overtly by one parent taking over the more mature functions of the other, who then becomes helpless and malfunctioning, and by either a "cold war" or a "frictionless but lifeless and idealized" relationship.

Theodore Lidz (4) has noted very similar boundary problems in families. In his "marital skew," as in Bowen's "over-functioning" and "under-functioning" marital pairs, one spouse presents a false image of competence and normality at the expense of the partner who accepts to contain the pathology for both. Alternatively, his "marital schism," like Bowen's "emotional divorce," demonstrates a self-centered and competitive struggle for the children's affections and for power over the partner.

Lyman Wynne's "pseudo-mutuality" and "pseudo-hostility" (5) similarly describe surface manifestations of either idealized or conflicted marital relationships which conceal and defend against an underlying avoidance of real intimacy or challenge. Wynne's method of clarifying the boundaries, in contrast to the detached, defined stance characteristic of Bowen, involves sharing in the family's confusion initially, usually by working with the whole family together in conjunction with a co-therapist.

We will examine the rationale for these different approaches later, together with the different ways of dealing with *hierarchy and control*, which are for obvious reasons a central issue in the technique of all family therapists.

Communication

Two main groups of family therapists who have been interested particularly in schizophrenia—the Palo Alto group of Bateson, Jackson, Haley and Weakland (6) in the United States, and Laing and Esterson (7) and Cooper (8) in England—have focused especially on issues of *communication*. The concept of the "double-bind" developed by the former group, whereby conflicting messages or instructions prevent the individuals receiving them from either finding a solution or escaping from the conflict aroused (e.g., "boys must stand up for themselves and not be sissies"; "don't be rough ... don't be rude to your mother") is now well known. Laing's "mystification," which postulates a systematic provocation of confusion and bewilderment by vague or incompatible information, with hostile and destructive intent, describes a similar process in more dramatic form.

Satir (9), who worked with the Palo Alto group, has developed from their ideas a technique based largely on clarification of communication which is applicable to a more general range of psychiatric problems.

The American group of communication theorists has shown little interest in individual psychopathology and therefore makes conjoint work, where communication and interaction can be directly observed, the rule. The British group, with its strong background of individual analysis, tends to focus more on individual pathology even in the family group; it is also prone to side with the member of the family deemed to be the patient, who is often seen as an innocent victim of deliberate persecution by the parents or even as a superior being endowed with greater wisdom than average (10). These views seem to me to reproduce the paranoid/schizoid "black-and-white" thinking which characterizes the families themselves.

Conscious attempts to alter behavior by learning processes, presenting different models for the family to internalize, are emphasized by a number of contributors to the field, though of course these mechanisms must always be in operation whatever the theory employed. Minuchin and his colleagues (11) and Robert MacGregor and the Galveston group (12) are outstanding examples, but a number of contributors have also developed the use of role-playing concepts from a background in the social sciences rather than in medicine and psychiatry. Spiegel (13), Pollak (14) and Scherz (15) are outstanding examples. There has also been some application of straightforward behavior modification principles in the family context by a number of workers (16).

Object-Relations Theory

Approaches based on object-relations theory, whereby the key to a family problem is searched for explicitly in the unconscious internalized models of dead or absent figures—usually the grandparents of the referred child—have understandably been more the choice of those with an individual psychoanalytic background. Framo (17), Boszormenyi-Nagy (18), Friedman and others from the Eastern Pennsylvania Institute (19) all seek to bring back to awareness the past experiences which underlie present projections and distortions; they are inclined to believe that unless this is done the repressed experiences continue to interfere with the development of the children or with the therapeutic process. Norman Paul (20), with his concept of "ghosts from the past," takes a similar view. In marital work, H. Dicks at the Tavistock Marital Unit (21) and the staff of the Institute of Marital Studies (22) at the Tavistock Institute of Human Relations, and, in family therapy proper, John Byng-Hall (23) at the Department of Children and Parents at the Tavistock Clinic, with his development of Ferreira's (24) concept of "family myths," have all been working in the same vein utilizing Kleinian principles.

Developmental Concept

The developmental concept, which seems to me such a fruitful way of ordering the phenomena of family interaction, has been less explicitly used. The Galveston group (25) has made the main contribution with their clear and explicit linking of different levels of developmental arrest in children with corresponding immaturities in the marital relationship of their parents. Their main findings have already been presented in Chapter 8 (see pp. 142–144). The Minuchin group (26), whose work will be discussed more fully in the next chapter, has also classified disadvantaged families in what is essentially a developmental sequence, which is outlined in Chapter 12. Unfortunately, both groups have produced developmental classifications of their own which makes it hard at present to compare and contrast their findings with each other or with more established concepts.

Two individuals remain who do not fit easily under any of these categories. The first is John Howells (27), one of the pioneers of family psychiatry in England, who perhaps has contributed most of all through his own experiences of setting up a comprehensive family approach in a general hospital setting, fully integrated with other local services. His interest in the conceptualization of family psychotherapy is, however, largely limited to his "vector therapy," whereby the environment is manipulated in the light of family diagnosis to alter the strength or direction of inappropriate emotional forces. Curiously enough, this obvious but vital aspect of intervention has been strikingly neglected in other writing.

The second is John Elderkin Bell (28), a unique figure whose early formulations anticipated and integrated many of the different aspects that other therapists made central in their own theories. He takes control of the family and establishes a format within which it can feel safe to experiment with the clearer communication which then becomes a central focus; he proceeds systematically from the initial problem in the referred child to the original difficulty in the marital pair; his modeling to the family of new types of relationship is clear if implicit; and more than any other exponent he combines attention to the intrapsychic, individual aspects with awareness of the group as a system, never forgetting either the parts or the whole.

Hierarchy and Control

I have suggested that issues of hierarchy, authority and control occupy a central place in the concepts and techniques of almost all family therapists, but their theoretical orientation or personality leads them to gain or maintain control in different ways. Beels and Ferber (29), who have not only surveyed the written work of the main contributors but also attempted to observe what they actually do, classified them into three main subgroups according to their methods of establishing control.

The first group, which they label "conductors," enter the family system with a clear and confidently held value system of their own about how families function best, and seek to re-educate the family in what they regard as more healthy and constructive attitudes to com-

munication, control and mutual exchange. They take the role of edu-
cators, of "super-parents," and openly confront and challenge the
family's pathological functioning (especially the defenses the family uses
against the therapeutic intervention itself). The type of pressure exerted
to effect change may be persuasive, seductive and manipulative in some
conductors' work, or critical, provocative and forceful in the work of
others. These two approaches can perhaps be seen as more "maternal"
or "paternal" respectively, though the best therapists, like good parents,
seem able to utilize both types of intervention as required. Conductors
are, as Beels and Ferber remark, usually vigorous, charismatic personalities. Examples of such conductors are Bell, Ackerman, Satir, Minuchin, Bowen, MacGregor, Paul, and Howells (30).

A second group is labeled by Beels and Ferber as "reactor analysts,"
and these include Whitaker, Wynne, Framo, Friedman, Boszormenyi-
Nagy and others of the Eastern Pennsylvania Institute (31). In England,
I would include many of the Tavistock marital and family therapists.
Members of this group have, as the name suggests, a background in individual psychoanalysis and a basic respect for the idea that both families
and individuals have within them the motivation and potential for growth
and change, if only this can be uncovered and released. If this is the case,
the imposition of the therapist's own values and life-style, which might
be inappropriate, or even pathological, for others, is obviously to be
avoided; these therapists therefore allow themselves to *react* to the family
system by lowering their own defenses (especially defensive control of
the interviews themselves) and letting the family attitudes affect them.

While the conductors probably defend themselves against receiving
family projections by maintaining a high level of activity, and the system
purists (described below) by distancing themselves emotionally, the
reactor analysts open themselves to the family's projective system and
use their resulting countertransference responses as vital information to
learn about the family's pathology by permitting themselves to be
"sucked into" it. They operate rather like the fishermen of the Gilbert
and Ellice islands, described so beautifully by Sir Arthur Grimble (32),
where one member of the team dives into the tentacles of the octopus
while the second follows immediately behind and, by a sharp tug on the
legs of his companion, raises them both swiftly to the surface where they
can be disentangled. For equally cogent reasons the reactor-analysts also
operate in pairs, one standing by to rescue his co-therapist as he is about
to vanish into the "dear octopus" of the family's pathology.

This group operates, it will be seen, more from the vulnerable role of the "child" or the "patient" rather than the protected one of the "super-parent," though they also confront the family with the truth about itself in a different way. However, as in psychoanalysis and psychoanalytic psychotherapy, a good deal more conducting probably goes on than is admitted or recognized by the therapists. The best family work, whatever the technique, is inevitably experienced as beautiful and elegant, but I often find the accounts of the work of some of this group deeply moving as well.

The third category is that of the "system-purists." It includes Jay Haley, the late Don Jackson, and Gerald Zuk (33). Their approach is more difficult to summarize briefly and meaningfully and the reader is referred to Beels and Ferber's paper for an outline of the principles, or to Watzlawick *et al.* (34) for more comprehensive accounts. In essence, however, they do not so much engage in a direct encounter with the family "from above" (like the conductors) or "from below" (like the reactor analysts) as seek to change the ground-rules of the game (the therapeutic interaction itself) in such a way that the family can neither continue to function in the same pathological fashion nor, should it decide instead to break these new rules, help seeing that they are doing so and facing themselves more honestly. Usually, the key lies in perceiving the way in which the family tries to influence the therapists to accept a relationship which will in effect be an extension of the family system and would, far from changing it, maintain its homeostasis. Once this is seen by the therapist, the rules of the therapeutic relationship are so arranged as to make this impossible. The family tries to get the therapist "against a wall" where they can control him, but he constantly avoids this and moves about and keeps them off balance instead.

Thus, the family which tries to perpetuate childishness and dependency by keeping it in the children—who then have to be perpetually nurtured by the parents (who are also vicariously nurturing their own dependency, through projective identification)—will try to take a similarly helpless, dependent role towards the therapist. "Tell us what to do and we will try to do it," they will say, maintaining their dependency by failing and implying that this is due to not having had enough "help."

One current patient in a marital group, for example, drove his previous individual therapist to ever greater lengths by making him feel useless and inadequate in this way. Advice, behavior therapy, abreaction under intravenous drugs and endless history-taking were tried in turn over two years while the patient lay comfortably on his back and complained that the therapist had not yet found the answer. In the group he tried the same passively expectant role, looking at me hopefully and complaining that he could not think of anything "useful" to say. I gave him the task of "ejaculating" some sounds into the group (the complaint with which he was referred was an inability to ejaculate sexually into his wife), instructing him to say anything, no matter how stupid, even making a noise or barking, as a prerequisite of receiving any help at all. After I said this he began to sit up uncomfortably instead of lying back blandly in his chair, for the tables were turned and he knew that it was his next move, not mine. This more positive attitude towards therapy continued and, after seeing that his wife was also controlling and castrating him (as he sought to do to me in a similar passive fashion), he not only took over control and responsibility in the marital relationship and attained full capacity for pleasurable orgasm (his wife was delighted at both changes), but also became the most active, constructive and respected member of the group prior to leaving.

Similarly, families where members need to defend their identity by fighting, and so try to provoke conflict with the therapist, are more likely to show therapeutic movement if they find that the therapist is always on their side of the argument instead of being driven into opposition and disapproval, where they would have him more under control. This type of approach requires one to be quick-witted, for patients change their tactics when these fail and one needs to keep one jump ahead all the time.

One objection to the more active conductor-type approach, which I often hear expressed when I lecture, should be countered. It is often suggested, particularly by those influenced by psychoanalytic techniques, that an active, controlling and forceful technique diminishes the patient's freedom to make his own decisions and encourages dependency, while the more conventional, detached, passive, nonjudgmental and nondirective approach encourages independence. Nothing could be further from the truth. Freedom and independence cannot be given but must be won, and they are far more readily achieved when the therapist's (or the parent's) attitudes are clearly, firmly, and even provocatively expressed, for then there is something definite to react against, something to struggle with in order to define one's boundaries. Excessive permissiveness, passivity or indulgence is much more enslaving and hard to escape from, partly because it is so seductive, partly because it is so formless, denying to the patient a clear challenge against which he can rebel and begin to define himself. The ever-loving, overpossessive, indulgent mother enslaves more inescapably than the strict, demanding but fair father.

This brief outline of the techniques of the main schools of family therapy must suffice (though further mention will be made later of some of those relevant to special types of problem or situation), and the reader who wishes to gain a more detailed perspective is recommended first to study the excellent paper by Beels and Ferber already mentioned (35) and the booklet by Joan Stein (36); then, perhaps, he should read the collections of seminal articles compiled by Howells (37) and Haley (38). All these contain extensive references from which the reader can follow up those approaches which strike him as most useful for his own purposes.

A GROUP-ANALYTIC APPROACH

In the remainder of this chapter I shall outline my own approach. This was particularly influenced by J. E. Bell (39) who, interestingly, was encouraged to begin his work, during a brief visit to England, by hearing of John Bowlby's work with families at the Tavistock, an account of which was later published in 1949 (40). Bell's papers, published in 1961 and 1962, led me to try to extend group-analytic concepts to work with the family group, seeking to continue the work of S. H. Foulkes (41), under whom I studied at the Maudsley and whom I later joined in practice.

Foulkes had been interested from the beginning in the family and social network and already regarded individual problems as points or nodes where group stresses manifested themselves overtly. However, though he had experimented with family meetings, his main interest had turned more to the artifically-constituted small group of strangers (usually seven to nine) within which the individual dynamics could be re-translated into group form and resolved in that setting. Neither he nor the other colleagues who subsequently worked with him had shared my experience of child psychiatry, except for E. J. Anthony (42), whose interest remained centered in psychoanalysis and the therapeutic use of the artifical rather than the natural group. Over the years, my own technique has drawn something valuable from almost every other contribution to the field, but it has grown organically out of the group-analytic principles developed by Foulkes. I think it is fair to describe my technique as group-analytic, despite the admixture of concepts from other fields, if only because of the following features it still shares:

1. A simultaneous study of the part and the whole are not seen in any way as incompatible, nor is one seen as a denial or rejection of the other. The psychological structure of an individual and of his family group are homologous, isomorphic, and changing one must automatically mean changing the other provided the parts of the system remain in contact. The case of Susan in Chapter 1 is a simple illustration of this principle. The therapist therefore has to listen to and observe both the individual contributions (which will all have their separate meanings, when taken together in relation to the individual concerned) and the communications of the group-as-a whole (disregarding who says what, and taking it all together), constantly attempting to relate them and understand one in terms of the other.

2. The family, like the small group of strangers, is seen as possessing inherent potentials for constructive understanding and for facilitating growth and positive change, as well as for creating confusion and blocking development. The main task of the therapist is therefore seen, as in the artificial small group, as the facilitation of these inherent growth-enhancing factors, and the creation of circumstances in which they can emerge and operate most effectively.

3. Though the therapist has a responsibility for leading the individuals composing the group, and so must accept a position of responsibility and authority in relation to them, the wisdom and understanding potentially inherent in the group-as-a-whole will exceed his own; he must therefore be attentive to, and respect, what it is telling him about himself, and be willing to be corrected by it in the course of his work with it.

The main difference in technique required when practicing family therapy lies in the fact that one cannot rely, as in the small group of strangers, on careful selection to provide a balance of attitudes and personality types from which a new and more effective social influence will emerge from discussion or sharing of views alone. The family is like a badly selected group, in that pathological attitudes, obstructions to communication and defenses against recognition of both are shared by all, and the therapist carries the full responsibility for somehow introducing new ideas and attitudes into the family system. Those who have worked with stranger groups according to group-analytic principles are naturally surprised at the greater prominence, in my work with families, of challenging confrontations, assumption of authority and control, and imposition of structure. But this is an inevitable consequence, it seems to me, of the different settings and the different demands family groups make on the therapist.

Turning to the relation of my own technique to those described above, I believe mine combines the approach of the reactor-analysts with that of the conductors, in a phasic sequence and varied according to the type of problem. I have also found very useful some of the communication-theory concepts of the Palo Alto group, and some of the similar ideas produced by R. D. Laing, but I tend to turn to these mainly when progress is blocked with a particularly manipulative family, since I find the seemingly detached, manipulative position of these workers personally uncongenial.

I begin each session (including the first) as I would with an artificially constituted group conducted along group-analytic lines, with no structure at all apart from the place and duration for the interview, as well as a roughly circular seating arrangement and the request that the whole nuclear family, at least, should attend. I prefer to have as little prior knowledge about them as possible, so that I am exposed to the family's communication problems and their selective account of their reasons for referral. The order in which the information is given, the sequence in which different people give it, and what is emphasized or left out are of particular relevance, perhaps more significant than the content of what is said.

I do not remain silent and wait for them to begin (which can be regarded as persecuting and become a pointless game) but introduce myself, asking them to do the same, and then explain my interest briefly and straightforwardly—e.g., "I understand from Dr. A. that you have some problem with the children; perhaps you would like to tell me about it?" As I say this I look expectantly around the group, taking care not to catch the gaze of any one person for more than a moment, thereby indicating that all are free to speak. I then let the interview develop its own form as far as possible, interfering and shaping it to the minimum in the early stages so that the pattern will be that of the family, not determined by me. My comments are mainly restricted to requests for clarification of the points which are unclear to me in their account, in the direction of encouraging greater detail. There is no attempt to "jump" to a "deeper" explanatory level; I stay close to the presenting symptom and carry out, as it were, a "square search" (43), widening very gradually the range of information in space and time, and asking them for details, in order to bring the context of the problem alive for me by a play-by-play account, like a commentator describing a football match to listeners who cannot see it. I often use such images to help the family grasp what I am asking.

If the problem complained of is that the child will not do what he is told, I ask for a recent example. If he would not eat his breakfast that morning, I want to know where everyone else was at the time, what mother said, what she felt like saying, why she did not say what she felt, what father did about it or didn't do, why he did or didn't do it, what mother felt about father for what he did or didn't do, and so on. Requests for advice or opinions are brushed aside at this stage with the explanation, if one is required at all, that I am only a doctor and that no one but a fool or a magician would give advice when he didn't even know the facts. There is rarely any problem about this, for the family can easily see that this is true and they are usually particularly pleased, especially if they have had any experiences with the helping professions before, to find someone who is actually interested in hearing about the problem they came about rather than things which seem to them at first quite irrelevant.

This focus on the *effects on others* of the symptoms, and the *interactions* which occur in the course of their *management* of them, as well as the *unexpressed feelings* about all this, soon provides a wealth of material about the family values and relationships. It also leads naturally to the past history and the parents' childhood, where this is relevant. Mother may say she cannot bear to be firm and an inquiry why this is so may reveal that the child concerned almost died in infancy, or that mother had an unhappy childhood with a rejecting mother herself. Father may say he would be firm but that mother stops him, and asking why he lets her stop him may lead to his relationship with women generally: Perhaps he sided with his own mother in childhood against an alcoholic father, or he may reveal a sexual problem producing an underlying tension. Thus, a here-and-now focus is maintained, but it leads into the past in a natural, connected and coherent way.

Gradually, in response to the gaps in the story, the silence of some members or the monopolization of others, I find myself becoming more active, stimulating some and quietening others, expressing puzzlement and other feelings of my own. There is no conscious plan at this stage, though I have come to trust my spontaneous responses and usually find later that they were more meaningful than I realized (others who have trained with me have soon come to have the same trust in their responses, so this is not just a personal aptitude). I begin to express my own responses more, to confront their pattern with my spontaneous, intuitive reactions and feelings, without worrying at first about the outcome. I may say that I am puzzled by something I cannot understand, or that

I cannot grasp the meaning of someone's facial expression even though I feel that it is relevant, or that I feel angry with someone, or confused by the whole situation. At this stage I am asking myself questions about my responses as I was earlier asking questions to try to understand theirs. At this stage I usually feel confused, frustrated and unhopeful that the interview will be of any value.

But if I can go through all this with patience, and some memory and trust based on previous successful work, I find that at a certain stage (having normally used one-hour sessions, this usually occurs when the interview has been running for about 40 minutes) the light dawns, things fall into place, and some coherent organization of the material suddenly and spontaneously occurs which makes sense of all that has gone before and which contains implications for therapy.

How this is dealt with will depend on other factors. If the family is intelligent and an analytic approach is appropriate, the understanding may be communicated directly to provide insight which they have the responsibility for developing and implementing. This insight may itself be given in more raw form, by reporting directly my countertransference or fantasy and seeking their help in understanding it, or it may be developed into something more organized and objective, something closer to an interpretation. On the other hand, if the family has limited understanding or expects and needs a more directive, managing approach, I translate my insight into a prescription for action and then become a conductor using my knowledge, influence and power to change the system.

An example may make this clearer:

In this case, the father had been unwilling to become involved in family interviews until the mother, who had previously accepted containment of the father's inadequacy as well as her own, had received individual psychotherapy from a psychiatric social worker (my co-therapist in the session to be reported) long enough to find some relief from her chronic depression and to demand that the father carry his share of the emotional load. Finally, the balance of power altered to a point where she insisted that he should attend for therapy as well, and a family session was then arranged.

Father looked ill at ease and defensively aggressive in the waiting room, mother more at ease and rather triumphant. In the joint interview Alan (aged 12 and referred for behavior problems, particularly a refusal to cooperate in washing himself and other similar activities) looked completely cheerful and in control throughout. The mother sat next to me, and I found both her physical proximity and intense gaze uncomfortable at times, as if I wanted to establish some boundary against her intrusion. The father sat opposite and his defensive aggressiveness continued. He immediately began by demanding, "What is the object of this exercise?" I fell into the trap and was almost treating him in the coercive angry way he treats the boy when my co-therapist rescued me.

Both parents soon relaxed when they were allowed to shift the focus of attention to Alan, when it became plain that the situation was reasonably secure and not punitive. The father insisted that the situation was completely unchanged, and elaborated this, on questioning, to say that he still could not get Alan to wash his hands or clean his teeth; it always ended by father frog-marching Alan to the wash-basin and making him do it, or father doing it for him. All parental commands ended in a struggle of this kind.

On inquiry, Alan pointed out that he had improved considerably as regards his other symptoms (sleep disturbance, nervous fears) which had bothered him more than the family, thereby contradicting father's allegation that no change had taken place. The attention then switched to the younger child, who suffered from a sleep disturbance. The parents said that when put to bed he screamed to a point where all the neighbors were disturbed. The father felt that he was naughty and stubborn, and talked about him in a harsh and rigid way; yet he admitted he ran up and down the stairs constantly trying to pacify him.

After we had allowed the parents to focus the discussion on the children for some time, and they appeared more at ease, the inquiry was widened to get a play-by-play account of what actually happened every evening. A picture of real pandemonium then emerged—father rushing up and down stairs to the screaming younger child, mother shouting at Alan to wash himself, father finally ending by frog-marching Alan to the sink and making him do it. They all sit and wait every evening for this series of events to begin! Alan had been grinning throughout this account and openly admitted that he enjoyed this kind of struggle; he said he liked his father and enjoyed fighting with him.

Exploring the details of these encounters, it emerged that mother, on father's return home, would complain that she had found the children difficult all day and demand that he take charge, but she kept repeating that father was quite incapable of taking charge and that no one listened to him. When asked who was really in charge of the family, father said that *he* was, but that no one actually listened to what he said! As we explored this, various points emerged. Father said he did not like to be a "sergeant major," felt that the children should instinctively want to clean their teeth rather than need to be coerced. Both parents seemed unhappy at the idea of having to face a really serious conflict with the children in which the children might reject and hate them. When it was put to them, they agreed that

Alan needed them less than they needed him, and could see that he was in command because of this fact. Father's failure to take an authoritative role with the family, including perhaps his wife, was sharply outlined, although he repeatedly evaded this fact. To redress the balance, we focused after this on the fact that mother did not really let him take charge, although she demanded it, and seemed to make him useless from the beginning.

At this point, both the PSW and I discovered that we were experiencing similar feelings in trying to identify with Alan. I suddenly noticed that her eyes, like my own, were flicking back and forth from one parent to the other. Discussing this, we realized that we did not know which parent to look at, who was really in charge. Also, we saw that the parents seemed to be waiting for something to happen and that no one really wanted to initiate an unpopular action.

Nearing the end of the interview, as we were speaking about the parents' needs for Alan to love them because of their own childhood deprivation, and the way in which he was able to control them through this, it suddenly dawned on me that the parents' own relationship to each other was strangely excluded from the interview. Once again, this came to my attention through the nonverbal interaction, when it became plain that the parents never looked at each other, only at the children or at ourselves. When I put it to them that their own capacity to give more to each other was the crucial difficulty, particularly in the sexual relationship, which should sustain and support them independently of the children, there was a long and thoughtful silence. The mother said "that went home last time," referring to a comment I had made at the initial interview over a year before, that Alan seemed to be jealous of the parents' sexual relationship and that this was the reason why he was so frequently intruding into their bedroom complaining of an inability to sleep. We seemed to have reached some real conclusion they could take away with them, and the interview was terminated on quite a friendly and constructive basis.

In this family, continued casework by the PSW with the mother, together with occasional family and later marital sessions, achieved a good result as regards both the children's difficulties and the marital relationship.

It will be seen how, after a bad start in which I was almost trapped into the kind of fighting relationship by which the father characteristically defended himself against the influence of others, and more deeply, I think, against homosexual fears (the value of a co-therapist of opposite sex is obvious here for I was clearly colluding in this homosexual defense by being provoked), the family interaction "came alive" in the session and led to a clear description, and simultaneous demonstration, of the parental relationship and its relevance to the children's problems. Finally, the connection between the difficulties the couple has in cooperating as *parents*, and their inhibition in sexual interaction as *spouses*, because of fear of the children's jealousy (the parents' own unresolved oedipal rivalry with *their* parents, projected into the children), suddenly became apparent to me, though it was potentially there all the time.

I think the explanation must lie in a figure/ground type of phenomenon. The real family problem is always contained in what is *not* communicated, what is *missing* from the content of the session. To begin with, it therefore cannot be located, and one feels a sense of frustration and inadequacy. Only when a good deal of conscious or "public" information has been accumulated, providing a "ground," can the "figure" —an empty space in the pattern of facts, what is missing from the facts—be observed against it. And as in visual pattern-recognition problems of this kind, the recognition is sudden, even though it appears so obvious, once seen, that one finds it hard to grasp why one did not observe it earlier.

Nevertheless, as in the present case, nonverbal exchanges which are less under conscious control often give the secret away first and one should always be alert for these, particularly movements of the eyes which say more than anything else about the real pattern of emotional bonds. This type of intervention is often characterized, as in the present example, by a profound response from the family. When the therapist allows himself to become part of the family system, and then struggles to grasp the problem "from inside," the solution when it comes can have a powerful impact. Members seem strongly affected, moved emotionally; there is frequently a deep and meaningful silence, and they leave in a quiet and thoughtful mood which induces further reflection. No doubt this is because the therapist not only sees the answer, but sees it through, and despite, the family defenses and communication problems from which he is allowing himself to suffer, so that he finds the position from which it can become visible to them as well.

To achieve this, however, one must expose oneself to the confusion, frustration and expectation of disappointment which is an inevitable consequence of entering the family system. This is why I prefer to avoid too much knowledge of the formal history beforehand, for though one can do good work despite this knowledge it is only human to want to "know where we are," to "know what we are doing," to cling to one's intellect defensively rather than to launch oneself into the unknown which each time feels like leaping into the dark.

Winnicott's technique of individual "therapeutic consultation" (44), which also achieves dramatic changes in a few sessions, even in one, seems to utilize similar principles, for he also insists on seeing the child first, avoiding information from the parents, and he allows his own feelings and spontaneous responses to be exposed to and interact with those of the child. His description of the process as "meeting the challenge of the case" rather than in terms of "helping," "curing," or "doing something to" the patient also suggests a similar type of interaction.

Cooklin (45) has recently expressed an essentially similar view, in concepts which help to explain why these therapeutic positions are so effective. He suggests that "the therapist's continuing work to define ... their roles ... facilitates the freeing of fixed family roles from attachment to a Shared Family Group Preoccupation [see Chapter 8] and ... to achieve this the therapist is required to share in the transitional consternation and role confusion." He sees as a main danger, in conjoint work, the possibility "that the therapist may embark on an increasingly Herculean attempt to master a multiple transference system of soaring complexity and may *avoid* the mastery of his own role." He uses the word "consternation," which he defines as "puzzled dismay," in much the same way as I use "confusion"; the only difference, perhaps, is that experience has led me to take it for granted that I will be confused, so that I am no longer dismayed by it even though the confusion remains painful.

In the case described above my co-therapist, who wrote an independent report of the session which showed no striking divergence from my own, made the following interesting comment at the end:

> The interview certainly left me with a feeling that it had quite a dramatic effect, particularly in relation to the parents' understanding of their own avoidance of each other. It was most interesting to see that an interview of this nature, which basically centered on the problems of the child in the immediate situation, fitted in extremely well with my long-term work with mother. I was surprised how little the relationship with mother interfered with the group interviews. At times I felt hampered by the information I already had and was not able to ask more pertinent questions as I knew them to be so volatile. As Dr. Skynner was not hampered in this way he was quite free to bring up many issues which I would otherwise have avoided, and once they had come into the open I felt free to join in. It had seemed to me for some time that I had been unable to help this family through mother in relation to the issue of Alan's washing, but that at the same time, until about this period, mother had been quite unwilling to allow the family the sort of involvement that this interview brought about, so that the two methods seemed to link extremely well.

11 TECHNIQUES: PRACTICAL CONSIDERATIONS

Freud is all nonsense; the secret of neurosis is to be found in the family battle of wills to see who can refuse longest to help with the dishes.

Julian Mitchell, As Far As You Can Go

It is amazing how rarely the question what? *is seriously asked. Instead, either the nature of the situation is taken to be quite evident, or it is described and explained mainly in terms of* why? *by reference to origins, reasons, motives, etc., rather than to events observable here and now.*

Watzlawick, Weakland and Fisch, Change

If a man will begin with certainties, he shall end in doubts; but if he will be content to begin with doubts, he shall end in certainties.

Francis Bacon, Advancement of Learning

The example given in Chapter 10 described a family interview arranged in the course of continuing therapy, but the following summary of a first interview similarly illustrates the way in which a focus on the presenting problem, on its effects on others in the family, and on the way in which others deal with the matter, leads from the presenting symptom towards more basic family pathology and ultimately towards the models of family life that the parents have brought into the marriage from their own families of origin. The interview came after a short history had been obtained by the psychiatric social worker, who also attended as co-therapist in this family session when we met the referred patient, aged 14, her sisters, aged 15 and 17, and her mother and step-father. According to the brief history, the youngest daughter had been referred because of sleep disturbance at home and tempers at school. To avoid identification and to make the description simpler, I will describe the daughters as youngest, middle, and eldest.

I started off on a false trail, thinking the problem of tempers in school was the main one. In fact, the youngest girl had reacted with explosive tempers to feelings of being rejected at her previous school, but since a change of school there had been no further trouble. The family then presented the main problem as a difficulty over sleep, saying that the youngest girl had nightmares every night and insisted on sleeping with her middle sister in a double bed, and also on putting on the light and disturbing both her sisters' sleep. It was difficult to get the youngest girl to speak about the nightmares, but the middle sister said that they were about *Dracula*, describing a film they had all seen which indicated that the anxiety centered around the idea of Dracula biting the neck of his victims. The youngest sister confirmed that this was her main anxiety.

We asked if there were any other difficulties and it was mentioned that the youngest girl frequently quarreled with her sisters. Exploring this, the eldest girl admitted that she sided with the middle girl against the youngest. On asking for examples of how a quarrel might develop the eldest girl said that the youngest often wanted to cuddle her but that sometimes she was not in the mood and would push her away, when a furious temper would follow. It was possible at this stage of the interview to make a connection with the anger and destructiveness over frustrated oral demands expressed in the Dracula dreams.

The mother had mentioned that the younger girl was very like her, and we asked if the sisters felt that the youngest girl got more attention from the mother through her difficult behavior, and, if so, whether this made them resentful. Both elder girls agreed that this was the case, and that somehow the youngest always got the better of them in this way. The eldest said that she had felt less upset recently and agreed that this was because she was moving away from the family, but the middle girl was obviously still much more involved and concerned about the difficulty.

This discussion of the girls' quarreling led naturally towards mother as the person over whom they were fighting. Mother acknowledged that she was like the youngest in being jealous and showing violent tempers if she could not get her own way. She also feared constantly that others might come to some harm, and the connection with her aggressive impulses and these fears was pointed out. Mother became anxious at this and suddenly began to attack the youngest girl, as if to defend herself. The youngest was now clearly cast in a scapegoat role in the family, at which she became increasingly agitated. A shouting match developed with the mother in which she complained that mother interfered in her life and refused to accept her friends. The older sisters appeared to agree that the youngest chooses friends who encourage her to be more independent, and that mother, being possessive, resented anyone coming between her and the children.

This was brought into the open and discussed. Soon the mother wept at her inability to cope with the youngest, saying she felt quite helpless.

The stepfather had remained very quiet, and at this point we turned to ask him about his place in this interaction—was he similarly withdrawn and quiet at home? The mother cut in angrily to say that the stepfather was not allowed to interfere in the management of the children: "They are my children! I won't let him touch them." We asked why she felt so strongly about this and it emerged that the mother had relevant experiences in her own childhood. She lost her own father at the age of nine, after which her mother married again. Her own mother and stepfather had rejected her in favor of her sister, and she had clearly been the scapegoat in her family of origin.

We pointed out how mother still seemed to be living in the past and reacting to the present situation as if it resembled her childhood one. Everyone looked interested and astonished at this, mother included, and clearly everyone felt that something important had been understood which might change the situation.

The stepfather now interrupted to say that he felt fed-up at returning each day to an unpleasant atmosphere. Recently he had come home to meet a veil of silence where no one would speak to him, and he had just withdrawn and given up because of this. We asked the family what they really wanted from him, and the girls said that the stepfather should take a much more active part. When we inquired what they meant by this they described instances in which he had been able to control them and had a good effect on the whole situation when he took a more definite role, whereas mother would always go to pieces and end in tears, behaving helplessly. All three girls agreed that mother should let the stepfather take over more.

During all this the three girls kept repeating that the mother and stepfather never seemed to "get together" over family problems, complaining that they seemed unable to discuss things, or to adopt a united front, instead acting independently of each other. The way in which this phrase "get together" was used, and the context in which it occurred, seemed to us at the time to indicate some underlying feelings about the sexual relationship, though neither co-therapist was later able to remember the details which led to this impression.

I asked the mother how she had felt when her own mother had remarried, and suggested that she must naturally have felt some sexual jealousy; did she perhaps fear that her children would in turn be jealous about the sexual relationship between herself and her new husband? Mother agreed that she had felt bitterly jealous over the sexual relationship between her mother and stepfather, and she had indeed feared that her children might feel the same about her remarriage. The eldest girl now cut in to say that she had felt very strong opposition to the stepfather earlier and frequently quarreled with him, but now she had a better relationship and wished that he and her mother could be happy together in their sexual relationship too. The two younger girls agreed with this, but clearly were not quite so free of oedipal rivalry as the eldest girl, who had already begun to grow away from the family and had a boyfriend of her own. The interview ended with a clear demand from the children for the mother and stepfather to get together as adults to develop a better relationship with each other, even at the expense of diminishing the close relationship with the children. The family left in a positive way, saying they had understood a great deal and that they wished to try out what they had learned before seeking another interview.

In the examples given it will be obvious, I am sure, that one must pay close attention to, and translate into more explicit form, both the *verbal content* of the interview (e.g., the Dracula dream, or the descriptions of the problems over washing mentioned in Chapter 10) and the *non-verbal content* (the movement of the eyes, the failure of the father in the preceding case to participate at all for a long period). But, in addition, one must also pay attention to the *power structure* and organization insofar as this determines the *communication* in the interview itself. Though I prefer in general to follow the natural pattern of family interaction in the earlier part of the interview, as I have described in the previous chapter and demonstrated in both examples, the *form* of the interaction and communication will sometimes need to be directly challenged and changed, by interpretation, request or manipulation, if the interview is to proceed at all, so that earlier control by the therapist may be indicated.

For example, where parents are reluctant to mention the problem in front of the children and ask to see the therapist alone (always best resisted, for the therapist would be trapped into a collusive avoidance of parent/child confrontation, which will be even more difficult later on); or where parents do all the talking while children are silent; or where children produce so much noise and distraction that discussion is impossible—in all such situations the therapist must act to change the structure if a family session is to be productive.

Such problems in the form of the interview should never be regarded merely as obstacles to discussion preventing one from searching for the "real" difficulty. They are always a fundamental manifestation of the problem itself, and if the *form* of the interaction can be changed the main work will usually have been done. Thus, parents who will not complain about the children in front of them usually prove to be over-gratifying and overprotecting them because of fear of the children's rage and rejection if they are frustrated. But the parents are in fact dealing with their own demands, and their own rage when these are frustrated, by projecting these into the children. It is therefore not surprising that they send the children out in order to keep such feelings at a safe distance from themselves and from the therapist, whom they fear, correctly, might seek to make them take such projections back.

Instead of colluding with a defense of this kind, which automatically ensures that the therapist has no chance at all of getting both the problem, and the persons who need to acknowledge the problem as their own, into the same point in space, the therapist can say mildly that while he would personally be happy to have a private talk with the parents he knows from experience that this will not actually help the problem, that he assumes they wish to solve it and that they would certainly not wish to waste his time by going against his advice. If he persists he will soon find the rage back in the parents, directed towards him (this is no doubt why we so often collude in this particular manipulation!), after which it may well be appropriate to send the children out and be supportive and nurturing to the parents, since their inability to cope with frustration may be due to their own parents' (i.e., the grand-parents') failure to provide this.

This is not the only reason why parents seek to exclude the children, of course. Another pattern frequently encountered justifies the wish to exclude the children by a desire to avoid exposing them to a discussion of the parents' sexuality. Once again, it usually proves that the real reason is the parents' fear of the children's jealousy of their sexual relationship, and that this fear in turn is due to a projection, by the parents into the children, of the parents' unresolved sexual jealousies from *their* childhoods. Where this is the case, sending the children out at the start colludes in avoiding the very challenge (the oedipal confrontation) that is usually necessary in order to solve the overt problems. By contrast, keeping the children in the room until the sexual issues are explicitly mentioned, and *then* sending them out while the details are being discussed, with the explanation that such matters are the private concern of grown-ups, provides exactly the challenge the children require and the parents have been avoiding, together with support and sanction by the therapists for the parents to make their marital and sexual relationship the primary family bond again.

TRANSFERENCE

I have already indicated that I prefer, as far as possible, to keep the system of projections, which comes to make up the transference in the formal analytic or group-analytic situation, between the family members rather than to draw it on to myself since this ensures that working through will continue actively between the sessions and so make the most effective use of available time. This is achieved in a number of ways. First, I do not encourage transference, do not draw it on to myself, do not set that kind of pattern for the family to follow. Transference is noted, often used, but not interpreted unless it begins to get in the way. Second, transference develops more readily when the therapist is passive and withholds his own natural responses; though he cannot actually be a "blank screen," he can stimulate fantasy as Rorschach figures or TAT cards (1) do by the vagueness and ambiguity of his responses. By contrast, active, spontaneous and natural behavior automatically diminishes the development of such fantasy in relation to him, and this is no doubt one reason why almost all family therapists manifest such behavior in their family work. Thirdly, the wide spacing of interviews that I have come to use also diminishes transference projection on to the therapist although it also increases real valuation for, and response to, the sessions. And fourthly, the *role* the therapist offers, implicitly and explicitly— that of an expert who helps the family to help itself rather than someone who is going to "take over"—limits both expectations of passive surrender and the aggressive defenses that fear of such regressive tendencies arouses.

Despite all this, marked transference to the therapist does develop at times, and when it does it is usually in response to defensive needs either in the family or in the therapist. If a family session has released more ambivalence, previously "bound" by successful defenses, than can be tolerated in the family system, the family will displace it and often defend themselves by shifting the hostility into the transference, thereby protecting their relationship with each other and perhaps also avoiding further contact with the therapist who was the cause of their discomfort.

In one such family, for example, where conflict between parents and children began to be perceived as originating in a previously denied marital conflict, the parents became re-united comfortably when the hostility between them was displaced to the professional who referred them, a displacement which was as close to a negative transference to myself and my co-therapist as they could bear. Fearing that this would develop into a powerful negative transference after the session was over, which might prevent further contact, it was interpreted as avoided hostility towards ourselves. The family was able to talk about this, and having done so they returned for one more session and left by arrangement, since the ambivalence between the spouses was too great for them to face at this stage. Because of this they were later able to resume therapy, which was ultimately successful. During the latter period they agreed with our earlier assessment that failure to interpret the developing negative transference would almost certainly have led to a premature and final termination of the treatment.

The other cause of transference problems is similar, but it involves the therapist's defenses rather than those of the patients. Members of the helping professions seem to show, as a group, a defensive system whereby a basic inner conflict is constantly resolved by taking (in Eric Berne's [2] terms) a "parent" role in relation to a client or patient, who in turn is seeking the complementary position and is willing to receive a "child" projection from the therapist as long as the latter will look after him. Thus the stage is set for the encouragement of what is called transference and is usually viewed as a relationship based on *voluntary*, *deliberate* passivity on the part of the therapist and *involuntary*, *unwitting* projection on the part of the patient, but which is in fact a two-way, mutual projective process meeting the needs of both individuals in varying degree.

The process may be examined in terms of three levels. At the most superficial the patient is aware of certain feelings towards the analyst, which are from the patient's viewpoint realistic and objective. At the next level the analyst is aware that he is concealing his own responses, and that the patient is projecting his own fantasies but perceiving them as real. At this level the analyst sees his own perceptions and responses as real, objective, and under his control. At the third level, usually unconscious to both but sometimes conscious to the patient late in therapy, the analyst is projecting an infantile aspect of his own personality into the patient. Where this is the case neither is really taking responsibility for himself, and both inevitably experience difficulty in terminating their relationship.

In a way this is, of course, recognized in existing analytic theory by the concept of countertransference, both in the older sense of activation of residues of the analyst's "pathology," and in the more recent use of the word to cover the analyst's normal emotional responses to the patient's behavior. But neither use of the word covers quite what I am trying to express, which is the defensive function of the professional role itself.

Family therapists are no exception to this general tendency, though I believe that they must have recognized and worked it through to some degree before they can even consider conjoint work, where this defense is, to some extent, prevented. Effective practice certainly requires a real resolution of the inner split which can be avoided in individual or even in artifical-group analysis and psychotherapy. However, when anxieties are aroused in the course of family therapy relating to unresolved conflicts of the therapist it is to be expected that he will behave in a way which will at least collude with, and even provoke, the development of transference to him as a defensive measure to protect himself.

My response to the aggressive opening remarks of the father in the case of Alan (Chapter 10), where I subsequently realized I was colluding with him in a defense against a homosexual involvement between us, is a good example. (This, in turn, may have been a defense against the intensity of the mother's emotions.) My colleague, being female, was quite at ease and was able to free me enough (she changed the subject, though she could just as well have pointed out the mutual defense) to enable me to recognize my anxiety and to deal with it internally in a more adequate way, even to use it as information about the relationship between the father and son. I am inclined to think at present that the development of marked transference manifestations in family therapy should always arouse the query, in the therapist, of whether he may be defending himself.

Work with families fortunately helps one very much with these problems, perhaps because the challenge of being confronted both with parents and children simultaneously, and having the task of aiding them to communicate, inevitably opens up communication within the person of the therapist. He can do his work only by using both aspects of himself to identify with the two generations of the family, simultaneously; by healing them, perhaps he heals himself also, becomes linked more healthily with his own internalized family group. Certainly I have reason to be grateful to the families I have worked with for they have taught me, among other things, to be prepared to accept responsibility fully and to "take over" when necessary, but also to hand it back completely, and to resume my own life, as soon as possible. We will return to this theme later, when we examine problems of training in Chapter 14.

GETTING FAMILIES TO COME

Some details of the more practical arrangements for family meetings should be described. And the first question most people ask, in my experience, is, "How do you get them to come?"

My grandfather, as a young man, was a senior salesman for a biscuit company, and in my childhood he recounted the story of a salesman who for some reason failed to secure many orders. Drawing this man aside, my grandfather asked him to describe exactly what he did when he approached the shopkeepers (it is clear that my play-by-play technique with families has itself a family history!). "Oh, I do just the same as everybody else," said the salesman. "I put my head round the door and say 'I don't suppose you want to buy any biscuits today?'"

In similar fashion the expectation of the professionals that the family will come, and their conviction that it is worth the trouble, are the main factors in securing attendance, since the attitude will automatically be communicated to the family. At the Queen Elizabeth Hospital for Children, where all referrals were medical, failure of the father to attend was so rare that such events were much discussed, and his absence always illustrated the crucial family problem. At the Woodberry Down Child Guidance Unit, despite many referrals of antisocial and delinquent problems by schools and social services, attendance was less universal but ultimately secured in most cases. In both situations the clientele were mainly working class, with many severely deprived, disadvantaged or borderline psychotic problems. It is, of course, much easier to secure the attendance of middle-class families.

However, this was the case only where the regular staff were concerned in the arrangements. When students with limited experience in family work made the initial arrangements failures were frequent, because they somehow conveyed their expectation that they "didn't suppose the father would want to come."

At the Queen Elizabeth Hospital, preliminary interviews were carried out by the psychiatric social workers, usually with the mothers, to explain the reason for involving the whole family; this seemed on the whole the more effective (if more costly) arrangement. The interviews were brief and limited to getting basic information needed for the family consultation (such as number of children, possible times of attendance, etc.). The PSW always acted as co-therapist in the subsequent family work.

At Woodberry Down we experimented with a different method, based on a series of carefully composed letters. Evening appointments were made available, but willingness to attend during ordinary working hours was rewarded with an earlier appointment. More use was made of the referral network than at the Queen Elizabeth Hospital, since the motivation for attendance often lay in the school or community. Home visits, either for the preliminary interview or for the family consultation itself, were used if other methods failed. Using this sequence of approaches, the family was usually assembled sooner or later, and the initial use of letters saved much staff time as regards the preliminary interviews though on occasion it wasted the precious family session where two therapists had made their time available. The combination of the two techniques would probably be best, beginning with letters and leading to a brief preliminary interview with the PSW, who would share the subsequent family session as co-therapist to the psychiatrist.* (I am speaking here of child psychiatric practice, based on the usual team functions. Other agencies would naturally arrange matters differently according to their structure and skills, but the principle of preliminary interviews, needing less time or skill, being used to avoid wasting conjoint family sessions, needing greater skills and the setting aside of more time, would still be relevant.)

Perhaps because they are uncertain, newcomers to the field often make the task of explaining the purpose of the family interview unnecessarily complicated and difficult. There is no need for long and detailed justifications; the idea is so obvious and readily acceptable to families, if they have not been trained to think in other ways, that a firm request is often all that is necessary. But if reasons are requested, a formulation in terms of "help" is useful and easily understandable. There is no need to argue with the family's contention that the referred patient needs help; he does, but the family can easily agree that the therapist also needs help in understanding the problem if he is to help the patient, and that the father, as well as the mother, and the siblings too, may have noticed things that were not brought to the mother's

---

* Specimen letters still used at Woodberry Down, together with a leaflet suitable for private practice to request the whole family to come, are given in Appendix C.

attention or that she may forget. Moreover, few families will reject the
suggestion that they, as well as the therapist, may wish to help the
patient if the therapist can share his understanding with them in the joint
interview to make this possible.

When I made these suggestions to a distinguished psychoanalyst who
wished me to see the family of a girl referred to him he demurred,
implying that such an approach was rather dishonest and that I would
accuse the family of collective responsibility for the problem when they
came to see me. When he later sat in on the interview (the first time
he had attended a family session) he changed his mind, for he saw that I
did indeed begin by accepting the problem as they first described it—
an inexplicable problem in one member for which the others were in
no way responsible—but led them by the methods I have described to
discover connections for themselves which made them see it in a different light. I always start in this way from the point of view with which
the family come, making no attempt even to oppose scapegoating, for I
find that exploring the detailed interaction surrounding the problem
leads soon enough to more open revelation of the general difficulties,
without any attempt to insist on the idea that there is a family problem.

FAMILY INTERVIEWS IN THE HOME

In the deprived and disadvantaged neighborhoods where much of my
work has been done, home visits have always formed an essential part
of the treatment provision, meeting the needs of a large and particularly
needy group which is never reached by agencies which demand office
attendance, by whom they tend to be classified as "uncooperative." If
this provision is available, should other methods fail, it is possible to
work with practically all families conjointly.

There are some advantages to working in the home. The physical
characteristics of the home itself give much information absent from a
clinic interview, while the family is usually more relaxed, open and at
ease on their home ground and so present a more natural picture. On
the other hand, the therapists are away from their own base and so
may be less comfortable and in command of themselves. Even when one
has more experience and confidence, there is still the real difference that
it is generally expected that a visitor will observe the customs and social
rules appertaining to a host. At the clinic the parents' roles and family
rules can be questioned and changed experimentally, without any im-

plication that the pattern should change at home, where the parents will be in charge again and will make the decision for themselves. At a home visit one is more concerned about the danger of undermining the parents' authority and inhibited about altering the pattern of operation, though the dangers can be reduced by making it explicit that the family interview is a special, experimental situation, like a game in which certain altered rules are accepted, and where the therapists are temporarily given authority by the parents' permission.

At the clinic, family members usually expect to stay in the same room with the therapist, and an overactive child can be prevented from escaping by requesting the parents to stop it or by blocking the door oneself; at home members will wander in and out freely, often with excuses one cannot refute even if they are clearly defensive in motive. Both television and offers of refreshments can be used for avoidance. It is necessary to ask politely that the former be turned off (*not* down) "so that I can really pay attention to what you are saying." The acceptance of refreshments may be taken by a family as a sign that one accepts those offering them as well. This may be a crucial opening communication, but in general one should discourage it when it is no more than a polite formality, perhaps responding to the positive intention in the message by expressing thanks and pleasure but saying that one has just eaten.

Visiting the home may also teach one much about the influence of neighbors and other important figures, and as Ross Speck (3) has pointed out, the behavior of the family pets often warns one of what to expect as one comes through the door!

PRACTICAL ARRANGEMENTS FOR FAMILY INTERVIEWING

During home visits one has to accept the arrangements provided, though it is helpful to ask people to sit in a rough circle so that everyone can see each other. At the clinic each practitioner will find his own best arrangement, but some remarks about my own method may be worth presenting. I provide a circle of chairs, and if there is to be play material I arrange this in the center, where all can see what is happening and where the therapist in particular can have the opportunity to link fantasies being expressed through the children's play with the verbal communications among the adults and older children. With very young children, around five and under, I like to have some play material to occupy them from the beginning, but with older children there is some advantage in keeping the play material in a cupboard and introducing it later, if necessary, in order to see in the early stages how the children behave when asked to sit and join in the discussion, and how the parents control them when they begin to become restive. Also, since I begin by asking about the problem for which the family has come, I like the children to focus their attention on the discussion at this point, and to give their views as well. Play at this stage can be used as an escape and denial of responsibility.

Whether available from the beginning or introduced later, play material should be such as to provide information about the children's fantasy in as clear a way as possible. Further, since much of the therapist's attention must be directed to the discussion among the older members of the family the play materials should not be such as to distract attention unduly through encouraging too much noise or movement. Soft family figures, plastic animals, rubber dolls, paper and crayons enable the significance of the children's play to be readily observed and create no practical problems, but toys which will distract through noise or which are potentially messy or dangerous and so need considerable supervision should obviously be avoided unless one of the co-therapists can give full attention to this aspect of the interview. If a child seems likely to run out, the therapist should sit by the door.

Importance of Siblings in the Family Interview

Some therapists, like J. E. Bell (4), exclude younger children who cannot participate in verbal discussion. Others like to have at least the whole nuclear family present. I also believe that this is vastly preferable provided the therapist is at least able to tolerate the distraction that younger children present, and even more desirable if he has some facility at understanding the symbolic significance of children's play. This will usually prove to be related to the verbal discussion of the older members, and the therapist may be able to link up the total family interaction by translating the play into verbal form, and possibly by also expressing the verbal themes in terms of the children's nonverbal activities. Two co-therapists are a great advantage here, for one can give attention mainly to the play, the other to verbal exchanges, a division of attention which is very hard for one therapist to achieve except from time to time.

The presence of the siblings is essential, partly because they often prove to be more disturbed, to outside eyes, than the referred person, and also because they have a certain independence from, and so greater objectivity to, the attitudes and interactions of the parents and referred patient, who are often more closely locked together in a pathological way and more blind to their interaction than the rest of the family. This is evident in the following case:

David, aged 12, was referred because of chronic mild depression, learning difficulty and inability to work to capacity. When first referred, the family had been seen separately along conventional lines, and though I had the impression from my interview with the boy on his own that he felt overshadowed by his more aggressive, driving elder brother, the parents strongly denied and avoided any suggestion that there could be problems of any sort in the family. A family interview was arranged for David and his brother, John, two years older, as well as both parents, on which I reported as follows:

"David said that although he had wanted to go away to the boarding school to join his elder brother and is getting adjusted now, after about a year, he was homesick for some time when he first began school. The parents showed me his school report, with adverse comments on his lack of effort and attainment by most teachers and the principal. I commented on something the parents had not mentioned—his favorable reports for wood-work, metalwork, art and history. Eventually, I used the opportunity to mention in the presence of the brother my impression, at the previous interview with the boy alone, that David was in a state of conflict and rivalry with the brother but was at the same time trying to avoid this, resulting in paralysis. The parents once again rejected my suggestion, insisting that there was no possibility of jealousy in the family, and David, apparently taking his cue from them, also shook his head. However, John remarked, 'It's a funny thing, but all those subjects he is good at are the subjects I don't take.' John agreed that it made sense that David must be jealous, though the parents still resisted this and repeatedly tried to change the subject. I wondered who the boys were really fighting over, suggesting that jealousy could have no meaning unless there was someone whose approval and affection one desired. I wondered aloud if David might feel that John had mother, but after a long pause John finally said, with some hesitation, that he thought it must be father since he and father had many interests in common and got on well. He thought David might feel shut out.

"Though the time for the interview was too short, it was interesting to see how the sibling had provided all the clues and seemed the only one to understand and to accept what I had to say. The parents seemed resistant even in the face of John's confirmations, and mother especially seemed not to like the way that things were getting out of her grip."

The following example, which has been given in a previous paper (5), illustrates beautifully the way in which children aid the therapeutic process, particularly in larger families where they can feel strong enough as a group to oppose the parents.

Sandra, aged 12, was referred to a child guidance clinic for persistent stealing as well as jealous and provocative behavior at home and school. Several months of separate treatment led to symptomatic improvement in the child, but complete deadlock in interviews with the mother, who rejected any connection between Sandra's problems and her own personality, despite the fact that she recalled she had been very similar in her own childhood.

Six months later the problem recurred, and this time the whole family was seen as a group—Sandra, her sister Susan, one year older, her brother Philip, one year younger, and two younger children, four and five, who played near the father and mother but took no active part.

Everyone began by blaming Sandra, who at first appeared to seek acceptance, then became stubborn and defensive, eventually wept and finally did in the group what she was said always to do at home—excluded herself and drew her brother into mischievous whispering. Mother then spoke of her closeness to the elder sister, Susan, and Sandra at this point said, "But I have got Dad." Father denied this, looking uncomfortable. The interview was otherwise unproductive, and for the psychiatric social worker, who took part, confirmed his belief that Sandra's difficulties were not explicable in terms of the family dynamics.

I found it difficult not to agree, but later recalled how hard Sandra had tried to establish a good relationship in the earlier part of the interview and how she had been driven relentlessly into opposition. At the next family consultation, two months later, everyone again treated Sandra as the family problem, accusing and reproaching her. This time Sandra did not attempt to defend herself and refused to take part, even when I invited her to do so. The other children said Sandra was carrying out her threat to keep silent and possibly to leave.

I pointed out how everyone was again focusing on Sandra as the problem, suggested that she was in some way functioning as a scapegoat, and acknowledged that I had colluded in this at the previous session.

At this mother put up a good deal of resistance, pressuring me to alter my assessment, but I reaffirmed it. The parents then began to talk about their own feelings of failure, father saying that Sandra made him feel frustrated, mother that she made her feel helpless and inadequate. Sandra still refused to join in even when I invited her. The other two children said she feared she would be picked on if she spoke, and at this point Sandra said she had been picked on by the whole family after the previous interview. The parents denied this, claiming the children had freedom to speak their minds, and Sandra began to sulk once more.

At this point an unexpected intervention came from the elder sister Susan (unexpected in that such interventions are always a surprise, even though in family therapy the siblings often play this crucial role). She hesitated, then plucked up her courage and said, "It will all have to come out now, it will all come in a rush, and everything will have to be said, even if people get upset." Susan then began to attack father, saying he was always picking on the children because he was so grumpy. Father, rather passive and withdrawn until this point, became animated and defended himself, while Susan's criticisms became more vehement. Sandra now entered the discussion again, giving up her role of the naughty child and defending her father fiercely against the criticism. From this point on she remained a member of the group, and only once fell briefly back into her previous excluded position. Mother now joined Susan in criticizing father. Eventually all the three children, including Sandra, were criticizing him, saying he was always complaining but never really firm; he would keep on at them about doing the cleaning up, but eventually do it himself; the three children all agreed that he should be more definite and make them do it. As all the children attacked father in this way, mother moved to his defense, though she seemed in fact to agree with their criticisms. During this exchange, the mother said among other things that the children were not as helpful as they should be.

It was at this point that the attack seemed to move to mother, and it came first from the boy Philip. He complained that even when they tried to help the parents wouldn't accept it. He instanced an occasion when he had offered to go and make the tea but mother had stopped him, saying that he would only make a mess. The other children began to agree that the mother had no right to grumble, since she wouldn't accept their help when they offered it. A sudden change now occurred in the group pattern, and it seemed only a few seconds before the whole family was once again attacking Sandra in the way they had done in the beginning, blaming her for being stubborn and unhelpful.

I now interrupted to point out how Sandra had been an active and constructive member of the discussion, accepted by everyone, until everyone had suddenly begun to blame her and drive her outside the family circle; this had followed immediately on some criticism of the mother, the only one who had avoided it until this point. The mother now began to argue stubbornly with me, saying that it was Sandra who had been sent to the clinic as the problem; they had all come to have something done about her. I said we had now clearly seen that the problem lay in the family as a whole; they could all be united against Sandra when Sandra was bad but when Sandra was not in this position as scapegoat, other family conflicts immediately began to emerge. At this point Susan said, "Yes, the real problem might not be Sandra at all, but someone else." Mother still seemed angry with me, determined to keep the problem in the children, and to disagree with the way I was formulating the position. After a short time, the parents and I noticed that the girls were making faces and whispering. We asked what this was about, and Susan once again took the role of family spokesman, this time criticizing the mother. Apprehensive underneath, but firmly and definitely, she said that the mother was not the same since the babies had arrived: "She is different, she has changed completely." All three older children gradually joined in the unanimous criticism of mother, saying she gave all her love to the two smaller ones and had little left for them. They felt the mother didn't realize they still had needs, just as the babies did.

After these criticisms of mother had continued for some time, mother began to attack Susan, usually her ally. One of the most interesting and moving moments in the interview came when Sandra then suddenly leapt to Susan's defense saying, "Now we are all doing to Susan what everyone was doing to me when we came in." The time allotted to the interview was nearing its end. I now suggested that just as the older children still needed something they had had as babies, mother might have her needs too. The mother said she wanted to give them all the affection she could but that they would have to help her more, so that she could in turn give more time. At this point Susan seemed to be less forgiving and to be dictating terms to mother, while it was Sandra who now defended mother, and supported her. Strong feelings of affection and need appeared to be released at this point, after the earlier feelings of resentment and rebellion. The older children seemed to be trying to come to terms with the fact that the babies now needed to have what they had had before, and Susan said, "We had all the love before they came. At first I was alone, and I had everything, then Sandra came and she had it, and now the little ones have to have it instead."

At the third family consultation, a month later, the situation had changed dramatically. Sandra had been integrated into the family and remained a member throughout the session. She seemed to have little need to speak, was warm and relaxed, and, significantly, looked after the two younger children throughout. Susan, by contrast, was now revealing a full-blown adolescent conflict with the mother, which at times would spread to a conflict between all the children and both parents, over the usual adolescent strivings for independence. The father was for the first time taking a leading role and both parents felt that all this was a natural stage they had to pass through. While they wished to be free to get in touch with us if necessary, they did not feel the need for further help for the time being.

Arenas

Family interaction is more readily understandable if it is recognized that different types of fundamental conflict are fought out through arguments which at first seem more superficial. It is as if the real issue is too threatening to family stability to risk a direct confrontation, so that the conflict is displaced to a different area or even to different family members. These stereotyped family disputes provide "arenas" within which the more alarming battles can be safely contained.

Authority problems, for example, are frequently expressed in disputes over who shall wash the dishes, or who should decide the matter. Arguments between parents and teenage children over the time at which the latter should be in at night are really conflicts about the degree to which the parents, or the adolescents, should be in control of the latter's sexuality. Conflict which regularly disrupts family mealtimes often indicates frustrated affectional needs; this may arise from a general difficulty in providing and accepting nurturance. Sexual frustration in the parents often becomes displaced to squabbling between the children, with the parents in addition venting their irritability with each other through scolding the children, or disagreeing about their management.

These arenas provide an outlet by which conflict can be expressed in a safe and limited way, but the fact that the real issues are disguised, and never clearly faced, means that they are never solved, and the arguments continue indefinitely. If the therapist recognizes these typical arenas for what they are, he can facilitate resolution of the real conflicts by bringing them into the open.

Constitution of the Minimum Sufficient Network

Practice varies about inviting members of the extended family or other figures who may be significant in the social network. Partly this is related to the difficulty in getting the people together or in managing the group as it becomes larger, and some compromise is necessary. The concept of the minimum sufficient network is useful in deciding on the composition to be aimed at, and if it is found that a grandparent, friend or neighbor plays a crucial and dominant role in family decisions, no progress can be expected unless that person is either included in the therapeutic efforts or at least rendered less influential through the therapist's somehow taking over that person's functions in the family system.

However, all is not necessarily lost if a crucial member of the network fails to come, provided the missing person is remembered and "brought alive" in the family session. The essential factor is for the group to be complete psychologically, in people's minds, and above all, of course, in the mind of the therapist. Fortunately, one is often helped by the fact that it is difficult to forget or "leave behind" some of the more disturbing members, when they are carrying projections, as the following example shows:

John, aged 10, was referred for lack of appetite, fears of vomiting, fears of going to sleep, and severe paranoid anxieties. At the first interview only the mother attended with him. She was described in the referral letter from her doctor as "hysterical" but she appeared to me a borderline personality and at times frankly psychotic. There was an impression of great ambivalence and provocativeness, and she seemed to be projecting these aspects of herself on to the middle child, Jean, aged 13, who was said to upset and dominate the whole household. Mother's separation fears appeared to be projected on to John. There was one older girl, Lillian, aged 15, who was said to be clever and successful at school.

I thought it unlikely that we could hope to do very much when the family disturbance was obviously so profound, but a family session was arranged. The notes state:

"Jean did not attend, and the session opened with all the family blaming her and describing her as being difficult and domineering. They said she had refused to come because she thought the psychiatrist would blame her, and we soon pointed out that Jean appeared to be regarded as the patient by everybody. Mother commented after a time on the way in which Jean appeared able to dominate the interview even when absent, just as she did at home.

"The mother said that John's symptoms had improved considerably since the first interview. However, John admitted that he had been sleeping with her or with the father recently. This led to a confusing description of how John sleeps with either father or mother, while the other parent gets into his bed. Often father and John go to bed together to read while the women all watch television.

At about this time in the interview Lillian accused the father of coming home late after drinking too much in a bar. Although she admitted to no pleasure at seeing him, it was clear that she really missed his company and at this point she burst into tears and asked for a handkerchief. All the family now accused father of going to a bar instead of coming home, and it was possible to help them to tell him how much they missed him and wanted him with them, and to help him to understand that they were usually too angry to say this in a positive way which could convey their need of him. This led to a complaint by father and mother that the children were always with them; because of this they had little time together and felt they had little pleasure or satisfaction.

My PSW co-therapist pointed out how everyone seemed to be expressing feelings of being unloved, and this led to considerable relief of feeling, particularly from the eldest girl, Lillian, who felt she got no appreciation for her success at school. The PSW focused on the jealousy the parents might feel towards Lillian over her school success, and the father admitted this might be true to some extent as he had missed all such chances in his own childhood. Soon John became restless and fidgety, and the similarity to his behavior at home, in that he seemed to be feeling left out and so was rejecting us all, was pointed out. Quite a positive position appeared to be reached by the end of the session and they appeared eager to come again, though the mother said she hoped she was not wasting our time.

The next interview offered was two months later, and the interval was probably too long. Only mother and John attended, though all the family had been invited. Mother said that the father had wished to attend but had not been able to manage it, but Lillian had felt too upset and decided not to come. Though the mother minimized any help she had received, which seemed a characteristic family attitude, it appeared that the main problems had been completely resolved and that John's nervous fears had improved to a point where they did not feel attendance was necessary. It also emerged that father had changed his job following the previous interview and was spending much more time at home. The mother was concerned only about John's persisting fussiness over food which seemed largely related to the mother's need to make him eat. Jean was not mentioned at all and was clearly not being scapegoated in the same way.

EXPRESSION OF FANTASY BY THE CHILDREN

A concern sometimes expressed by those accustomed to individual-centered psychotherapy is that family interviews would prevent the expression of fantasy by children which occurs readily in the free and productive atmosphere possible in individual psychotherapy. I shared this anxiety but have gradually come to be less sure that it is justified. The fantasy may not emerge quite so quickly (though I am not even sure of this), but it is certainly expressed in one way or another, and the therapeutic effect of this emergence with the family present has profound therapeutic consequences, not only through the effect of the increased understanding of the parents, but also through the child's awareness that a previously hidden part of himself has been accepted by them as well as by the therapist.

Stuart, aged eight, had been referred by the general practitioner because of poor progress at school (despite good intelligence), extreme slowness in all activities so that he had to be helped in dressing and undressing himself, together with disobedience and stubbornness, inability to go to sleep, and poor relationships with other children. His obsessionality was matched by similar obsessional and compulsive traits and symptoms in both parents, although the two younger children seemed more normal and relatively happy.

Stuart's regression and difficult behavior stemmed from the age of two and seemed to coincide with the birth of his sister, but later it appeared that hospital admission for surgical treatment of a testicle at the age of 18 months (six months before his sister was born) had also had important effects. Seen alone during the diagnostic interview (before family diagnostics became routine) he said, "I came here to make sure I still know enough from my operation." ... "I had my operation to make sure I haven't forgotten anything." ... "My operation was very low down on my body." ... "I worry I might get a seed out by accident before I am married."

The first three family interviews (all at monthly intervals) produced little fantasy but considerable change occurred. At the first I confronted the boy with the way in which he was making demands on me but using me in a dishonest way, not acknowledging the help I was trying to make available or accepting what I gave, which was exactly the pattern he showed with his mother. Stuart became somewhat upset and disturbed at this but gave up his defenses and interacted more openly. The interview was also used to point out to the family how they all kept themselves isolated from each other so that there was little communication or real interaction among any of them. At the second interview the boy was quieter, had lost his previous exhibitionistic behavior and many of the compulsive movements, while the mother was a little less withdrawn. At the third session the situation was much improved, demonstrating a calmness, relaxation and quiet warmth which had been quite lacking before. The parents appeared more tolerant and accepting, had dropped some of their earlier rigid control, while the boy was relaxed and quiet and seemed to enjoy the discussion. The parents commented on the great improvement they noted in him in all respects. Towards the end of the session references began to appear to the family's obsessional attitudes, which were seen in terms of a need to keep something destructive at bay by control and orderliness. This led to associations to death wishes to siblings, but this had to be postponed to the fourth session.

At the fourth session all the improvements had been maintained. After some hesitation about how to start, Stuart mentioned his fear of going to sleep because of dreams. On inquiry, he mentioned three dreams:

1. This was a recurrent dream dating from the age of three or four where he finds a worm on his hand and feels worried about it. He wipes it off with a tissue (at this point he began to play with his fingers).

2. His little brother falls into the toilet and is flushed away.

3. The car gets out of control and falls over on its side in the garage. (This was associated with his little brother, who actually had played with the brake and let the car run away.)

Throughout these descriptions Stuart was grimacing again, and repeatedly holding and shielding his fingers as if protecting them from something. I focused at first on his ambivalence towards his little brother. There was intense denial of any wish to get rid of him and he said he would like mother to have more babies. Indeed, he said, he would like to see the babies and know what they were like. I suggested that he would probably like to know how they were made and he agreed, saying that he thought the parents did something in secret, and he would like to watch the secret. I asked how much he knew about the making of babies and he told me, leaving out just the fact of intercourse. I added this, explaining how the penis was placed in the vagina and that this was enjoyable and exciting, so that the parents loved the baby and each other more in remembering it. He seemed very pleased with this, but admitted on suggestion that he felt jealous and wanted to do it himself with the mother, adding that he knew that this was not right and he must wait until he was older to make a baby with someone else.

I now linked his dream and his play with his fingers with his anxiety over his father's possible retaliation and wish to castrate him. During all this, his play with his fingers had diminished gradually and he became more relaxed. The father said that he too had wanted to know all these things when he was a boy, and both parents seemed to find it as helpful to discuss these matters openly as the boy himself.

Seen again three months later, the progress had been maintained and the parents reported that he was improving in all respects and beginning to make real progress in school. Though still a rigid and obsessional personality, he was much more relaxed and spontaneous and there was a warmth and relatedness in the whole family situation.

Further follow-ups confirmed the improvement.

Although, as in this case, there is usually development from one session to another, my approach to later interviews is the same as the technique I follow at the first. Though I make some notes after each interview, these are mainly for research and teaching purposes and I do not regard it as at all necessary for me to remember what has gone before. Indeed, there is something to be said for the principle that one should start fresh each time, for exactly the same reasons as I have already given in regard to the first interview. I expect the family to have made some progress since the previous interview, or at least to have thought or talked about it, and so I ask them to start from where they are now, not from where we left off. If there is any remembering to be done about previous interviews, I make it plain that this is their job, not mine; if necessary, I tell them that I see many families and can scarcely be expected to remember all the details, while they are presumably seeing only one family therapist and should surely be able to recall their own lives better than a stranger who sees them briefly every month. My object is to enter the system once again and help them to take another step, withdrawing at the end and leaving them to proceed on their own until we meet again. Every session is thus in some way like the first one, a step into the unknown, complete in itself. One advantage of this approach, and no doubt one reason why I developed it, is the fact that it enables one to treat far greater numbers of patients than is possible using techniques limited by the need to remember past history or previous interviews.

However, it is at the same time helpful to keep some brief record of the main points of the interaction and to refer to these from time to time since one can more easily avoid falling, through one's counter-transference, into the same errors on successive occasions. Also, it is important to make notes of the main findings of the first interview and to refer to these occasionally, since the whole problem is often presented in outline at the beginning even though one does not perceive it at first.

12 INDICATIONS AND CONTRAINDICATIONS

There are only two families in the world, my old grand-mother used to say, the Haves *and the* Have-nots.

Miguel Cervantes, Don Quixote

Thinking to get at once all the gold that the goose could give, he killed it, and opened it only to find—nothing.

Aesop, The Goose with the Golden Egg

The best of all would be a person who has all the good things that a poor person has, and all the good meals that a rich person has, but that's never been known.

Thornton Wilder, The Matchmaker

As is common with all new techniques, the indications and contra-indications for the conjoint family approach have received less attention than other aspects of this relatively new field. It is inevitable in the early stages of the development of new methods that they should be used in a relatively global, undiscriminating way, for reliable criteria cannot be established until each has been widely applied both in situations in which it proves to be effective and in those in which it does not. Indeed, it is in some ways desirable that it should be tried on every type of case, for only in this manner can it be assessed and ultimately used in a more discriminating and effective fashion.

However, being human we all too often avoid facing the complexity and confusion of life, and the necessity for struggle and professional growth, by a partisan selection and support of one approach against all others. If we can be enthusiastic enough about its merits, we do not need to learn how to use the alternatives, or to decide in each case which is preferable. In the case of existing therapies, whether psycho-analysis, behavior modification or physical treatments, we are only too aware that the choice is more often based on what the therapist happens to have learned, or feels more comfortable using, than on what might help the patient most. Family therapy stands in the same danger; in the

223

United States in particular one gains a general impression from the literature that some groups practicing the method apply it unselectively, as if they have abandoned other techniques in their enthusiasm for this new approach, or embraced it because they have not acquired expertise in individual or other group therapies first.

Systematic attempts to integrate conjoint therapy, stranger-group therapy and individual psychotherapies seem not only to be significantly lacking in the North American literature, but recognition of this deficit is also strangely hard to find. One rare instance occurs in a recent contribution by Bowen (1):

> It is noteworthy that specialists in group psychotherapy have had no more than secondary interest in family therapy. There were no group psychotherapists among the originators of the family movement.... The group therapists doing family therapy attend the group therapy meetings and they publish in group therapy journals with relatively little overlap between the groups.... Most of the influence of group psychotherapy on family therapy has come from people who had some early professional training in group psychotherapy but who did not consider themselves to be group therapists.

After I expressed a similar impression at the National Conference on Training in Family Therapy in Philadelphia in November 1972, when addressing the opening session in company with Bowen, Minuchin, Satir, Serrano, Whitaker and Wynne, no disagreement was expressed either then or later by them or the 800 delegates, while many expressed their agreement in private conversations.

This tendency has fortunately been less evident in Britain, particularly since family and marital therapy, though developed later than in North America, has nevertheless eventually taken firm hold in major teaching centers like the Institute of Psychiatry and the Maudsley Hospital, the Tavistock Clinic, and the Hospitals for Sick Children, where it has had to find its place among the full range of psychiatric interventions. As for myself, since my student days I have worked in close association with a wide range of professional disciplines. Consequently, although in the early days of my conjoint work, as in my early work with stranger groups, I experimented with the technique in all kinds of situations in order to learn what was appropriate to it, I soon became interested in defining more clearly the limits of each kind of intervention. This study became a special focus of interest, both for me and for the colleagues with whom I became associated, and I hope the conclusions set out below will be useful to others, supplementing other information available.

CONJOINT SESSIONS FOR DIAGNOSIS

We need first to distinguish between the use of conjoint sessions for diagnosis—securing information about the family system and its relevance to the problem as presented by the referrers—and for treatment—the attempt to change the state of affairs thus clarified.

For diagnosis there are no objections at all to conjoint sessions, and ideally an attempt should be made to see a family together at least once at the beginning or at least in the course of any form of treatment whatsoever. Only in this way can one be sure that one has not missed a family involvement crucial to the treatment of the presenting problem. To fail to see the family is equivalent to a physician deciding not to carry out a full physical examination in the case of organic disorder—permissible for the experienced, but a calculated risk nevertheless.

Sometimes intractable, vicious and destructive attitudes in some family members have been given as reasons for avoiding conjoint sessions. For treatment this may often be correct, but it is not a contraindication to a conjoint diagnostic session. If the family members have survived living together till the diagnostic interview they are likely to be able to survive another hour of interaction. Further, there is no reason why the relationship should be worse after the interview if attempts at intervention are avoided, and the therapist's attitude is supportive to all, uncritical of any individual, and neutral as regards the conflict. In case of doubt the conjoint session can be stopped at any point with the explanation that it has served its purpose and that individual history-taking will now be necessary. Separate interviews may be carried out in any case, either before or following the family session, or on other occasions where detailed medical or other history is needed, or where material is emerging that it is not appropriate to share at a given stage with the whole family (e.g., detailed information about parental or adolescent sexual activity), or where the therapist wishes for some reason to gain more information about the "inner world" of one family member. One can be quite flexible about such arrangements, and each practitioner will wish to work out the pattern of diagnostic interviewing that suits him best, varying it in his own way for different types of cases.

CONJOINT APPROACH TO TREATMENT

For therapy, the value of continuing with the conjoint approach, as compared with individual or stranger-group therapy for one or more family members, or with practical provisions, environmental manipulation or vector-therapy, has to be decided. These different interventions are not mutually exclusive, and in our experience a judicious combination of a number of these approaches usually has the best chance of success. Much will depend upon whether goals are limited or more far-reaching, whether therapy is to be short term or long term, and whether it is to be crisis oriented and intermittent or carried out through regular sessions planned well in advance. Nevertheless, at the Woodberry Down Child Guidance Unit this problem of selection for different types of therapy—conjoint, individual and stranger group—was an issue of deep interest to us over several years and some conclusions emerged from our study and discussion of cases which have since proved most helpful to us.

The problem was illuminated from two unexpected directions: First, I was at the time chairing a subcommittee at the Queen Elizabeth Hospital for Children which was studying the problem of permitting unrestricted visiting of hospitalized children by their parents. Because of this, I read all I could about early child development and the problems created by separation from the mother at critical stages.

Second, I was concerned in my stranger-group therapy of adults with the problem that certain patients did not respond even to twice-weekly groups, though they were helped by individual psychotherapy. These patients all proved to have suffered early parental deprivation through such causes as death or hospitalization of the mother, a succession of "nannies" in infancy, early placement at boarding-school because parents were abroad or in the army, and so on; they all responded dramatically when placed in a special group where individual sessions replaced one of the two twice-weekly group meetings.

Traveling between these three situations—Woodberry Down, the subcommittee at the Queen Elizabeth Hospital, and my stranger group, I gradually became aware that certain issues were common to all the problems we were meeting, and they appeared to receive a satisfactory explanation in the ideas of Melanie Klein, about which I had until then been skeptical. I have already outlined Klein's developmental concepts in Chapter 2. What I began to notice was a kind of "sandwich" distribution regarding suitability for group therapy, whereby the most primitive levels of development and the more sophisticated levels could use group situations fruitfully, though in different ways, while the level intermediate between these "top" and "bottom" levels required a dyadic relationship.

Individuals and families representing the "bottom layer of the sandwich" make extensive use of paranoid/schizoid functioning. Boundaries are vague and fluctuating. Parts of the self are readily projected into others, who as easily accept them and perform certain functions for other members. These mutual projections may change repeatedly, so that roles change and the problem appears in different members at different times. Pleasurable and painful feelings are split and kept apart, often by projecting the former into a "good" child and the latter into a "bad" scapegoat. At this level the members forming a group or family are thus not true individuals with separate identities and boundaries, but rather functions, roles or part-objects which are located in particular physical bodies on any one occasion.

Such individuals feel comfortable in a group, not because they are having true relationships with others as separate people, but because the relationships are essentially on a part-object basis to the group as a mass, as in the infant in the first three months who is little harmed by multiple mothering and can accept changing nurses because he cannot yet recognize his mother as a person.

At this level families relate to organizations rather than to particular individuals within them, and are not unduly disturbed by changes of staff provided the unit as a whole remains available to them. To be allowed to enter the building and sit on the stairs may be as supportive as a formal interview, even a great deal more supportive if the former is available on demand and the latter involves delay. At this level conjoint therapy is not only possible but essential if progress is to be made, since only then will the overt problem be visible as the function it is connected with passes from one member to another. Only then, too, will there be a minimum sufficient network capable of autonomous functioning and able to use constructively the help provided.

The "middle layer of the sandwich" is made up of families whose functioning corresponds in some measure to that of a child who has developed some capacity to contain its negative feelings without projecting them, who is able to integrate love and hate and tolerate the ambivalence and depressive anxiety which results, and who is able to perceive others as separate individuals with needs of their own who also require concern and care. This layer corresponds, in other words, to Klein's depressive position, but to the earlier stages in the emergence of such capacities where the synthesis is still insecure and the capacity to keep the image of the loved ones present and intact is precarious and easily threatened by arousal of frustration and rage through absence and rejection. Such individuals and families, like infants between about six months and two years of age, are deeply dependent on positive relationships with each other and with the therapist, and are made severely anxious by any threat of loss, separation or rejection. Uncovering of strong negative feelings in the course of family sessions can lead such families to flee, and even the awareness of differences of attitude and of separate identities can be experienced as a threat of abandonment.

At this level, the emphasis needs to be on secure, reliable dyadic relationships. Conjoint diagnostic interviews are possible if used with care, and conjoint therapy sessions can still be utilized if they are accompanied by individual sessions for all the members or for a key figure (usually the mother) who is thereby helped to play this supportive role in the family as a whole. If the individual therapists attend the family or marital sessions they should maintain their personal relationships to their own family members, each representing his point of view rather like a legal advocate and letting other therapists support their own family members in the same way. A compromise is also possible, whereby the individual relationship is provided in the conjoint session itself without separate individual interviews, through the co-therapists' acting in a similar partisan way. Gradually, as the family members mature and gain in capacity to preserve their inner models or objects in the face of frustration and loss, the individual contact becomes less necessary and ordinary conjoint techniques can be utilized.

This middle layer is more difficult to recognize than the others, but a history of loss of loved ones in infancy or other evidence of deprivation or separation, or of depressive episodes, or a clinging "babes-in-the-wood" mutual supportiveness, or other obvious inability to sustain loss and separation should make one alert to the possible need for individual contact.

The "top layer of the sandwich" represents all those other individuals and families in which the capacity for relationships represented by the depressive position is securely established. Ambivalence, aloneness and separateness can now be faced squarely, so that the emergence of negative affect or of difference and conflict in the family sessions can be coped with and used constructively. Individual, family, or stranger-group methods can be used at this level, depending on other factors such as time available and other resources, treatment goals, problems over attendance and so on. But individual therapy is no longer essential or even preferable, and the conjoint session, which at this level becomes an assembly of individuals rather than an "organism" of which the individual is a part, often produces more rapid change. Stranger-group therapy comes into its own, also, especially with latency-age children and adolescents, where the main task is to leave the family and integrate with the wider social setting, and where the principal help in achieving this normally comes from the peer group. At these ages separate peer stranger groups for children and parents, combined with multifamily sessions, are probably most effective of all.

These conclusions, which I first reported in a tentative way in a lecture to the British Association for Social Psychiatry in 1967, and published in 1969, have since received strong support from similar investigations at the Institute of Marital Studies, reported by Lyons at the recent Tavistock Jubilee Symposium (2).

VARIATIONS WITH SOCIAL CLASS

Writing from the viewpoint of a psychoanalyst, Bychowski (3) noted that the conceptual defects, poor ego strength, primitive and punitive superego development, diffuse hostility and chronic apathy and depression found in his deprived patients appeared to make conventional individual psychoanalytic treatment ineffective. The apparent exceptions he found to this rule proved to possess in their backgrounds a positive attitude to learning and education in at least one parental figure or family member, together with a reasonably stable family structure and some satisfactory early nurturance, permitting adequate ego development. However, reviewing the research literature on outpatient treatment of the lower socio-economic classes, Cobb (4) found much evidence that successful intervention with these patients was related to the degree of acceptance and empathy, as well as the capacity for understanding and communication, in the therapists. Not surprisingly, these qualities were often greater in those lower in the professional hierarchy or of similar cultural background, though experience could help to bridge greater cultural differences. With group, as with individual techniques, methods must be adapted to the patient's needs.

Christmas and Davis (5) point out:

> The expectation of lower-class patients for concrete answers, direction and guidance can be satisfied through the use of groups focused on the counselling level, with group problem-solving as a technique. In some groups based on common problems or needs, the emphasis has moved from problems to coping mechanisms in general, and from the present to the past and to the future. As a process which is social rather than primarily verbal, group methods seem to us to help those patients who have difficulty in communication in the dominant middle-class language. Communication among group members in the language of the deprived community may broaden the awareness of the therapist, not only in terms of the culture of the patients, but also in terms of deepening his understanding of both the reality concerns and inner conflicts of the individuals (p. 471).

Bloch (6) found that an open-ended, crisis-oriented stranger group was used effectively by deprived and disadvantaged individuals. Despite irregular attendance, a large pool of patients provided a changing group composition which nevertheless functioned vicariously and effectively for the whole. Active interventions by the leader, "bridging" differences by emphasizing similarities between members, and encouraging sharing and problem-solving, was necessary. Beck *et al.* (7) also found that group work with the poor could be successful if the leader actively facilitated group interaction and sharing of problems rather than intervening and giving advice directly, which instead stimulated envy, resistance and inhibition. White *et al.* (8) demonstrated a greater drop-out rate in individual interviews in lower-class as compared with middle-class patients when therapists were passive and silent rather than active and encouraging.

Similarly, McKinney (9) concluded that conjoint family therapy could be even more effective than individual approaches with the poor, disadvantaged and deprived where it was modified appropriately to include the following: "reaching out" to make contact instead of demanding application and attendance as a measure of motivation; advocacy, in the form of practical help and support towards obtaining needed resources and services, in order to demonstrate real care and concern; other forms of active engagement in the early stages; limited goals tailored to the family's wishes; and emphasis on positive aspects and on growth potential. Because of these demands a high degree of involvement and participation was required of the therapist.

SEVERELY DEPRIVED, DISADVANTAGED AND DISORGANIZED FAMILIES

Though working-class families generally have differing expectations, values and modes of communication, which demand of the therapist different skills from those he finds appropriate with the middle-class, families at the lower extreme of poverty, education and social acceptance require approaches tailored even more carefully to their special needs and ego strength. Minuchin (10) and Montalvo and his other colleagues have done more than any other group to understand the problems and needs of the latter and their book *Families of the Slums* (11) is essential reading for all professionals working with severely disadvantaged families. They concluded that such families were characterized by a general atmosphere of impermanence, unreliability and inconsistency, with no clear rules to internalize and no enduring structure. As a result, the children, instead of following any rules, reacted to the parents' fluctuating moods, which determined responses, rewards and punishments bearing little or no relation to the children's behavior.

A poor capacity for sustained focal attention also prevented learning from experience, permitted impulsive motor discharge without delay for reflection, limited the capacity for self-awareness, self-analysis and self-monitoring, and made impossible sustained, persistent discussion of a particular topic to a conclusion in the face of distracting and disruptive forces. Vocabulary and capacity for abstract thinking were meager. The members of such families showed, in short, a capacity for attention and self-control normal in very young children, trying with this to cope with a physical strength and drive appropriate to their real age. And because there was a lack of consistent structure or coherent rules to internalize, they remained dependent on others to organize and control them, failing to develop such inner controls themselves.

These were essentially one-parent families, usually with a mother and an unstable succession of father figures, but even when there were two parents they seemed able to relate to each other only through parental roles rather than as spouses with satisfying marital bonds. They tended to alternate between rigid, autocratic control of the children and helpless abdication, handing responsibility over either to the most powerful of the children (the "parental child" in Minuchin's phrase), or to society at large by abandoning the family altogether, physically or emotionally. The sibling subsystem thereby became the main socializing force, often on a bullying, gang-like basis, while the parents and children grew further apart and the latter developed attitudes of increasingly rebellious opposition as communication broke down.

Minuchin confirms our own findings in his conclusion that the basis of the pattern lies in the fact that the parents themselves have experienced backgrounds of deprivation, and have not received real love and care or internalized a system of rules and self-control which could enable them to operate autonomously. Thus, they desperately desire above all to be good parents, to give their children what they have not received themselves, but not having received it they cannot give it, except in fantasy or in clumsy, inappropriate ways. In any case they are really giving it vicariously to themselves, responding to their own projections rather than to the real children's needs, so that the children react negatively to the inappropriate care. Minuchin does not say this, I think, in so many words, but it is certainly implicit in what is described.

As regards therapeutic intervention in such families, Minuchin's group believes that abstract, conceptual interventions—conventional "interpretations"—are largely ineffective. Moreover, they consider that the *structure* of the family has to be changed, by interventions of a more concrete nature. The therapist must first reduce the "noise," must become a chairman who actively controls the interchange and renders it orderly and constructive, making people speak one at a time, preventing interruptions and diversions, generally setting a model of attentiveness and respect by listening attentively and respectfully to each person in turn and preserving continuity by remembering the theme when they forget it, acting as a monitor and memory until they begin to internalize these functions for themselves. He rewards cooperation and constructiveness by praise, and highlights positive achievements so that they reinforce changed behavior. Instead of merely reflecting feelings, he changes the structure in a concrete way by setting tasks (e.g., "Can you get your mother to talk to you?" instead of, "Why doesn't your mother talk to you?") and altering the communication pathways (e.g., if all communications usually go through the mother, he will block this and talk through the father).

One of the most effective and unusual techniques developed by this group—a beautiful example of providing a concrete external pattern as a model for a family to internalize—is the use made of one-way screens.

One of the two co-therapists takes a parent behind the one-way screen to watch the rest of the family interacting. This situation physically enforces observation, reflection and containment of impulses, particularly as the watching parent is able to identify with the reflective comments of the co-therapist sitting beside her (the parent's self-esteem is also bolstered by seeing that the other co-therapist has similar difficulties to her own in coping with the children!). Parents usually spend several sessions behind the one-way screen, in order to foster a process of reflection and introspection which is an almost undeveloped function in such families. The family is helped gradually to make distinctions, to differentiate over-inclusive categories and themes instead of functioning in global, all-or-nothing terms; this is done by interrupting and examining the interaction in the here-and-now, rather than by discussing reports of what has happened elsewhere in the past. The therapist also seeks to identify the prevailing mood and to change it, either by introducing some feeling that is missing or joining in the characteristic family emotion and either exaggerating it so that it becomes obvious, or gradually changing it.

It is hard to describe the tremendously positive, supportive relationship established with families by members of this group, but to experience it is to be convinced that it is the main ingredient in their success. Something positive is always found to encourage, instead of defects to criticize (they believe that interpretations are always experienced by such families as wounding criticisms), and interventions are carefully phrased to make this possible. Instead of criticizing a mother for shouting angrily at her son the therapist will praise her for her wish to help him behave better, but offer help to find a more effective technique.

Work with such families requires considerable flexibility and capacity for role playing, without losing respect and concern. Minuchin (12) states:

> We consider it extremely important for the therapist to be able to gauge the threshold of attention in a family in order to calibrate the intensity of his messages to the family's affective requirements at any particular moment. At certain times the therapist must yell more vigorously than the family members, dramatize his affect by making his silence audible, change his seat to increase or decrease proximity, introduce examples from his personal life, or use audibly the four-letter words that the family members use secretly among themselves. It is in the artistry of appropriate selection and timing in the use of such maneuvers of mood control that the therapist's messages achieve a palpable reality for family members (p. 286)....

The therapist activates conflict and increases tension by "testing the limits" and "rocking the system." To test the limits he challenges the customary direction of pathways, the usual flow of communication along these pathways, the concurrent stereotyped mood level etc. This brings out the mechanism through which tension and conflict are usually masked in the family. To rock the system, the therapist *over-exposes* conflict. He deliberately sides at different moments with different participants, and he tugs and pulls at the positions that the members customarily take around areas of conflict. While he is studying the family system by these means, he is also changing it (p. 291).... The problem with this procedure, of course, is determining how far the family can move beyond its customary limits. In our view, this is best solved by observing the family's own processes and its own capacity for flexibility ... we prefer to rely on observing the family's own performance rather than measuring it against some average or norm (p. 292).

Minuchin emphasizes the difficulties the therapists may feel in working with such families (13):

Therapists who work with these families should be alerted to certain processes that are inherent in this clash of cultures. The affective entrapments on the part of the therapist can lower his self-esteem and cause him to feel superfluous and impotent. He can respond with a series of reparative acts unrelated to the psychological growth of the family.... The therapist can also find himself exhausted when a session ends. He has gone through the stress of trying to talk through and over an unaccustomed level of noise. He has tried to maintain a theme in making himself heard by either over-active or listless family members. He has had to awaken members of the family, or to physically control a child's acting-out during the session, and has had to do all of this while being bombarded by multiple stimulation. A variety of transactions have occurred at the same time, seemingly without any connection to each other, and he has tried to weave what was being transacted into some unity, hoping to maintain a theme with some family members while keeping others engaged in active listening. And he has been continuously thwarted in the process.... Clashes between the therapist and family members with regard to the value of talking also challenge the therapist's affective endurance. Talking has very little usefulness and prestige in these families.... The resultant devaluation of thinking in words threatens the therapist precisely at the core of his clinical armamentarium—his ability to talk in a special way. He may cope with this feeling by overemphasizing his concrete "giving" (pp. 289–290).

Minuchin and his colleagues divide up these families into categories based on their level of development. It will be clearer, perhaps, to begin with a description of the least immature and work downward, for the sense of chaos and confusion increases as one descends the scale.

Most developed are the "families with juvenile parents," where both parents are essentially pre-adolescent in attitude and have their main relationships in peer groups outside the family rather than to each other or to the children. The wife is often promiscuous and fickle, finding her sexual excitement outside the marriage, dominating her husband and classing him as "another child." The father is more often dependent and inadequate (though defiant to external authority) and there is considerable exchange of sexual roles, the mother being more effective as a manager though less adequate in nurturance, the father taking over part of the mother's nurturing functions. The family interaction is characterized by a bantering, non-serious quality which interferes with problem-solving, and the children show divided loyalties and confused sex-role identities.

For these couples, Minuchin recommends a co-therapy team with the male therapist assuming pre-eminence, siding with the husband as a chum and confronting the wife over her arrogation of control. The female partner similarly sides with the wife and confronts the husband with his taking over of the nurturing functions. Individual sessions may be necessary with the same-sex therapists, and the co-therapists must be careful to avoid being split and reproducing the parental rivalry.

In the next group, "families with non-evolved parents," the mother behaves more like an elder sibling to the children, while the maternal grandmother fulfills the maternal role. The main work needs to be focused on the mother/maternal grandmother relationship, assisting maturation and separation of the mother and strengthening the marital bonds if there is a husband in the picture.

"Families with a peripheral male" form the next group. These have a father role available even if the man is mostly based outside the family in the peer group, and therapy has to be concentrated on combating the mother's need to command the central position and exclude him, while making the father more central in the interviews.

The most primitive and undifferentiated families of all are usually composed of mother and children only with male figures excluded altogether. Minuchin describes such families as arranged along an axis characterized by "disengagement" at one end and "enmeshment" at the other, some families oscillating between the two poles.

"Disengaged" families are characterized by apathy, unresponsiveness and a lack of relationship and connection to one another. The mother is depressed, feels hopeless, suffers from depression and psychosomatic problems and abandons altogether the task of controlling the children. This function is taken over by the "parental child." She perceives control as bad, likely to make her unloved, and reacts with passivity and dependency not only to the children but to outside agencies, which tend to take over too completely if the family is reached at all.

In such families the therapist should "mother" the mother, sustaining and nurturing her and, while avoiding taking over her role, patiently helping her to improve in her performance of it. The therapist needs to block the dominance of the "parental child"—perhaps establishing an individual relationship with him to do so—and tries to "reconnect" the family members with each other and with supportive figures in the environment, from which these families are also isolated.

In "enmeshed" families, on the other hand, the mother fears weakness, helplessness and loss of control and is overcontrolling in consequence. Family interactions are intense, immediate, and focused around power conflicts rather than affection, so that the children are driven to obstinacy and rebellion. Agencies involved with these families are typically manipulated and seen either as "tough antagonists" (if authoritative) or "depriving suckers" (if nurturing and supportive). Therapy needs to concentrate on decreasing the intensity and tempo of interaction, while power struggles are diminished by one co-therapist taking the mother behind the one-way mirror while the other works with the children. But as with the mothers at the "disengaged pole," the main focus needs to be the support and nurturance of the mother herself.

The focus by Minuchin and his team on the here-and-now rather than past history, on action rather than expression of feelings and on conjoint interviews at the expense of individual work results in some neglect of the underlying common factors in the histories of these parents. However, the impression from their evidence (which agrees entirely with our own work) is that there is a fundamental defect in maternal care and nurturance perpetuating itself over generations. The mothers desperately want to give their children what they lacked, but have not been able to internalize an adequate model by which they could do so. Because of this, they desperately attempt to "impose" care, becoming more like controlling fathers and excluding the males (enmeshed families) or withdraw into depression and apathy when this fails (disengaged families). In his most recent book (14), Minuchin has clarified concepts regarding the most primitive families just described. Enmeshed families are seen as having inadequate boundaries, disengaged families as having boundaries which are excessively rigid and impermeable. Thus, to combine Minuchin's concepts with those developmental principles already outlined here, "enmeshed" families could perhaps be seen as trying to solve some of their problems over establishing inner controls and separate identities before they have completed the earlier task of establishing satisfactory involvement at the level of nurturance, so that they repeatedly collapse back into a more and more primitive state of "oral" fusion.

In England the teams with which I have been associated at the Queen Elizabeth Hospital for Children and Woodberry Down Child Guidance Unit, serving areas in East and Northeast London with a high incidence of poverty, housing shortage, delinquency and psychosis, have paid particular attention to the therapy of deprived and multi-problem families. For various reasons, the approach is different from that described by Minuchin. At Woodberry Down, where I succeeded G. S. Prince as Director, I inherited a situation where many years had already been spent in a unique attempt to modify individual psychoanalytic techniques to the treatment of the deprived and disadvantaged. Entering this situation, I sought to add the group dimension (both artificial and natural) to the work while preserving the dyadic techniques already successfully employed. This is perhaps the reason (together with the fact that I also discovered at this time in my office practice the need for combined individual and group therapy for patients who had suffered early parental deprivation) why individual as well as small-group methods, alongside and integrated with conjoint family techniques, have played a much larger part in some British work than in American work.

Apart from this, we (15) have reached similar conclusions to American writers and found no difficulty in applying individual, group or family psychotherapy to working-class patients provided the approach was: (1) crisis-oriented, or focused clearly the presenting problem; (2) short-term but with the opportunity for further contact when needed, with flexibility over time of attendance, rather like the service offered by a good general practitioner; (3) communication in simple language, free of jargon and utilizing modes of expression familiar to the social class concerned; (4) based more on an educative model, utilizing identification processes, modeling and role-playing rather than on an intellectual, analytic, explanatory, verbal approach; (5) supported by and related to practical and material forms of help, such as hospitalization, drugs, "convalescent" vacations etc.; (6) based on a more directive, authoritarian relationship, at least in the early stages, than would be appropriate or acceptable to educated middle-class patients; and (7) based on the values, needs and desires of the patients, rather than those of the therapists.

We have found the same principles to apply, in even greater force, to the deprived and disadvantaged. Practical help is even more important, as well as "reaching out" through visits to home and school. Appointments must be available at short notice or on demand even if they are brief. Since self-esteem is low, interventions need to be supportive, encouraging and positively phrased, avoiding criticism and any interpretation that could be negatively construed. Firm control and guidance are experienced as the provision of security and caring, and the tendency to chaotic and impulsive expression of emotion requires warm but determined containment rather than the encouragement of abreaction and expression of impulse and fantasy, which may be more appropriate with more mature individuals.

The disintegration and fragmentation of these families on social as well as emotional levels demand greater attention both to the provision of supportive individual relationships, and to the reestablishment of connections to the wider network with which the family needs more fulfilling interaction. Like others, we have found that male and female cotherapists can provide role-models for families where these are lacking due to parental inadequacy caused by conflict or absence. In particular, we found that scheduling periodic multi-family sessions every one or two months, in which a male therapist is included, is a way in which the male, paternal role-model can be included in the treatment of fatherless families by clinics with predominantly female staff.

Our work suggests that the label "unmotivated," often applied to these families by child guidance clinics, might better be applied to those therapists who are unwilling to put themselves out to meet their special needs. This is a pity for the professionals as well as for the families themselves, for though family therapy with the disadvantaged requires effort and emotional involvement it is among the most rewarding and enjoyable I have encountered. Just as a small sum of money, by American or European standards, can make a profound difference to the practical health and welfare of a family or community in an undeveloped country, so a measure of interest, warmth and support which may seem hopelessly small to the "advantaged" professional may result with deprived families in an astonishing and at first unbelievable reaction.

DELINQUENCY

Families manifesting delinquent or persistent antisocial behavior may suitably be discussed in relation to the deprived and disadvantaged, for the underlying dynamics and treatment are in many ways similar even though delinquency may arise, of course, in families where there is material affluence as well as in those afflicted by poverty, the deprivation being wholly at an emotional level. The main difference lies in the fact that the more seriously the delinquent individual has suffered, in H. S. Sullivan's (16) terms, a "malevolent transformation," the more he will have decided to exact from those around him, by force, deceit or manipulation, the needed emotional and material supplies denied to him in ordinary ways.

Bowlby (17), describing the stages passed through by a child in response to deprivation of maternal care in infancy, speaks of an initial phase of "protest" characterized by anger at the lost loved person, followed by one of "despair" where this gives way to depression and hopelessness, leading finally to one of "detachment" where the suffering seems to have been relieved at a cost to the capacity for permanent relationships. The first two phases follow from the child's valuation of its attachment to the loved person and are remediable by restoration of the relationship provided there is time to work through the pain, anger and sadness the separation has caused. In "detachment," however, the pain and suffering appear to have been overcome but only at the cost of forfeiting the capacity to love. This step is understandably taken to avoid being hurt again but from this point on, in varying degree, the individual avoids further attachments, "looks after number one," seeks to gain without giving, to control without commitment, to exploit and manipulate others without regard to their own needs and welfare.

Once this critical step has been taken, straightforward attempts to remedy the deprivation usually prove ineffective. Generosity in others is perceived as weakness, and those who manifest it are "suckers" to be exploited. Kindness arouses at best fear and at worst contempt rather than gratitude and trust. Love can no longer heal because the delinquent, to avoid further pain, has cut his links with, and, indeed, seeks to destroy, the loving part of himself which might respond. Like a mouth disconnected from an empty stomach, where the food never reaches the place where appetite might be satisfied, he is insatiable.

Much antisocial behavior is an expression of the suffering characteristic of the anger of the "protest" phase or the depression of the "despair" phase, both of which respond in time to patient acceptance and affection. But treatment of the seriously delinquent individual or family must begin by recognition, challenge and control of these manipulative, destructive defenses which the phase of "detachment" involves. In milder cases this may require no more than a gentle but firm reproof at deceit and cheating, a demand to look one in the eye and to "level" with one emotionally; in more seriously damaged individuals the merciless tongue-lashing used by ex-addicts to redeem their fellows in such organizations as Synanon (called there a "haircut") may be necessary. Until the hard protective shell is made permeable in this way no real change is possible, but once the vulnerable core is reached, and the terrible pain of deprivation which led to its encapsulation is experienced again, all the help required by families which have remained at the level of simple deprivation will be needed. The therapist must be able to switch quickly from a tough, determined, challenging attitude to one of warmth and support immediately when this true underlying sensitivity appears, taking care not to be deceived and disarmed by the false remorse and pseudo-capitulation which is only another defense to protect it from being reached. The possibilities of manipulation become greater as the number of helpers involved increases, and delinquent personalities are highly skilled at achieving their own ends by playing off against each other the professionals working with them, arousing jealousy by praising or condemning one to another, giving different information to different people, and so on. To work successfully with such families involved members of the helping services network need to keep in close touch and to regard any serious disagreement or conflict among themselves as a possible effect of the family's manipulation.

A delinquent attitude in the family will not always show itself overtly in every generation. Some families, particularly those belonging to the middle-class, present a delinquent child as incomprehensible and the very opposite of all the values they claim to stand for. On inquiry, one usually finds that the parents feel they have been deprived themselves, that they blame their parents for it, and that they have determined to do better with their own children. This often arouses sympathy in members of the helping professions, but the effect of such parental attitudes is actually to encourage greedy, inconsiderate and delinquent attitudes in the children. The children are naturally led to feel "if *they* think they are not giving me enough, surely I have the *right* to steal from them."

The children are thus really acting out a latent delinquent attitude in the parents and usually continue to do so until the parents change their attitudes and not only give the children no more than they really need, or their behavior has earned, but also make it plain that this is all they think the children deserve.

Another dimension which is relevant to technique is that of *ego-strength*—a concept which indicates the stability of the defensive systems and boundaries, the flexibility and variety of roles and coping mechanisms available, the general adaptive potential and resilience to stress available to the individual or family. This is to some extent related to other dimensions already considered, but it also cuts across them. Poverty and deprivation may lead not only to limited education and adaptability in general, but also to an ability to do without material and emotional supplies which might be inconceivable to the more fortunate, and which can in some ways be a strength. The invulnerability and "hardness" of a delinquent may enable him to cope with situations which could break a more open and responsive individual. By contrast a wealthy, educated family may have defenses so precarious, and roles and coping mechanisms so rigid and inflexible, that comparatively minor stresses threaten the equilibrium of the whole system or precipitate psychosis in one of the individuals.

In the treatment of such vulnerable, unstable families, whatever the social level or outward appearance of success or failure, one needs to intervene with particular care and attentiveness, setting limited goals which are constantly re-examined and adjusted in the light of the family's response. First of all, it is important to enter the system in a quiet and unobtrusive manner. Such vulnerable families are like xenophobic countries, where one must cross the rigidly defended border by stealth, disguising oneself to become as much as possible like one of the natives and adopting their customs, attitudes and appearance. In borderline psychotic families this means appearing to share the family attitudes and behaving as if one considers them perfectly normal, however absurd or unhealthy they may actually seem to an outsider. The therapist at first colludes in the system of denial, reassures and disarms the family by agreeing with their protests that they are just ordinary, nice people, perhaps misjudged by others.

Such families, though deeply distrustful of strangers in case their hidden fears about themselves may be confirmed, are nevertheless also in great need of acceptance and support, and if one can be with them in this way, providing a warm, comforting, accepting and relaxed relationship, they cautiously begin to offer their fears and fantasies for examination and help. This is usually done tentatively, testing out the therapist, who needs to proceed with equal gradualness and circumspection if they are not to become frightened and withdraw. The family is allowed to choose its own pace, perhaps by the therapist at first minimizing the problem and making the family slowly convince him that there is anything seriously wrong at all. Only one aspect of the problem at a time is tackled, treating everything else as satisfactory, and avoiding too much exposure of the ramifications of the pathology. The emphasis is throughout on maintaining a basic attitude of confidence and trust, within which the family may be able to tolerate and contain small exposures to their anger, rejection and other negative attitudes.

This process is necessarily slow and may seem disappointingly limited in extent to those therapists accustomed to dealing with more normal families, but such work is immensely rewarding, just as is work with deprived families, once one measures the changes against the family's expectations or desires rather than against one's own. I have developed a deep affection for many of my "crazy" borderline families, which is perhaps no more than a reaction to and measure of their own deep needs and consequent positive response to real acceptance. However, one must feel comfortable at entering and sharing in the family "craziness"; therapists who feel uncomfortable and threatened by what the situation arouses in their own psychology tend to do more harm than good through their need to protect themselves by defining the problem immediately and fully, in order to keep it clearly in view and safely outside themselves. Such anxieties in the therapist lead either to excessively rapid interpretation of the problems in the family-as-a-whole, or collusion in the attribution of them to a subgroup while denying their presence in the others. Both interventions are experienced by the family, or by a vital part of the family, as attacks by the therapist, which they are—a kind of "pre-emptive strike" designed for his self-protection.

Much conventional psychiatry tends to deny problems in the relatives, and to keep them in the designated "patient" in this way. "Radical" psychiatry does the reverse. But both seem to me to have the same object, to prevent the problems from getting into the therapist.

However, effective *family* therapy cannot be done from a position of self-protection, "blaming" and superiority. Indeed, the most effective position from which help can be given is one which is, from the family's viewpoint, even more pathological than their own: The therapist must be in touch with, and speak from, his own infantile and psychotic aspect *for himself*. Nothing, I find, works better with my borderline families than to preface an interpretation with a comment such as, "I'm afraid you'll think I'm absolutely crazy if I tell you about the feeling I just had about what is happening here . . ." "No, no!" they usually say, "Don't worry, you're all right really, there's quite a lot of truth in what you have just said."

PSYCHOSIS

A large part of the early research on conjoint family interaction was carried out in relation to families containing schizophrenic members, and the literature on this subject is greater than on any other. Because of this, and also because my own experience is limited in the field of schizophrenia, I shall have little to say upon it. My work has been carried out mainly with neurotic adults in office practice, and with the whole range of children's problems in child guidance clinics and children's hospitals. Neither situation brings one into contact with schizophrenic disorders in the compelling way that work in adult mental hospitals does, and it has always been my policy to direct limited resources mainly towards the more treatable cases rather than to deprive large numbers of curable people of help by concentrating time on small numbers of more intractable disorders. What limited experience I have had convinces me, like colleagues more experienced in this field, that it is even more vital to work with the whole family when one or more members are schizophrenic, whether the work is supportive and symptom-reducing or aimed at underlying change and growth. However, if basic change is aimed at, one must be prepared for intensive and long-term work, for stressful and crisis-ridden interaction, and for repeated frustration and disappointment over relapses and withdrawals from therapy.

The only case I have recorded in any detail and which might have served as an example—a schizophrenic adolescent for whom I could not find a place in a suitable adolescent unit or hospital—did well, but it was relevant, for someone accustomed to using widely-spaced interviews a month or more apart, often for a few sessions only, that it was necessary to see the family twice a week for over a year. Also, the crucial incident involved the boy chasing the mother through the house with an axe, hotly pursued by the father, who brought him down with a flying tackle in the nick of time. This was the moment the father took over the active and controlling role in the family he had until then avoided. No doubt the boy arranged matters so that he was caught by the father before he came within range of the mother, but I felt much anxiety nevertheless and many times wished I could hand over responsibility to an institution, despite my belief that family therapy offered a better chance of a real solution.

For those who have made this field their own the work is deeply satisfying and worthwhile. The reader wishing to develop skills in this application of the family method is referred particularly to the work of Lidz (18), Fleck (19), Bowen (20), Wynne (21), Jackson and the Palo Alto group of investigators (22), Friedman *et al.* (23), Langsley (24) and Scott (25). Boszormenyi-Nagy and Framo (26) have brought together contributions by leading authorities relevant to long-term, intensive therapy of families with psychotic members. The next section summarizes a crucial comparative study which provides some outline of the different pathology to be expected.

COMPARISON OF FAMILIES OF SCHIZOPHRENICS, DELINQUENTS AND NORMALS

In one particularly interesting attempt to compare the family structure and interaction of different types of families, Stabenau *et al.* (27) examined the families of young people referred for schizophrenic and for delinquent pathology, comparing not only the referred patients but also their siblings and parents with each other and with a third matched group of families containing a well-adjusted child. Stabenau *et al.* report the results of a test designed to reveal the ways in which the families handled conflicts of attitude and opinion as follows:

> The major differentiating features were found to be in family roles, in the expression of affect, in family interaction, and in communication patterns. Overcontrolled affect, often inappropriate to content and behavior, was exemplified by families with a schizophrenic in which bitter, angry affect inappropriately pervaded the discussion on the question and was accompanied by equally inappropriate, calm behavioral restraint. In other families with a schizophrenic, though the behavior was that of hostile rejection or

exclusion of some members in their attempt to participate in the discussion, the affect was an inappropriate one of controlled, saccharin sweetness. The rigid family organization of these families, with distortion of role differentiation and expectancy, was characterized by imbalance in the leadership with frequent isolation, withdrawal, and blockage of assertiveness by the various family members. This rendered some members impotent in the family interaction or resulted in distortions of the socially expected alignments and roles.

In the families with a delinquent, affect was relatively uncontrolled, sharply intense, and at times counterfeit and artificial. Interactions showed a teasing manipulation with frequent open conflict among family members. Family organization was unstable with an absence of clear role differentiation. Members frequently competed for roles or abdicated from their expected roles. Interaction occurred between the parents, but they were frequently at odds with each other.

Finally, in the families with a normal control, affect tended to be appropriate, modulated, positive and warm. Interaction featured considerable autonomy, a coping rather than manipulative or controlling pattern in dealing with the family members, and a goal of mutual understanding and satisfaction. Family organization was flexible with clear role differentiation and expectancy. Empathic awareness with each other's role was evidenced, and the father and mother tended to interact in a complementary manner (p. 50).

Hierarchical authority patterns tended to confirm the suggestions already made about the dominance patterns which appear to work best. Families presenting delinquent problems "seemed to lack organization and clear role differentiation. This led to an unstable relationship in which it was uncertain who would be the father, who would be the mother, who would dominate or be the leader, since each person was operating in conflict with the others, alternately competing for or abdicating his appropriate role. . . . It appeared as though the index child was more involved in this competitive, conflict-ridden, unstable relationship with his parents than was his control sibling" (p. 55). In these families no member took the initiative in trying to resolve differences when they arose but "differentiation was clearest in the N [normal] family where the father was most active in initiating discussion, the mother next, and the children least" (pp. 55–56). It was found that the father in the family presenting schizophrenic problems was less active than the father in the normal family, but in a rigid and controlling way which denied autonomy to others.

Summarizing their findings, Stabenau *et al.* conclude that in families producing schizophrenic patients "family organization was seen as rigid, roles were inflexibly maintained, affect was overcontrolled, and interpersonal interaction was closely bound to external standards and was characterized by forceful control of others." In families producing delinquent members "there was loose, unstable family organization, shifting of the family roles, undercontrol of affect, and an open conflict among family members" (p. 58). In the manifest themes produced by projective testing of the families with schizophrenic members (the latent content was not interpreted) "discipline was seen as harsh. Parent-child interaction was intense but was mainly in terms of parental-need satisfaction, and the child was often seen as inactive and as an 'extension' of the parents." In the stories produced by families containing delinquents "parent-child interaction was superficial and impersonal. The demand was for expedient action, and when parental 'standards' were not met, the child was automatically rejected" (p. 58). In the normal families the tests examining conflict-resolution, and the fantasies produced to TAT cards "reveal the presence of warmth and empathy, the promotion of autonomy, complementarity between the parents, and encouragement for differentiation of the child" (p. 58). Finally, results showed that

> the family organization of the delinquent offspring was unstable, and roles were not reliably executed by the parents. In contrast, the family of the schizophrenic was rigidly stable, but often with resultant isolation or distortion. The families of normal offspring exhibited a flexible relationship with a consistency of family organization and reliability of role fulfillment.
>
> It also appeared that in the "normal" families affect expression was predominantly genuine, and expressed freely and without anxiety. In the families with a schizophrenic offspring, warmth was lacking and affect was overcontrolled, but anxiety and hostility were nonetheless expressed frequently. In the families with a delinquent offspring, affect was quite artificial and uncontrolled (pp. 58–59).

13 MULTI-FAMILY AND COUPLES' GROUPS

The Group tends to speak and react to a common theme
as if it were a living entity, expressing itself in different
ways through different mouths. All contributions are
variations on a single theme, even though the Group are
not consciously aware of that theme and do not know
what they are really talking about.

S. H. Foulkes and E. J. Anthony, Group Psychotherapy;
The Psychoanalytic Approach

By the crowd have they been broken;
by the crowd shall they be healed.

Cody Marsh, Mental Hygiene

Once the members of the family or the marital pair are brought together for treatment, it is but a short step to multi-family and couples' group therapy wherein a number of families or couples are treated simultaneously. Not unnaturally, the experiment seems to have suggested itself more readily in association with inpatient units, where a number of children or young people are already living together on a ward and their families may often be visiting simultaneously (or in some cases invited to live in as well). Here working with the total group, already well established as regards the nominated patients through the principles of milieu or community therapy, requires only the asking of the question: Why are the different families and couples being kept apart? Bowen (1) appears to have begun in this way, for example, and has recently reported that couples' groups (for him this *is* a multi-family approach, since he prefers to work with the parents once the total family situation has been observed for diagnosis) are now the preferred mode of treatment because of their greater effectiveness.

Outpatient psychotherapy which makes use of traditional group methods also readily leads to the multi-family approach once conjoint work is established. Where the diagnostic procedure includes an interview with the family together, and children or parents are assigned to separate stranger groups, continued occasional conjoint interviews with separate families permit a regular review of the changes occurring in the members and ensure that the separate therapies are progressing harmoniously. If the different therapists also attend, each has the opportunity to become better acquainted with other parts of the system, while fantasies in the family members about possible harmful effects of the therapists seeing other members can be dispelled.

Once again, the desirability of periodic multi-family meetings of *all* the families involved in the small-group work together, as well as all the therapists, in order to observe and coordinate the total situation, soon becomes obvious. This method of working has become a regular choice at the Woodberry Down Child Guidance Unit and at the Queen Elizabeth Hospital for Children, where much use is made of stranger groups for children, adolescents, and mothers. In a predominantly working-class area where it is rarely possible for fathers to take time off to attend weekly groups themselves, but where they can usually change a shift and attend every month or so, the multi-family sessions have been found to be the ideal way of involving the fathers in a manner which makes the most effective use of their limited capacity to attend. Also, in a clinic where the majority of the staff are female it is nevertheless usually possible to include one of the male staff in the multi-family sessions, thereby striking a better gender balance and providing the fathers with a same-sex model for identification.

My original training under S. H. Foulkes (2) was as a group analyst working with small stranger groups of adults, and it was the curious therapeutic power of the group situation, when facilitated according to the group-analytic principles he advocated, which fired my interest once I had confirmed this for myself. Provided the group is well selected (we will examine this requirement in a moment) and the members begin to feel relaxed and secure in an essentially experimental situation where no harmful consequences to their real-life situations can follow (this is the reason for choosing people who are strangers to each other as far as possible, and advising against meetings outside the planned sessions), it becomes possible for controls and defenses to be sufficiently relaxed to permit the development of what Foulkes calls "free-floating discussion." Members are encouraged to respond to each other as spontaneously as possible, without worrying too much about logicality or conscious attempts at problem-solving (though these activities are equally acceptable if this is what the spontaneous responses prove to be). Reactions become less obviously related to each other and move in the direction of the free association aimed at in psychoanalysis, though they are necessarily less idiosyncratic and self-preoccupied since members are encouraged to remain aware of each other. But if the therapist listens attentively to the group *as a group*, irrespective of which member says what, a new meaning and pattern becomes discernible in the seemingly chaotic contributions, just as the blocks, silences, and sudden alterations of topic in the course of an individual psychoanalytic session suddenly prove to be meaningful in terms of a deeper, hidden preoccupation. It is as if a collection of boats, all sailing hither and thither in a harbor, are suddenly perceived as having a common element in their movement, indicating a tidal current not at first visible.

However, in individual psychoanalysis, the work of deciphering the significance of the initially meaningless associations rests largely with the psychoanalyst, and will be subject to his limitations. A well constituted group, by contrast, does much of the work for him, acting like a sounding-board which "resonates" (Foulkes' word) with the common elements in the varied contributions and expressing these through the overall group pattern or through some key contribution—fantasies, dreams or reports of past or present experience. The task of the therapist is to listen attentively to the contributions with "free-floating attention" and then to recognize and to decipher the solution, when it appears, for it is presented in symbolic form and its significance is not at first understandable by the group. The therapist thus serves the group process by translating its conclusions back into a verbal form that the group members can utilize, rather than attempting to do all the work himself as in some other types of group technique.

It is this possibility of using the group-as-a-whole as a sensitive problem-solving instrument—a computer which is constantly producing answers to the questions fed into it by the individuals it comprises, but producing them in a code which requires a specially trained operator to convert them into ordinary language—which provides the main advantage of group over individual therapy. Despite the greater personal difficulties for the therapist, in the form of confusion, of apparent loss of personal control of the situation, and need for additional knowledge, the rewards of having such a powerful tool at one's disposal more than compensate for the extra effort. Most valuable of all, the therapist has a constant source of new knowledge available to him which will continuously expand his understanding, if he will listen to it and make the group his teacher.

For a therapeutic group to function in this way it needs to be carefully constituted. First, the members must be sufficiently evenly matched to ensure that no one member or subgroup can dominate the whole; this will ensure that the individual value systems (which underlie the neurotic problems for which treatment is sought) all become subject to scrutiny and ultimately contribute to a new and more reality-based consensus. For the same reason the initial selection aims to provide, within limits of difference sufficient to ensure adequate communication, rapport and mutual supportiveness, a range of personalities, attitudes and value systems great enough to allow mutual scrutiny, challenge and criticism from a variety of points of view.

A group composed of individuals who are too similar will become too much like a group of friends, who usually chose each other partly to reinforce a particular set of values and self-beliefs. The members will soon join in a collusive defense to avoid examination of the problems they have in common. (This is why group analysts receive their therapy in groups where they are mixed with ordinary patients; a group composed of psychiatrists or psychoanalysts exclusively would inevitably avoid examining the pathology which made them take up psychiatry or psychoanalysis in the first place.) I have also pointed out elsewhere (3) the similar danger in therapy groups in general tending to become like neurotic families, colluding with the therapist to preserve his value system once they sense his blind spots.

However, if the group is carefully selected according to these principles, the conductor will not often have to intervene to challenge the value system of the members, since this will be done by the group-as-a-whole: Indeed, the therapist may find that his own value system is beneficially modified by his participation in, and acceptance of, the new group norms as they emerge. The therapist's role will be more that of a technical expert—setting the group climate and translating the group themes—than that of an authority or educator, and as he will also be freer to provide support for a member under criticism a faster pace can often be tolerated.

The crucial difference between stranger and natural groups has already been touched on in Chapter 10. From the point of view of those principles used in selecting stranger groups, the family or marital pair could hardly be more unfortunately chosen. Either by assortative mating in the case of spouses, or by transmission of the parental value system in the case of the family, each member shares a set of beliefs, values or family myths as well as a collusive system of defenses designed to preserve these common attitudes and protect them from examination and criticism. In addition, far from being evenly matched, the members of the family group show very great differences in power, both by virtue of their age or strength and by the authority conferred on them, legally or through social custom, by their roles. If change is to occur in such a tightly-knit, collusive system, it can only happen through the agency of the therapist, who must enter the family system and challenge it, confronting the family's values with those he brings with him from the world outside.

Gradually, as I have become aware of these important differences between stranger and family groups, I have realized that it is not possible to transfer the group-analytic principles developed in stranger groups directly to family and marital situations. Nevertheless, I believe that couples' or multi-family groups hold a promise of the best of both worlds. Because they contain one or more members of the same natural group, the pathology is immediately visible through the nonverbal interaction. The motivation for change is high because the relationship is a real one, with real and immediate rewards in the form of basic gratifications if progress is made. And the working through of new insights continues actively among the partners or family members between sessions at home, leading to rapid progress.

At the same time the situation also has many of the advantages of the stranger group (provided selection is careful) in that challenge and criticism of the value systems of each couple or family are mainly carried out by the group-as-a-whole, enabling the therapist to take a more detached position much of the time and relieving him of a good deal of the educative or authoritative role required of him in the treatment of separate families or couples. Instead, he can give his attention to the group themes since these groups, combining features of both natural and stranger situations, prove to have the same miraculous capacity to resolve problems as groups composed of strangers alone.

MULTI-FAMILY GROUPS

A number of authors have described the multi-family approach, and for more detailed accounts the reader is referred to these sources (4).

My own use of multi-family groups (as opposed to couples' groups) has been limited to monthly or two-monthly sessions supplementary to other forms of therapy for different family members, particularly separate groups for mothers and for children. These multi-family sessions have therefore included about three to six families, or up to 30 individuals altogether, apart from the several therapists.

The management of these sessions, which come into the large-group category, has posed rather different problems in the early stages compared with small stranger or natural groups. At the beginning, a greater degree of structure is necessary to reduce the likelihood of fragmentation and chaos, and although active leadership is ideally carried out by the therapists as a team it may be desirable to assign one member to the role of active chairman, to provide a focus in the early stages. The therapist playing this role needs initially to explain the purpose of the meeting (e.g., sharing ideas and experience within and among families so that they may help each other find solutions), to act as a communicative link between one contributor and another, to encourage the silent and timid as well as to interrupt the over-talkative. Gradually, as the families become interested in each other and in their emerging common problems, the group itself develops a cohesion and purpose of its own and the leaders can stay more in the background, serving a more analytic, interpretive function but remaining ready to take a more active part if further support or control should be needed. As this happens, the leadership task will be shared increasingly between the co-therapists.

At first, the separate families tend to keep their main links among their own family members, presenting a united front to the other families as in any social gathering of strangers. Gradually links develop on the basis of other identifications—among the fathers, or the mothers, the adolescents, or the younger children. These cross-family subgroups provide considerable support for the members, who can be seen to be actively identifying with and learning from others, subsequently showing evidence of a greater confidence and more secure identity in relation to their own family. This change is most obvious in the children, of course, but mothers and fathers also benefit from the support of others occupying the same role.

In a multi-family group centered on the symptom of school phobia there was a striking fear of aggression and conflict, while the fathers were passive and allowed the mothers to dominate. The fathers gained in confidence by recounting their war and other stress experiences, where they agreed that even the bravest men experience fear in battle. They then combined to criticize the (male) psychiatrist, something they had never dared to do without this mutual support, and subsequently they became more involved and assertive with their own families in a beneficial way. A description by one mother of having finally struck her daughter across the face after mounting conflict, following which the girl returned to school and the family relationships improved, at first aroused gasps of horror in the other families but led eventually to an increased acceptance that such anger and conflict could sometimes be beneficial and indeed an evidence of caring.

This particular multi-family situation was combined with a weekly group for the children and another for the mothers, the fathers joining in as well in the multi-family sessions which were held every six weeks.

Another therapeutic mechanism peculiar to multi-family therapy, noted by several family therapists who have written about the method, is the communication which takes place among different roles *across* families. Thus, a boy and his father, both too angry and disappointed with each other for rational communication to be possible, may, nevertheless, be able to talk to another father who can identify with both points of view and, from his more detached emotional position, help each to understand the other better.

COUPLES' GROUPS

Compared with multi-family groups, whose considerable size and range of ages produce rather special management problems, the couples' group is considerably simpler technically. From three to five couples are usual: Therapists who tend to work with each couple separately while other couples wait their turn and learn by identification—e.g., Bowen and Framo (5)—understandably prefer the smaller number, while those like myself who see the main therapeutic agent as the *group*, and the therapist as facilitating this function, find the larger number an advantage. As with other stranger groups, meetings last for about one and a half hours and usually take place weekly, though Bowen prefers monthly meetings, an interval which accords with my own preference in the case of single families where the needs for support are not too great.

Much less attention is necessary to selection in couples' groups than in stranger groups and a very wide range of personality, problem, and degree of disturbance seems possible. This may be because each participant is a member of at least one pair which has been carefully if unconsciously selected; the possibility of becoming a real isolate, at least until very considerable progress has occurred, is therefore minimal. One selection criterion on which there is some agreement is the age or stage in the life-cycle of the couple, whereby participants are chosen on the basis of facing similar developmental tasks (e.g., younger couples uncertain whether to start a family, or older couples with children growing up and leaving home, etc.). However, even this is not essential and groups with wide age differences can have other advantages, the younger members admiring and learning from the older, and the older perhaps remembering happier earlier years through the younger.

Two therapists of opposite sex offer some advantage through the provision of role and relationship models, since much learning occurs by conscious emulation or unconscious identification as well as by the support and mutual aid the co-therapists give each other in understanding the group process. This mutual support proves more important than one anticipates, for the emotional intensity of the exchanges and atmosphere can be much more powerful than one encounters in groups where members do not have such intimate relationships outside.

Further, in a group composed of pairs engaging in the most intimate and potentially gratifying of all relationships, it would not be surprising if a solitary therapist felt somewhat isolated and out of place, and suffered some distortion of judgment because of this. Perhaps the tendency of marital group therapists to work in pairs is partly a recognition of this very human predicament and a means of protecting patients against its ill-effects. I have gone a step further now and, like several colleagues, work with my wife as co-therapist in all the couples' groups, a solution which puts the therapist on the same level as the patients as regards the sexual relationship as well.

Existing literature on couples' groups, which is almost all American, exhibits a wide range of theory and technique. Much of it is concerned with presenting and countering arguments against seeing relatives together which have been put forward by psychoanalysts whose primary allegiance is to individual techniques. Such controversies have never played an important part in British approaches, perhaps because individual psychoanalytic methods have never achieved the wide acceptance they temporarily obtained in the United States, so that there has been less entrenched resistance to new developments. A further possibility is that experimentation with groups in Britain was carried out from the beginning by distinguished and respected psychoanalysts in the two main teaching institutions, so that serious splits have not occurred in the same way.

For those interested in these issues, the short but informative paper by Gurman (6) provides a good summary of the situation and includes an extensive bibliography. For those who have followed my argument, I hope it will be clear that these disputes about the dangers of departing from the traditional individual psychoanalytic technique are misconceived and need not be taken very seriously.

For the group analyst, the intrapsychic world of the individual is a subsystem of the couple or family, so that change in one must necessarily involve change in the other, if both remain in contact and continue to communicate. Some followers of systems theory like Bowen and Framo are fully aware of this, but they seem nevertheless to neglect one logical consequence of their beliefs: If change in a couple's relationship must be accompanied by change in their self-differentiation and other intrapsychic functioning, and vice versa, then the production of certain changes in the functioning of the therapy-group-as-a-whole should produce changes in the members, both personally and in their separate marital interactions. In fact, both Bowen and Framo, because of some apparent fear of losing control of the group situation (the reasons for which do not emerge in their accounts), hardly use the group process or harness the group therapeutic potential at all. Instead, they exercise a rigid control in which the therapist works with each couple in turn while the others remain onlookers, obviously learning by identification but denied the opportunity to bring their healthy attributes and intuitive understanding to bear as a factor in the therapeutic process.

I think it is likely that the technique of these authors is based on a very appropriate recognition that marital interactions are driven by the most primitive, powerful, and so potentially destructive emotions of all, and I can imagine that such a highly structured method could at least be a very good way for an inexperienced therapist to start. Nevertheless, by restricting the interaction between couples so completely in order to minimize these dangers, they lose the creative, therapeutic interaction as well. My own experience indicates that there is, in fact, no difficulty in maintaining control despite encouragement of group interaction and "free-floating discussion," provided the therapists are prepared to intervene much more forcibly and directively than is usually necessary in ordinary stranger groups, if ever the destructive interaction of a couple escalates undesirably, or a partner monopolizes in an aggressive or destructive way, or if some other destructive situation threatens the therapeutic work.

CASE ILLUSTRATION OF A COUPLES' GROUP

The following example shows in outline a series of sessions of such a group, illustrating some of the ways in which it operates.

The group is composed of four couples.* *Hank* and *Harriet*, an American couple residing temporarily in England, are older people whose marriage has been chronically difficult. The sexual relationship has always been unsatisfactory and they have separated several times. *Jack* and *Jill* also have an unsatisfactory sexual relationship. Jill is domineering, critical of Jack's passivity and very fearful that his previous homosexual tendency will always make real heterosexual passion between them impossible. *Bill* and *Bunny* have left each other for a period before joining the group, but are now trying to restore the marriage. He has engaged repeatedly in indecent exposure and has had many extramarital affairs, while she is seen by him as cool and unexciting and indeed acknowledges that she is more interested in safe and cozy domesticity. *Peter* and *Phyllis* were seen together because Peter's recurrent hospitalization for psychosis (schizo-affective psychosis beginning each time with manic features) seemed related to precipitating factors in their relationship, while his lack of insight and motivation suggested that psychotherapy on his own would not be worth attempting. The group as a whole has been running four months at the time these extracts begin, with three couples, but Hank and Harriet have just joined at the beginning of this series.

First Session After Extracts Begin

All members present. Jill is late and kisses Jack on arrival—an unusual display of affection. This is followed by small talk whereby Hank and Harriet are drawn into the group by the others. As this gives way to continuing discussion of previous themes, Phyllis scolds Peter for his restlessness and for not paying attention, while Peter responds by asking why he is coming for treatment at all, saying he can't see any reason for it. Jack speaks of how the group has helped their marriage, saying how they are both able to have disagreements and to clear the air, instead of the previous sulking and withdrawal. The members wonder why the group is able to help more than discussions with friends, and all agree that it is not possible to burden friends with personal problems in the same detail. It would be too embarrassing, and might threaten the relationships.

Phyllis once again attacks Peter for not being prepared to expose his problem. Peter says he finds the criticism by others of their parents too farfetched. When the group presses him he admits that his father was hard and distant, his mother "flighty," but he has never been able to remember any negative feelings towards either or any serious problems or conflicts in his early life. Harriet, who has had a great deal of previous individual analysis, states that Hank also tends to deny problems in his past, but Hank

* The names of each couple have been altered, but given the same initial letter to make it easier to remember who is married to whom.

says he hopes it's not too late for him to explore his past also. Harriet, obviously identifying Peter with her husband, explores his feelings about his family in a sympathetic but persistent way, and the group questions whether Peter behaved with his family as he does in the group—turning up and going through the motions of complying and having a good relationship, but in fact refusing any real involvement and frustrating all efforts to relate to him and help him. They experience him as "good" in his superficial behavior, but very frustrating and hostile at a deeper level.

Harriet describes difficulties with her adolescent child, saying how difficult it is to cope with the alternation between love and hate—young children are so much easier.

The group speaks about the great demands young children make on their mothers and the women identify with each other, saying how they bear the brunt, how easy it is for men who are out of the house, and how fathers should share the problems more and help them. A "women's lib" contingent is developing at the end of the session and my wife and I, who realize that we are sitting opposite each other in the middle of same-sex subgroups, join in the contest and encourage constructive and forthright argument by modeling it.

Session Two

The group begins with talk about the women's liberation movement (where it ended the week before). Harriet speaks of her deep involvement in the civil rights movement from the age of 14. In discussing some articles about the women's lib movement Jack mentions some reference in them to cutting off men's testicles. At this point Phyllis giggles and remarks on the male therapist's tie.

Jack describes his discomfort during the week. He has felt inadequate as a husband, as if he had a mental age of 13—he says he stopped developing at that age. He relates this to the fact that he finds boys of that age attractive and queries whether he could ever be a real husband to Jill—he has felt totally withdrawn for days. He appeals to Jill to help him to remember any important points he may have left out of his description of the week.

Jill, who has always blocked previously at the mention of any possibility of homosexual interest on her side, says she feels obliged to tell of an experience of her own. Once, when on a climbing expedition with the junior counsellor of her school, they slept in the same sleeping bag. She fainted outright when this woman made some advance to her, and she recalls fainting in the same way on being touched in bed by a young man at her first really sexual encounter. The group suggests that she was frightened by the intensity and pleasure of her sensations on these occasions, that she has repressed them out of guilt.

Hank and Harriet describe how they have parted several times but rejoined each other with good feelings, as if they have also had to flee from excessive pleasure.

Phyllis attacks Peter for his general lack of feeling and for the way he always forgets his experiences during his depressions and hospitalizations.

To summarize the two sessions reported above, we see that the first begins with the problems of relating to the new people, and small talk as they seek to find common ground. The existing members seek to reassure each other by saying the therapy is working, in the face of the questions of the new members. Ambivalence to parents is the central theme, with two members (Hank and Peter) denying any problems, as if their needs for parental affection are too great to acknowledge that their parents are unloving. This discussion leads on to the beginning of recognition of the intense unsatisfied infantile needs of all the partners, with which the women, as mothers, feel excessively burdened. The references to "women's lib" appear as a response to this, as if to say, "Why should women meet all these needs? Why shouldn't women have theirs met by the men?"

At the next session, this leads to a recognition by one of the women of her needs for nurturance from her own mother, expressed in terms of homosexual excitement, and the whole group appears to express the feeling that, because early childish needs have not been fulfilled, the demands and expectations of the sexual relationship are too great to cope with, so that all members have to "switch off" and deny them.

Session Three

Still responding to the emergence of infantile needs for mothering by the group, Harriet begins at once to describe how she has just had flu and has also been very depressed for two weeks since Phyllis described her as "too demanding." She describes how she left Hank for four years to marry someone else, then returned to him. From this she goes on to criticize his passivity, his failure to lose his temper and be more of a man, and the way in which she needs to take all the responsibility. Hank says little during this, leaving Harriet to talk about the problems they have with their children, in which Harriet seems quite incapable of dealing with their demands since her own are so great.

The session then centers around Jack and Jill, Jill saying in a histrionic way that she is desperate since Jack has once again withdrawn into a passive, resentful dependency upon her. Despite her expression of distress, she seems quite triumphant, as if she has once again defeated him, while he also appears secretly pleased at the way in which he can frustrate her by not being potent and giving her what she wants. Eventually she breaks down and weeps, as she begins to face the consequences of her arrogant need to dominate him. At this point the women in the group are extremely supportive and helpful to her, sharing similar experiences about their own difficulty in loving and trusting their men, urging her to be patient with herself, yet at the same time keeping up a firm confrontation over Jill's manipulative tendency.

Jack eventually speaks of his deep resentment of his mother for the way in which she dominated the family and made demands on everyone, and his desire to get even with her and to break the relationship. With help from the group and the therapists, he begins to see how he places Jill in exactly the same position as his mother and punishes her for all his mother's faults.

During all this the therapists point out the manipulative control that all the members try to exert on their partners, by which they seek either to force the partner to be the mother and gratify them, or alternatively to take the controlling mother's role in a manipulative and exploitative way, where the other members of the family have to pretend to be mothered and supported but are actually yielding to the mother's manipulative demands.

Session Four

Peter is in a state of greater denial than usual, demanding to know why he is in the group, why he needs to come. The therapists feel very uncertain about how to deal with his intractable denial, but Hank identifies with him and following this Harriet, seeing the similarity between them, helps Peter to admit that he has difficulties by acknowledging they share these with him. He is able to acknowledge that he feels deep shame over his hospitalization and that he feels his parents reject him for it. Later in the session Jill suddenly says that she has been suffering from vertigo—could this be psychosomatic? The therapists are not certain how to deal with this sudden intervention, since it is not clear whether it is simply a bid for attention or has a more fundamental and specific meaning. After some discussion in which she acknowledges that Jack is "coping wonderfully," though he is obviously retreating from a more satisfactory relationship with her, the conversation changes to sexual experience. Harriet suggests that the women don't try hard enough to excite the men and the whole group discussion suggests a general fear that sexual excitement will become too great to cope with, each partner nevertheless tending to blame the other for the inhibition which results.

Sessions Five and Six

The next session is dominated by Harriet, who obliges the group to spend much of the time talking about her problems with her adolescent daughter. She has felt obliged, as part of her "helpfulness to others," to invite a dying friend into the house. At this Hank had retired to bed and the daughter had made repeated verbal attacks on her. Gradually her own deep deprivation and need to gratify it vicariously by giving others what she wanted herself is brought to the surface; she is confronted firmly but kindly over this, but finds it difficult to give up the idea that she is helping other people rather than herself. The following session is dominated by Peter's seeking to stop treatment and saying he has no idea what his problem is. The other main theme is concerned with the men needing to prove their masculinity, speaking of sports and other active pursuits while the women remain silent.

Session Seven

The subsequent session, which followed a week's break when the two therapists were away, begins with small-talk about their holiday experience. Harriet reports a happy dream about the group which had comforted her. Jill describes how Jack had talked with her about his early life, during which he had broken down and wept, remembering many things he had forgotten, including the fact that he had been absent from school for two years. He had spoken of being able to remember his relationship with his mother, which had in fact been much warmer than he had thought. Jill had been able to comfort him, to hold him close, had finally put him to bed, but the following day she had not been able to cope with this dependent and child-like state and had turned on him and attacked him. He had recognized that Jill was angry because he was unable to make love to her, when she had become excited by the closer relationship. It then emerged that Jill, when visiting a woman friend the week before, had obviously come closer to seeing her own homosexual involvement. During the course of the conversation she had discovered that the friend was frigid and realized that the sexual difficulty in her own marriage was basically due to her frigidity, not to Jack's impotence.

Bunny also seemed to have got in touch with positive feelings towards her mother, having visited her recently when she was ill and found her attitude was quite different from what she expected. Much warmth had been shown and the relationship was changing.

Peter allies himself with Hank and they find many similarities between their parents and early lives. Harriet cuts in to describe a "terrible week" in which her son has been getting drunk, ruining his business and attacking her. She rejects the group's insistent suggestion that she enjoys these painful experiences, though she comes under increasing pressure because of her intractable resistance.

Bill reports that he has had flu and though Bunny has been warmer towards her mother she has found it difficult to show him sympathy. Later on she acknowledges that she cannot bear illness in those from whom she expects support, and she clearly cannot cope with both her mother and her husband being ill at once.

Jack, who is becoming more confident and outgoing, announces that he feels that he can never satisfy Jill sexually though she expresses more positive feelings and says she loves him.

Phyllis reports a dream of stabbing a friend. Peter suggests a motive based on jealousy, since the friend is more successful than Phyllis at one of her interests. The male therapist links her destructive attitude to her husband's weakness and his mental breakdowns, and these, in turn, with the intense jealousy and incestuous emotional involvement of Phyllis with her brother and Peter with his sister; previous sessions having shown that the marriage was based on these ambivalent sibling transferences and the mutual competitiveness each had brought to the relationship. The need for the women in the group to control the men, in order to keep their own painful feelings of demand and frustration projected and contained in their husbands, is very evident.

Session Ten

Three sessions later, after a break when the two therapists had been absent on holiday (until this point the themes of needs for mothering and fears of disappointment and frustration continue), the group is very ambivalent and the focus is much more on feelings about fathers. Peter is in a cheerful but manic mood. Bill is negative and critical towards therapy, complaining about the cost of psychiatry, the bad treatment he has received, how all doctors give different opinions. The "badness" is generally kept outside the group in criticisms of his previous treatment, but his ambivalence towards the therapists is interpreted and acknowledged. Bill and Bunny agree that they are looking for a reliable father and Jack and Peter express the same feeling. Hank excludes himself from any expression of this group attitude, saying he sees himself as a father, however inadequate, as if trying to keep the father-role within himself for fear of being disappointed if it is allowed to be vested in the male therapist. Phyllis says how fatherly and strong Hank appears when Harriet is not present in the group. (Harriet is absent with colitis, a defense to which she always retreats when her dependency needs are threatened by confrontation. She eventually left the group altogether after a prolonged bout.) Jill queries whether their fathers were really inadequate, or whether they simply imagined that they were so. The men talk a great deal about father-figures, expressing positive feelings about the male therapist's role in this respect.

Peter is lively, triumphant, rather provocative to Phyllis who is bitter, angry, and attacking towards him. The group and the therapists focus on the power struggle in this marriage, which is expressed in the group discussion in terms of "who controls the car." Much of the conflict is seen in terms of Phyllis's desire for a reliable father, so that she demands this from Peter but sabotages him whenever he becomes more adequate.

Throughout these extracts a lack of satisfactory experiences of nurturance and trust in the early relationships of these spouses with their mothers is an obvious feature around which much of the discussion centers. We see how these unsatisfied demands, and the pain associated with their frustration, are dealt with in many ways: by maintaining emotional distance, projecting them into the marital partner or (particularly in the case of Harriet) into the children; by making constant demands but avoiding an open and honest relationship in which they might be satisfied—instead, taking a "nobody loves me" position in which the partner is blamed; by seeking nurturance through illness and manifestation of psychosomatic problems, and so on.

We see how the spouses are able to talk about the origins of these problems in disturbed early family relationships and how the members facilitate each other's recollection and acceptance of these problems by sharing in the exploration and providing mutual support. Even in the most heavily defended cases another member, with similar but less intense defenses, is likely to aid in the process of the "return of the repressed" or "the return of the projected" (i.e., Hank's ability to get through to Peter, in terms of their shared family history, when the latter's resistance is most intense).

The interference of these early unsatisfied infantile needs with the marital and sexual relationships, through the manner in which the mutual demands multiply to a point where they are too frightening to expose, is demonstrated clearly, together with the increased ability to face both homosexual and heterosexual impulses more straightforwardly as the complicating infantile demands are uncovered and partially gratified in the group situation. As the spouses become increasingly able to contain and cope with their own feelings of love and hate, the need to project feelings into the partners or the children diminishes, and they become steadily more capable of mutual aid and support. And as the members gradually work through and repair their unsatisfied need for mothering, their lack of adequate and reliable fathers becomes a more central preoccupation and they begin to deal with this, using the male therapist as a transference figure.

The sessions also demonstrate how the capacity to use such a situation depends partly upon the positive resources that individuals bring to the situation and the extent to which they are honestly able to face their own difficulties. For example, while most of the couples in this group were using each other to contain their unaccepted parts, Harriet was using her children as well to a much greater degree, while Hank had accepted a position of dependency and submission towards her more fully than the other men had done. In fact, when Harriet was increasingly unable to use this defense in the group and began to be confronted more directly by the other members, she escaped completely into illness and retired to her bed with colitis. Hank continued to attend for several weeks, after which he made plausible excuses supporting termination on behalf of both of them and they returned to the United States.

Peter continued to be heavily defended against any form of insight at all, and was admitted several times to the hospital with further psychotic breakdowns. During this period it was possible for the group actually to witness the precipitation of these episodes by Phyllis, in which she would become morbidly preoccupied with his behavior and gaze at him with an increasingly intense, hypnotic stare from which he sought to escape by increasing withdrawal. The projection of her own psychic contents into him was almost visible, and the process was several times reversed, whereby Peter lost his thought disorder and came more into contact with others, when the group and the therapists countered Phyllis's pressure and offered support to Peter. However, Peter never acknowledged any serious problem in himself and Phyllis finally separated from him during one of his admissions, having changed very considerably herself and lost to some extent her need to use Peter as a container for her own madness. Soon after this she was moved to a stranger group (we have found it to be bad policy for one spouse to continue to attend a couples' group after separation) where she continued to make progress and eventually terminated therapy.

Bill and Bunny made very considerable gains, both in their personal adjustment and in their relationship to each other, becoming able at the time they left to be much more accepting, responsible and giving towards each other, while the sexual relationship had become more satisfactory. It was thought that they may have left somewhat prematurely, because of difficulty in meeting the fees, but it was felt likely that they would continue to work out their difficulties together.

Jack and Jill continued to attend for over two years altogether, and reached a very satisfactory conclusion. Jack gained steadily in independence, confidence and manliness, and was at last able to offer Jill the support, control and affection she desired. The marital relationship at the end appeared very satisfactory to both.

The next example shows in more detail the sequence of group-associations in a couples' group throughout one session, and demonstrates how a group both presents and solves its problems if the therapist(s) can trust it to do so, feeding in further questions and understanding without feeling it necessary to provide solutions or conclusive interpretations. The session, which was the next to last group meeting before the long summer break, begins with a report of disturbing symptoms developed by a member since the previous session. As with dreams reported in groups, these receive more explanation from the continuing group-associations than from direct inquiry to the member concerned, and the whole group is soon facing a common fear of jealousy, and a tendency to avoidance and emotional manipulation when facing a situation where jealousy may be aroused. This soon becomes revealed as a common problem in the participants' families, and as participants become more conscious of the way in which they have taken over their parents' possessive attitudes, or projected these on to their spouses, there is an increasing sense of freedom and capacity for enjoyment.

SUMMARY OF TAPE RECORDING OF MARRIED COUPLES' GROUP

Present: Bill and Billie; Chris and Chrissie; Eric and Erica; Frank and Frankie. One couple absent, already on holiday. Robin and Pru Skynner, co-conductors.

Problems all center around sexual difficulties—frigidity, impotence, difficulty in ejaculation or premature ejaculation.

Erica begins by reporting a number of amnesic episodes. The group explores this issue but seems to find no relevance in the content. Erica speaks of her "insanity" at the last group. (Although the tape was listened to several times it was difficult to see any significance in the content of these amnesic episodes, as the relevance seemed to lie more in the fact that she was losing her attention through emotional preoccupation. However, the group-associations which follow suggest that Erica's symptoms and fears of "insanity" or loss of control are one expression of a current group preoccupation with emerging problems of possessiveness and jealousy.)

Bill describes how he has found himself "wild with jealousy" of his girlfriend and her possible relationship with another man—his imagination takes hold of him and he "goes berserk." He feels similar intense jealousy when he visits his wife's house (he is separated from her by agreement) and sees the curtains closed and her lover's car outside. The group explores the problem of his jealousy and sees this in terms of his fear of rejection. I make an interpretation that he cannot cope with *sharing*, and so manipulates others to avoid being exposed to this.

Frank resonates to this issue and describes how he "gets physically sick" with jealousy. (Bill had used the word "sick" too.) Frank justifies his response, emphasizing that "one *cannot* stop it." Several members agree, saying, "You can't help feeling jealous," as if they are feeling guilty about it but clinging to the right to be jealous, somehow putting their weight behind it. My wife agrees and also reminds them of the possibility of *accepting* the situation—recognizing that jealousy is natural but that one should learn to cope with it.

Billie describes how she has always protected Bill from this experience of jealousy he finds so difficult. For example, she explains how she tells her lover to hide his car so that Bill will not see it if he passes the house. She says she has realized from the discussion how she overprotects him and enables him to avoid facing this problem.

I suggest that Bill has not had sufficient experience in coping with jealousy—perhaps because he has been exposed to it too intensely at some point, or was shielded from it, or perhaps even both alternately. I mention my experience that, when children are referred with a problem of jealousy, the difficulty usually lies in the fact that the parents have tried to avoid making them jealous—"cutting the cake with a ruler to ensure absolutely fair shares." I emphasize the manipulative aspects of their response to a situation in which jealousy is aroused, and suggest that the manipulative response can be changed even though the feeling of jealousy does not itself need to be removed.

Bill says that this is "exactly it." He realizes that in some way he "switches women off" by his response, makes them think, "Poor Bill, he's so sensitive, we must be gentle with him." It protects him from the painful situation, but also kills any sexual excitement.

This is followed by a pause.

Frank cannot see that he is clinging to and justifying his jealousy—he says it is natural to be jealous. Bill replies that, even if Frank cannot avoid being jealous, he can at least stop enjoying it, making it grow inside him, stirring it up. He thinks Frank is similar to himself in this problem. Although Frank has been speaking in the third person, as if talking about other people's problems, we point out his obvious personal involvement in the issue.

Frankie talks of her problems over competition—why does she put herself in a "one-down" position? Why does one lose? Why not enjoy winning?

Chris says it is easier to drag the other person down than compete and try to win. Therefore he doesn't try, and tends to end up jealous and defeated.

Eric describes his difficulty in "standing up for himself" and fighting for his share. We indicate the positive aspect of envy, jealousy and competition, which often get things done. Why do we focus on the destructive aspect? We suggest that this depends on what hope there is of success in attaining the desired goal; if possession seems too hopeless, then to destroy it seems the only alternative.

Chrissie mentions that when she was eleven or twelve her father said how worried he was that she was not more outgoing and had no friends. She had never felt free to invite her friends home before but after this she felt she had permission to do so. Chris resonates to this issue, says how he felt he had to conceal his relationships from his parents, hide his friendships, didn't want to take his friends home. Frankie agrees, saying how resentful she felt that her parents made her feel unable to share her friendships with the family. Chris says there is something destructive about his mother—she would always try to destroy his friendships or steal his friends from him. Chrissie adds that Chris's mother has friends of all ages—"there seems to be no generation-gap with her."

An interpretation follows about their parents' apparent possessiveness and jealousy, whereby they cannot let them have friends outside the family. They appear to be repeating the parents' pattern by demanding complete possession.

Chris responds to this by saying that he realizes he is always competing with his mother, fearful she will steal affection from him. He says, "I don't know why I want to compete."

I suggest this is a strange way of putting it—why doesn't he resist his mother's stealing of his friends—surely it would be more natural to compete?

Bill resonates to this by saying how he feared making his mother jealous, and Chris adds that he sees his mother in himself—his mother won't compete either, she always drags others down just as he [Chris] does.

Erica describes how her mother never has any friends, is totally absorbed in the family, is interested only in family meetings and thinks they are "lovely" even if they end in storms. Bill says, "Families like funerals." Erica continues by talking about her parents' unhappy marriage and her mother's recent separation from her father. She recalls how at school she discussed with other girls the reactions of other mothers to outside contacts, and found that several girls described how they escaped from an unhappy home atmosphere by sitting in the park on their own. Chris says his mother "had to be king-pin." Erica continues by saying that her mother could not let her children be in a room on their own for half an hour, would have to come in and find out what they were doing.

Chris reports he had his first fight with his mother in his life the previous week. After some disagreement his mother accused him of "splitting the family up." The emotional pressure from her had stopped absolutely since the fight; he feels much better and no longer jumps every time the telephone rings. Since then his mother has been trying to manipulate Chrissie instead, but without success.

Billie suddenly speaks of a warm and loving letter she had from her daughter which had given her pleasure.

Both Chris and Chrissie talk of their childhood. Chrissie realizes hers was unhappy, and Chris says that he "had a marvelously happy childhood until he came here and everybody spoiled it." There is much laughter at this.

It is suggested, following this, that they are all speaking as if their mothers feel like children themselves. Perhaps it is difficult to compete in a fight with childish, helpless parents, who have no friends or pleasure, who are depressed and simply follow their children around to get what happiness they can. They all agree with this and it obviously strikes home— that their parents' power lies in their weakness rather than their strength. Erica says how difficult it is to conflict with her mother, because all her friends are on her mother's side, see her as a "sweet old lady."

Bill says, "We seem to have taken over our parents' problems—jealousy, possessiveness, inability to share and mix." This is followed by a very long silence. Finally someone says, "Bill's gone quiet."

Bill speaks to Billie about her mother's envy. Billie says, "I can't bear my mother pumping me, so I won't give anything away." She says her mother therefore tries to pump Bill instead, to get the information she wants, and becomes importunate. Billie's mother has always been subtly negative to her; for example, she said recently, "Is that the same awful perfume you are wearing?" and when Billie said she was wearing none, her mother added, "Well, it must be old perfume." Billie speaks of her mother as being interfering, nosy, angry but always denying that she is angry and trying to put herself in the right. Bill speaks of his "real hate" for Billie's mother when she is like this, and says he "could kill her," but he realizes that these are feelings transferred from his own mother.

An interpretation follows, to say that it seems that all negative aspects are being safely kept outside the room in parents, outside the participants and away from the therapists. Alternatively, members seem to be using their spouses' parents; they cannot use their own for this purpose.

Chrissie says that Chris is still under his mother's influence. She describes how his mother used to defend him against his father. However, since talking about his mother in the group he has become more independent and his mother has been upset about it.

Another interpretation suggests that the reason they are making their parents bad and creating a negative relationship with them is to avoid breaking with them. They don't really want to leave their parents, cannot be independent, but simply transfer their attachment to their spouses, in the same negative way.

Frank responds to this by saying how Frankie is always wanting a reason to ring his mother, or saying, "Don't you think we ought to have her to stay?"

Billie bursts out saying, "I get fed up listening to you all talking about your parents, I don't want to hear about it." She says again how she cannot bear her own mother's childishness and negativeness, so she doesn't want to connect with it at all, doesn't want to have to face it.

The way in which these negative, manipulative relationships between parents and children perpetuate a very close bond is once again emphasized. Billie's discomfort with her mother and fear that she will play on her emotions and guilt is explored, and she realizes that she reacts to Bill in exactly the same way.

The guilt and worry over their parents are once again interpreted as a way of maintaining a relationship and avoiding a real separation. This time it seems to be accepted and produces a response of relief and relaxation. Erica says she suddenly "feels much better." Others agree. Chris says he feels "great relief," as if he has permission to "saw the branch from the tree"— nothing disastrous will happen if he succeeds in separating.

Chrissie begins to undermine Chris by an overtly supportive but covertly destructive reaction to him, which includes the words, "Poor Chris." My wife points out how Chrissie is undermining him just as he is improving. Chrissie denies this and goes on to speak of an unsatisfactory session in bed the night before when they had tried to pleasure each other. She says she "doesn't enjoy his body; full stop!" Chris says, "Why did you marry me?" and she then admits that she never felt any sexual attraction for him at all.

Chrissie agrees that she chose Chris because he didn't attract her. She adds, "I can't believe father would be attracted to mother." Sex had been taboo in her family. She adds: "The taboo has been passed down." Chris says, "You want me to be impotent, and the trouble is that I want that too."

They ask about our holiday, and there are some jokes about this. The session ends in a warm and relaxed fashion. Chris says, "I feel ever so good." There is a good deal of laughter. Billie says gratefully, "It's helped me too." Everyone agrees as they leave that the session has been unusually productive and freeing.

This session proved to be a turning point in this group, and was followed by considerable change in the participants.

In the preceding accounts that part of the therapeutic process has been emphasized which depends less on deliberate modeling influence than on more conventional therapeutic interaction, such as facilitating the rediscovery of early experiences in the family of origin which were interfering with current relationships, interpretation of the transference distortions in relationships with the therapists and each other, and so on. Though behavioral, modeling influence is present all the time in subliminal ways, the interaction, it will be seen, is very much like that in a stranger group run on group-analytic lines, with the exception that the main transference distortions remain between the spouses most of the time and other members take a more supportive, objective role in relation to them.

However, the model provided by the relationship between the cotherapy pair is profoundly important and at times perhaps the main factor influencing change, provided the co-therapists recognize the situation in which this is occurring and, far from trying to avoid the intense ambivalence and envy the group manifests on such occasions, take care instead to sharpen the issue and to maintain the confrontation.

MODELING IN A COUPLES' GROUP

The following summary describes a session in which recognition and envy of the relationship between the therapeutic couple became unusually intense and was the central topic throughout the whole discussion. It was felt to be a turning point in the progress of this group and in subsequent sessions there was often reference to the idea that members had at last managed to internalize good models (though that word was not necessarily used) which could form a source of comfort, strength and guidance in dealing with the world.

Present—all five couples, and both therapists. This was the last session for Jim and Joan, to whom we'd given notice a month before, because of their professed inability to pay their fees (they had been given six months' grace).

We entered to find only Tony and Tessa present, sitting next to each other and looking affectionate and relaxed. (They were planning to leave the group, by agreement, in two months' time.) My wife sat next to them, and I sat next to her. I was not aware of any particular motive in sitting in this fashion, though whether we sit together or apart usually proves to have some relevance to the current group constellation, which later seemed to be so in this case. Next to us Tony and Tessa carried on their conversation, after smiling at us in a friendly way. Next, Ray and Ruth entered, and sat as far as possible from each other and from the four of us, making up a triangular shape, with Ray in the big "womb" chair. Ray remarked sarcastically that the four of us looked like a "cozy group." I think Jim entered and sat next to Ray, then Ken and Kate who sat next to each other, Kate seeming deliberately to choose to sit next to Ruth. Finally Alan and Alison sat on my left, Alan next to me. A space had been left between the chairs occupied by Alan and Alison for people to get in from the door, and it seemed relevant that Alan pulled the chair away towards Alison, leaving the space between himself and me instead. Finally Joan came in and sat on the sofa next to Tony.

The group started in a desultory way. Someone asked Jim and Joan whether they were still going to leave, and they said they were. Ruth commented that she would not be able to go on without treatment, and would have to arrange some individual therapy to help her with her new work in the psychiatric field if they both left the group. However, she said she only came because of Ray. Various people questioned her about this, querying her motives. Tony then asked Ruth about her relationship with the doctor she is working with, an older man to whom she has felt some sexual attraction. Ruth said she always felt sexually attracted to men in this situation, but the attraction wore off gradually and was doing so in the present case. However, she enjoyed putting herself in the care of a man in this way, and would like to do so by having individual treatment; it made her feel sexy when a doctor paid attention to her. Normally she was not a "consumer" in this sense, and she had never allowed herself to become a "consumer" in this group. Someone asked whether she felt the same sexual stimulation when she went to her hairdresser, but she denied this. I pointed out the transference implications, for she had shown a great deal of sexual interest in me through her nonverbal behavior, but had never been able to acknowledge this.

During all this Jim and Joan were questioning Ruth and commenting on everything that was going on in a very superior, arrogant, dismissive fashion. I found myself irritated by their behavior, which seemed defensive and designed to prevent themselves from becoming hurt or upset by the fact that they were leaving. It also seemed to be destructive towards the therapy with which the others were continuing. Finally I reported my reaction, expressing this in terms of a feeling I had at that moment that psychotherapy based on talk was really of no use since it allowed people to avoid interaction. I said perhaps we needed something like an encounter group, but that I thought even this would be escaped from; I suggested, indeed, that even actual sex in the group would somehow not be real or honest. In particular, I pointed out how Jim and Joan were talking in a very intellectual, brittle, "trendy" way, which seemed to be destructive towards the total situation and to be preventing any real progress. This provided a shock to the group which moved it on to a more real, emotional level. Jim and Joan looked chastened, particularly Joan, Jim appearing black and angry at being confronted in this fashion, though he seemed to have absorbed the criticism.

Soon after this Ken said how bad he felt that, as a teacher, children looked to him for some kind of example and inspiration, particularly where their own parents were inadequate; he felt very bad that he had nothing good inside him from which such an example could be provided. He followed this by saying that he wished that we, the co-therapists, were his parents, though he did not amplify this. I asked him what he felt we had that he needed to take from us. He blocked at this and said he didn't know, and the whole group seemed to be vacillating, indecisive about whether to follow this up or to avoid looking at the question. Tony in particular obstructed discussion of this issue by encouraging Ken, reassuring him and saying that he could "do it himself" if only he had the confidence. My wife cut in to point out how

Tony was trying to avoid recognizing the role of the co-therapists in the group, and was displaying jealousy of them. Tony denied this but several other members agreed that they felt this was what he was doing.

Ruth commented on the fact that my wife and I were sitting together, and wondered if we had planned it to make them aware of us. The whole group went on from this to talk about their unsatisfactory parents, how there had been tense and unhappy atmospheres and how their parents had not seemed able to get along together or provide support, so that they had not felt able to identify with them and use them as examples in their own life.

During all this the focus was on the co-therapists. Ruth, who always blocks in any situation in which her envy is aroused towards us, said she could see us as a couple but couldn't imagine us being in bed and making love. Joan said she could, that she felt it was good between us and that she felt frankly envious. Alan said that we were "lucky we had no problems." (My wife mentioned later that she had wanted to remind him that we had, and had displayed them, but she felt I had blocked her from expressing this. I had in fact interrupted her for fear she would dissipate the envy before we had clearly looked at it.) The whole group seemed to struggle with the issues we presented by sitting together, and, forced to pay attention to us, seemed to express a positive view of our relationship which they wished to emulate, despite the envious destructiveness which was also interpreted.

Alison, who had always managed to keep herself apart and uninvolved during the long period she had been in the group, broke down during this and cried for the first time. She described how earlier in therapy she had had very disturbing dreams every night, but had been able to cope with them and feel secure because, in the dreams, the co-therapists were always sitting "on the side" so she could feel safe. She mentioned how we had been "very big" in the dream and in the discussion realized that she had felt therefore like a child. I suggested that to feel like a child, and to see us as parents, must make her feel ambivalent also; on the one hand she was secure, but on the other it took away her freedom. She said she had not thought about this before but realized the two feelings were there.

Alan expressed skepticism and teased us, as usual, though his positive attitude was clearly present behind this.

There now occurred some differential attitudes towards my wife and myself, particularly from Ruth. She said she felt different feelings towards me and towards my wife. In particular, it upset her that she felt I "negatived everything that my wife said," that I "put her down." Despite this, she said she believed that we had a good sexual relationship, and this was important to her. She said she also felt critical of my wife, claiming that her reactions were "slow," that she felt she often didn't understand and was "stupid" in expressing strongly approving or disapproving attitudes rather than making "clever" interpretations like myself. Nevertheless, she admitted that she took more notice of my wife, whose responses were far more important to her than mine. She was aware that she was using my wife as a mother, and transferring to her many competitive feelings she had felt for her own mother, from whom she had been able to win her father by sharing intellectual interests.

When it was time to stop, all the group said goodbye to Jim and Joan, all the women embracing Joan and kissing her affectionately, since she was weeping. My wife also embraced her and comforted her. After this we explained that they could return for further treatment at a later date, but that it was important for them to get their affairs straight. They left in a positive way and later settled their account, but have not yet returned for therapy.

Those accustomed to group-analytic psychotherapy with stranger groups will notice in these accounts striking differences from the groups they work with. This is also the case in my own work, where I work more extensively with stranger groups than with couples' groups, mainly without a co-therapist. In these stranger groups transference is far more in evidence, particularly in relation to the therapist but also in the irrational projection of psychic contents on to all group members. The discussion is also more free-floating, more symbolic, less concerned with real relationships and day-to-day external events, and the atmosphere is more formal and artificial, the relationships more experimental.

Nevertheless, it will be evident that in couples' groups as in stranger groups, the group as such takes over many functions that would otherwise have to be exercised by the therapist(s), for example as regards support, or criticism and control, or the provision of insight and understanding. Intervention by the therapist(s) is essential only when the group becomes blocked (though they will usually also share in the group interaction between these points), and the fact that the therapist(s) attention is greatly freed by the way much moment-to-moment therapeutic activity can be left to the group enables them to perceive the overall pattern of the group process more clearly, and to anticipate and deal with group resistance, or facilitate the transition to deeper levels when critical points are reached.

14 CO-THERAPY, TEAMWORK, TRAINING

No preaching seems to me more profitable than that which reveals a man to himself and replaces in his inner self, that is in his mind, what has been projected outside; and which convincingly places him, as in a portrait before his own eyes . . . Whoever has the duty of teaching, if he wishes to be perfectly equipped, can first learn in himself, and afterwards profitably teach to others, what the experience of his inner struggles has taught, which is much more abundant than we can express, according to the way the successes and failures which he has experienced have impressed themselves on his memory.

Guibert of Nogent, quoted in Colin Morris,
The Discovery of the Individual 1050–1200 A.D.

Knowledge is proportional to being. . . . You know in virtue of what you are.

Aldous Huxley, Time Must Have a Stop

The development of conjoint family therapy has been accompanied by a striking increase in the use of co-therapy, both by pairs of therapists and by teams. Sager (1) considers this change a very significant one and remarks that ". . . as recently as 1949 it was considered revolutionary for an experienced instructor to present one of his own psychoanalytic cases to students in a continuous case seminar. At that time, the process of psychoanalysis or analytic psychotherapy was taught only through the use of students' cases. The 'master's' work was revealed only in his own carefully edited summaries in the literature or through illustrative snatches in class, never through a presentation of the total process." He further suggests that "the fact that open communication of process takes place more frequently among those who do family therapy than among other psychotherapists may be related to the inquisitive, experimental bent of those who have pioneered in the field. It may also have to do with the fact that the family approach usually

273

means a break from the traditional isolation of the individual therapist" (p. 304).

It seems to me that this change in the therapist's functioning is an obvious parallel to that expected of those undergoing treatment, and an inevitable consequence of the change to thinking of families and other natural groups as open rather than closed systems. We have come to realize that growth takes place through challenge and response, through the intrusion into a system of information from its surroundings which disturbs its stability, demands the development of new capacities and coping skills, and so alters its repertoire of programs in a more flexible and adaptable direction. But this change in fundamental principle must affect the therapist, the therapeutic team and the helping profession generally as much as those they seek to help. If the family can change only through an increased permeability of its boundaries and the entry of new values and concepts from the wider world carried by the therapist, so personal and professional growth in the therapists themselves can continue only insofar as they are open to constant criticism and correction by their colleagues.

Our previous static, closed-system concepts led naturally to ideas of "training" which had to be "completed" and certified by a qualification when "enough" knowledge had been acquired. Self-examination was also necessary in the training period, but could be regarded as largely behind one when one had "completed a training analysis" or was even "fully analyzed." Thereafter, professionals often felt obliged to conceal their ignorance and hide their symptoms and problems (psychoanalysts most of all, in my experience) and though lip-service was paid to the need for continuing study, self-examination and growth, the prevailing concepts led automatically to an opposite attitude. The "do not disturb" notice outside the consulting room, in consequence, protected the therapist's boundary from penetration, and his theories and self-concepts from disturbing change, as much as it insulated the patient from impingement of unnecessary disturbance at a time of inner preoccupation.

The change to open-system concepts led just as naturally to awareness of the need for exposure, confrontation and challenge of the therapist by his colleagues and by the differing values within his wider supra-system, just as much as this was needed by those he sought to change.

Co-therapy has its rationale, therefore, in the changed views of human functioning and of therapy that conjoint family work has brought about. But there are also many other reasons for its popularity. It is in the family, once we leave the mother/child symbiosis, that we learn to share, to give and take, to perceive our place in a greater whole. For those who have not mastered these challenges, the witnessing of the interaction of co-therapists or therapeutic teams provides an immediate and living model, something that the conventional psychoanalytic or other dyadic treatment situations can never offer, however valuable they may be for remedying disturbances at more primitive, mother/child levels.

A pair of co-therapists of opposite sex can also provide more adequate gender role-models for spouses and children in families where these have been confused or conflicting, and the relationship between the co-therapists can demonstrate principles—even though these are expressed within the context of their professional cooperation—which also govern successful marital and sexual interaction. The mutual trust, and the combination of personal spontaneity with attentiveness and responsiveness to the partner, essential for really effective co-therapy, mirror closely the relationship necessary for the most satisfying sexual intercourse.

The value of co-therapy for certain types of intervention where one therapist allows himself to be "sucked in" to the family pathology, and to manifest the family disorder while the other stays detached as an "observing ego" and ensures that the total situation remains constructive, has already been mentioned. Where firmness, challenge and control need to be presented in a context of support and acceptance—a difficult task for a single therapist—a co-therapy team can offer both types of intervention simultaneously and can do so at levels of intensity impossible for one person to combine without danger. Or one therapist can give emphasis to intuition and emotional response, while the other makes more use of information available to intellect and logical thought. These roles may be exchanged, of course, even though each member of the therapeutic team may be more comfortable with one or other of them.

I personally experience a much greater freedom and can "let myself go" in revealing or reporting my reactions when working with someone else, because I have found that one's partner automatically compensates. Working alone is much more like walking a tightrope, for if one reacts too strongly it may be difficult later to redress the balance.

Though all this applies particularly to situations where therapists work with a family jointly and simultaneously, such experience tends to have profound effects even on more conventional forms of psychotherapy. Just as it is hard to see an individual alone, after working with families, without being aware of his effect upon his network and its influence on him and on the therapy, so the experience of co-therapy lessens one's possessiveness and personal investment in a patient even when one is seeing him alone. One speaks less of "my" patient, and remains more aware of colleagues seeing other members of the family separately, of the need to fit one's work to theirs, and to keep the therapeutic network in good repair. Though there is undoubtedly some loss of satisfaction through lessening of personal identification with the patient one is seeing separately, the rewards that follow from increased sharing and involvement in the therapeutic team or network more than compensate for this.

COMMUNICATION

It should be mentioned that many years' experience of co-therapy and combined work (multi-family, marital, stranger group, individual, etc.) has led my colleagues and myself to rather different conclusions about professional communication from those commonly held. The case conference is such a basic part of conventional child guidance practice that its value is not often questioned, at least where several colleagues are cooperating in the treatment of a family, and communication between colleagues is usually seen as unreservedly helpful and desirable except in the considerable time it demands.

Our own experience, however, has revised this view. Just as the receiving of "secrets" from one member of the family, seen separately, can inhibit one's freedom to respond to nonverbal material and other clues in later joint family sessions (for fear of breaking expectations of confidentiality), so can the receiving of similar information from a colleague working individually with a family member handicap one. This is particularly so where the approach I personally advocate—exposing oneself to the confusion of the family interaction without too much prior information—is being attempted, for then any information received about separate interviews may impair one's receptiveness even if problems of confidentiality do not arise. A case example may illustrate this.

In one family session, I was aware of somehow failing to respond adequately, without being able to understand why this was so. Six months later, when I played the tape recording of the session in the course of preparing an account of the family's treatment, the explanation was clear. Part of the discussion centered around the height of one of the daughters, which caused the mother some anxiety. (This daughter, the "good" and idealized one, was six feet tall.) As I heard the tape I remembered that the PSW, who was seeing the mother separately for individual sessions, had told me the day before this family interview that the mother had said she had married the father only because he was so tall—in fact, taller than the mother (six feet herself), who had experienced difficulty in getting boyfriends in adolescence because of her height.

I then recollected the point in the interview where I had hesitated to follow several leads because I could not bear to confront the father with this fact, which seemed certain to emerge. Without this prior information, I am sure I would have tried to follow and expand the "tallness" theme which arose in connection with the daughter in the interview, and had we honestly explored it, the mother's "secret" would probably have been disclosed and then made possible a deeper examination of the parental relationship, which was limited more by the mother's need to regard the father as inadequate than by any real fault on his part.

In the case just described the PSW concerned did not attend the family sessions, which I conducted without a co-therapist. More recently, we have come to see that the family interview should ideally be attended by all therapists working with the family, to ensure that the work is coordinated. Insofar as it is possible, this is also the time for the therapists to communicate with one another, for the family will help to correct misperceptions and bias on the part of the therapists, usually with quite amazing objectivity and fairness, if the therapists make it clear by their ability to disagree constructively and amicably with one another that disagreement and criticism are acceptable.

Such behavior by the therapists diminishes fantasies of their omnipotence, and so corresponding attitudes of dependency and passivity in the family; it therefore encourages family members to become active partners in the treatment task. Such "case conferences" held in front of the family can also provide for them a profoundly influential model, dissipating fears that disagreement and conflict will destroy relationships and enabling them to talk about themselves more objectively at home.

What has been said must be qualified in several ways. First, the suggestions about avoiding communication outside the joint sessions apply more to experienced therapists who are accustomed to working together; for beginners, or therapists learning to work together for the first time, communication outside the sessions should be full and frank, since it is serving the function of learning and of establishing their therapeutic relationship as well as of therapy. Secondly, communication in front of the family must be done with sensitivity to their developmental stage and ego-strength, particularly their readiness to relinquish magical expectations (which protect and support them in the early stages), and to cope with the therapists' limitations. The family should never be exposed to really serious conflict between the therapists which they (or the stronger of them) cannot control and handle; such problems should be brought to a supervisor, consultant or larger staff group for arbitration. In any case, the needs and safety of the family must come first, and the desire of the professionals to resolve their own personal or professional difficulties should be gratified only if it serves the primary aim of therapy.

Although care should be exercised in communication between the therapists outside the sessions, it is vitally important to keep the professional *relationships* in good repair. Personal contact and cooperation in other activities, in an atmosphere of mutual respect, help to achieve this, though the experience of co-therapy is itself pleasurable and involving and tends, over time, to develop attitudes of mutual trust and regard which are not easily attained in conventional work. To expose oneself and put oneself in the hands of another colleague can bring out the best in us, as the encounter movement has demonstrated. But to do this in mutual fashion multiplies the effect many times over.

PROBLEMS IN CO-THERAPY

A good deal has been written about the problems which may arise in co-therapy situations (2) and some authorities discourage it altogether. The latter seem either to have had too little experience of it to judge (considering the years of practice it requires to use it effectively) or are emphatically "conductors," individuals who need to take the center of the stage and do not find it easy to share.

Provided basic willingness and interest with regard to co-therapy are not lacking, the difficulties are most easily understood, in my view, in terms of the sequence of developmental levels already outlined for individuals and families. Therapists with strong oral-dependent needs may find cooperation difficult, and may be comfortable only when they are passive and inactive, leaving the partner to take the lead and make the decisions, or, alternatively (where they are paired with a less experienced or less dominant colleague), when they take over altogether and monopolize the therapeutic role. Co-therapists with strong anal traits tend to engage in struggles for control and dominance, and have an excessive need to hold to their theories and attitudes as if fearful of losing their personal or professional boundaries and sense of identity. Predominance of phallic levels of function results in competitiveness and tendencies to champion one sexual role at the expense of the other, so that co-therapists of opposite sex will often take sides with the same-sex family members and reproduce any marital conflict they encounter. Genital-level functioning, by contrast, can lead to highly effective and enjoyable co-therapy, with cooperative and mutually supportive but different and complementary modes of functioning in the therapeutic pair, especially if they are of opposite sex.

Of course, a developmental sequence may be anticipated if two professionals work together over a period. Especially when one is teaching the other, the less experienced member may be expected to pass through the natural stages of dependency, disagreement and finally constructive sharing in the therapeutic work. And a family which emphasizes a certain type of developmental conflict in its operation will tend to reactivate the residues of similar fixations and conflicts in the therapists, no matter how constructively they work together. Such reawakened conflicts can be a valuable source of information, provided they are recognized as related to the family dynamics; ideally, they should be discussed by the co-therapists in front of the family, examining the possibility that they are relevant to the subject of the interview.

Diana, aged twelve, had refused to attend school over a period of about 20 months, dating from the death of her mother's co-habitant just after she moved to the senior school. The father had deserted the family early in the child's life and when the co-habitant, who was almost permanently ill with multiple sclerosis, came on the scene the girl showed an ambivalent relationship to him. The (male) school inquiry officer had been visiting the home regularly, as well as another male social worker, but they seemed uncertain how to deal with the situation. There were three younger children, aged nine, seven and five, none of them showing any particular problem.

The mother and all four children were seen by myself, a female PSW co-therapist, and the male school inquiry officer. The notes of the joint interview state:

"The mother did most of the talking, at first describing the refusal of Diana to go to school, but by attracting our interest and attention she was, as the PSW pointed out, deflecting it away from Diana, who was absenting herself from the conversation and appeared sullen and blank rather than depressed. It was clear early in the interview that we were being affected by some family constellation, which first became obvious when the PSW and I held quite long separate conversations, she with Diana and I with the school inquiry officer.

Diana opened up and spoke quite freely with my female colleague, but when I later inquired, as I thought sympathetically, into the girl's experience over the year she had spent away from school, she said that she was bored, denied that she was depressed or anxious, and said provocatively that she was not going to school because she just didn't like it. This angry outburst was clearly directed at me, and, following the principles established by that time in our treatment of school phobics, I tried to establish quite clearly that she would have to return to school, whether day or boarding, no matter what mitigating factors there might be.

My PSW colleague clearly felt that I was taking a one-sided view and presented the other side of the situation like an advocate, emphasizing Diana's support of her mother and her underlying depression and anxiety. The most relevant part of the interview consisted of a discussion of the way in which the professionals had become polarized, and this led to a realization that Diana completely rejected and attacked the males, but could open up and confide in the females. It was then revealed that the same thing had happened as regards the school inquiry officer and social worker (both male), who had taken a similar position to myself in the past, and who had found themselves in conflict with a female social worker who had also become involved. I was aware that it was impossible for me to have any useful function as regards the supportive and insight-facilitating side of the work, and that this would have to come from my colleague or some other woman.

After the family had gone, we continued to discuss the situation and realized that we were responding to various sexual problems in the family, whereby Diana had to protect herself against incestuous fears by rejecting, provoking and castrating males, and also needed in some fashion to get the parental figures of opposite sex to quarrel so that they could not "get together."

My PSW colleague was at this time a strong advocate of "women's lib," and though the interview was highly beneficial as regards both the girl's symptoms and her school attendance (she was reported to have been more lively and to have more friends, and also had returned to her previous school where she appeared to be happy), my colleague, who continued to see the girl and mother, and I both found a continuing tension in our relationship over this and similar cases. After a period this was resolved through our perceiving the dynamics while working together on another case, realizing that the form of our interaction was similar to that described by Eric Berne (3) as "Uproar," where father and daughter argue with each other as a defense against sexual attraction.

I was unable to remember the name, or find the notes, of another family which was interesting from a similar point of view.

In this case, three therapists were involved, two females and myself. At a family interview at which all three of us were present, together with both parents and the children, the children at one point were enacting scenes of violent jealousy with the play material on the floor, the parents were talking about the jealousy which preoccupied their relationship, while the rivalry which infected the therapeutic trio was only too evident.

Another example occurred in a group of married couples in which my wife and I worked together as co-therapists.

A couple who showed a particularly profound overprotective/destructive relationship, based on the experience in both spouses of extreme ambivalence at the hands of essentially psychotic mothers, was placed for therapy in the married couples' group. Here their endless ambivalent bickering and mutual provocation seemed unresponsive to any intervention, though the other couples, who all showed less severe mutually destructive relationships (we called it our "Who's Afraid of Virginia Woolf" group), were improving. At one session another couple, who had made good progress and were planning to leave, complained that they had returned home after the previous group session to find themselves "having this couple's fight," and said that this couple "should have their own fights instead of getting others to do their dirty work for them." Like the rest of the group, my wife and I were amused by this event, but during a meal together after we got home, usually a pleasant relaxation at the end of the day, found ourselves also having a blazing, unexpected fight. I accused her of not appreciating me, while she countered that if I really appreciated her she would have an automatic dishwashing machine. We slept back to back at opposite sides of the bed, but as soon as I woke up I realized that we had ourselves "had the fight" for this couple. It at once became obvious that the conflict was based on our both taking positions of jealous siblings, placing the partner simultaneously in the position of a parent from whom approval was desired, and also of a sibling competing for that approval.

The group was amused when we reported these events to them, but the understanding gained from our internalizing and working out this conflict within the group based on their relationship-models enabled them to understand the basis of their arguments also. The incessant quarreling of this couple at this point yielded to continued therapy, while our automatic dishwasher was delivered two weeks later!

Family pathology is often reproduced in the operation of larger professional groupings, causing conflicts between staff subgroups, as Brody and Hayden (4), Main (5), Kafka and McDonald (6) and others, as well as myself (7), have emphasized. Two or more separate organizations or agencies involved with a family may find themselves critical of each other, thereby acting out a marital conflict for the parents. The social service department may, for example, find itself playing the part of an overprotective mother, shielding the children from the school, which is cast in the role of an insensitive and punitive father.

Wherever two therapists work together in treating a group or family, they must expect to be cast into paternal and maternal roles. This is the case whether the therapists are of opposite or of the same sex, though in the latter case one therapist will necessarily be treated as if of the opposite gender. Much co-therapy with same-sex therapists runs into difficulties because this is not understood, and both men struggle to avoid being cast as the mother, or both women as the father. Once these transferences are recognized, no serious problems need arise. However, if problems do arise, discussion of them in the family session is often highly illuminating. It should not be thought that the more senior or active therapist will necessarily be cast as the father, for in many families the mother performs the executive, controlling functions while the father is seen as the weaker but more affectionate, nurturing figure.

Behind the allocation of parental roles to co-therapists lies all the related fantasies about parents, particularly the assumption that sexual intercourse occurs between them when they are alone. Co-therapists will often feel unaccountably uncomfortable when such fantasies are active if they are not aware of this issue, especially when they are of the same sex. Once the presence of these sexual fantasies is taken for granted, and the signs that they are active watched for, the discomfort disappears and their presence becomes a further source of valuable information.

In stranger groups fantasies about the co-therapists' sexual relationship will appear in the form of curiosity about what the co-therapists do after the group finishes, and if the group is run on analytic principles it may be helpful to interpret such fantasies directly. Material of this kind may be dealt with similarly in family therapy, but if transference to the therapists is not being encouraged it may be better to recognize the significance without making it explicit, treating it more as an avoidance of discussion of sexuality within the family. The therapists' task may then be to *model* more open sexual communication, by the way they speak to each other and to family members.

In the course of joint work of this kind, especially where it is intensive and prolonged, the co-therapists inevitably find themselves facing the question of what is the normal—or the most effective—relationship between man and woman, husband and wife, father and mother. There is little help available in the literature, since this problem is not only unexplored but seems actively avoided in most writings. The contribution I have found most helpful—as well as deeply moving and beautiful—is a description by Sonne and Lincoln (8) of their work together in prolonged and intensive conjoint therapy of a family with a schizophrenic member. They concluded that the earlier stages of family therapy need to concentrate on strengthening the father, helping him to assume the responsibility and executive dominance he has hitherto avoided. During this period, the female co-therapist needs to take a secondary place and to support the activity and assertiveness of her male colleague. But later, when more order and a sense of safety is restored in this way to the situation, the mother's role becomes the principal focus, and then the female therapist takes the central therapeutic part with the male companion in support—very much as the husband supports, protects and gives precedence to his wife when she is pregnant and after the birth of her baby. This paper should be read and re-read with an open mind by everyone involved in co-therapy.

SUPERVISION

Clearly, there are dangers and difficulties in the constructive working-out of such co-therapy relationships which require that some form of help be available when required. This can be provided in several ways. Most straightforward is ongoing supervision by a more experienced colleague, either of the pair of co-therapists seen together, or of the pair with other professionals similarly involved in joint work in a supervisory group. In the earlier stages of training, this is probably the best solution, but for more experienced people different solutions may be preferable. The Department of Children and Parents at the Tavistock Clinic has developed an interesting function in their team chairman role. This is a member of staff, not engaged in treating a particular family, whose function it is to chair and moderate the conferences of the various therapists who are involved, providing a neutral figure who is more capable of remaining objective, and who is also outside the hierarchical, authoritative relationship usually associated with a supervisory role. Indeed, the roles may reverse, and the team chairman for one therapeutic team may be chaired, in the conference to discuss his own co-therapy, by one of that team.

Several institutions in the United States (see Friedman *et al.* [9], MacGregor *et al.* [10]) have given the main responsibility for co-therapy supervision to the whole unit team meeting as a group. This arrangement is in line with systems-theory concepts since particular co-therapy pairs are thereby subject to the control of the whole unit of which they form part. Such team supervision is less likely to be limited by the prevailing theoretical models, or by personal idiosyncrasies, than conventional supervision by one senior person. A process of growth and development flourishes more readily in the group situation, in theoretical as well as in emotional ways; however, in my experience the group process needs nevertheless to be facilitated by a skilled chairman whose leadership is in the service of group function and who also submits, like others, to the authority of the group.

This potential of larger group situations (given good chairmanship) to contain and resolve conflicts in their subgroups can have good effects in meetings between units or teams. For several years the units with which I was associated at the Woodberry Down Child Guidance Unit and the Queen Elizabeth Hospital for Children held yearly day-long conferences with colleagues from the Department of Children and Parents at the Tavistock Clinic and some other units with common interests. It was always astonishing to see the way in which the conflicts and tensions within my own units, or in others, were able to be more openly and constructively expressed in the safer context of the conferences, usually with persisting benefits and continuing separate discussion after the conference had ended.

At the Institute of Group-Analysis, staff conflicts tend to receive expression each year at the large group experience of the General Course in Group Work, in a context where the staff members are meeting together with over 100 students, most of whom are experienced in their own different fields (11). The larger group provides a container, a moderating or reconciling influence, within which these tensions can be recognized and coped with. Also, the students inevitably form a sensitive indicator of staff disagreements, just as children in a family are bound to suffer from, to express, and to desire the resolution of parental tensions. In such circumstances students tend to locate and express the staff's tensions with remarkable accuracy, delicacy and therapeutic skill, if the staff can suffer them to do so without blocking the process in a defensive way.

Similarly, much of the monitoring of co-therapy is provided by the families under treatment if the professionals can listen to what the family is saying about them "between the lines" and can allow themselves to be helped. Often staff members (especially the less experienced or less secure) feel some guilt at receiving help and understanding from their patients, but such reversals of the usual roles can have profoundly beneficial effects on the quality of the relationships, the willingness of family members to accept their own dependency needs, and the intensity and integrity of the therapeutic process as a whole.

CONFLICTS SPECIFIC TO MENTAL HEALTH PROFESSIONALS

Apart from the common developmental problems that professionals in the helping professions share with others, they also tend, as I have already suggested in Chapter 9, to show rather special difficulties in integrating harmoniously their more infantile and childish aspects with their more adult and responsible selves. Instead, these are kept split and separated, the childish aspects being projected into patients or clients, who are then looked after by the more adult aspect of the professional's personality. Over 15 years' experience with training and therapy groups containing almost every type of professional, including psychoanalysts and group analysts, has repeatedly confirmed this pattern on which I have reported in several papers (12).

This point is of particular importance in conjoint family therapy. Work with families confronts the professional with this split and demands that he overcome it if he is to master the technique as well as to offer much help in doing so. This is because conjoint family therapy, especially if carried out in the manner I have called here "group-analytic," *requires that the therapist identify simultaneously with all the family members,* and carry them in his mind in their relationship to each other. To do this the infantile and adult aspects of the therapist must necessarily be utilized at the same time and brought into contact. It is precisely this simultaneous activation of and interaction among different elements of the therapist's psyche that constitutes the main difficulty for one beginning the technique. If this dynamic interaction is coped with it leads, inevitably, to a more integrated personality in the professional, as well as more successful family therapy.

The problem of training is thus of special importance in the developing field of family therapy. The acquisition of theory presents no special difficulty, for the lack of a coherent, agreed-upon conceptual scheme is a feature common to most other forms of psychotherapy and ideas can be conveyed by reading selected books and papers, by lectures, discussions and theoretical seminars (13).

The practical side of teaching needs, however, to be differently organized if attitudes and techniques appropriate to conjoint work rather than to conventional psychotherapy are to be encouraged. The passive, neutral, non-judgmental, uninvolved position developed with so much care and effort in conventional individual and group therapy has to be avoided and, if already present, overcome. Though the family therapist must be open, flexible and receptive, he must also be able to involve and commit himself without losing his balance and independence. He must be capable of taking on and relinquishing just as easily the maternal functions of acceptance, nurturance and support, as well as the paternal functions of authoritative demand, challenge and control. Further, he must identify with the needs of the children of different ages and step outside the family altogether and see them through the eyes of neighbors, teachers or policemen. This cannot be achieved by emotional distance, by avoiding involvement; instead, he must learn how to move swiftly in and out of emotional involvement, to change rapidly from one identification to another and to maintain several identifications together simultaneously even when they conflict.

Fortunately, the demands that family therapy makes on its practitioners have brought about many new techniques ideal for such training. Conjoint therapy is by its nature essentially public so that one-way screens, closed circuit television and videotape recordings can be used to enable pupils to learn from more experienced practitioners. Videotapes can be edited to break down and demonstrate nonverbal sequences too complex for students to perceive without clarification and often not fully conscious to the therapist, even when he is dealing with them effectively. The videotapes edited by Braulio Montalvo (each took, he told me, about 80 hours to edit) are masterpieces of this art (14).

Again, because of the public nature of family therapy, supervision need not be a separate activity from treatment, relying on the student's memory or notes. Just as the student can watch the supervisor at work, the supervisor can watch the student working with the family through the one-way screen and enter periodically to join the group and provide active supervision. In a similar way, co-therapy can be used as a vital teaching tool, whereby the student can begin in the role of a relatively passive observer, gradually taking a more active part as confidence and understanding are gained.

These teaching methods all provide the student with more direct practical aid in developing effective techniques than is usually available in training for individual work, and by their very nature they oblige him to confront and work through many relevant unresolved problems in his family of origin. One cannot facilitate the release of death wishes towards the mother of a family by the children without facing at the same time one's ambivalence towards one's own mother. Similarly, one cannot take control of a family and challenge the father over his passivity and withdrawal without feeling all the anxieties one would have experienced at criticizing one's own father and fearing to find him impotent. To discuss the parent's sexual relationship in front of the children will revive all one's guilt over early primal scene fantasies and incestuous wishes, and to work with a co-therapist, or as part of a team, will bring one up against unresolved sibling rivalries or desires to be "special" and "the only one." Because of this, I believe one cannot continue to engage in conjoint therapy, and strive to improve one's skill, without some growth also taking place in one's general maturity in relationship to oneself and others. Certainly one notices very remarkable changes in people who take up the work.

How much does this experience require supplementation by a personal therapeutic experience, and how is this best achieved? There is no doubt that understanding and acceptance of one's own inner world are even more important in conjoint therapy than in the practice of individual therapy, but a personal individual analysis does not seem the best approach to this; in some cases it appears even to diminish the wide vision, flexibility and spontaneity that family work demands. The group approach seems preferable, either through a personal group analysis or, if this is not possible, in sensitivity groups organized as part of a training program. Even so, the group-analytic techniques normally employed for training therapists to work with stranger groups do not provide quite the right model, based as they are on the encouragement of regressive transference fantasy in relation to a relatively passive therapist. A model is needed which does more to keep transference projections between the members and away from the leader, in which too much regression is discouraged and in which the leader is more active, challenging and involved.

The new Course in Family and Marital Group Work at the Institute of Group-Analysis is at present struggling with this problem, attempting to combine the power of the group-analytic technique, where unconscious group themes and transferences are interpreted, with some of the newer, active approaches from the United States. In "simulated families" —to which the Tavistock Department of Children and Parents introduced us, and a member of which (Ms. Rosemary Whiffen), with experience at the Nathan Ackerman Family Institute in New York, advises us as one of the leaders of the course—a number of professionals are assigned family roles and, after going outside to agree on a "family problem," are treated for it by others playing the role of therapist. The way in which such sessions develop a validity and life of their own is quite astonishing (perhaps suggesting that we have all the necessary "roles" available dormant within us). Their value lies in the way in which each individual can take different family and therapist roles in different sessions as well as in the feedback the therapist gets about his interventions, which a real family could not give him even if they were willing to do so.

In "family sculpting" (15) an incident is taken from a person's family experience, and after he has assigned poses to the others playing the various roles in order to depict the scene he wishes to present, they begin to report on their own responses and reactions to each other. Not only does the main participant learn a great deal more about his own family situation, both by facing his own attitudes more clearly and by being obliged to put himself in everyone else's shoes, but also the "freezing" of the situation in the form of static poses, and the subsequent intellectual examination of its meaning, "cool" the problem depicted in a way that makes it possible for highly disturbing feelings or relationships to be examined without fear of loss of emotional control. Others involved, and also those observing (who add information by reporting their reactions) usually feel a deep relevance to their own family situations and may benefit as much as the main participant even though their involvement is vicarious. All these points make family sculpting very suitable for training situations as well as for family therapy.

Both these techniques—simulated families and family sculpting—utilize action methods drawn from psychodrama or encounter methods to help individuals to externalize, understand and come to terms with their internalized families of origin. Such methods are used in the small groups of the Family and Marital Group Work Course, alternating with discussion of the students' cases or examination of the group dynamics, to help students to move easily to and fro between active intervention and encouragement of transference fantasy, between interpretation and modeling techniques, between the inner and the outer worlds. So far the results seem favorable, though there is constant re-examination and experiment at this early stage.

Another technique used in the United States, particularly by Murray Bowen (16) and Norman Paul (17), is that of giving students the task of investigating their own families of origin. Memories or impressions of family events are checked against detailed histories obtained from relatives, and the findings reported back in supervisory sessions. Bowen believes that real maturation can take place only by trying to "differentiate a self" while remaining in contact with one's own family; a beautiful account of such an attempt, by an anonymous author using Bowen's concepts, has been published (18).

We find that discussion by students in the small groups of their families of origin is undoubtedly valuable, and usually arises spontaneously from the simulated family and family sculpting work, but we have not yet embraced the concept that students should *treat* their own families as part of their training. At present we are inclined to regard the latter, in the absence of a request from the student's family for help, as a manifestation of a "rescue fantasy" which must be outgrown as part of the training process.

Morse (19) has outlined the ways in which a desire to change the parents serves as a resistance to personal change in psychotherapy. I have usually found it to be due, at root, to the desire to have the benefits of personal growth without the acceptance of separation and aloneness that true adulthood and autonomy inevitably entail.

More promising methods for helping the professional to get in touch with his internalized family, in order to relate to it from a more adult, detached position, to resolve "frozen" attachments and attitudes, and thereby to make his own family experience available as a reservoir of knowledge available in the service of professional work, have recently been developed. They aroused considerable interest when they were demonstrated recently during a visit of representatives of the Nathan Ackerman Family Institute to London (20).

The first is a combination of some of the role-play techniques already mentioned. In the course of acting as therapist to a simulated family, the professional tries to note the point at which he blocks. Instead of struggling on and changing to another approach to the problem, the therapist associates to some event in his family history and the group of professionals now cease the simulated family exercise and help him to sculpt this original family situation.

This exercise has an astonishing tendency to locate traumatic events or unresolved family conflicts central to the typical countertransference difficulties of the person playing the therapist role, though others involved often benefit remarkably also. One young woman, for example, felt confused and incapable of dealing with a simulated family when the "father" began to walk out. Sculpting the period of her life that she associated to the block revealed a family constellation in which an absent father was crucial, connected with a disturbance in her relationship with her mother. In the course of the exercise the professional playing the mother, previously immobilized on the periphery of the scene, was asked to enact a solution. She rushed to the girl and embraced her, when both burst into tears, like a mother and daughter reunited after a long and painful absence. Following this the woman was able, during a "replay" of the simulated family, to deal confidently and successfully with the "father's" attempt to leave the interview.

The second technique is really an encounter method with a family relationships emphasis, called a "family systems exercise." The group of professionals is asked to circulate about the room, each choosing another person who either resembles someone in his own family of origin or whom he would have liked to have to fill a missing role in it. After exploring the reasons for their choices each pair then links up with another pair, and the four then negotiate roles to form a "family" of some sort. The profoundness of the unconscious perceptions which guide these choices, as they emerge in the course of subsequent discussion, is at first almost unbelievable and the exercise is an ideal way of helping professionals to become aware of the mutual projective systems by which marital partners are chosen and family collusions are perpetuated. The "families" thus formed are also particularly suited to simulation exercises.

Another method, developed by my colleagues and me in the Family and Marital Group Work Course at the Institute of Group-Analysis, is "guided group regression." The leader gives the group the task of discussing the experience typical of a particular age or stage of development, and in this controlled situation, where the group as a whole is participating and everyone is "letting their hair down" together, the participants begin to discover the universality of childhood experience.

All these techniques which aim to connect the professional with his own family experience, in group situations where revelation is simultaneous and mutual, perhaps have their most valuable effect through the way in which they replace the idea of separate, shameful family pathologies with the experience of common, shared patterns which are dealt with in different ways in different families.

One skill which is almost completely neglected in medical, psychiatric and social work training is that of interviewing when sexual topics are the main focus. Professionals have been subject to all the taboos and inhibitions from which the general population suffers, and, though younger entrants who have passed more of their formative years since society has become more permissive regarding sexual matters are notably more relaxed about such matters, specific training is surely needed in this as in all other techniques. This training is even more essential for older professionals. In the past, professionals usually received no systematic help but were left to shift for themselves, so that they were often more uncomfortable and evasive than the patients who were seeking advice. The frequent complaint by patients that their doctors are unable to help them with sexual problems is probably due more to this evasiveness than to any other cause, for often all that is needed for the resolution of sexual problems is to make possible a really explicit discussion.

Recently, specific programs have been developed to cope with this difficulty. The medical faculty of the University of Minneapolis, for example, now runs periodic four-day courses (21) using visual aids, including, at one point, films of every imaginable kind of sexual activity projected simultaneously onto three screens. This desensitization by flooding is followed by other material depicting sexuality in the context of tenderness, responsibility and love, and the audio-visual material is accompanied throughout by discussion in large and small groups where reactions can be shared and professional experience exchanged. The fact that the courses were not offered until the full confidence and support of the other medical teaching staff, the university, and local civic and religious leaders had been obtained is no doubt an important factor in the program's success.

Similar training now exists in Britain (22) and various other helpful visual aids are available, as for example a delightful film (23) where two professionals alternately role-play patient and doctor discussing sexual problems, combining the modeling effect of very explicit yet relaxed discussion with the tension-releasing effect of moments of great humor.

Apart from such aids, seminars in which the leader sets an example of frank and detailed discussion of the sexual aspect of cases, and exerts pressure for similar openness and naturalness in the other members, within a professional rather than a personal context, can do much to liberate participants from the residue of inhibitions derived from their childhood training.

15 RESULTS, FREQUENCY OF MEETINGS

The fairy tales of Science, and the long result of Time.

Alfred, Lord Tennyson, Locksley Hall

. . . there are other modes of knowing that are not strange and mysterious but do require taking seriously: forms of perception which do not fall within the experimental model . . . This form of knowing, which I would want to call existential knowing, depends upon certain conditions. It depends upon the presence over a period of time of people capable of drawing perspectives from one situation and applying them as projective models to another . . . They require that both the projective models and the situations themselves be treated as open-ended in the sense that they are susceptible of being changed, exploded or abandoned in the face of what we find. It follows from this that expertise and professionalism, as we have known them—that is to say, with closed theories—are no longer of very great use . . . It requires that we be willing to use ourselves as informational instruments, to be attentive to our own feelings as sources of data, as good as and in many instances better than any source of data presented to us by the situation that we're in.

Donald Schon, Beyond the Stable State,
Reith Lectures 1970.

Family therapists, like most clinicians, have shown little interest in the scientific validation of their results, and while their work has been relatively public and open to examination, and though most practitioners would probably have welcomed outcome research by independent, unbiased assessors, the opportunities have not been taken up. In a comprehensive review of reported results, Wells *et al.* (1) found 18 which met their minimum criteria of (a) reporting on at least three cases and (b) clearly specifying the outcome result. Of these, only two were methodologically satisfactory, the others failing mainly through their lack of a control group.

The two studies considered satisfactory, by Langsley *et al.* (2), both reported on the same research project at the Colorado Psychiatric Hospital, Denver, where 150 patients whose families had requested their hospitalization were randomly assigned to short-term, crisis-oriented, outpatient family therapy and compared with a matched control group admitted for conventional inpatient care. Time lost from normal functioning in the experimental group was less than a quarter that of the controls, and the total hospitalization rate for the experimental group over the six months' follow-up was less than half the *re*hospitalization rate of the controls. Attempts to assess improvement in social and emotional functioning showed no significant difference between the two groups over the six-month period. The cost of the conjoint family approach was less than one-sixth that of the conventional methods.

These striking results demonstrated that crisis-oriented family treatment could be as effective as conventional measures, such as individual and group therapy, milieu influence and removal from life-stresses to a protected environment, at considerably less cost in time and money. However, it did not measure the effect of conjoint family therapy against the changes that might occur with no treatment at all.

Most other studies lacked a control group altogether and results can only be assessed, therefore, by comparing them with what is known about the likelihood of improvement without any formal treatment. Averaging the results of the various non-controlled studies, the improvement rates of 69 percent for adults and 79 percent for children are very close to the familiar spontaneous improvement rates, so often quoted in critiques of psychotherapy, of about two-thirds for adults and about three-quarters for children. Gurman's (3) recent review of reported outcomes in marital therapy produced a similar average improvement figure across a range of techniques and orientations.

What is not taken sufficiently into account, however, is the duration of such conjoint family treatment. For though some conjoint techniques compare in the number of interviews and length of therapy with conventional individual or group psychotherapy based on psychoanalytic concepts—Friedman *et al.* (4) describe seeing families at least weekly for a year or more and Bowen (5) speaks of four years as the order of time needed to achieve the degree of differentiation he aims at—many family therapists have emphasized the rapidity of change and consequent small number of interviews needed. In the Colorado study quoted above, for example, therapy for the experimental group averaged six family sessions extending over about three weeks, while the treatment offered by the Galveston "multiple impact" group (6), which claimed improvement in 86 percent of cases, was completed in two consecutive days of intensive family therapy. Change which follows hard on the heels of such brief contact must obviously be evaluated against a quite different baseline from the two-thirds figure for spontaneous improvement reported over two-year studies, relevant though the latter may be to psychoanalytic individual and group therapy which expects at best to bring about gradual but deep personality change over that period.

Gurman emphasizes this point in his review of outcome reports of marital therapy, where the average number of interviews—when this was specified at all—was under 18, or four-and-a-half months of weekly meetings. Gurman calculates the expected rate of spontaneous recovery over this period, using Eysenck's (7) formula, as only 16 percent. According to this formula, the expectation rates for spontaneous recovery are as given in Table 15.1.

TABLE 15.1
Predicted Percentage of Spontaneous Recoveries Using
Eysenck's Formula (Extrapolated)

Weeks elapsed	2	4	8	13	26	52	104
Expected spontaneous recovery	2%	4%	8%	12%	23%	41%	65%

In the absence of control groups and other information necessary for a statistical, objective judgment, the reader must be left to examine the original material and come to his own conclusions (full references are available in the papers by Wells *et al.* and Gurman already mentioned). No doubt one factor hindering clinicians in carrying out the more valid, painstaking research needed is the dramatic rapidity of change which sometimes occurs in conjoint work, which is clear from the anecdotal material. Because it is so obvious to anyone engaged in this work that something of an entirely different order is happening, practitioners are understandably more interested in gaining enough understanding of *what* this difference is, in order to facilitate it more predictably, than in trying to convince others that it is happening at all.

My own techniques, which seem to aim at even more limited expenditure of professional time than any others I have seen reported, have also not been subjected to rigorous examination (though a study to be described, by M. Crowe, is remedying this deficiency at least in its application to conjoint marital therapy). Nevertheless, some information about what we think is happening—even though it is mere counting of clinical judgments—may be of interest. The late Miss Patricia Brierley made a retrospective study of all cases seen during the year 1969 in the psychiatric department of the Queen Elizabeth Hospital for Children, which was at that time routinely using conjoint family interviews for all diagnostic work and as far as possible for treatment also, seeking to clarify a number of issues. As part of this work she produced figures for outcome on the 133 cases seen that year by my own team, which are given in Table 15.2.

TABLE 15.2

Outcome in All Cases Seen for Family Interviews by Authors' Team at Queen Elizabeth Hospital for Children During 1969

No. of Family Interviews	No. of Cases Seen	A	B	C
1	69	30	13	26
2	38	12	11	15
3	17	13	2	2
4	4	3	1	0
5	5	3	1	1
Total	133	61	28	44

Above results expressed as percentage of total cases (to the nearest whole figure), for 1–2 and for 3–5 interviews.

Interviews	Cases Seen	A	B	C
1 or 2	81%	32%	18%	31%
3, 4 or 5	19%	14%	3%	2%
Total	100%	46%	21%	33%

A = Cases where change followed rapidly on the family session, and in the manner predicted.

B = Cases where family sessions did not appear to have the intended effect, but where information led to other forms of help, such as individual psychotherapy, special education placement, reception into care, which produced or at follow-up seemed likely to produce desirable change.

C = Cases where no change in the patient's problem occurred despite our efforts (though the information derived from the interviews was usually helpful to referrers).

Her results are based on a study of the case notes, supplemented where possible by evaluations from the school, from other professionals still involved, or from the case notes of the referring pediatrician (the latter notes were often a valuable source of information as many cases continued to be followed up by other hospital departments after they had been closed by our own). We normally followed up our cases to the point where adequate improvement was noted, or where it was judged not to have occurred and where further investment of time was thought to be wasteful or uneconomic, but there was no other special attempt to follow up the cases concerned and the duration of follow-up was variable and not related to the purpose of the study. Furthermore, drugs were used where considered helpful as part of the psychiatric treatment plan; in about a quarter of the cases, Librium (chlordiazepoxide) was prescribed, and occasionally antidepressants. Also, though conjoint family therapy was used as the only treatment with the majority of cases, this was sometimes combined with occasional individual interviews or groups for children or mothers. Although it has not been possible for me to clarify these details because of Miss Brierley's tragic death in a car accident in 1973, the main interest of the figures lies in the striking result of many families seen only once or twice, which almost certainly received no other significant treatment. A more thorough follow-up of two to three years was, however, carried out through the schools on cases of school phobia seen during that year, and this is reported in Chapter 16.

As will be seen, no families were seen together more than five times. Column A, which refers to those cases where change followed rapidly on the family session and in the manner predicted, shows that 46 percent improved sufficiently to satisfy the family (which meant complete or at least very substantial improvement in the symptoms originally complained of) within five interviews and 32 percent of these were satisfactorily improved within two sessions.

Column B refers to cases where the conjoint family interview did not appear to have the effect intended, but where the information obtained led to the provision of other forms of help—individual psychotherapy, special education placement, reception into foster care, etc.—which either produced desirable change or was judged likely to produce it on the basis of the information available at the time of follow-up.

Column C lists the families in which no apparent change occurred, despite our efforts. However, this is not quite a "failure" category since most of the 31 percent seen for one or two interviews were actively screened out within that time as unlikely to benefit from further intervention. In many of these, the motivation for treatment lay in the referrers rather than in the family themselves. In almost one in three of these families (about 10 percent of the total) one of the parents proved to be either a borderline personality or suffering from a recurrent psychosis currently in remission, and functioning as well as could be expected in the community. The referring professional had enough psychiatric experience to recognize the presence of mental disorder, but not sufficient to know when to leave well enough alone. Because we did not attempt therapeutic intervention in these cases to bring about change, they had to be listed under no change, but we ensured that the referring professionals understood the situation, that they or some other agency were able to provide ongoing and indefinite support (if not, we offered this ourselves) and that the family and the referrers understood that we would offer another appointment at any time if the situation worsened and medication, hospitalization or other assistance were needed.

In the case of some other families in this category, it had obviously been judged desirable by the referrers, usually from another social class with different values, that the families should change their ways, even though they were apparently happy with their mode of functioning and no different from their neighbors. The enjoyment of sexual intercourse or physical aggressiveness by adolescents, both normal enough in working-class families, was often the target of middle-class professional disapproval.

A third group in this "screened-out," no-change category were those families where the parents demanded change in their children's behavior but were not prepared to pay for this by sacrificing some of their own selfish attitudes. Family interviews were particularly valuable in demonstrating early on that the parents were making impossible demands and that a viable therapeutic contract or alliance was not attainable. In such cases, we made it clear that the parents were demanding the impossible and that we could not provide it, but we tried to leave matters open so that they could reapply later.

A few of this early no-change group sought appointments with a misunderstanding of our function—one immigrant was seeking legal advice over a housing problem, for example, and was helped to obtain this. It will be clear that these no-change interviews were in most cases normally useful to the referrers, through the reports and advice they received, and often eventually of value to the families themselves.

The accuracy of the assessment in these first or second interviews, where 31 percent of cases were screened out, may be judged by the fact that those that continued were very likely indeed to achieve a positive result through further conjoint therapy (14 percent). The undisputed failures (2 percent), who continued for three, four and five conjoint sessions without improvement, are a particularly interesting group, though rather small to generalize about. Such cases, both those in Miss Brierley's study and those seen in other years, foundered at the point where the children's problems became clearly linked with marital difficulties, and where the parents were unwilling to contemplate closer examination of this area. Usually this came as a surprise to us, following upon apparently productive and positive earlier sessions where the focus was more on the children. The following example is rather typical:

Jeremy, a boy of six when first referred, had been admitted to the hospital several times with severe asthmatic attacks. As on previous occasions, he recovered rapidly away from his mother. The whole family appeared to have difficulty in dealing with certain types of feeling and suffered psychosomatic symptoms instead when these could not be expressed. All members were hot-tempered and self-willed, and suffered no symptoms when aggression could be released. The mother had suffered from migraines and abdominal pains until she changed, some years earlier, and began to express her annoyance more freely no matter how much she upset the others. The father coped with his frustration by smoking, had developed asthma when he had tried to give up this comfort and lost the symptom when he began smoking again. The other children showed rather similar problems over the management of frustration and aggression.

In the family interviews, the basic problem which ultimately emerged was the failure of the parents to achieve an adequate sexual adjustment. The relationship was summed up by the typical pattern of mother upstairs in bed reading a book, father downstairs looking at television. Mother found this situation more unsatisfactory than he did, and sought excitement and masculine company by going out to bingo rather frequently. The father repeatedly opted out of sessions when his inadequacy as a man and his own intense desire for nurturance became the crucial issue, and so no fundamental progress was made. Treatment was terminated by agreement, the parents deciding they did not want to risk the consequences of facing up to any fundamental problems in the marriage.

Solomon (8) has reached very similar conclusions about five families who similarly terminated when the marital relationship came under scrutiny, and suggests that these families may be wiser than the therapist about what is best for them. My own experience supports this view, for although the marital relationships in these cases might appear limited and even dismal to those more fortunate, they were usually the best relationships the couples had encountered in their largely deprived and miserable lives. However, re-reading Solomon's paper in preparing this chapter, I am struck in his examples by a feature which was present in my own cases though I did not see its significance at the time. Solomon's couples and our own all displayed evidence of intense affective needs at an oral level, consequent on early deprivation, which were adequately "bound" and met in a tolerable way by the marriage as long as the needs were partially denied and held in check by maintaining emotional distance. Successful therapy leads in the early stages to increased recognition of the needs and so to greater overt demands on the partner or the children. When the uncovered demands are disappointed, there is a retreat into further defensive withdrawal, together with splitting and projection which often includes paranoid attitudes towards the therapists. It may well be that such parents need fairly intense individual support to meet the hidden demands as they appear, in order to remedy the deprivation and protect the equally needy partner from a relationship with which he/she cannot cope. This possibility has not yet been put to clinical test.

FREQUENCY OF MEETINGS

Scheduling of interviews may also be important here in view of my tendency to favor a longer interval between conjoint family sessions than most workers, in fact, three weeks. The use of this interval developed from my having first used conjoint family sessions, at a time of staff shortage in 1962, for diagnosis and thereafter for family meetings every two months. Though first utilized for diagnostic, supportive and supervisory purposes only, I was surprised to find startling changes occurring even at this frequency of meeting, and set out to find the most satisfactory interval. The consensus reached by most families was that an interval of three weeks between sessions was preferable, since with a lesser gap they did not have time to digest and apply the consequences of each meeting, while with much longer intervals the continuity was broken. However, a spacing of a month between interviews is also suitable, as well as more convenient administratively, and, as will be evident from the case illustrations, I sometimes use a spacing of two or three months or even longer. Long intervals are sometimes effective with these families who tend to wait until the next session before making any effort themselves, in the hope that the therapist will produce some new answer and solve the problem for them. Sometimes, indeed, I have felt it necessary to tell the family that I would not be offering a second appointment at all, explaining that I have already said everything that could be said, when I have felt that only in this way would they really accept responsibility for tackling their own problems. One can always follow such cases up by writing to the family six months later, asking how they have been getting on. Malan has demonstrated (9) that somehow getting the patient to take responsibility for seeking a solution to his problem, and preventing him from placing the therapist in this role, is a crucial factor in the successful short-term (especially one-session) psychotherapy of individuals.

Most family therapists have been curiously uninterested in this question of the most favorable interval between meetings, seemingly taking it for granted that weekly sessions represent a minimum frequency, as in individual analytic therapy, and appearing very glad to get good results from as little as that. However, Bowen (10) has recently reported similar findings to my own, claiming to achieve more rapid therapeutic effects in couples' group and couple therapy with monthly as compared with weekly meetings. It may be that the optimum spacing is dependent on the technique used, and that longer intervals are more appropriate where the therapy catalyzes family interaction which is then carried on as "homework," rather than focusing interaction around the therapist by encouraging transference fantasy.

However, the "failures" described by Solomon and myself make it particularly necessary to stress that such spaced-out sessions may be undesirable or harmful where there is a history of deprivation or depression against which family members are successfully defending themselves. As stressed in earlier chapters, these families require (in order of ascending need) either more frequent family meetings, perhaps with multiple therapists maintaining a primary relationship to their "own" family members, or separate individual sessions at least for key members and, above all, for the mother.

The 31 percent "screened-out" category also needs some further mention. I have indicated that even where no change was expected and no immediate help offered, we ensured that support-systems were available should they be needed, either through the referring source or from ourselves, unless some other agency was better equipped to fulfill this task. Nevertheless, any service is always a function of the finances and facilities available, as well as of the needs of those served, and I am sure that more could have been done for some of these families using conventional methods, given more staff time. The negative attitudes of some could, for example, probably have been changed by formation of a positive relationship through long-term, patient casework. The fact that we attempted this in only a limited number of cases does not mean that we undervalued such work, but that we could not often supply it from our limited resources and judged it better, given our particular interest and expertise, to devote these resources to ensuring that the greater number received adequate help swiftly, without languishing on a long waiting list where the opportunity for rapid change by short-term intervention presented by the immediate crisis would be lost.

Heard (11), following Caplan (12), has emphasized that the period of greater responsiveness to outside intervention characteristic of a family system in crisis lasts only up to five weeks. There can be no doubt that the striking proportion of rapid changes shown in the figures for the Queen Elizabeth Hospital for Children cases was made possible by the fact that the waiting-time for the first family consultation was rarely more than four weeks, and much less where there was particular urgency. Furthermore, it was the rapid change made possible by the early intervention that enabled us to keep the waiting list at this level; in fact, the cases dealt with tripled over a four-year period without any increase in resources.

Also, these figures apply to cases where the main presenting problem concerned the children and when these could be aided with only minor changes in the marital relationship. Where the therapy progressed to more thorough investigation and treatment of the marriage itself, it usually took longer, of the order of five to twenty sessions rather than one to five, as evidenced by the 16 sessions in the longer case illustration that makes up Chapter 17.

Apart from this it is more difficult to give any clear impression of the results of marital therapy, either of couples alone or in groups. In the first place, I have been studying this systematically over a shorter period—seven years as against fourteen for the family work; in the second, so many of the cases seen—between one-third and one-half—have been difficult and intractable and referred for marital therapy as a last resort, often by psychoanalysts who had been working with one or both partners as individuals and had found progress limited.

Allowing for the latter circumstance the results appear so far, to a clinician accustomed to practicing other forms of treatment, to be very encouraging. The outcomes in the couples' groups are particularly heart-ening, and even though the most difficult marital problems are assigned to this form of therapy (this is not the only reason for placement in couples' groups—many accept it because I believe it to be the most effective therapy available), the rate and degree of change compare favorably with that in my stranger groups. Other colleagues who practice group-analytic methods appear to find, as I do, that from two to four years is the time usually required to achieve a degree of person-ality change satisfactory to the patients. In the couples' groups, where emphasis is similarly on individual maturation rather than adjustment in the marital system—a successful and amicable separation may prove as satisfactory an outcome to some couples as a viable marriage does to others—an equivalent level of personal change appears to be reached in 12 months to two and a half years. The difference is probably ac-counted for by the continued interaction between the couples outside the group sessions, as well as the fact that the defensive projective systems are fully available in the treatment situation, even if not within the transference. However, these groups have not been running long enough for this impression to be reliable.

Though a rigorous examination of the techniques I favor for conjoint family therapy remains to be carried out, M. Crowe (13) has recently compared the effects of an interpretive approach (based mainly on this aspect of my own work, but including techniques of other therapists such as Minuchin and Ackerman) with behavioral, directive methods (based on the work of Stuart and of Masters and Johnson) and with a support-only control group, in the short-term treatment of a series of cases referred to the Maudsley Hospital for overt marital problems or individual symptoms which appeared to have a connection with the marital relationship.

Though follow-up of the cases has not been completed, a number of conclusions appear well-established. Within the pre-established limit of ten interviews all three groups showed a significant improvement in gen-eral marital adjustment, and there was a trend in favor of the behavioral methods as regards improvement in specific sexual problems. Target symptoms showed a significant degree of positive change with the be-havioral as compared with the support-only approach, with the inter-pretive approach intermediate between them (14).

The study indicates clearly that short-term treatment of marital prob-lems can be effective, at least where the conjoint method is employed (unfortunately, testing of the effectiveness of conjoint interviewing *as such* was not a part of the research design, and in the absence of a further control group treated by *separate* interviews the importance of the conjoint method in producing these results must remain speculative). However, in evaluating each of the three treatment methods, an attempt was made to avoid using either of the others at the same time. Thus, many techniques described in this book, which seek to *combine* analytic, systems and behavioral principles, would have spoiled such a research design and were as far as possible avoided. Also, nearly all the cases were treated personally by Crowe who, though he studied with me over several years, received his basic psychotherapy training in behavior modification rather than analytic methods; it is possible that this had some preferential effect on the cases treated behaviorally, just as the reverse might follow if treatment were given by someone grounded in psychoanalytic and group-analytic principles but less experienced in behavioral approaches.

The most interesting conclusion suggested by the results concerns a more detailed examination of the outcome within each group, rather than overall improvement rates. The former appears to suggest that for the *majority* of cases simple behavioral methods sufficed, and that these methods were also widely acceptable and did not cause couples to drop out of treatment. Interpretive analytic or systems interventions appeared less widely acceptable and provoked the greatest drop-out rate before completion of therapy, but, on the other hand, also showed the highest individual improvement scores in measures of general marital satisfaction.

Crowe's results suggest that both kinds of treatment have their proper place, and that there is a need for closer collaboration between dynamic and behavioral psychotherapists to provide complementary rather than (as at present is often the case) competitive treatment services. He states:

> ... my recent approach to marital problems tends to rely at first on the more simplistic, behavioral model, which is easy to explain and apply, and which produces clear-cut results, or lack of results, within a short time. Sometimes, however, the problem does not seem amenable to such methods, and indeed one may in some way be able to detect the kind of couples who will not respond, perhaps by their tendency to reject simple explanations for their problems, to talk in more sophisticated psychological terms, and especially in their failure to carry out the tasks if they are given to them. In those cases, I tend to use the more dynamic and evocative approach and I feel very strongly that in the field of marital therapy, one needs above all to be flexible and to have several different forms of

therapy available, in order to help the couples to the maximum extent (15).

At the time of writing, a further study of brief therapy carried out at the Brief Therapy Center of the Mental Research Institute, Palo Alto, has appeared (16). Though treatment was based primarily on the systems concepts developed at that institution, and though it was often given to individuals alone, the family or network was always considered and often treated, the focus was around the presenting symptom, resolution was aimed at within ten sessions, and responsibility for solving the problem was kept with the patient(s). There was no control group but the results compare favorably with those reported by Miss Brierley on our own cases. Complete relief of the presenting complaint was achieved in 40 percent of cases, substantial relief in 32 percent, and 28 percent showed no change or (in one case out of a total of 97) deterioration. These figures need to be considered with the brevity of the therapy in mind, the average attendance being seven sessions.

16 APPLICATION OF FAMILY TECHNIQUES TO THE STUDY OF A SYNDROME: SCHOOL PHOBIA

Love goes toward love, as schoolboys from their books;
But love from love, toward school with heavy looks.

Shakespeare, Romeo and Juliet

We postulate that the major task of the mother, qua
*mother, is to love unconditionally, to gratify, to heal
and comfort and smooth over; and that the major task
of the father,* qua *father, is to support and protect, to
mediate between the family and reality (the world),
and to prepare his children to live in the extra-familial
world by discipline, toughening, instruction, reward and
punishment, judging, differential valuing, reason and
logic (rather than by unconditioned love), and by being
able to say "*NO*" when necessary.*

A. H. Maslow and R. Dias-Guerrero, Adolescence
and Juvenile Delinquency in Two Different Cultures

The syndrome of "school phobia" (also since called "school refusal")
was first named and clearly differentiated from truancy by Johnson
et al. (1), a distinction later confirmed by Warren (2) and Hersov (3).
The view of Johnson and her colleagues that the essential problem lay
in an unresolved, mutual dependency relationship between mother and
child, with arousal of intense separation anxiety at the prospect of school
attendance, has also been supported by most subsequent investigators.

Differences in symptomatology and outcome have been accounted for
mainly in terms of differences in the child's general level of development and personality integration; Coolidge *et al.* (4) speak of "neurotic"
(regression from oedipal-level conflict) and "characterological" (pre-
genitally fixated) types, while Kahn and Nursten (5) add a third, still
less integrated, "psychotic" group as well. This traditional view of
school phobia, which I shall call here the "child/mother-centered

This chapter is a slightly modified version of a paper by the author which first appeared in the *British Journal of Medical Psychology*, 47, 1, 1974. It is reprinted here by
kind permission of the editor.

306

model," has perhaps been most lucidly expressed in a classic paper by Davidson (6), who concludes in her summary that "school phobia occurs in children who have a strongly ambivalent relationship with the mother when the balance of this relationship is disturbed and the hostility takes on a dangerous meaning. This may occur quantitatively with the renewal of the oedipus conflict in prepuberty, or qualitatively when the existing level of hostility takes on a dangerous meaning because death is seen to be a real possibility owing to death or illness in the family" (p. 287). Bowlby (7) has recently reformulated this traditional child/mother-centered view in terms of the ethological concept of "attachment" behavior.

While the need to view the child's disorder in the context of the *family* relationships is often emphasized in the literature, it seems that psychotherapy has usually been offered to the mother and child only. Malmquist (8) has drawn attention to the relative neglect of the role of the father in previous studies of this disorder, and to the limited extent to which the father is offered treatment even when his relevance is to some extent appreciated. Nevertheless, though Malmquist emphasizes the need to include the father in the diagnostic and treatment plan and gives examples of conjoint family interviews illustrating the father's close involvement in the child's problem, no clear general principles emerge regarding the father's characteristic part in the genesis of the syndrome, equivalent in clarity to that already established for the mother.

Almost all studies which have included an examination of the fathers of school phobic children have remarked on their typical failure to play strong, supportive, and responsible paternal roles. Some investigators have perceived them as having an uncertain sexual identification (9) or as being more like anxious mothers themselves, competing with their wives for the maternal role (10, 11). The few exceptions reported to this rule of passivity and dependence are not very convincing. Some fathers described by Thompson (12) were domineering but were also anxious, while those found by Goldberg (13) to be rigid and controlling were highly insecure as well. Hersov's (14) study included one subgroup with "a firm controlling father who plays a large part in home management," but these were reported in association with "an overindulgent mother closely bound to and dominated by a willful, stubborn and demanding child" where the mother "over-indulged the children to offset the father's firmness" (p. 140)—scarcely a picture of a father providing secure and confident guidance and control to his family, and in fact, a pattern consistent with the view of school phobia to be presented. As will be seen in the case study which shortly follows, the exceptions to the general rule of a weak and dependent father are more apparent than real and what at first appears like forceful management is often no more than a defensive rigidity in which other members of the family collude as part of a denial of the father's inadequacy.

It will be suggested that another feature of the school phobic pattern, usually over-shadowed by the emphasis on the child's anxiety, depression, and helplessness, may be related to this inability of the father to fulfill his paternal role. Waldfogel *et al.* (15) comment on the school phobic's "inflated need for narcissistic gratification, which he achieves mainly through the continuous exploitation of his subservient parents. Their inability to limit his demands, which at times assume tyrannical proportions, nurtures his omnipotent fantasies. . . ." They conclude that "the parents, by their own vacillation in regard to his impulses, fail to provide the child with any basis for a stable system of inner controls" (p. 759). Hersov (16) reports that "those mothers who are not completely dominated by their child at home, but are able to make some demands upon them, appear to have the best chance of success" (p. 143) in returning them to school, while Kahn and Nursten (17) state that "a framework of discipline has been lacking and therefore must be supplied" (p. 713), at least with the more seriously disturbed cases.

Several other authors have expressed similar ideas, including Colm (18), who viewed phobic children as reacting with anxiety to parental inability to set clear and firm but flexible limits, and Levenson (19), whose series of ten older school phobic boys were covertly hostile and obstructive, but avoided open challenge over issues of authority. Leventhal (20) perceived the problem in terms of an "over-estimation of power" whereby the child comes to possess, with parental encouragement or collusion "a highly perfected self-image that involves exaggerations of the ability or potential ability to master personal and external events." There is "an alertness to, and avoidance of, situations that threaten the over-controlling self-image" so that "helplessness, including being delicate, weak, nervous, afraid, is not only experienced when the preferred self-image is threatened, but is also used to facilitate avoidance" (p. 686). The school phobic pattern therefore develops when incidents occur, generally at school, that threaten collapse of the preferred self-image, leading the child to strive to remain at home in a situation where his fantasy is not challenged. Radin (21) similarly suggests that the evaluation of realistic performance at school threatens the omnipotent self-image which has been fostered previously at home, leading the child to avoid school situations in order to re-establish his strong and magical position at home with parental collusion. His suppressed rage, felt largely towards the school for its presentation of reality and the consequent inevitable humiliation, but also towards the parents for their weakness, deception and need to gratify their own omnipotent fantasies through their child, becomes more frightening in any context involving death, injury or loss, necessitating further regression to a level of greater helplessness.

I do not wish to suggest that these later studies contradict or supplant the earlier ones. All authors appear to agree that a basic disturbance exists in the relationship between mother and child, arising from the mother's own immaturity and insecurity in the maternal role, and leading to an ambivalent, insecure and clinging relationship. What is missing in the earlier reports is a clear recognition of the crucial role of the father, and so a relative failure to involve him as a key figure in the syndrome, indeed the key to its solution. I believe this failure is an inevitable consequence of the child/mother-centered approach traditional in child psychiatry and that a family-centered approach, to which we now turn our attention, at once demonstrates more clearly the nature of the problem and points to the remedy. The description of this approach will follow the historical sequence in which the ideas and techniques were developed, beginning with an account of a research case studied intensively by the conjoint family method which, though a relative therapeutic failure, revealed thereby new perspectives which led to the theoretical formulations which follow. Examples are then given of the manner in which these principles are applied to different situations, in sufficient detail for the methods to be replicated and tested by others.

AN EXCEPTION THAT PROVED THE RULE

As part of a research program designed to investigate the special characteristics of different presenting syndromes as manifested in the family group situation, in order to clarify the special needs and techniques appropriate to each, a psychiatric social worker and I undertook the treatment of a boy referred for typical school phobic symptoms in the case which follows:

This case was chosen because of two special points of interest. First, it was the father who initiated the referral and brought the boy to the clinic, offering to involve himself in any way required because he considered his wife too anxious and unstable to cope with clinic attendance. By studying this apparent exception to the pattern described by most authors up to that time (a weak father and relatively dominant mother), it was hoped to clarify further the crucial issues of the parental pathology in this syndrome. In addition, a brother two years older had also suffered school phobic symptoms at the same age (12 years) so that the family situation had already been thoroughly investigated by more traditional means.

The father was persuaded to allow his wife to attend with him and the referred child but our limited experience at that time led us to yield to the parents' resistance over involving the older brother, almost certainly a grave mistake. However, my colleague and I met weekly with the referred patient, Richard, and both parents for a total of 30 sessions of conjoint family psychotherapy, each lasting one hour.

Reviewing the notes, the theme of authority and control appeared central throughout the discussions. In the early sessions, the boy's fears of vomiting (a symptom which formed a central anxiety during the school phobic episode, but which had always been present during his school life *except* when his brother had been school phobic and under treatment) were clearly linked with fears of being immature and childish, including losing control of "bad" regressive impulses and harming loved ones, perhaps causing the death of needed figures. At the same time, the main anxieties appeared to stem less from a fear of being controlled and frustrated than from an expectation that those in authority or in a parental role would be defeated and destroyed. Because of this, hostility and aggressiveness were dealt with by projection or displacement so that all dangers were seen as lying in the outside world safely excluded from the family, except in the case of sibling rivalry which was intense and clearly encouraged as a solution to the dreaded conflict between parent and child.

In later sessions the theme of genital sexuality emerged with fears of being a baby and lacking something, together with equal anxieties over becoming dangerously potent. It was revealed that pains in the testicles had been a premonitory symptom of the phobic episode. Fears of "madness" were linked with anxieties over being excluded and made to feel jealous and rivalrous towards the parental couple—"mad with rage and jealousy."

Meanwhile, as these themes developed the family relationships changed considerably. The mother showed the most remarkable progress. At first she appeared completely identified with Richard, living in and through him, but as she gradually became able to express hostility towards him and to work through her fears of damaging him, she became a separate person, developing considerable strength and independence and beginning to lead a life of her own. Richard also showed a steady improvement in confidence, with loss of his initial depression and anxiety; as the mother became stronger he was able to separate from her after experiencing anger and pain at her possessiveness, which he saw as one primary cause of his problem. He was soon going to school with his father, later alone, but although he began to mix with his friends, joined in football at the sports field, and appeared perfectly normal in all other ways, he was unable to manage the last few yards through the school gates until the critical confrontation, to be described.

Even by the sixth session Richard was clearly demanding a firm line over school attendance from his father—described by the boy as a "push"—which the father felt totally unable to provide; the latter spoke repeatedly of fears of damaging the boy and making him into a "broken animal." By the eighth session, my PSW colleague was demanding from me the firm control the father felt unable to give but my response—I first mentioned the possibility of boarding school about this time—was half-hearted and aroused such anger and reproach in the family that I hesitated to persist.

Both Richard and the father avoided any real confrontation over authority, either with each other or with us, by placatory subservient attitudes which concealed rigid resistances, rebellion, and the threat of withdrawal. At the same time, my colleague and I noted that although active criticism by us aroused stubborn resistance, always denied, the anger they felt in response would usually be admitted the following week when they would have "swallowed" the criticism and would appear both stronger and less resistant. Richard was able to attack the school, next the therapists, then the mother, but could never bring himself to confront the father. The father revealed an increasingly panic-stricken, almost psychotic core lying beneath the strong façade the whole family helped him to maintain, and acknowledged that he had suffered periods of phobic anxiety himself, sometimes preventing him from going to work.

Towards the end of the treatment, the unresolved authority conflict between Richard and the father had moved into the relationship between the father and myself. He was clearly determined to defeat me in the same way that Richard was defeating everyone else, but terrified that this would be discovered and avenged in some harsh way. Interpretations to this effect were denied and were clearly regarded as further manifestations of my weakness and inability to act.

Finally, after experimenting with a few separate interviews for Richard and the parents, which were even less fruitful, I informed both Richard and his father that I saw no medical reason for further failure to attend, that medical cover would be withdrawn at once, and that if he did not return to school immediately I would see to it that he was brought before the court and that residential placement was arranged. It so happened, because of the changed arrangements, that this ultimatum was delivered first to Richard and then to the father two days later. It is of particular interest and relevance that Richard returned, not when I told *him* this, but the day after I confronted the *father*. The family refused further appointments but the boy returned to school, and indirect information indicated that he was settled and happy.

The general impression gained of the family dynamics in this case was reinforced by the way in which the co-therapists were used in the transference. My female PSW colleague was described several times as "soothing," and seen more as an indulgent mother who would intercede with me; I was cast more in the role of a harsh father and punitive authority, and spoken of as "probing." In fact, this distinction was based much more on transference expectations than on reality, for we both tended to alternate between roles of firmness and attempts to understand. The family found it easier to speak when one therapist only was present (there were occasions when one or other of us was obliged to be away) and, for example, mention of genital sexuality and the premonitory symptom of pains in the testicles first emerged in an all-male session when both mother and female co-therapist were absent. This led the parents to suggest that the co-therapy situation might be more difficult for Richard, but although he agreed that this was so he was quite insistent that he made more progress when both therapists were there.

Although my colleague and I were cast in different and mutually incompatible roles, the family seemed to keep us abnormally free of conflict in the co-therapy situation by the preoedipal, dependent position they adopted. Their needs to deny jealousy in the family, or difficulties in the marriage, appeared to be mirrored in their need to see the co-therapists as always in agreement and to avoid provoking any conflict between us. However, in the twenty-fourth session, in a context where the father was being actively confronted and had threatened to leave treatment, I criticized the PSW openly for trying to identify with me rather than being herself. This had a profound and dramatic effect on the members of the family, who all attacked us and were able to express real ambivalence for the first time, as if reassured by our own "marital quarrel," and perhaps by the firm position I was taking towards my colleague, that it was possible for spouses and families to argue and fight without inevitable destruction and loss.

A NEW MODEL

Looking at development as the mastery of a series of challenges presented by the social environment, as outlined in Chapters 2 and 3, it appeared from the case described (later supported by the more recent papers in the literature already reviewed), that the essential problem in families producing seriously school phobic children lay in the parents' failure to help their children relinquish omnipotent demands for exclusive possession of the mother. From this arose the persisting difficulties over separation from the mother and home as well as the subsequent need to establish similar exclusive and controlling relationships either with teachers (enabling the child to cope in the "one-parent" situation of the elementary school, but not in the "multi-parent" environment of the junior and senior high schools), or with friends (making the child exceedingly vulnerable to the loss of its one exclusive peer attachment).

This crucial challenge appears to be avoided by the parents. Typically the mothers maintain exclusive and possessive relationships with their own mothers until these are transferred, in turn, to their own children. Bonds between individuals are, as it were, "vertical," running from parent to child, the emotional forces being essentially the same whether a given individual is in a subordinate or superior position. There is a corresponding failure to establish "horizontal" peer-group or genital-level bonds, i.e., mutual attachments between individuals functioning on an equal level. In such families, therefore, the primary attachments always remain between parents and children rather than between spouses.

In a normal family the primary attachment is between the spouses, expressed partly by the sexual relationship but also by all the other mutual, complementary interactions which accompany this. When a child is born, the mother needs temporarily to enter into an intense and exclusive relationship with it, regressing to a state of what Winnicott (22) has termed "primary maternal preoccupation" in order to perceive the infant's needs directly through reexperiencing that stage herself. The father, if sufficiently mature, is prepared to forgo his previous unfettered enjoyment of his spouse to enable her to carry out the maternal function, while he fulfills his responsibility by "holding the life-line" and supporting the mother in her biological task.

An adequately mature father will, nevertheless, be prepared to forgo his normal demands on his spouse only as long as necessary and in the child's interest. All being well, as soon as the child no longer needs the mother's exclusive attention, and when indeed the attachment needs to be weakened, he will automatically begin to intervene and disrupt the exclusive mother-child dyad by demanding that the mother resume her relationship with him and make the marital relationship primary again. There are two ends to any piece of elastic, and by cutting the attachment at the mother's end the father puts the child in the position where it has to cope only with its own attachment, rather than the mother's as well, in order to escape and gain the next developmental stage (23).

In school phobic families, by contrast, genital primacy is not achieved by the parents; the marital relationship is weak; the father is either a peripheral figure or a dependent child, rather than a supportive and protective figure during the child's infancy; the mother-child bond remains intense throughout life and is only swung from the grandmother to the child rather than being outgrown; and the father is typically unable to disrupt or weaken this primary attachment.

Having reached this conclusion, the next step was to find ways of presenting this challenge to the school phobic children referred to us and to support them in mastering it. Since we were more interested in facilitating maturation than in relieving particular difficulties, and also because we were driven through limited resources never to do anything for a family we could teach them to do for themselves, a number of techniques were developed for dealing with school phobic children and their families, depending upon their maturity, ego-strength and motivation.

Where possible, change is achieved by increasing insight and understanding through interpretation, enabling the family itself to supply the skills and resources it lacks. Where this does not appear possible, however, the therapist either supplies the missing parental functions through his own responses, or arranges for them to be provided by some other agency outside the family (social worker, club leader, court, etc.). Some examples follow illustrating these different types of approach.

TYPE 1: CASES WHERE THE PARENTS CAN PRESENT THE CRUCIAL CHALLENGE TO THE CHILD, GIVEN INTERPRETATION AND SUPPORT

Case A

Jacqueline, aged ten, was referred with the complaint of nausea and occasional vomiting over about three months, fear of which was greatest in the morning assembly; she had been away from school for several weeks. There was a variety of the usual precipitating factors noted in school phobic children. I interviewed the child with both parents in the company of a social worker student and the supervising psw, who had both seen the family for their initial interview. For teaching purposes, the student was encouraged to take the lead but neither he, nor later the psw nor myself could get a fruitful discussion going. The child saw the problem as lying entirely in some unwholesome tomato sandwiches she had eaten before the onset of her symptoms. The parents saw the problem as lying entirely in the child and avoided all possibility of a connection with their own attitudes or relationship. There were some complaints of an interfering and possessive maternal grandmother, but the mother denied any resentment or jealousy and this line of inquiry also proved fruitless.

After three-quarters of an hour, with no progress and 15 minutes left, I focused on the nonverbal interaction and commented on the doting look the mother showed towards the child, as if Jacqueline were a great treasure with everything valuable the mother possessed locked up inside her. The mother confirmed my comment by her response—her face crumpled, she appeared on the verge of weeping, shut her eyes, and kept her fist tightly against her mouth, being unable to speak for a time. When I asked what effect this intense attachment had on the family as a whole, the father commented that the mother had experienced an insecure and miserable childhood; her father had been brutal, her mother had rejected her, and it was therefore terribly important to her to make a success of bringing up this child and to give her a different sort of life. To confirm my point, I said to the mother, "Who are you married to?" Immediately the mother looked at the child, not the father, and this further nonverbal communication, which summarized the underlying problem, was pointed out.

This led to a discussion of the sleeping arrangements, in which it proved that the girl slept in the parents' bedroom still. When I asked what effect this had on the sexual relationship, the mother said that it did not matter because she was "not bothered" and agreed on inquiry that she was frigid. At this the father interrupted angrily to say that he was highly dissatisfied with the present relationship although he had not complained before for fear of upsetting his wife. The mother countered by complaining that she had always wanted to lean on her husband, but that he did not support her emotionally and it was always she who had to make the decisions. The interview ended at this point and I suggested that if the husband could satisfy some of the needs his wife had not had met by her father, she might not need to re-live her childhood through this intense identification with her daughter.

The family was not seen again as they lived far from the hospital and requested referral to a local clinic. Four months later, the child and mother were seen by the psychiatrist there who reported that Jacqueline had returned to school after the interview described; she was more able to stand up for herself and cope with stress that previously had been too much for her. Further treatment was not judged necessary, and follow-up two years later showed no further problems over attendance.

Case B

Lindy, aged eight, was referred to us because of school phobic symptoms after she returned with her family to their district of origin near our hospital. By then she had been out of school altogether for 13 months, having been given a bad prognosis at the child guidance clinic serving the area in which they had been living. Psychotherapy had been recommended there for Lindy, but she was still on the waiting list.

A family interview was attended by both parents and Lindy, who was the youngest child, together with a sister of 12 and a brother of 14. A 15-year-old brother had just started a job and was not pressed to come.

After getting to know the family, I inquired of Lindy about the onset of her symptoms. She immediately looked at mother several times but when I pressed mother not to answer for her, Lindy cried weakly, refused father's offer to take her on his lap, and clung to mother like a passive baby for the rest of the interview. The father appeared rather tense and nervous, but was insightful, straightforward, and more objective about the needs of the children than the mother. He had wanted to return Lindy to school soon after her refusal began even if it upset her, but had been advised by the psychiatrist not to do so. Father said that he had put pressure on the 14-year-old boy when he had suffered a school phobic episode near the same age as Lindy, and in the interview this boy acknowledged that, although he had been angry with his father at the time, he was now grateful for his firmness.

Both parents described how they tended to focus their love and attention on the youngest child, finding it almost impossible to perceive that it was getting older until a new baby came along, when they would suddenly see it more objectively. In this connection, it was interesting to learn that the brother's resistance to attending school had ceased the day Lindy was born, as if some projection had been withdrawn. In connection with the typical onset around six years the father described how he enjoyed babying and cuddling them until that age, when his feelings would suddenly change and cause him to push them away, demanding a sudden move towards maturity. Both the other children present thought the parents were much too soft with Lindy, saying that she was spoiled and got away with things. Lindy appeared to accept all this discussion without distress and in response to questioning said that she worried about accidents befalling her mother when she was away from her, and that her main fear of school was of teachers shouting at her.

We agreed with the siblings that Lindy was fit to return to school, emphasized as the crucial problem the difficulty both parents had already described about allowing the youngest child to grow up, and encouraged them to pay more attention to each other and their own relationship, and less to Lindy. The main responsibility for this was put upon the father who was much the more insightful parent. As Lindy had seemed quite upset during part of the interview, we were reassured to learn, from a psychologist from another clinic who later saw Lindy at our request in order to decide which local school would be best for her, that Lindy had appeared "quite positive about returning to school" and did not give any impression of being simply coerced. Lindy in fact returned to school without difficulty, but mother, whose motivation appeared uncertain, joined a mothers' group for further support. Follow-up three years later showed normal attendance.

Both these cases illustrate very clearly the way in which these children receive a projection of a split-off, denied, infantile aspect of the parent's personality and the way in which this ties the parent to the child in a regressive way (and vice versa), with a corresponding weakening of the marital bonds.

TYPE 2: CASES WHERE THE THERAPIST NEEDS TO SHARE THE
TASK OF PRESENTING THE CHALLENGE WITH THE PARENTS

In this second category, the parents are adequately motivated to gain control of the situation and separate from the child, but are unable to bring themselves to do this even with support. Usually the mothers are more rigid and ambivalent, the fathers more passive than the parents in the first category and unable to take a firmer line. The task of confronting the child with the challenge of relinquishing its omnipotent demand for a total attachment to the mother has to be carried out by the therapist, although this has the parents' support and they are allies in the task. This may be done by making it clear that residential placement will be arranged if a return to school does not take place, a technique which not only fulfills the function the father has failed to perform (of intervening between the child and the mother and disrupting the original attachment, as part of his family and marital role) but does so in terms both of the form in which the underlying problem is being expressed, and of the therapist's real authority and power within the medical and educational systems.

Case C

Susan, aged 11, had been refusing school for 13 months at the time of her referral to the hospital for a second opinion. She lived in a distant area and had previously received psychotherapy from the psychiatrist at the local clinic, but had refused to attend again after he had been critical of the mother in a joint interview. The mother was continuing to attend the local clinic for interviews with the PSW. There were many features of the usual school phobic pattern.

At the initial family interview with us the mother presented as a rather rigid, ungiving and critical woman, who was nevertheless unable to be really firm. The father was passive, placatory and had himself been school phobic as a child; he was clearly unable to take a more active role himself. While the marital relationship was a limited one it was clearly satisfactory to both parents and unlikely to change. They described Susan as being anxious and depressed, but she showed no striking sign of this and in fact looked willful and manipulative, failing to answer some of my questions, looking out of the window, and behaving in a generally unhelpful and uncooperative fashion. When I focused on this nonverbal communication, rather than the family's description of her, she looked furious and became even more stubborn and resistant, evidence which was also used to confront Susan and her parents with her wish to control the situation. Her elder brother, who also attended, said that he believed Susan was manipulative and that she usually succeeded in dominating the parents.

I stated that Susan was clearly not suffering from any illness and that medical cover would be withdrawn immediately. I added that I was quite sure she would be able to return to school, prescribed some medication (to be described later) in order to reassure the parents that any residual anxiety would be removed, but said that I would be very pleased to help by recommending a residential school if there should be any undue difficulty. Despite Susan's fury when confronted with firm authority she appeared friendly, open and relaxed towards the end of the interview, smiling warmly at me over her shoulder as she left.

Seen for the second time two weeks later, the parents reported that she was "completely changed," a "different person." She had returned to school, was happy and showing no problems over attendance. She did indeed look very different, appearing cheerful, lively, bright-eyed, confident and considerably more mature. Her parents reported that she had shown increasing open aggressiveness, saying "no" to everything during the week following the first family session, culminating in a furious fight with her mother over wearing her coat. The mother finally lost her temper and had been able to use her anger constructively. The following day, Susan had appeared cheerful and relaxed and had asked her mother to take her to school. The mother said that it had been the "worst week of her life" and felt she would not have been able to maintain a firm position throughout had she not been clearly warned that such a reaction was likely and supported in advance in standing her ground.

Follow-up revealed that Susan's attendance remained secure for over a year, when the mother telephoned the hospital as Susan was refusing to go to school again. An appointment was offered with another psychiatrist (because I and the PSW co-therapist who saw them with me had left the hospital) but this was cancelled a week later by the mother who reported that Susan had resumed regular attendance. Fifteen months after this (27 months after the interview described above), she was again referred by the GP for school refusal. The notes state that Susan refused to attend the interview, but the parents were seen by my successor who reported that "both parents described their fear of Susan, who gets in such terrible tempers if she is ever opposed by the parents, that mother feels helpless and ill."

After attempting further family interviews including the brother (whose departure for a distant university had deprived the parents of support in handling Susan), my colleague recommended residential placement as Susan still declined the appointments offered. This recommendation was not acted upon by the local authority, which allowed itself to be manipulated into offering changes of day school, without result. Eventually, Susan was referred back to the local psychiatrist from whom she currently receives certificates of her unfitness to attend school, despite her refusal to attend interviews.

This is a good example of the difficulty in dealing with such cases if one is not able to influence the relevant medico-socio-educational network through trust built up by regular collaboration.

TYPE 3: CASES WHERE THE PARENTS ARE COLLUDING FULLY WITH THE CHILD

A more difficult problem is presented by those cases where the parents see no problem in themselves or the child, but seek to prevent conflict in the family by siding with the child against the school or external authority. In such cases, the therapist needs to challenge the parents' own omnipotent fantasies. The power to do this is available through the fact that only medical sanction prevents the implementation of the law regarding school attendance.

Case D

Pamela, aged 12, had shown school refusal at two secondary schools and the parents were demanding yet another change. She appeared sulky, angry and manipulative at the initial family interview, but there was also more depressive symptomatology than in most of the other cases and the mother was also particularly anxious and inadequate, trembling with fear throughout the interview. An antidepressant was prescribed for the child and she was encouraged to return. After the interview, the PSW who had acted as cotherapist asked me why I had not taken the usual firm line and I found myself unable to explain adequately why I had been so permissive.

Pamela did return gradually and claimed the tablets helped her, but seen a month later was still only partially involved in school activities and appeared to be making limited efforts to overcome her difficulties. The PSW once again remarked on my gentleness with the family and queried my motives.

Three months later the principal complained that Pamela was still manipulative and that the mother was repeatedly coming into the school, criticizing, interfering, and creating problems. At the next family interview, both parents openly colluded with Pamela in criticizing the school, the teacher, and indirectly the hospital and myself. I then challenged the manipulative and resistant attitude of the parents as well as Pamela, "read the riot act," and said that if Pamela did not return to school on a normal basis at once, I would see that they were all taken to court. At first there was violent protest and denial of their non-cooperation, which gave way to cooperation as soon as they perceived that we were not to be manipulated.

A month later, Pamela was attending normally and appeared well. A month after this (the last interview before I left the hospital) she was attending regularly and fully, said she was enjoying school, and both she and her mother reported that there were no further complaints or symptoms. She was cheerful and friendly, looked tougher instead of immature and soft, and said that she could hold her own better with other children. They said they had forgiven me for the painful confrontation and felt that this had helped in the long run. It was arranged that they or the school would contact my successor in case of need, but nothing further was heard.

TYPE 4: TRUANTS REFERRED AS SCHOOL PHOBICS

This group is really composed of truants, in the way that word has been defined by Hersov, but they either show some admixture of school phobic symptomatology or are referred by schools or agencies which prefer to avoid a disciplinary challenge by using a diagnosis which will transfer the child to medical responsibility. There is little evidence of depression, anxiety or guilt, and the parents are often openly encouraging the child to remain at home for their own advantage. The parents are usually uncooperative with psychiatric services, the father often failing to attend at all.

Case E

Margaret, aged 12, had not attended school for four months, with intermittent attendance over a long period. Since moving to her secondary school she had become defiant and had begun to stay out late at night so that the parents often had to search the neighborhood to bring her home. An older brother had a similar history and was on probation after being charged with larceny. The father failed to attend a diagnostic interview (a very rare event and usually the most significant feature of any case in which it occurred), and the mother—a tough, domineering woman—appeared to be openly colluding with the girl against father and school.

Use of a similar technique to that already described for the Type 3 cases resulted in a return to school, but the education department and school were warned that the problem was one of truancy and that close supervision should be kept on the girl's attendance with normal disciplinary measures if this began to falter.

In fact, the school neglected to watch her attendance, and we later learned that Margaret was frequently kept out of school to help the mother at home. Attempts to re-refer her as a medical problem were resisted.

NEED FOR THE THERAPIST TO ACCEPT A ROLE
OF REAL AUTHORITY

It will be clear that the approach described here requires that the therapist be prepared to accept a position of real authority in relation to these families, parents as well as children, if he is to be effective. Even in cases of the first type, where the therapist does not actually play a parental role, he is nevertheless introducing a clear value system about what that role should be. Many who work in the medical or social work fields might find this type of action difficult to undertake; it certainly went against the inclinations and ideas I favored when I first entered the field of child psychiatry, and it took several years to feel comfortable in the role I now adopt: This change has come about through using conjoint family techniques generally, which obliged me, like so many others, to perceive the vital but neglected place of authority, hierarchy, and issues of power and control in families and social systems.

Not only does the therapist need to accept an authoritative role, and a position of personal responsibility within the social hierarchy, but he is also dependent upon corresponding views in related parts of the social network—the education officer, the court and so on. Unfortunately, the pendulum governing this issue seems to be swinging to its extreme point at the present time and it becomes increasingly difficult to persuade many teachers, magistrates, and members of social service departments that appropriate cases need an intelligent use of authority and limits as much as others require permissiveness and encouragement. Recent legislation changing the function of the juvenile court has made the position still more difficult.

The family therapist is particularly dependent on the support and common understanding of any colleagues who may have become involved with separate members of the family containing a school phobic member, since any conflict among the professionals concerned is skillfully exploited. In particular, the psychiatric team needs to guard against the danger, already mentioned in Chapter 14 on problems of co-therapy, that the family pathology may be reproduced in their own relationships. Inter-professional conflicts over the timing of a return to school can be a warning sign of this.

Moreover, to treat school phobic cases adequately, the therapist must himself be in an appropriate position in the social system, i.e., employed by, and ultimately responsible to, the wider community even though the therapeutic aim is to meet the needs of its "deviant" members. I have not found it possible to apply the above principles successfully in private practice, for there the therapist is paid by, and so under the control of, the family who fails to return and often fails to pay the fees if its manipulative demands are not met. Clearly, school phobia is best understood as a psycho-social problem rather than as a purely medical, intrapsychic or even intrafamilial disorder.

CONTROL OR COERCION?

It may be objected that the techniques described simply put the clock back to the time when coercion, force and fear obliged the child to return to school, no matter how terrified and disturbed he might be. Short of providing an opportunity for those who possess such doubts to see with their own eyes the increased health and happiness of the children and parents concerned, or to hear the families' own positive comments at follow-up, it is difficult to refute this. Perhaps the other main argument lies in the fact that coercion and fear were never very successful and most people are familiar with examples of children against whom the full legal sanctions were applied without success.

The fact that the techniques described here are usually both successful and psychologically beneficial rests on the psychological *meaning* of the action taken which is designed to assist the family to cope with a developmental challenge they have previously failed to transcend. It is not the threat of the court or of residential placement which produces the essential modification but the fact that someone in a position of parental authority is both concerned and friendly, yet prepared to use sanctions which will arouse hate and rejection if it is nevertheless in the family's interest to bring about a certain change in their functioning. That change is an increased tolerance for the experience of separation, through an ability to contain and cope with the rage that the threat of separation provokes. Some approaches explicitly based on behavioral concepts may be employing similar mechanisms. Kennedy's (24) successful return of 50 (less chronic) cases includes the instructions: "Have the father take the child to school . . . allow the mother to stand in the hall, if she must, or to visit the school during the morning, but not to stay" (p. 288).

MEDICATION

It should be mentioned that medication was routinely prescribed to cover the period of return to school in these children. Even a placebo effect has some value in reassuring child and parents, and giving practical evidence of support and interest, in these families which function so much at primitive, near-psychotic levels, including magical thinking, and any method which eases the transition back to school and reduces unnecessary distress should obviously be utilized.

Frommer (25) found a combination of an antidepressant (Phenelzine) and chlordiazepoxide (Librium) helpful in such cases and I have mainly used the latter, finding it effective where there is excessive fear and inhibition of aggressive and hostile feelings, a state of affairs which is especially prominent in this condition. One typical effect, seen clearly in

Case C, is for hostility towards the parents which has been displaced on to teachers to return to its real object and to cause increased, overt conflict in the home. Parents need support in coping with this, and usually there is a change in the level of tolerance of aggressiveness within the whole family which persists after the drug is stopped. It is often helpful to prescribe the drug for the mother, or for both parents, in addition, if they are also frightened of aggression. For children, the dose of chlordiazepoxide required is larger than that normally recommended and I usually give 5 mg t.d.s. for children under 7 and 10 mg t.d.s for those 7 and over, continued for a month after return to school. I believe that this medication by itself greatly improves the chance of return and often averts development of school refusal in early cases; while there is as yet no scientifically acceptable support for this view, the placebo or other effect should obviously be taken into account in any attempt to replicate this method.

OTHER THERAPEUTIC MEASURES

In addition to medication, other forms of help were arranged whenever this was judged necessary. Although it was taken for granted that the first step was to return the children immediately to school, excessively timid children were sometimes helped by inclusion in psychotherapy groups and some mothers were helped to become more independent of their children by attending psychotherapy groups for mothers. School changes or other special educational arrangements were rare since demands for these seemed usually manipulative and part of the symptomatology.

Another promising technique, preferably combined with therapy groups for mothers and for children, is multi-family therapy. As described in Chapter 13, the understanding gained in the interviews continues to be worked out by the families at home, but during the sessions participants are able to be more objective about other families than about their own and the therapeutic task and the issue of authority and control can for this reason be left more to the group as a whole. One particular advantage is the way in which the parents of one family can understand and help a child in another, because they are able to be more detached and neutral than the child's own parents; another is the possibility for the children in all the families to support each other and so enable each to speak more freely. Mothers and fathers also benefit from this kind of mutual support.

RESULTS

A retrospective study of the outcome of all referrals seen over a year (1969) at the Queen Elizabeth Hospital for Children was carried out by my colleague, the late Miss Patricia Brierley. Of a total of 20 children showing a problem of school refusal and assigned to my team, one returned before the diagnostic interview. A further 15 returned within a month of the initial consultation (most of these returned within one or two weeks, after only one interview, but some needed a second interview and there were occasional complications delaying return, such as finding a suitable school for Case B, on her return to our area). One girl showed irregular attendance at first and did not return securely until after the fourth interview, ten months after first being seen; this was a Type 3 case, in which the behavior of the family and our own errors in dealing with them closely resembled Case D (who was not in fact seen during the year studied).

Three cases returned, but failed to establish regular attendance. One was really a truant from a family with delinquent attitudes in which our advice regarding management was not followed by the referrers. The second was a schizophrenic girl, both hallucinated and deluded, who was being supported in the community for lack of suitable inpatient facilities. The third came from a chaotic, multi-problem family in which failed appointments were not properly followed up through an error on our part; this boy came to our attention again a year later, when he was admitted to the hospital with an organic disorder, by which time he had come under the psychiatric care of his local clinic so that we were not further involved with the case.

Follow-up of these cases treated in 1969 was carried out in the second half of 1972, through the education welfare services which were requested to inquire from schools about subsequent attendance and also about any problems of adjustment and general behavior noted by the teachers (26).

Apart from Susan (Case C), who was by then out of school again and whose subsequent history has been described, all the 15 children who returned at once after treatment were attending school regularly at the time of the follow-up or, in the case of those who had already left, had been doing so prior to leaving (27). One girl was reported to be anxious and mother-attached, and two more had suffered brief periods of resistance to school; of these latter, one (from a distant area) relapsed three years after returning following the interview with us but had attended regularly after being placed in a day unit for maladjusted children; the second (from our local area) had needed only encouragement from the education welfare officer, who was familiar with our methods, in order to resume attendance, and subsequently received a glowing report from his head teacher. The other members of the original group of 15 whose treatment was judged successful all received positive comments from their school about their regular attendance. The majority also received positive comments about their ultimate adjustment and social relationships; where this was not the case the report was brief and related to attendance only, omitting any answer to the inquiry about general adjustment.

Of the three cases considered relative failures the psychotic girl in fact settled well in a school for delicate children recommended for her because of its success in dealing with borderline cases; she attended reasonably well and is now reported to be enjoying her work in an office. The truant's (Case E) attendance continued to be irregular. The third "failure," who came under psychiatric care elsewhere, has continued to attend school irregularly and has needed periodic support and pressure to return. His psychiatrist describes a collusive relationship between the boy and his mother, and an inadequate father who is at present excluded from the home and seeking unsuccessfully to be accepted back.

Rodriguez *et al.* (28), using a technique emphasizing early return to school with the use of the appropriate sanctions of authority where necessary, found that, while almost 90 percent showed a successful outcome in children under 11, this fell to just over one-third in children of 11 or more years. It may therefore be worth recording that of the 20 children reported upon here, ten were below 11, ten were 11 and above. The results showed no difference in outcome related to age.

RESERVATIONS AND POSSIBILITIES FOR FURTHER INVESTIGATION

Both the model put forward here to account for normal child development, and the hypothesis regarding the distortion this may suffer in the development of the school phobic syndrome, are clearly too simple and will need elaboration. Nevertheless, simplicity is no disadvantage in a preliminary hypothesis, permitting as it does clearer testing and recognition of its deficiencies.

A more serious criticism could be leveled at the rather stereotyped definition I have put forward regarding normal parental and sexual roles, which corresponds imperfectly to the truth even in the most "normal" families. In families producing the school phobic syndrome the most difficult cases to deal with, even using the methods described, have been those where both parents show a marked reversal of sexual and parental roles, in that the father seems to have taken the "maternal" position from the beginning and resists any loosening of this attachment, while the mother is the firmer, more detached parent, attempting unsuccessfully to weaken the bond. No doubt the explanation will be found in the form of the identifications made by the parents with the grandparents, but for lack of adequate material this aspect has not been explored in the present study. Clarification is most likely to come from a combination of conjoint family interviews with individual psychotherapy, in order to relate the interpersonal and intrapsychic processes; the most effective combination of conjoint and individual treatment also remains to be discovered.

17 OUTLINE OF A FAMILY AND MARITAL TREATMENT

I was angry with my friend: I told my wrath, my wrath did end.
I was angry with my foe: I told it not, my wrath did grow.

William Blake, Songs of Experience

He daren't quite bite. Not that he was really afraid of
the others. He was afraid of himself, once he let him-
self go.

D. H. Lawrence, St. Mawr

In order to provide a wide selection of case material, illustrating many different types of problem, it has been necessary to select cases where treatment was relatively brief. These brief interventions are by no means untypical of the approaches described, as the last two chapters have demonstrated, but this form of presentation has led to an underrepresentation of more extended treatments, particularly those which begin as a problem ascribed to the children and gradually turn into marital therapy.

To make good this deficiency, this chapter presents a longer treatment—one comprising 16 consultations. Sessions were recorded on audiotape, with the family's permission and the understanding that the material might be used for teaching purposes. Because presentation in written form requires a family that makes high use of verbal communication, an articulate, middle-class family was chosen. (Where a session can be conveyed through use of videotape, which records the nonverbal communications of family and therapists, this need for verbal sophistication is not important.)

Though the tape recordings were listened to in order to check and amplify the notes made after the session, considerations of space have demanded that the interaction be presented in summary form, though hopefully in sufficient detail to convey some impression of the lively transactions described. Needless to say, the identity of the family has been thoroughly disguised, though changes in details have as far as possible been made in such a way as not to alter significantly their psychological implications.

A middle-class, intelligent family with a bias towards an intellectual approach to problems. Both parents in their early forties.

Father—a teacher in a practical subject at a polytechnic school, devoting himself more fully to his work than was in the family's interest, and perhaps somewhat disappointed that he was not teaching at a more academic level.

Mother—had a part-time job as a bookkeeper.

Mary—aged 18, a daughter by mother's previous marriage, was away at a university at the time of the series of interviews.

Matthew—aged 14, the referred patient.

Mark—aged 11.

Luke—aged two.

PROBLEM AS REFERRED

The clinic's educational psychologist was asked by the school to see Matthew because of concern that, despite a high intelligence and academic potential, he was failing to work anywhere near his capacity.

His teachers felt that he should be transferred to a more academic environment in which he would be "stretched" more than was possible in his current school, but the father was said to be opposed to this because of strong egalitarian principles. Apart from doing the minimum amount of work required, Matthew was also said to be extremely argumentative and arrogant.

The psychologist found Matthew to be an able boy who did not feel he had a problem. In his view the adults were exerting too much pressure. The psychologist noted in him considerable fear of being boastful and a readiness to feel inadequate and inferior, accompanied by strong feelings of envy. Though his inconsistent attainment did indeed appear to stem from personality difficulties, the psychologist felt that his lack of motivation might make him unsuitable for therapy.

The father subsequently contacted the psychologist and was clearly hoping to be seen. She therefore arranged an interview with both parents, at which the father did most of the talking. He expressed concern that his relationship with Matthew was poor and that he, like the teachers, found the boy's arrogance so difficult to tolerate that he tended to "slap him down." The father showed considerable admiration of Matthew's cleverness and gave the impression of being quite envious.

The mother was by contrast rather over-protective; she tended to minimize Matthew's problems and felt they were partially explained by the fact that she herself had suffered frequent illnesses and that the boy had reacted badly to these.

When the question of transfer to a more demanding school was raised the father in fact seemed more willing than his wife to consider the possibility, though he appeared to be hoping the psychologist would help him by taking responsibility for the decision. The mother was reluctant to agree to a move because this would separate him from Mark, also at the same school.

The parents appeared to be hoping for some form of psychological help, yet also to be fearful of this. Mother was concerned that Matthew might feel singled out if psychotherapy was arranged for him, reporting that he had wept after the psychological testing and said to her, "I'm not schizophrenic."

SUBSEQUENT PROCEDURE

After discussion at the referrals conference, it was agreed that the family would be offered a diagnostic family consultation. In the course of inviting them for this a letter was received from the mother indicating that she felt some considerable anxiety about what this might involve, and the effect on Matthew. A preliminary interview was therefore arranged for the parents to see Miss Roberts, the psychiatric social worker who was to share with me the task of interviewing the family and to act as co-therapist should ongoing family interviews be offered.

At this preliminary interview the mother seemed quite agitated; though her anxiety was overtly concerned with fears that Matthew either was, or would imagine he was, seriously disturbed emotionally, it was clear that this was a projection of her own anxieties about herself. At this interview father invited mother to describe the difficulties, and she reported that the relationship between herself and Matthew had always been an unhappy one though she felt it had improved recently when father had been more often at home. Mother said she felt Matthew had first changed after the birth of Mark and attributed his current difficulties to jealousy, first aroused then and never subsequently outgrown. She clearly felt she had let Matthew down by placing him in a day nursery while she was hospitalized for Mark's birth, and also because she had herself become ill upon her return and, far from being able to comfort Matthew, had needed additional attention for herself and the baby. She went on to describe Matthew as having been a very difficult toddler, to a point where she found herself hating him. Her eyes filled with tears and Miss Roberts suggested that she felt very concerned and guilty about the boy, which she acknowledged.

Father took over at this point, as if to relieve mother in her distress, and said what a shock it had been to learn of the school's concern about Matthew. He said he felt equally to blame for the problems because he had, until the past year, spent a great deal of time away from home involved in his work, and had often excluded the children from his attention because he was preoccupied with it even when at home.

The rest of the interview was taken up with the parents' concern that, though they have read a great deal of psychology and done all they could to learn how to be good parents, their emotions had not allowed them to behave in the way they knew was correct. The mother said, with some feeling, "Now that I am going to psychology classes, it is even more difficult."

Though still ambivalent over the idea of individual therapy, feeling that this would single Matthew out and make him feel worse, they responded readily to the idea of conjoint family therapy. They agreed that the problem concerned the whole family and that even the youngest child played a part in what happened at home and should be included.

An initial family consultation was arranged three weeks ahead and the mother subsequently wrote to say that the family had agreed to attend, even though Matthew had again denied that he had any problems and had said that though he would come, he would not talk about himself.

INITIAL FAMILY CONSULTATION

The mother was unable to come as she had been admitted to the hospital for treatment of a minor surgical ailment, but the father came with all three boys to see Miss Roberts and myself.

Father, a cheerful, outgoing man who talked easily and fluently—
almost too easily, at once outlined his view of the problem. In his view
the main difficulty was the constant rivalry and quarreling between
Matthew and Mark; he gave examples of their arguments about doing
the dishes, and said that these were so time consuming that he ended
by doing the dishes himself! Matthew's learning difficulty was also
mentioned later on but this symptom, which had been the overt reason
for referral, took a secondary place in his presentation.

Asked to elaborate his account of the difficulty, the father described
how they had recently arranged to go on a vacation using two cars with
one boy in each, because it was so difficult to deal with the quarreling in
any other way. Matthew at once disagreed with the father's description,
saying there were other reasons for using two cars. He looked depressed
and resentful, and when I pointed out his obvious anger with his father
he seemed disturbed by this suggestion, saying he "certainly didn't feel
like chopping his head off" (no one had suggested anything of the sort).
Mark agreed with Matthew that the father was misinterpreting the relationship between them, and we were at once struck by the solidarity
of Matthew and Mark against the father, while the father was avoiding
the question of his relationship to the boys and focusing on the friction
between them.

Matthew's irritation seemed directed also towards ourselves, and when
this was explored he expressed a great deal of resentment about coming
to the clinic at all, saying he felt the problem did not justify it. As this
was discussed the conflict between father and Matthew began to emerge
more clearly into the open, since father obviously felt more dissatisfaction with him than the boy felt with himself, and at one point the
father spoke of "not really wanting to hit Matthew with a cricket bat"
(no one had suggested this either). Their relationship appeared to become more alive and real when this mutual hidden antagonism was
made clear.

Mark tended throughout to opt out and sit on the sidelines, and we
commented on this and also on his look of pleasure as the quarrel between father and Matthew developed. Matthew agreed that Mark appeared to take advantage of any quarrels for his own ends, and it appeared from the discussion that Mark behaved at home much as he did
in the interview, failing to involve himself or to take his share of responsibility for the family problems. Another fact which emerged, in relation
to this, was Matthew's strong conscience, which makes him unhappy
if he does not please others and miserable if he upsets Mark or his

mother. He agreed when we suggested he felt constrained and coerced by his own anxiety and guilt as much as by others' expectations. Mark, on the other hand, was seen by the family as not guilty enough—as having been allowed to become too selfish and to exploit situations to his own advantage.

We seemed to be making some progress in elucidating the family pattern, and towards the end the father described how Matthew had been neglected at the age of three when Mark arrived, particularly because the mother had developed pneumonia at that time. The parents had made a good deal of this at the previous interview with Miss Roberts and there was obviously much guilt about it.

The most striking points to emerge in the interview were Matthew's depressive anxiety, his rivalry with his father which he could not face, and the father's rivalry with both the boys which he tended to displace away from himself and to see instead in terms of rivalry between the two of them. Also, I wondered if Matthew might be rather like his mother, depressive and conscience-ridden, while Mark's selfishness and cheerful unconcern were perhaps copied from the father's similar pattern of opting out of the family difficulties.

SECOND FAMILY CONSULTATION

Both parents and all three children were seen together by Miss Roberts and myself.

There was a considerable pause to begin with as if there were some struggle by the children to force the parents to take the active role. The father reported that the situation had been much improved following the last discussion, which had continued afterwards at home. Both Matthew and Mark agreed that the discussion had helped, and that they were getting on better. However, it seemed that the family had in some way not brought the mother in on the discussion, and she said that she had not grasped what had happened at the interview; she mentioned that one of the children had told her that she was a "lot less neurotic."

The father did most of the talking to begin with, but we had the impression that he was being forced into an active and controlling position which the children, especially Matthew, could then feel justified in resenting. This was pointed out, but Matthew's reluctance to contribute continued and he seemed to go on provoking his parents to be active and critical towards him, when he would respond by resisting them, and by complaining that he felt "flattened" by father's clever arguments. The mother complained that she felt equally "flattened" by Matthew; her helplessness and vulnerability were very striking throughout, as also was the way in which these seemed to provoke a desire in Matthew to attack her, coupled with anxiety about doing so and a strong compensatory restraint. Early on, when he said something aggressive to her she almost went to pieces and her face crumpled, after which he looked depressed and guilty.

For some time the interaction centered between Matthew and father, mainly over whether it was necessary for parents to be "reasonable." The father felt strongly that parents always should be reasonable, but Matthew obviously exploited this by making his father feel in the wrong when he tried to "lay down the law." (I remembered that before I had met the family professionally, the father had reacted strongly against my statement that it was necessary at times for parents to be firm without worrying about being reasonable, at a parent/teacher meeting he had attended at Matthew's school, where I was a guest speaker. The father was obviously challenging me, trying to defeat me by making me feel in the wrong, just as Matthew did to him.)

It was striking how much the mother and Mark were left out of this exchange, but they both seemed to be excluding themselves. When this was commented on the mother explained it in terms of needing to give attention to the baby, but after this comment she joined in more and the father paid greater attention to the child. Mark also now began to be drawn into the discussion.

The parents next focused on the constant fights between Matthew and Mark; Matthew, they said, was always jealous and attacking him, causing Mark to withdraw and to put up defenses against others. However, we pointed out the way in which, during the interview, everyone actually attacked Mark and how no one gave him much chance to speak. At this point a constellation which had occurred in three successive interviews suddenly had meaning for me: They were all behaving as if Mark's birth had never been accepted by Matthew, and as if both parents felt guilty about conceiving him. As I interpreted this it seemed to have great meaning for them, and the situation became much more alive. The father admitted that he was, as it were, married to his work, and that he had never really wanted Mark. This was news to mother, who looked quite shocked. Matthew was able to express annoyance that the parents had not consulted him before they conceived Mark. We felt some regret that there was not time to discuss this further, as time was up, but had little doubt the discussion would continue constructively at home.

The whole family was seen by Miss Roberts and myself.

The family arrived late, and explained this by saying that they had wanted to leave Luke at home as he disrupted the session, but the baby-sitter had failed to turn up. There was a long pause again at the beginning, with obvious anxiety and tension. I said it was like a "slow bicycle race," where the last person to begin was the winner. Father initiated the discussion but complained that he did not know how to include Miss Roberts and myself, since so much had happened that it must be difficult for us to understand the point the family had reached unless they told us. This seemed based on his own need to understand and control the world through his intellect, so that he could not grasp the way we use the here-and-now. Also, there seemed some element of resentment and jealousy towards our co-therapy relationship, as if he wanted to understand it in order to control it, just as he and his wife allowed the children to control them.

He said he felt the problems derived as much from his wife as from him, and the mother finally began the session by reporting a dream in which she was Matthew who, with a former close friend he had since grown away from, was going to be executed by a firing squad. I thought this concealed a close and positive involvement, probably oedipal, but though we helped them to clarify their feelings it did not seem appropriate at this stage to interpret it directly in sexual terms.

However, in this session Matthew, previously depressed and hostile in a sullen, fearful way, seemed to have become much more openly determined and aggressive, dominating the whole family. Mother said that the main friction in the past had been between herself and Matthew, but that this had now changed to a conflict between him and his father. She linked this with the fact that Mary, the elder half-sibling by her previous marriage, had left the family to go to a university. While Mary was at home she had been the "chopping block" and there had been fierce conflict between Mary and her stepfather; mother linked this implicitly with sexual feelings by saying that fathers tended to worry more about the sexuality of daughters than of sons.

Since Mary had left home the conflict changed its position and now occurred mainly between father and Matthew. Mother next stated that she understood her daughter well enough, but could not understand boys "for obvious reasons." This seemed a further indication that we were on the verge of a sexual discussion.

The argument between father and Matthew now became more intense, and the father expressed increasing distress about it. He said it made him feel ill, and on inquiry said the symptoms were "like I think a coronary might be, my veins all close up and so on." I suggested Matthew might feel very inhibited at father's suggestion that an attack on him might kill him, and wondered whether Matthew inhibited his aggression for this reason. Following this interpretation Matthew seemed able to attack more directly, and taunted his father by saying that the symptoms were really due to the father's envy of his (Matthew's) greater educational opportunities.

At the beginning of this session Mark had seemed eager and expectant, joining in much more than he had previously done, but he had gradually withdrawn and played with the younger child. Matthew expressed anger that Mark was opting out of the discussion again and brought him in several times. In response, Mark complained about Matthew's domination and aggressiveness, in a way which suggested that this mirrored the relationship between father and Matthew, whereby he always suffered from their conflicts as the one at the bottom of the pecking order. He spoke with considerable feeling.

At this point in the interview father, mother and Mark were all lined up, both psychologically and physically, against Matthew, who was increasingly treated as if he were a tyrant of whom the whole family was frightened. This was pointed out, and the mother admitted that she felt opposed to Matthew, but also identified with him. This led the father to complain that he and the mother could never agree about things, and we pointed out how a discussion between the parents had been the missing factor up to this point in our interviews; we seemed to be now entering another stage. There were further indirect allusions to the parents' sexual relationship when the father said they wished they could have a room to themselves on their vacation, but that Matthew would resent being in with the two younger boys. Father said he was worried how the mother would cope when he went off on his sabbatical studies, which would take him away from home except at weekends, but the mother smiled and said she was looking forward to it—there were no problems when the father was away from the family! I suggested that the mother enjoyed having two men to play off, one against the other (father and Matthew). Though this was said twice, she seemed not to understand it at all. Matthew, however, seemed to confirm this interpretation by making fun of father and calling him an "old man of 95." The father looked rather disconsolate and the whole family tried to cheer him up by saying some positive things about him.

Throughout this session we had been on the verge of open expression of the oedipal conflict. I decided to wait to let them see it in their own time.

FOURTH FAMILY CONSULTATION

Both parents and both elder boys were seen by Miss Roberts and myself. This time they had succeeded in leaving Luke at home.

The seating was particularly relevant, for the father came and sat next to me instead of next to Miss Roberts and said to me, "I am changing places today, so I can hold your hand." There was the usual struggle to avoid taking the initiative at the beginning and the father suggested jokingly that I should lead as "director of communications." He then quoted a joke of Matthew's, which Matthew amplified, to the effect that Matthew was glad they were not going to a private psychiatrist on Harley Street and paying money for nothing, but were coming to see us instead and "getting nothing for nothing."

The father now seemed to make an attempt to open up the subject of the marital difficulty, referring back to the previous session where we had stopped at the point where the difficulties between himself and his wife had emerged. The mother did not offer him any help in continuing the discussion, and Matthew also appeared to be holding back; this time it was the father and Mark who appeared to be more honestly involved.

When I pointed this out the mother said that this was because the problem really lay between herself and Matthew. There was a good deal of rather violent imagery as this was described (e.g. "lightning flashing around the room," etc.) and the mother recounted how she had broken a broom over Matthew's head during a quarrel one day while the father was out. The sexualized relationship between Matthew and mother was again striking and it was relevant that Matthew described the argument as "one of mother's fucking fights." It was reported that the children got on better with either parent singly, but not when the parents were together. Miss Roberts pointed out how they seemed able to operate in pairs, but never in threes, and this expression of their jealousy and inability to share summed up much of the interaction. We seemed over and over again to be approaching the parents' marital difficulties but they behaved as if they could not see this implication at all.

I had felt throughout the session that I had "missed the boat" last time by not interpreting more directly the oedipal rivalry between Matthew and father. In this session the issue again kept recurring in indirect ways but the opportunity for an interpretation never seemed clearly to come. Nevertheless, Matthew gradually began to act as the healer of the marriage, and both boys said they wished the parents would have more fun, would go out more, instead of devoting so much attention to themselves, the children. The parents still seemed to avoid a direct relationship, even avoiding looking at each other. Finally the children took a more active part to unite them, Matthew even offering his pocket money so they could go to the pictures together, saying, "Dad! Would you like to see more of Mom? . . . Right! You would! . . . Mom! Would you like to see more of Dad? . . . Right!"

The parents still seemed to avoid the issue of their own relationship throughout this exchange and after it, despite the children's efforts, but the mother was gradually able to express much pent-up bitterness that the father had been absorbed in his work in the past and had given her little time and attention. The father spoke of his new plans to spend more time with the family, after his sabbatical was over. It became more and more obvious (except to themselves) that the parents were avoiding the issue of their sexual impotence and frigidity, but all interpretations met the same massive denial.

Matthew's final solution to father's problem, that they should "buy him a power drill" provoked roars of laughter; the children and the therapists clearly understood each other perfectly, but the parents were still somehow avoiding the issue and were laughing without quite appreciating the joke.

(*Note*: The last two sessions raised for me an important question. Although I felt I had "missed the boat" by failing to make an oedipal interpretation last time, my failure to do so seemed to lead to Matthew's taking the initiative in mending the marriage; does this mean that the interpretation was not only superfluous but could even have been harmful?)

A week after this interview the father wrote to say, "My wife and I have much appreciated the sessions we have had with you, but as you no doubt expected, they have acted as a catalyst with regard to our own relationship. The position is very difficult. We are both anxious to put it right but cannot do so without outside help. Are you in a position to discuss this with us separately from the rest of the family?"

The letter was addressed to me personally and sent to my home, not the clinic; we were not clear what this mode of communication signified, unless the father really wanted to see me without Miss Roberts also. However, an interview was arranged at the clinic in the usual way, but with the agreement that they would not bring the children.

FIFTH FAMILY CONSULTATION

The parents were seen in joint interview by Miss Roberts and myself, without the children, one month after the fourth consultation.

The father began and talked for about 15 minutes, giving a very clear and articulate summary of the marital history—much too clear and articulate to contain real feeling and involvement. He mentioned how his two previous marriages had broken up, but that each one had lasted longer and that the present marriage had endured for 15 years, seeming to imply both anxiety about his capacity for marriage and some claim that this must be improving. A daughter by a previous marriage had been given up by him to her mother's custody, and he clearly felt this a great loss. He also appeared to feel excluded by, and jealous of, his present wife's relationship with Mary, her daughter by a previous marriage, describing the mother as "protective," as if accusing her of defending the girl against himself. He then went on to describe an extra-marital affair he had been involved in five years previously, after which his wife had become disillusioned and had withdrawn from him, as well as suffering frequent depressions. From this point on the sexual relationship had become unsatisfactory.

When he finished speaking his wife as usual waited as if hoping that someone else would fill the space and "let her off the hook," but finally she said, "Now you want me to talk?" She then described her recurrent depressions since her discovery of the affair. It was clear from her account that she had not wanted to know the truth and had avoided recognizing what was happening at the time, though she now realized that she had sensed something and feared she had taken it out on the children, particularly fearing that she might have harmed Matthew.

Other themes then began to emerge. For example, father's absence from the home through overwork, and his absence of mind even when at home through preoccupation with his work, seemed related to his resistance and rebellion against his feeling that he was under his wife's control. This in turn was linked in the discussion with his dominant mother against whom his passive father had failed to help him free himself. His absorption with his work seemed a safe and controlled intellectualized expression of the rebelliousness he felt towards his parents, and we linked this in the interview with the passive nature of his rebelliousness towards his wife.

On her side, the mother revealed her need to have things organized, controlled and planned, and showed how upset she became if these were changed. The obsessional, managing and restrictive qualities of her interaction with the family became more obvious, and we were particularly struck by the way in which she appeared to control others by looking hurt and wounded, though when this was pointed out she seemed quite unaware of it. Father complained about the way his wife always began to worry about something the moment she got up in the morning, and we linked this with the hidden and denial mutual destructiveness in their relationship, and the way in which their fears of this led them to protect the relationship by withdrawing from each other.

Throughout the whole session, the mother still seemed to be reproaching and punishing the father for his infidelity, as if refusing to accept his guilt and self-reproach and to forgive him. The implication of her behavior was that the marriage had been viable until this extramarital affair spoiled it, but I challenged this and said it sounded to me as if the marriage had never really begun, that there had been nothing to spoil, and that she was now using the event to justify her failure to involve herself. The father obviously found these comments liberating, and the mother understandably did not like them too much.

(*Note*: Without the children, and particularly without Matthew's refreshing directness, the pace seemed to be much slower and we appeared to find it much harder to get down to reality. I wondered afterwards whether there was really anything important that could not have been said in front of the children.)

SIXTH FAMILY INTERVIEW

After an interval of two weeks, the parents were seen together without the children, by myself only as Miss Roberts was away.

The situation had changed and this time the father looked less cheerful, self-satisfied and comfortable; instead for the first time he seemed angry, determined, almost desperate. He opened by saying that his wife had been very upset at my having said, and Miss Roberts' having agreed, that their marriage had never started. His wife agreed that she had been very disturbed by this comment, adding that it sounded as if 15 years had been completely wasted. The father nevertheless firmly expressed the view that the statement was essentially true, and that one could also take the statement positively, as suggesting that a beginning was at least possible.

This time the father was much more openly critical of the mother, describing quarrels they had experienced over the children in which it seemed that he had in the past allowed her to be the controlling influence in their upbringing and education, fearing to oppose her, but that he had recently begun to take control, to stand against her, and to exert more influence over the children. I became increasingly aware of the way in which the father was inhibited and rendered helpless by the mother's controlling masochism, whereby she looks so helpless and vulnerable that she disarms others and makes them feel it would be cruel to attack her. I focused on this repeatedly during the interview, and said I felt the need to report a personal reaction to the way she was behaving since it seemed to contain relevant information about the marital interaction. I emphasized that this response was not intended as an expression even of a personal attitude towards her, still less a professional view, but rather as a response that I needed her help to understand and which might illuminate her understanding of herself.

I then reported my fantasy that, if I were married to her, no real relationship could exist as long as I allowed myself to be controlled by her expression of fear, vulnerability and pain, and that the only solution would be to behave so cruelly and ruthlessly that her illusions would be shattered.

The father found this comment releasing and illuminating. He said that he did indeed feel inhibited in just this way, and that through this the mother always controlled him.

The mother described how much of the time she felt like a child wanting to remedy the deprivation she suffered in her own family of origin through arranging happy family outings, which she felt the father spoiled. I linked her need to see him as an omnipotent, all loving parental figure with her simultaneous incapacity to allow him to be a man, particularly in the sexual sense. The father described how he was some-

times frightened of driving the mother mad, and she acknowledged that
this was indeed a real fear for her, and that at times she becomes quite
depersonalized. (This was presumably the origin of her fears of coming
to the clinic and exposing the family pathology, which Matthew was
expressing for her at the start of the therapy in his fears that he might
be "schizophrenic.")

Throughout the session I deeply felt the lack of Miss Roberts' presence, because on this occasion mother's need to control, limit and in
effect to castrate the father was so intense that I felt obliged to support
the father in his stand against her. I felt the mother needed a woman
to take her side in this difficult situation.

(*Note*: Again, nothing seemed to be said that could not have been
discussed in front of the children, whose absence still appeared to reduce
the effectiveness of the sessions. I asked the parents what they thought
about this, and left them to decide in what manner they would come
next time.)

SEVENTH FAMILY CONSULTATION

Three weeks' interval occurred since the last session. This time the
parents turned up with the two older boys, and were seen by myself and
Miss Roberts, who had been absent because of sickness from the previous
interview.

The parents began by inquiring about Miss Roberts' health, then
commented on the fact that they had brought the children with them. I
thought I had left this quite open, but the parents implied that I had
said they should come, or at least that they had felt that I wanted
this to happen because I had said I "felt we needed the children's common sense," which may have been the case.

The discussion started with the focus on the children, and in their
presence the previous overt discussion of the marital problems was no
longer explicit, though still implicitly present in an argument about the
children's schooling. Father had gotten his way and Matthew had been
moved to a school more able to cater to his high potential, separating
him from Mark (the boys had both previously attended the same
school and mother had said she "would never tolerate" a change of
school for Matthew).

The children were several times invited to speak but did not participate; we had the impression that they were resisting an attempt by the

parents to make them the focus and project the marital conflicts on to them. Miss Roberts commented on how lively and bright Mark appeared this time, and the father then described quite striking recent changes in both boys in the direction of improvement.

The discussion continued to block as if the parents were avoiding a confrontation, but the mother, clearly very angry still about the way I had supported the father and been critical of her at the previous interview, expressed some very aggressive comments to me. She said she thought I was "like a sea anemone" in that I appeared at first a warm and comfortable person who made people trust me, but then I suddenly stung them, pulled their insides out and spat them out again! I suggested that the mother was angry with me but complimented her on her more confident and assertive bearing, saying that I welcomed her ability to attack me and defend herself rather than to behave masochistically and look hurt. The mother seemed pleased by this response; the father was also looking more confident, and when this was commented on he agreed, saying that he had not felt able to assert himself before.

I asked if the rest of the family had noticed similar changes in the mother to those I was describing, but at first everyone evaded this question. However, Matthew later attacked her quite strongly and all the family not only agreed that she was bad-tempered and difficult when she got up in the morning, but that she could also get into violent rages—something that no one had dared to say openly before. The mother took this well and seemed quite able to stand up for herself, quite a change from her previous defensive vulnerability.

This discussion was interrupted by father's saying that he would like to understand Matthew's jealousy of Mark. Matthew resisted becoming involved in this discussion but Mark attacked him quite strongly, and the whole family seemed much more comfortable as this constellation developed. When we suggested they were avoiding a more general problem, particularly as it affected the parents, this was ignored. Finally, when I insisted that the *whole* family had difficulties with jealous feelings, but that they always dealt with this by keeping the jealousy safely concentrated between Matthew and Mark, the mother admitted to intense feelings of jealousy in childhood, while Matthew said he believed the family used him as a scapegoat for this type of problem.

The discussion continued to block and I finally expressed my feeling that we always avoided discussing the fact that the primary relationship in the family seemed to be between Matthew and mother, that he treated her as if she were his property, and that it was therefore understandable if he felt jealous of mother producing a baby (Mark) by another man (father). This interpretation was dealt with by further blocking and avoidance, but it seemed to influence what followed, for father and Matthew then displayed a capacity for a warm, mutual, masculine relationship which had never been revealed before. During this Matthew attacked both mother and Mark for refusing to join in intellectual discussions between him and father. He said they showed "empty faces" when he and father were getting on well and discussing something interesting, and asked, "What's behind them?" Mark replied, "If only you knew!"

Miss Roberts made the interpretation that mother and Mark felt envious about the good relationship between Matthew and father and therefore tried to destroy it; I agreed and added that Matthew and father seemed in fact to destroy it themselves before the others had a chance to do so, because they were so frightened of envy.

It was left for the family to decide the manner in which they wished to come to the next interview and the mother said, a bit provocatively, that she would bring Mary, the daughter by her previous marriage, as well, since she "might have something to add."

EIGHTH FAMILY CONSULTATION

Four weeks later, both parents and both elder boys were seen by Miss Roberts and myself. Mary, the mother's daughter by her previous marriage, came late, attending for the first time.

Matthew took the most comfortable chair and was laughed at for this. Father said he had heard from others in the family that Matthew had announced that he was going to dominate the session, but in fact Matthew sat with his head down, reading a book and ostentatiously withholding any comment.

After the usual long pause father expressed his wish to continue exploring the interpretation made last time that he and Matthew were rivals for the mother's affection, but that beneath this lay the possibility of a deep and positive relationship. There was no response from any of the family and this theme was completely avoided by everybody throughout the session in a most striking way. Matthew made a joke about "the congregation joining in the hymns," and we interpreted this in terms of his making his father into an authority or preacher and then ridiculing him. Matthew then made some jokes about psychoanalysis, saying that he was "guilty but pleading insanity," and it seemed as if the authority conflict between him and his father was now moving into the transference with me; this was interpreted.

A tense period followed in which all appeared to be avoiding contributing anything, but the father seemed able for the first time to keep silent, eventually forcing the others to show themselves. During this tense, silent period Mary arrived late, but did not contribute either.

Eventually some conversation developed fitfully around the plans for the family vacation (a seaside vacation in a foreign country) which Matthew was opposed to. Mary said that she thought it would be quite normal for him to wish to be away from the family, but Matthew seemed unable to express this feeling openly and to be in some conflict between his wish to remain attached and his desire to be independent. He spoke of the way he enjoyed playing ball games with all the family, including father, when they had once been on a deserted beach, as if expressing a wish for intimacy, and he objected to the vacation plans because he felt there would be too many strangers about. Mark made a joke about people "rubbing shoulders and producing friction" which resulted in much laughter.

Matthew did, in fact, appear to dominate the session, attacking Mark and mother after he had finished with father and me, though he never attacked Miss Roberts or Mary, the latter seeming at the moment to be his ally in his wish for autonomy.

Both Miss Roberts and I became aware about the same time that we were both feeling mystified and excluded by the intimate family jokes and small-talk, which prevented us from entering into things or understanding what was happening; having realized we were both experiencing this, we shared our joint response with the family and explored its meaning. Miss Roberts said she felt as if there was a conspiracy between mother, Matthew and Mark; this made sense to me, and I realized that this collusion had at first been directed against father, and later against me. I interpreted it in terms of my being cast in father's role and attacked and derided as he usually was. Mother partly confirmed this and later, when Matthew was deriding me again, she appeared both to enjoy the way he was attacking me and to protect me at the same time, much as she does with the father.

This confused situation seemed to go on for a long period with the family continuing to demonstrate this kind of interaction but refusing to discuss it, to become conscious of it, or to accept any interpretation from us. Towards the end I felt it worthwhile to express the feelings that Matthew was arousing in me, which I thought might well correspond to those he produced in father but which the father did not like to express. I said that Matthew made me feel frustrated and impotent, as if I somehow had to be cleverer than him and not be defeated by him. At the same time, I said, I had felt relieved when I was able to rebuke him and to say I felt that he was cheeky, irritating and boring, covering up with his jokes and contempt the deep need he felt for me to help him understand himself better. I asked why all the family seemed to let him get away with this, and this had great meaning for Mary. Matthew was able to admit that he did want something but could not understand what it was, and the parents were able to express how much they wanted to give it to him.

(In our discussion after the interview, Miss Roberts mentioned that at this point she was struck by Matthew's intense envy, and its resemblance to mother's. This suddenly clarified the situation for me and also explained the discomfort I had felt in this session. I realized that the essential key to the interaction which I had been seeking, but had been unable to discover because I was in fact denying it, was the penis-envy that had previously been directed towards the father, and which was now turned towards me.)

At the end of the session Mary asked if we had another appointment after the interview ended, and, looking appealingly at Miss Roberts, asked if she could have a talk by herself without the family. Since it was the last interview of the day, it was arranged that she should have a brief talk with Miss Roberts alone. This did not directly concern the family but centered around her anxieties about an ex-boyfriend of hers, who was planning to attend a homosexual party, and her fears that the experience might "rub off" on him. However, this fear of homosexuality seemed highly relevant to the total family situation.

NINTH FAMILY CONSULTATION

After four weeks' interval both parents, Matthew, Mark and Mary were seen in company with Miss Roberts.

The seating arrangement was quite different and this was commented on early in the session. The father asked if there was something missing in my corner of the room which had been there previously. I could see no change but this was quickly explained when the father decided that *he* was missing because he had changed his position and was no longer sitting next to me. In fact, Mark was on my right, where he usually sat, but father had moved away from my left and was next to Mark, between him and mother, so that the two parents were closer. Then the circle continued with Matthew, then Mary, and finally Miss Roberts on my left so that the therapeutic couple were also united. The pattern seemed in some way important and to represent some general change.

There was again the usual long silence and father was left to struggle to open the discussion while everybody left him to it. He mentioned that Matthew had not wanted to come and had been cross with me for attacking him last time. Matthew actually did look angry and said he did not want to discuss anything or argue, and I commented that he was clearly still annoyed at what I had said to him. He continued by saying that nothing had changed through their coming to the clinic, admitting that things had improved in the family generally but denying that this was anything to do with the interviews. Mark surprised us by disagreeing firmly and saying that the interviews had been helpful, in which he seemed to be expressing similar views to father. Mary said something about "water flowing under the bridge," which we took to mean that even if changes had occurred the interviews had not produced them.

For some time father kept up the attempt to get Matthew to talk, as if he somehow had to get the interview to work and take the lead, though his leadership is of a kind that takes too much responsibility for others and allows them all to opt out in an unhelpful way. Mother in particular looked as if she were withholding her contributions in a rather mischievous way. When I mentioned this there was some comment about the annoyance she had felt when I had criticized her previously, in the same way as Matthew was annoyed this time. I felt that the interview was blocked because the value of the interviews was not being questioned openly; even though Matthew and Mary were expressing veiled criticism they could not do this directly.

This led on to discussion of the jealousy between Matthew and Mark, during which a very real and warm relationship between them, beneath the frequent squabbling, began to emerge just as a similar warmth had revealed itself previously between Matthew and father. I found this quite unexpected and moving, and wondered if the jealousy and conflict were being fomented, perhaps by mother.

Later Matthew began to talk of his fights with mother, and of the great intimacy which existed between them when they were arguing and when they had made up after their quarrels. I began to feel that the real aggressive interaction in the family was between them, or at any rate between mother and other members of the family apart from father, one at a time. When I expressed this, Mary lost her previous boredom, sat up and grinned, and one had a clear impression of a hidden alliance whereby the rest of the family were describing secret and interesting things which happened among them when father was not there, and from which he was excluded. Father tried to take this in good part but looked uncomfortable and out of things, which we commented on.

A little later the talk turned to fears of destructiveness—for example, occasions when the children had taken overdoses of tablets, had suffered accidents and so on—as if such fears underlay their inhibitions. At this point the family turned to the attack and asked Miss Roberts and me how we resolved our differences, as if we also might be fearful of conflict and use masochistic defenses to avoid it. Later the whole family asked me whether I had suffered accidents as a child also. We did not deal with this part of the interview well, somehow not tuning into the transference implications but, instead, re-enacting the parental anxieties about their personal vulnerabilities and about the relationships among them.

The main theme throughout the session seemed to be the exclusion of the father, whereby the mother and the children shared intimate relationships into which he was not allowed. The father, on the other hand, appeared unable or unwilling to insist on his proper role and to break up this collusion. I realized after the interview that they had been treating me as they normally treat the father, as well as perhaps trying to split Miss Roberts and myself, and that I had found this difficult and had responded in a rather feeble way.

TENTH FAMILY CONSULTATION

After four weeks' interval, father, mother and Matthew were seen by Miss Roberts (I was away), who made the following notes:

"Father began by saying that Mark was on vacation, that Mary was caring for Luke and that the family had felt it would be an opportunity for the parents and Matthew to come alone. Matthew sat in Dr. Skynner's chair and he and the parents laughed about this, commenting on his wish to be Dr. Skynner. Matthew confirmed this by taking up a paper from the desk and reading it until father reprimanded him firmly.

"Throughout the interview Matthew alternated between swinging around in the swivel chair with a nonchalant expression and becoming seriously involved in the discussion.

"Father said that he had suggested to mother that she should be 'provocative' this week, whereupon all the family lapsed into silence. I made a comment eventually about this, indicating that Dr. Skynner's absence seemed to be linked with the family's wish to express provocative feelings. Mother said she could not get started without help, so father then began talking of the fights at home among them all.

"The interview continued in a very active way and I was required to do very little. Father adopted a 'protective' attitude towards me throughout and Dr. Skynner's absence was frequently referred to. Father spent some time talking of the need to protect mother who was exhausted because of many demands made upon her by the family and by her job. Matthew was clearly concerned about mother's well-being and showed it quite openly, but then expressed bewilderment because despite her 'exhaustion' mother will suddenly announce, for example, that she is going to take in a foster child. Matthew was particularly upset about this kind of suggestion because it meant that he would be denied the room of his own that he had been promised. There was much material around this theme, and I suggested that this was evidence of mother's provocation which father had wanted her to express. We went on to discuss the lack of communication in the family about events which could affect them all."

ELEVENTH FAMILY SESSION

After five weeks' interval both parents, Matthew and Mark were seen by Miss Roberts (I was away).

Miss Roberts' notes state:

"Father immediately began by saying that he was speaking for the family and continuing a discussion they had been having on the way to the clinic. This concerned the future. Both father and mother said they had found the meetings very helpful and felt that they had been able to see things in a different light which had improved family relationships. Mark also said he enjoyed coming, and his improvement was attributed to the sessions. Matthew said he did not want to continue and that he thought the sessions had made no difference.

"This led to talk about the future, father in particular expressing anxiety about the family conflicts with which mother would have to deal alone while he was away on his sabbatical, which would begin in just over two months, when the family consultations were to cease. I pointed out how father was again acting as spokesman for the family and wondered whose anxiety he was really describing; father took the point and said that this tendency to attribute his anxiety to others was one of the things he had learned through coming here.

"Mother appeared upset and said how difficult she found it to talk without being helped to do so. Father and the boys became quite angry with her but she only muttered that she was worried about the future. I took up these comments in relation to the future interviews and the father at once showed that he had calculated that there would be at least two more interviews and, if we were willing, that a third could be squeezed in before he left.

"The talk turned again to the possible problems that would arise when father was not at home and there was some attempt to visualize what these might be; however, Matthew felt there was nothing to be concerned about. I said they seemed to be talking about the future in order to avoid speaking of problems in the present; the parents both agreed but still continued to express fears in the same way as before. Again I tried to relate this to anxiety about the future of the therapy and asked what they had in mind in this respect. After some discussion it was generally agreed that mother would like to feel that they could come and see us if and when difficulties arose and that they would all (except Matthew) like to feel that an occasional session could be arranged during future vacations.

"This having been dealt with, the parents began to speak of Matthew's greed and his 'grasping' attitude. Mother said that she avoided this problem by not becoming involved in shopping expeditions with him. Matthew expressed much anger and kept asking for evidence to support the parents' accusation. The parents were only able to speak in terms of food and material possessions, but I said I thought they were really referring to feelings, and I suggested that people often felt that they had to grasp when they felt deprived. This led to some discussion about Matthew having perhaps felt rejected when Mark was born, and mother commented that Matthew had been a very demanding toddler. Father added that Matthew always had to interrupt and draw attention to himself if father was engaged in conversation with someone else. He went on to blame himself for giving too little attention to the family in the past, but mother did not express any feeling of responsibility herself. Mark, who had stayed out of much of this discussion, defended Matthew and tried to explain that his demands did not have the meaning that others gave to them. As the family spoke about him Matthew became more and more angry, and the session ended with him walking out of the room followed by Mark. The parents followed in a way which made me feel that they were together in their feelings about this.

"I felt that this session centered around Matthew's problem of greed and was struck by the fact that he was the only one of the family who had to deny that he had received any help. The parents had spoken earlier of a number of improvements in both Matthew and Mark, and in the family in general. I felt Matthew's attitude to be an indication of his envy and saw this session as a development from earlier sessions which had centered upon oedipal conflict and other problems of a later stage of development."

TWELFTH FAMILY CONSULTATION

Three weeks' interval intervened. Both parents, Matthew and Mark were seen by Dr. Skynner. Miss Roberts was away on this occasion.

There was little direct reference to my absences, though they were offered opportunities to comment on this. This time father openly declined to let others force him into the position of doing all the talking, and the whole family sat in awkward silence for over five minutes. The father appeared to be more comfortable in the situation, more able to take the initiative, while the others seemed to be more at a disadvantage in relation to him.

Eventually Matthew said he saw no point in coming, adding that people tended to say things they did not really mean, which upset everybody afterwards. Both parents seemed to want the children to say that they had found the sessions helpful, though they really gave no reason why they should expect this or, indeed, why they felt it was worthwhile coming themselves. Mark made one or two comments early on but was soon swamped by the conflict which developed between Matthew and father.

This was the same battle as before, but more in the open. The father was gradually becoming stronger, more assertive and direct, so that it was Matthew who finally refused to give his opinion of others in the family, when challenged, saying that he felt it would be damaging; he restricted himself to calling father a "silly old bugger." Gradually it appeared that Matthew's position contained a contradiction, whereby, on the one hand, he felt that when the family tried to change him or make him happy they were taking away his individuality, while, on the other hand, he seemed to prevent the positive exchange he really wanted by making clever and meaningless replies to any comment. He was attacked a great deal by both parents, and was still smarting from father's accusations at the last interview that he was mean and grasping. Mother tended as usual to sit outside the discussion but did point out how the other children would ask whether something could be afforded, and do without if necessary, whereas Matthew would always demand the limit.

Matthew argued and stonewalled by denying and countering everything that was said, as if to destroy its meaning rather than to answer the charges. I eventually interrupted this by using a systems manipulation. I suggested that any attempt to change Matthew or even to discuss the problem with him was in some way making him feel that his individuality was threatened; I suggested that he must be permitted the right to be hopeless, unchangeable, a "dead loss," or, if he wished, to destroy everything positive in the interview as he did at home. This appeared to unlock the previous pattern and Matthew was left without his former hold over his parents, who were able to see that their wish for him to be happy, successful and well-rounded was a subtle form of control and domination which he did in fact have some right to resist, and which in fact put them under his control.

Though the interview was very tense half-way through, they all left in reasonably good spirits.

THIRTEENTH FAMILY CONSULTATION

After an interval of one month, both parents, Matthew and Mark were seen by Miss Roberts and myself.

After the usual hesitation about beginning, the father began by saying that they had "all agreed not to waste the first 15 minutes of this valuable hour." He was much more relaxed and composed, obviously determined not to let the others force him to do all the work, and he let them sweat the silence out. Matthew pulled his chair back aggressively at the start, and Mark read a book which Matthew later took away from him. Father said that mother had declared that she would attack me (she was reported to have said "let's lam into him"), but mother denied this and said that she had suggested they should all "attack the problem." She did nevertheless seem quite hostile and aggressive beneath this sweet veneer, and demanded that I "ask nice leading questions I can get my teeth into!"

Eventually father expressed his concern that the mother would not discuss with me the main problem, which was really her distress about the fact that he would be away from home during his sabbatical. Mother said it was hard to discuss the matter because she was so worried about current events in the world—a recent earthquake, the invasion of a foreign country—clearly displacing her fear of distress into outside events. Matthew seemed to oppose the idea that his mother was really concerned about the separation, complaining that the main problem was that she worked too hard at her job and had little energy left when she came home; he suggested she might get worse and have a breakdown, have nothing left for them at all.

Mother's typical avoidance of her own problem was once again successful and Matthew and father began to argue and criticize each other's stubbornness; though valid in itself this seemed to be escaping from the primary problem between the parents and letting the mother off the hook. I pointed out this recurrent tendency to protect the mother by starting disputes between other members of the family. From this point on, Matthew repeatedly pointed out similar avoidances of parental interaction and put the problem back in the marriage every time it became displaced.

Mother finally began to acknowledge her inner distress, saying it was too difficult to talk about the separation and that if she did speak about it she might break down. Shortly after this she began to weep and then recovered, saying that she always reacted badly to separation but hoped she could survive her husband's absence as she had done before. She believed the only way she could cope was to avoid talking about it.

This led to her speaking for the first time about her frigidity, which had become worse at the prospect of the separation. Father also expressed distress at mother's sexual rejection of him. I suggested that she was angry about the separation and was dealing with it by withdrawing her attachment to her husband in advance. She admitted that she cannot avoid rejecting him, cannot explain why she does it.

The parents appeared to experience no difficulty in talking about this in front of the children, though Matthew kept saying that it was really a problem between his parents and that the children's presence was not necessary, as if he found it difficult to acknowledge the sexual relationship between them.

Father said that the relationship between him and mother had become steadily worse since they first came for treatment, and that at present they seemed to have nothing at all in common and nothing to share. He attributed this to the "bloody mess" of the past. I said that although the mother presented herself as helpless and suffering, as if others were hurting her, she seemed at the same time, beneath this, to be hard, bitter and unforgiving, punishing father for his previous infidelity. The father appeared supported by my comment and able to express similar direct criticism of her. Matthew also criticized her more openly, and when the father spoke of the mother's brief periods of elation, which he said were always followed by trouble, Matthew added that they all had to be grateful to her whether they liked it or not.

We agreed to arrange one more interview before the father went away, and we left it to the family to decide how they would come to the last session.

(*Note*: In this interview for the first time the mother's problems have come fully into the open, particularly her depression and her rage at rejection, of which her sexual frigidity seems to be one element. In the past the family has repeatedly colluded to avoid facing this and to present some other issue upon which to focus attention. It seems as if the father, who needs her to be a good mother, had to collude in this avoidance until he felt stronger, and that when he became firmer the children were also able to refuse to let the marital problems be displaced on to them.)

FOURTEENTH FAMILY CONSULTATION

Three weeks' interval intervened. Both parents were seen by Miss Roberts and myself.

The parents came without the children, mother thinking that this was obligatory, father remembering that it was left for them to decide. The father sat next to me, while mother and Miss Roberts sat opposite each other towards the other end of the room. The father began the discussion, and for some time offered various ideas and starting points in an effort to get his wife to involve herself, but each time she looked helpless and appealing, said she had forgotten or that she did not know what to say, etc. Father had started by saying that mother had announced before the interview that she would "lam into him" but she denied this too.

This continued for some time until I queried its meaning, when the father said that this had been the fundamental pattern throughout their lives together. He would initiate discussion, but his wife would never respond or reciprocate or engage in a dialogue which could lead anywhere. During this I mentioned that the mother looked helpless and miserable and she denied this, tapping her foot in an irritable way as if she were denying anger, which was again commented on. Our efforts continued to be blocked by this excessive passivity on her part, which seemed to be her feminine way of defeating the father's masculine activity.

After some further exchanges in which Miss Roberts and I appeared to be taking an impartial position which facilitated agreement between us, but which somehow put us between the marital pair, I pointed this out and suggested that we somehow needed to be more involved with the couple even if we took sides on the basis of male and female positions. (Though I omitted to mention it in my report at the time, the mother had said, at the session following the one at which I had challenged her and at which she had felt very attacked, that she had subsequently discussed what I had said with some other women. At first they had felt that what I had said had been harsh, but later they had agreed that the feelings and problems that mother had described were things that all women shared. I felt that the mother was asking for support from Miss Roberts in a similar way, as a woman, and that this might mean that they both had to take sides against the father and myself.)

Miss Roberts then mentioned that she had always found some difficulty in the seductive way the father talked to her. This appeared to free the situation and most of the succeeding comments were made by Miss Roberts, mainly in interaction with the mother. Miss Roberts said that the mother somehow concealed her emotions and made it hard for others to respond and sympathize; this led the mother to open up and reveal her experience in a much more direct and simple way than she had been able to do before. She expressed fears that her husband would leave her if she showed her moods fully, but on the other hand, she said, she was sure that they were very close and would never leave each other.

At this the father said the mother was too complacent, that the marriage could go on the rocks if they did not struggle for it; he declared that he often felt fed up with it and wished it would end.

The mother looked crestfallen, but instead of the father's remarks producing resentment, withdrawal or masochistic behavior she seemed to listen and to take the criticism seriously, in a way that might produce a change both in her and in their relationship. For the first time they appeared to be listening to each other, open to each other's unknown qualities and to the marriage as something which could change and grow —or fail. Twice they became anxious and turned to us as if unable to tolerate the uncertainty and helplessness which facing one's existence and the issues of a real relationship must entail, but we supported them and the interview appeared to end with some possibility that this real dialogue and questioning of the relationship might continue afterwards. Both Miss Roberts and I noted independently that during this stage we both felt almost like intruders, as if we should quietly steal away and leave them together.

Towards the end there was some anxiety, no doubt caused partly by the long break they would be facing from each other and from the treatment situation, since the father was to depart the next week. They expressed a wish to resume the family consultations during the next vacation break, in three months' time, and we agreed that they could come in whatever fashion they felt most helpful.

(*Note*: This interview seemed a real breakthrough, and a crucial factor appeared to be the capacity of Miss Roberts to identify with, and support, the mother as a woman as I had previously done with the father as a man. This naturally meant that Miss Roberts and I had, as it were, to move apart from each other and it may have taken us some time to feel secure enough to do this because we were still learning to work together.)

During the break the mother wrote to Miss Roberts and myself saying there were certain things that she found it difficult to say in the joint interviews. She described her husband's past history and that of their relationship in some detail, but the main point to emerge was that she felt his sexual potency was vulnerable and might be seriously threatened by any criticism from her, particularly by the fact that she had not felt real sexual desire towards him since the time of his affair five years before, though the letter also suggested that this dated from a puerperal depression she had suffered after the birth of Luke. They both seemed to make it difficult for each other by worrying too much about each other's response, thereby inhibiting a spontaneous expression of feeling and sexual desire.

The other point was that there had been a brief resurgence of sexual passion in both of them after she had discovered the husband's affair. It was agreed that Miss Roberts would offer mother a separate interview, before the next family interview planned for the vacation. Miss Roberts reported:

"The mother seemed rather apprehensive and I focused on her problem of bringing the material in the letter into the joint interviews rather than on the problem presented in it. She expressed fears about upsetting her husband by talking about not wanting to have a sexual relationship with him. I tried to help her understand why she believed this would be more upsetting than her actual rejecting behavior. It was fairly evident throughout that talking is felt by her to be attacking, in the same way that she often feels attacked by comments made by others to her. She gave indications of her fears of becoming mad and we talked a little about the difficulty that can come from reading books on psychology, as she does, when one is not actually in the profession and one's imagination has no check. We talked about the two possibilities of resolving the present problem: (1) for her to go on coming weekly to see me; (2) for me to help her to bring it into the next joint interview. I pressed for the latter, saying that I thought that the former might lead to other problems, particularly regarding father's feeling about it. We left it that she would think about this and decide what she wanted, and also let me know if she needed me to help her to bring it into the next joint session."

FIFTEENTH FAMILY CONSULTATION

Ten weeks' interval intervened. The parents came without the children, and were seen by Miss Roberts and myself. She reported that mother had whispered to her as she entered the room, "It's all right," as if to indicate that she had been able to discuss the sexual problems with her husband. When we inquired why they had not brought the children, they explained that they had left the older boys to look after Luke, and that in any case Matthew's problems were resolved and they wished to talk about the marital difficulties out of the boys' hearing.

The father began by speaking about the marriage in a rather verbose and longwinded way which left both Miss Roberts and I confused. We reported this to them and the mother began to talk much more straightforwardly than usual, describing the discussion she had on her own with

Miss Roberts and the subsequent talk with her husband about the marital difficulty. She was upset particularly, she said, about the lack of
real relationship and sexual enjoyment in the marriage. The latter had
become more and more flat as they had collapsed into a cozy but boring
domesticity. Mother mentioned the father's fears of impotence and he
acknowledged that he had experienced similar difficulty in his former
marriages. He than began to complain about the present marital relationship, saying it was "almost non-existent" and that they only
stayed together because of the children. The discussion gradually became more direct, but it was very striking how dull, boring and apathetic they both were in the way they related to each other as they
spoke about their relationship, never interacting in a direct or lively way
or even looking at each other. This led on to a discussion of how the
marriage had really "got off the ground" when the father had his affair
five years previously, and the mother confirmed that this had produced
a much more lively capacity for sexual response in her (she spoke of
"six months of bliss").

During all this the father was criticizing the mother in a somewhat
unconvincing way, though seemingly reassuring himself at the same time
that they really had a good relationship underneath, while she sat with
a rising flush, looking more and more emotional. She attacked him
strongly for not taking responsibility for the family; we had never before seen her so assertive, but the father did not reply and, as if she had
to inhibit herself because he could not cope with her, she subsided to
her previous pleading, masochistic attitude.

We focused on this aspect of their relationship. Miss Roberts felt the
problem between them was being demonstrated in their interaction—
mother unable to be assertive or angry for fear of making the father
feel castrated, father feeling impotent but defending against this by
becoming a "puffed-up wind-bag" (Miss Roberts' description in her
notes).

I recall feeling quite exasperated with the way the father avoided his
inadequacy so that everyone had to protect him, and I criticized him
very directly, saying he somehow compensated for his feeling of sexual
impotence by trying to be potent in his head, blowing himself up into
a great balloon of words and ideas. He continued this verbal "masturbation" although confronted several times, and at the end, when he
went off into a great oration, summing up the whole interview and once
again trying to control the situation by intellectual understanding, I
told him it was all "hot air" and deflated him again.

SIXTEENTH FAMILY CONSULTATION

After five weeks' interval both parents were seen without the children, by Miss Roberts and myself.

Both parents looked more relaxed and comfortable, and a better relationship was evident throughout the session. The father began by acknowledging that he had been upset by my sharp criticism of him at the last session, but that it had made him think and it led to a serious discussion at home. He had perceived that he is really very selfish, wrapped up in his own world, and that this had caused problems for all the family. He felt that this general problem was more fundamental than the more limited sexual one we had focused on.

Mother agreed that they now felt closer together. She felt she understood father better, felt closer to him, warmer and more affectionate, and the relationship had improved considerably. They both reported that the children also improved, and that father said he thought this was partly because he had learned something from me about being more direct in what he said to Matthew. They made several comments which suggested that they were thinking of terminating, and said that they felt they had got the help they needed and were functioning adequately, though they expressed some uncertainty as to whether they were still avoiding more difficult issues. We clarified this question with them and agreed that their decision to stop was an appropriate one.

We spent the remaining part of the session clarifying some of the issues. Mother's need to castrate father in the past received an explanation through her account of an uncle who had in her childhood made advances to her which were too overtly sexual and had made her embarrassed and frightened. Father recognized this as explaining mother's excessive control of his sexuality and also her fear and jealousy of his relationship with Mary and with Mary's adolescent friends. Father's fear of homosexuality, which had led him to distance himself from his sons as they became older, had received some attention in earlier sessions but now was fully explored and recognized by him as a relevant factor. We had the impression that they would be able to go on working out many of these problems on their own.

At the end of the session the mother seemed anxious and wanted another interview in three months, at the next break, but the father said firmly that he felt they should stop, as otherwise they would always put things off and not take responsibility for solving the problems themselves. As the father stepped forward to take responsibility, it was interesting to see how mother was able to accept his decision.

They left with warm expressions of gratitude, and we felt equally warm feelings of pleasure at the outcome of the work we had done together.

This account of the sessions will not be further summarized or elaborated, leaving the reader to form his own conclusions and criticisms. However, a few brief remarks may make this easier.

First, the fact that a number of themes appear overtly in the last session, when they had not been explicitly dealt with before, might be taken to indicate a failure to recognize and interpret them earlier. I think, nevertheless, that they were worked with throughout in the non-verbal, interactive way I prefer to use, and their verbal expression in the final session is more a "history-taking" after therapy is completed, for the benefit of the therapist's general understanding and future work, and a way of filling in time through conversation when the work is already completed.

Secondly, I expect it will already be obvious that my co-therapist and I were still relatively unused to working together, were "feeling our way" and so did not at once exploit all the opportunities for modeling relationships that presented themselves. My colleague, who was at that time still learning from me, hesitated, for example, to form a female coalition with the mother, as I had earlier formed a male alliance with the father, until I encouraged her to do so.

And thirdly, the fact that the sessions were being taped for teaching purposes (with the family's permission) led us to accept a slower, more leisurely pace and to avoid taking "short cuts" based on intuitive insights, in order that the therapeutic sequence might be allowed to unfold in a clear way and to come as far as possible from the family itself.

APPENDIXES

A SOURCES OF FAMILY THERAPY CONCEPTS IN OTHER THEORIES OF CHANGE

Prove all things; hold fast to that which is good.

St. Paul, Thessalonians

The family is a meeting ground for many sciences, an area where the boundaries of many fields of knowledge overlap. It is this condition which makes conjoint family therapy such a fertile and interesting area of study, but from it also arise two serious problems in teaching the subject. First, the fact that the family stands at the interface of so many fields of knowledge requires some basic grasp of a wide range of concepts and theories. Fortunately the basic principles involved are simple enough and are not difficult to cover, but it would ask too much of the majority of students to expect them to study these basic sciences directly and to abstract the relevant principles themselves, at least in the early stages of their training. Secondly, the field of conjoint therapy is attracting would-be therapists from widely different disciplines—psychiatry, pediatrics, general practice, social work, psychology, psychoanalysis, counseling, nursing, occupational therapy and so on—each with a grounding in different basic sciences. Pediatricians or psychologists are often poorly acquainted with psychoanalytic theories; psychoanalysts are often ignorant of the principles of behavior modification, modeling and role-playing; many nurses and teachers have little basic knowledge in psychology and other behavioral sciences.

Because of this we have found it helpful, in the Family and Marital Courses arranged by the Institute of Group Analysis, to begin with a series of notes and lectures outlining the main basic concepts in the fields of study related to family therapy, before examining conjoint techniques themselves. Inevitably, this information will appear obvious and indeed oversimplified to those whose previous training has covered the field in question, even though it may be new and useful to others whose earlier training has taken a different line. Nevertheless, we have found that these introductory notes and lectures are welcomed by most participants in the courses, both because they enable them to gain a rapid impression of the ideas and theories underlying family work, and also because they provide an outline to guide their further, more detailed study of the basic sciences, when there is time to attempt this.

What follows, then, is a very brief summary of some of the fundamental concepts from psychoanalysis and other psychodynamic theory, psychology, communication theory, systems theory, ethology and so on. This is intended to serve as an expanded glossary available to those readers whose professional education has not included some of the concepts taken for granted in the presentation. Though based on a personal view I hope it will indicate, nevertheless, the broad base from which family therapy has grown.

GENERAL

In approaching psychology, it is helpful to distinguish two types of contribution to the field. Until around 1850, psychology was a branch of philosophy, and some psychologists have continued to produce general systems of ideas, essentially philosophical in nature in that they are speculative, generalizing far beyond any known facts, in an attempt to provide some total explanation of human behavior.

The other type of contribution derives from careful, painstaking observation and research. Theories are submitted constantly to the discipline of fact, such as microscopy, electrical studies in physiology, or at least the need to relieve suffering and to cure symptoms in the medical treatment of mental disorders. The ideas of this second type of contribution, however much admixed with improbable generalization, seem steadily to accumulate sound and valuable principles.

Unfortunately, much psychological theory is a mixture of the two, for there is a frequent tendency to overgeneralization whereby principles well-established by experiment in a limited sphere are then extrapolated to create an all-inclusive "system." Behaviorism and psychoanalysis are particularly striking examples, often leading to rejection by others of the core of fact on which the speculative structure was based. Much of the apparent conflict of schools in psychology is due to this type of contest over territorial claims rather than to any real conflict of fundamental principle.

The subject is, moreover, less like a unified nation than a confederation of independent states which have developed more or less independently, often without much communication or even with an "iron curtain" of hostile disregard separating them (though at the present time the barriers are suddenly breaking down and each branch is beginning to illuminate the others in relation to certain current studies, especially in the field of family therapy). At least the following separate streams can be distinguished.

ACADEMIC AND EXPERIMENTAL PSYCHOLOGY

Psychology as a discipline on its own, separated off from philosophy but excluding psychological studies which have their origin in related fields, such as zoology, physiology or medicine, has been concerned with three main types of investigation. These are:

(A) *Studies of Perception*

From about 1850 onwards, when psychology became a separate science, investigations were carried on into the laws governing perception of the external world by the senses. Such experiments, which could be based on introspection and measured by simple instruments, led to such discoveries as the logarithmic relationship between increase in sensory stimulus and the resulting sensation experienced.

In recent years some investigations have concentrated on the way in which sensory experience is determined as much by learned expectations and unconscious attitudes as by the external world, facts which have some relevance for those of us who are concerned with helping others to alter their views and expectations of others and the world generally. This aspect of psychology has aroused little controversy and is perhaps closest to the other natural sciences.

(B) *Psychological Tests*

The second main area which academic psychology has made its own is the measurement of human capacities and skills, particularly those functions labeled "intelligence."

This aspect of psychology proper is more concerned with practical problems and the behavior of ordinary people, than the two other branches described, which have been concerned mainly with animals or with limited human functions, under artificial and experimental conditions.

Apart from controversies over the relationship between intelligence and social class, race or ethnic group, arising from emotionally charged political issues, disputes in this area have resembled those common to all developing sciences, based on resolvable issues of fact.

(C) *Studies of Associative Processes*

Beginning with James Mill, in about 1800, while psychology was still a branch of philosophy, there has been a central interest in the laws governing associative processes. Throughout the nineteenth century this involved studies of human subjects, using introspection to examine the ways in which ideas in a sequence were related to one another, with such factors as *contiguity* (association of two ideas in time or space), or *repetition* leading to increased tendency to recurrence of the association. However, even around 1820 Hebart had expressed the view that sequences of ideas were determined by unconscious factors, not accessible to conscious introspection, and such difficulties led, at the turn of the century, to a rejection of the introspective method (which was left to the medical psychologists and psychoanalysts), and to the rise of behaviorism.

Around 1900, Thorndike and later Watson (in the United States) and Pavlov (in Russia) produced psychologies based only on observable events—the presentation of a stimulus and the observation of the resulting muscular or glandular response, seeking laws governing the connection between them. This work, based mainly on animal learning experiments, has since been developed in great detail, particularly by Skinner, Tolman and Hull. The laws determining the formation of associations by conditioning (the association of a neutral stimulus with an instinctive one, e.g. salivation by a dog to the sound of a bell, previously rung at the feeding time) and by operant conditioning (the association of an action, at first random or accidental, with a reward, as when a dog repeatedly presses a lever after this is followed on the first occasion by the presentation of food, or where a man learns to relax and reduce his blood pressure after he has been provided with visual or auditory feedback about its level) are now very accurately known, as also are those governing the removal or extinction of such responses. This knowledge is extensively applied to behavior therapy, whereby such principles are used to help sufferers from undue anxiety or specific phobias (and recently psychosomatic disorders) to unlearn harmful habits and learn others considered more appropriate.

This body of knowledge is also now as well-based as that in other sciences, and begins to illuminate other branches of psychology. However, difficulties constantly arise when laws relating to the simplest forms of learning or association, adequate much of the time in the study of animals and in the simplest human associations, are pressed into service to explain all human behavior. This limitation, which leads not only to constant theoretical difficulties, but also to naïve generalizations and recommendations regarding the control of human conduct (cf. B. F. Skinner), appears to me to have its roots in an emotional resistance, in many of those attracted to this field, to the idea that human behavior is not all potentially rational and controllable. Many, therefore, show pronounced hostility to the ideas of psychoanalysis, though a rapprochement is gradually developing between these two approaches, especially in the field of family and marital therapy.

ETHOLOGY

In 1872, Darwin, interested in the psychological consequences of his theory of evolution and seeking links between the behavior of men and animals as well as in their morphology, published *The Expression of the Emotions in*

Man and Animals. He gave detailed accounts of the muscular movements involved in various "emotional" responses and found close correspondences between human (both infant and adult) and animal reactions. He provided evidence that these responses could represent preparations for action appropriate to the situation producing the stimulus (e.g., fight/flight in situations of danger) as well as other ideas fundamental to recent developments in psychiatry and psychosomatic medicine. His ideas could have been produced yesterday, so far are they still from being generally understood and applied, and it is instructive to see the different approach of a biologist, used to viewing behavior as a whole in a wider context and seeking its broader meaning, compared with the narrower view of the learning theorists towards their laboratory animals. That Darwin was so far in advance of his time can be judged by the fact that little was added to his ideas until the last 25 years or so, when Lorenz and Tinbergen gave the study of ethology (the behavior of animals under natural conditions) a new impetus. Since then many workers in the field of human psychology have seen its value and ethologists and psychoanalysts now work side by side in the study of human behavior in some institutions, while Harlow's studies of monkeys deprived of mothering have illuminated, for example, the problem of battered babies where human mothers have suffered similar deprivation in early life. This field is only beginning to influence psychology generally but is likely to play a crucial and increasing role in the future, through the principle it follows of viewing all functions within a context of the whole organism within a social setting. It is particularly relevant to the understanding of nonverbal communication, which is of increasing importance as one begins to work with groups, especially natural groups like families.

PHYSIOLOGICAL PSYCHOLOGY

Soon after 1800 Rolando suggested that the cerebral hemispheres of the brain were the seat of "higher" mental functions. This was confirmed by Flourens, who demonstrated by animal experiment not only that different parts of the brain had special functions, but that the whole nevertheless operated as a unity and that functions of damaged parts could often be taken over by those which were unharmed. By the 1850s the cell structure and fiber connections had been discovered and the neurone theory emerged around 1890 giving, in the variable properties of the junctions or synapses, a possible basis for learning and habit.

The concept of hierarchy, in which higher levels modified through inhibition the action of lower ones to permit more subtle responses, was put forward by Hughlings Jackson, a physician and neurologist, before 1870. Sherrington, around 1900, developed the concept, seeing the nervous system as essentially concerned with the integration of information, man's more developed higher centers making possible the integration of more complex and comprehensive information and permitting subtler and more appropriate responses.

Interest was at first centered on the "higher" centers of the cerebral cortex (roughly intellectual functioning) and the "lower" centers of the spinal cord and brain stem (roughly instinctive and motor function), but in the past 20 years research has clarified the operation of the intermediate centers or limbic system which seems more concerned with functions denoted by such words as emotion, drive, need, etc.

Though physiological psychology has, like other sciences, involved much study of detail, the tendency of its more eminent contributors has been to see the nervous system as an integrated whole which cannot be understood unless it is viewed as a "field" which is influenced by, but which also controls, its parts. The idea that it is organized in hierarchical fashion with lower centers subservient to, but providing information for, and influencing, higher centers, seems to be inescapable to those who study it. However, the detailed information about brain function is still too coarse and approximate to permit much correlation with the subtlety of human experience.

MEDICAL PSYCHOLOGISTS

Two main lines may be distinguished: (*A*) The physician/humanitarian and (*B*) the physician/hypnotist/psychotherapist.

(A) The Physician/Humanitarian

The last witch was burnt in 1775. Evidence from that period suggests that many, if not most, were mentally disordered individuals and that they were used as scapegoats into whom unacceptable aspects of the "normal" population were projected and then "destroyed" by proxy. Pinel, who was given charge of the Bicetre Asylum in 1793 and began to substitute kindness, understanding, and re-education for the chains, shocks and punishments previously used on the insane, probably represented a more general change in the attitudes of people towards their own less rational aspects. His action began a steady change (despite periods of resistance and reaction still widely apparent) towards a view that mental disorder was understandable and perhaps even open to alteration by scientific investigation, and that it represented a difference in degree rather than kind from the normal range of behavior, needing normal attitudes in response. The "open-door policy" and the "therapeutic community" concept, in which patients are encouraged to share responsibility for their own care, re-education and government, are present sequels.

(B) *The Physician/Hypnotist/Psychotherapist*

Around 1780 the physician Mesmer proposed the name "animal magnetism" for a method of healing by exorcism, previously used by the priest Gassner, attempting thereby to substitute a rational and scientific explanation for the supernatural rationale of the latter. His techniques, which became widely known, were given, in about 1840, an explanation based on brain physiology by the Scottish physician, Bain, who renamed the phenomenon "hypnotism" and made it acceptable in medical circles. Reports were made of its use in surgical operations soon after.

Libeault and Bernheim (at Nancy) and Charcot (at Paris) studied the phenomenon of hypnotism extensively, focusing particularly on the phenomenon of hysterical dissociation and multiple personality on which they reported independently around 1880. Hypnotism became a temporary fad in the medical world, to be rejected equally irrationally soon after Charcot's death, but two men, Janet and Freud, were led to investigate the phenomenon more deeply.

In the 1880s, Janet, the Frenchman, developed the idea that hysterical symptoms were due to split-off parts of the personality, dissociated ideas which continued to have effects although the patient was unconscious of them. He coined the term "subconscious" and anticipated Freud and Breuer in demonstrating that the symptoms could be cured by restoring the dissociated ideas and emotions to consciousness by means of "psychological analysis"—the examination of dreams and of automatic writing and talking in the hypnotic state. In addition, Janet developed several ideas which are absent in those of Freud and his other successors. He was particularly interested in the idea of attention—almost neglected by other medical psychologists—suggesting that hysterical dissociation took place more readily in people who had weak powers of attention and so found difficulty in holding their experience in a synthesis. He also developed the idea of levels ("tensions") of energy, regarding mental symptoms as akin to "release" phenomena, breaking loose in the absence of higher organizing functions. Thus, the cure of mental disorder was not to be found merely in passive acceptance of previously unconscious ideas; re-education through work and active stretching of ordinary abilities were necessary in order to develop an increasing capacity for sustained attention and control, when the symptoms would disappear of themselves through more appropriate use of the energy in the mental apparatus. Janet's ideas contain clearly the concepts of hierarchy or level, including quality of energy and its generation by effort and sustained attention. Janet was, however, later eclipsed by his rival Freud and his work neglected by Freud's followers, though Jung and Adler acknowledged their debt to him. Until recently, Janet has remained unappreciated, his works largely unread.

Freud's ideas contain at least three main models of human functioning. The first, anticipated by Janet, views consciousness as an integrative force, so that ideas or emotions excluded from consciousness through anxiety exist autonomously and interfere with the function of the whole organism, producing symptoms of some kind. Like Janet, Freud at first used abreaction (release of repressed emotion) under hypnosis to cure disorders, but soon developed the new technique of psychoanalysis, whereby the patient was encouraged to associate freely while the analyst looked for clues to the interfering unconscious factors in the otherwise inexplicable jumps, breaks, or changes of theme in the associations. Dreams were also seen as a "royal road to the unconscious," once the distortions used to conceal their true meaning were understood. Above all, Freud utilized the phenomenon of transference—a tendency of patients to behave towards the analyst as if he were an important figure who influenced their attitudes in childhood in ways leading to their difficulties—as a vital source of information rather than a tiresome interference with the necessary doctor/patient relationship, as it had been viewed by others.

In this first model, the conscious mind was roughly equated with self-control, the unconscious with instinctive forces. Difficulties with this led to the second model, in which the mind was represented by three parts: the id, representing instinctive forces, the "animal heritage" in terms of the Darwinian theory that Freud espoused; the ego, representing the mechanisms of self-control, the "civilized man," essentially *reason*; and the super-ego, representing the social attitudes, values and standards that the child takes in through identifying with his parents. Consciousness represented another dimension, in that all these parts had both conscious and unconscious aspects. Therapy was seen, at least in the middle-class patients with whom Freud and his followers mainly dealt, largely as bringing about the relaxation of an over-strict superego, permitting the release of pent-up instinctive drives. Later, towards the end of Freud's life and after his death, the focus came mainly on the ego and the necessity to help people to cope better with conflict and stress, rather than to encourage them to escape from it. But Freudian theory, unlike that of Janet, has always lacked any *active* techniques for strengthening the character and achieving this aim.

The third model is based on a concept of development. The child is seen as passing through a number of stages in its psychological growth, in which it has to meet and master a series of challenges. The first year, roughly, is the oral stage, in which the task is to take in food and impressions to build the body and personality. The child is largely passive, receptive, concerned mainly with sensation, and no demands are made on it. The second or anal stage, from about one year onwards, begins when the child starts gaining control of its musculature and develops the possibility of activity, response and choice. It can now say "no," can obey or do the opposite of what is requested or it can perform its excretory functions in ways acceptable or offensive to the parents. In this "age of stubbornness" a compromise must be achieved between the demands of society for conformity, and the need for adequate independence and autonomy, so that clear and definite limits, to provide sufficient freedom for experiment within a context of security and safety, are needed if a child is to develop a clear identity, confidence and cooperativeness. The third stage is concerned with the working out of sexual identity, through the oedipus complex, whereby the child eventually renounces its attachment to the parent of the opposite sex by identifying with the same sex parent. There follows from about the age of six the so-called period of latency, where energy is turned to tasks of social and other learning until the biological pressures of adolescence bring fresh demands for independence and sexual maturity, causing a re-emergence of the unsolved problems of the earlier stages. In this model, neurotic disorder is seen as the arrest, or fixation of an individual's development at a particular stage or a regression to that stage because of difficulties in coping with the later ones.

The recognition of this sequence has probably been Freud's main contribution, and has had profound effects on many fields apart from child psychology. For example, all group situations tend to recapitulate a sequence of phases of this sort—first dependency and submissiveness, later argument and unconstructive opposition, finally cooperation and exchange, provided the leader can, like a good parent, recognize and respond appropriately to each pattern.

Freud's followers have tended to work out details within the framework laid down by him but with a gradual shift towards a focus on the ego and its weaknesses. His daughter, Anna Freud, has been especially productive of ideas regarding the defense mechanisms whereby the ego protects itself from facts too painful to face. The other main original contribution has come from Melanie Klein, also a non-medical analyst, who founded what has come to be called the British School of Psychoanalysis. Klein focused mainly on the developmental processes of the first year of life—Freud's oral stage—which were left relatively unclarified by him and other followers. The ideas were produced partly by extrapolating backwards from the study of adults and older children, but also by studying infants and psychotic patients apparently regressed to infantile states of mind. Her findings have had profound effects on current theories. Briefly, she distinguishes two stages in the first year of life. Given adequate maternal care there is a progressive capacity, from about three months onwards, for the development of awareness of personal boundaries, of the mother as a whole and separate person, and for the integration of the feelings of love and hate which are a natural response to her gratification or frustration of the infant's desires. Achievement of this degree of integration of experience leads to the beginning of concern, protectiveness, and personal responsibility, called by Klein the "depressive position" because the capacity to feel depressed about one's possible destructiveness, and so concern for others, was seen as an important achievement. To the extent that this stage is mastered, greed and envy give way to gratitude and concern for others. Failure to attain this stage results in the individual remaining in the "paranoid/schizoid position" in which the individual is confused over personal boundaries between himself and the world, tends to use others as objects for his own ends, with extensive use of splitting, projection and introjection—for example, blaming others for his own defects or letting others live through him because he lacks a clear identity of his own. Some grasp of these ideas is essential, not only for the understanding and treatment of children and psychotics, but of groups as well. These developmental concepts of Freud and Klein are explored in more detail in Chapter 2.

Adler became Freud's collaborator from 1902 to 1911, when he broke with him and founded his own school. His main contribution was his view of man as "all of a piece," the shape of whose personality would show itself in every thought and gesture as a stick of rock carries its label from end to end. This shape he called the "style of life." He anticipated developments 30 years later in his awareness of the extent to which man was a product of the social matrix, seeing disease as often due to excessive self-preoccupation and avoidance of a true meaning and usefulness within the larger group. He emphasized the importance of aggressive and competitive drives as well as sexual ones, which Freud later incorporated into his own theories, and his concept of the inferiority complex and the resultant tendency of striving to compensate by success have entered the language. He was a generation ahead of his time in the way he worked with whole families and with teachers rather than with children alone. Nevertheless, his influence, although profound, remains largely unacknowledged, which is an interesting psychological problem in itself.

Jung, another collaborator of Freud's between 1906 and 1913, had already distinguished himself before they met. He shared Freud's interest in unconscious functioning (he coined the term "complex"), and the significance of dreams, but regarded the unconscious as more than a container for repressed experience, seeing it as containing a high intelligence which could give meaning to life and complement what was lacking in a person's conscious awareness of himself, or, through a deeper level, which he termed the "collective unconscious," could put man in touch with a higher level of existence. At the same time, premature contact with such experience could shatter a man (like Freud he underwent a "self-analysis" which at times threatened his stability). It was this fundamentally religious attitude which eventually became inconsistent with Freud's positivistic atheism, and provoked the break, although he continued to accept much of what was useful in Freud's ideas, as also those of Janet and Adler to whom in many ways his views were closer. Like Janet, his therapy involved from the beginning a re-educative element and the setting of tasks. He was the only medical psychologist to develop a clear idea of psychological types divided according to emphasis on functions (intuition, thinking, feeling, and sensation), and his further division into introverted and extraverted types has been fully validated by the most hard-headed experimental psychologists. From the beginning he also regarded children's psychological problems as usually expressive of difficulties in the total family system, whereby relief of symptoms in one individual might lead to the development of symptoms in another member.

In the United States, Freudian psychoanalytic theory has perhaps been subject to more radical criticism and modification than in Britain.

W. Reich, though adhering to Freudian concepts of psycho-sexual development and indeed extending these in an increasingly irrational manner towards the end of his life, was a pioneer earlier both in the analysis of the character-as-a-whole and its bodily manifestation in physical postures and tensions. This was a further step from the medical model of a localized disturbance in a psyche assumed to be generally healthy (like a boil on an otherwise healthy body) to a view that the whole organism was likely to become involved in the effort to conceal and compensate for some trauma or imbalance of emotion. His preference for a "frontal assault" on the defensive system (and on the "character armor" which was its expression in the form of tensions in the muscular system) rather than the slow analysis of resistance, anticipates the more active, challenging engagements so characteristic of family therapy today.

Around the beginning of the Second World War, the influence of cultural anthropologists, like Malinowski, Mead and Benedict, drew attention to the different effects of different forms of upbringing in other cultures, leading to modification of psychoanalytic ideas to include more recognition of social factors. Horney, Fromm, and Sullivan were influential examples, and though they were labeled "neo-Freudians" they included many ideas of Jung and especially Adler (who had paid more attention earlier to social forces) in their theories.

Eric Fromm, a social psychologist and psychoanalyst, was interested in the relation between cultural influences and individual development, particularly the human dilemma involved in trying to reconcile the desire for independence and autonomy with the fear of aloneness and the desire for acceptance by society. Karen Horney, a psychoanalyst, was one of the first to emphasize the importance of the here-and-now in therapy and of the patient's real life situation, as well as to recognize that recall of the past and of the origins of disorder could be irrelevant to change and could even become an escape from attempting it. Like Reich, she explored the manner in which the whole character became involved in layers of defensive systems or "vicious circles," each compensating for earlier defects but producing new problems and anxieties in turn, all needing to be unwound in therapy.

H. S. Sullivan, with a background in American general psychiatry rather than European psychoanalysis, was influenced by the analytic concepts emerging from Europe but sought to work these principles out anew, staying as close as possible to clinical observation and seeking to avoid what he called the "doctrines" of the earlier analysts. His developmental concepts, based on level of socialization and the capacity for love—the ability to consider and respect the needs of another as much as one's own—are of special relevance to those dealing with children and families, and for me supplement Freudian and Kleinian ideas. He regarded the "self" as being formed from those inborn tendencies to which the parents gave approval. Parental disapproval of other tendencies led to their being rejected by the individual and seen as "not-me," though they still remained in consciousness. More severe disapproval led to avoidance of awareness of these parts of the personality altogether, or of those external events which might stimulate them into activity, by means of "selective inattention." They then functioned completely outside the awareness of the person concerned (though not necessarily of others) and could emerge as meaningless symptoms, including psychotic delusions or hallucinations. This idea of unconscious factors as more akin to a torch-beam avoiding illuminating certain objects in a dark-ended room, than to a box in which repressed material is concealed, is easier to link with learning theory and what occurs in behavior modification techniques. His formulations anticipate and explain many of the later findings of family therapists concerning the transmission over generations of shared systems of denial and of family myths, as well as the manner in which psychotics become the members who cannot keep the family skeletons in the unconscious cupboard and so have to be split off and shut away in a cupboard (mental hospital) themselves. Sullivan's work with psychotics and obsessionals led him to recognize the necessity for more active support and concern for the therapeutic relationship in the former, and more active control of the evasive intellectualization of the latter, again heralding the more active, challenging approaches typical of family therapy.

The "neo-Freudians," as Fromm, Horney and Sullivan came to be called, tended to throw out the baby of infantile sexuality and particularly the oedipus complex with the bath water of the libido theory as a whole, but there is little doubt that they left an awareness of, and interest in, the relationship between the individual and his social environment to which the conjoint family approaches were a natural sequel. Their work has been as neglected in Britain as Melanie Klein's has been in the United States, and I am sure this is an important reason why family therapy developed so much more rapidly in the U.S. than in Britain. Perhaps it is also a partial explanation of my own adoption of the conjoint approach sooner than many others in England, since my interest in psychotherapy was first stimulated by reading the neo-Freudians, even though I later came to embrace the main ideas of Freud, Klein and others.

Without going outside the broad framework of psychoanalytic ideas, other psychoanalysts have perhaps brought about even greater changes in techniques. E. Erikson approached psychoanalysis from the background of a social anthropologist. He emphasized in particular the notion of *development* and saw much emotional disturbance as a necessary consequence of the "identity crises" that occurred when old patterns of functioning became inappropriate, as the individual was obliged to develop new skills to deal with changes in the world outside (e.g., going to school, marriage, retirement) or in himself (e.g., puberty, pregnancy, etc.). This greater interest in developmental issues, and in providing support for normal processes of growth and adaptation, rather than in pathology and its repair, led to the "crisis-coping" techniques of Caplan in which transitional points between developmental stages are seen as times when individuals or families are not only suffering and vulnerable to stress, but also unusually open to beneficial change and growth, given adequate social support-systems and information conducive to more effective adaptation. H. Searles, D. W. Winnicott and M. Fordham have all demonstrated the possibility of briefer and more effective intervention, if the therapist can learn to involve himself more personally and use his own unconscious, intuitive responses in a spontaneous and constructive way. Winnicott's technique of "therapeutic consultation" expects to produce beneficial change in a few interviews, often even in one. Malan has demonstrated statistically the value of short-term, focused psychotherapy and has recently confirmed that single interviews can sometimes facilitate profound and lasting personality changes, provided the therapist is sufficiently active and involved, can present a clear and accurate formulation of the essential problem in terms of the transference repetition of childhood patterns, and can find a way of stimulating the patient to take responsibility for doing something about his life.

GROUP PSYCHOTHERAPY

Though the dynamic psychologies described above all sought to understand the individual in terms of the influence of the social environment, particularly the nuclear family structure, this interest in the *group* aspects of human behavior was at first confined to theory. With a few exceptions (notably Alfred Adler, who was interviewing whole families together early in the century), the group existed only in the minds of psychotherapists, if at all, while intervention was largely limited to interviews with individuals separately. Even in child guidance practice, where the explanations of children's problems were usually sought in terms of the family context, it was customary for child and mother to be kept apart for history-taking and for treatment, and even routinely provided with different therapists. Fathers were not treated at all in most cases, and siblings were not even interviewed for assessment even though it was recognized early on that they might be more disturbed than the child referred. As far as action was concerned, the focus was still on the individual, even though dynamic psychology had stimulated therapists to think about the group. Freud was no exception, and his seminal writings on group psychodynamics were not accompanied by studies of actual group or family interaction. Indeed, he seems to have shown some resistance to this, and psychoanalytic techniques, which came until recently to have such a dominant influence on psychotherapeutic practice, not only failed to provide for direct investigation of the patient's family and its influence but even regarded any contact between the analyst and the patient's relatives as undesirable in principle.

There were probably deeper and more adequate reasons for this individual-centered focus than those advanced by psychoanalysts at the time. The medical model of a physical body containing a diseased organ, or invading organisms within its boundary, powerfully influenced thinking about human behavior and mental illness even though such a model is usually inappropriate in this field or at least, even in cases where it can be applied successfully, partial and inadequate. More important still, perhaps, was the immense complexity of the social systems being studied, so that it was necessary to examine individuals in isolation, and to establish some basis of knowledge from what could be learned in this limited way, before there could be any hope of dealing with the vastly greater challenge presented by groups and families, where one was obliged not only to consider several individual organisms simultaneously but at the same time to grasp their complex pattern of dynamic interaction. Almost fifty years were to elapse after the study of the individual was begun by Freud and Janet, before the group began to be widely employed for the investigation and treatment of mental disturbance.

There were a number of pioneers, including Pratt and Cody Marsh (who utilized the power of group support in the treatment of physical and mental illness, such as Alcoholics Anonymous does today), and Trigant Burrow, Redl and Schilder, who all studied group interaction from the point of view of analytic ideas. But the main impetus came from the Second World War, which not only focused interest on family relationships through the effects of the evacuation of children, of mothers working in munitions factories and fathers serving in the forces abroad, but also brought psychoanalysts out of their consulting-rooms into the armed services and obliged them to turn their attention to the treatment of cases too numerous for individual psychotherapy and flung together, by necessity, in a hospital ward. In England this led to the two Northfield Experiments, where first Bion and Rickman, and later S. H. Foulkes, experimented in an army hospital with the treatment of neuroses by means of group discussions. The former learned much about the psychological forces operative in the setting but Foulkes, who followed them, was more successful in gaining the cooperation of others and this second Northfield Experiment lasted much longer. Bion later introduced his group methods at the Tavistock Clinic, while Foulkes did the same at the Maudsley Hospital; these two centers have, through Bion and Foulkes and those they taught and stimulated, had a profound influence on the development of group approaches throughout Britain and all over the world. Both men have led others to view the group as a *system*, an organism with a life of its own which is not just the sum of the individual contributors.

Bion's ideas were based mainly on his observations of "leaderless" groups. Having set the group the task of observing and understanding its own intentions and behavior, he perceived the "work group" (the group struggling rationally and purposefully to perform this task he had set) alternating with other phases where indulgence in strong emotionally-determined patterns would interfere with this. Three main patterns were noted: one characterized by dependency (an attempt to make the leader behave omnipotently and take all responsibility), a second by fight-flight (attempts to find solutions by escape or conflict), the third by pairing (the establishment of relationships between a pair of group members while the rest of the group hopefully anticipates a solution from the interaction between the pair). Bion also studied group behavior in terms of the psychoanalytic concepts of Melanie Klein and his most valuable contribution is perhaps derived from this extension of our understanding to primitive "psychotic" levels of group behavior. However, his emphasis on the performance of intellectual tasks (rational understanding, insight, etc.), rather than on processes of growth and integration, makes his technique of questionable value for psychotherapeutic purposes, despite its undoubted contribution to the study and facilitation of task-oriented situations, such as training and factory organization. This view is shared by Yalom, an independent American observer who spent a year at Tavistock studying their methods.

The other Tavistock model, developed by H. Ezriel, views the group in terms of the tripartite psychoanalytic model (superego, ego, id), whereby at any moment the group as a whole is seen as undergoing a conflict between a wish for some form of instinctual satisfaction on the one hand, and a fear of the consequences on the other, the actual group behavior demonstrating the compromise reached. The special needs of the individuals are met more fully than in Bion's methods by interpreting, in addition to the common group theme, each member's particular way of handling the group conflict and the implications this has regarding his intrapsychic dynamics.

Both these models associated with the Tavistock Clinic have been worked out with considerable clarity and they not only provide frameworks for understanding events in the group but also theories and techniques, lacking in the early American analytic models, for making simultaneous use of both intrapsychic and group dynamics. My personal criticism of them is mainly that they tend to reproduce the hierarchical and non-mutual structure of individual psychoanalysis, and by viewing the group too much as a unit turn the group situation back into a two-person, dyadic type of relationship in which comments tend to be focused around the relationship to the leader and the transference towards him. This limits the extent to which the more positive and mature qualities of the patients can be encouraged and developed by handing over to them increasing responsibility for the therapeutic task. In addition, the artificial and withdrawn position of the leader, while valuable for stimulating projection, is capable of a defensive use which excludes him from the treatment process and can prevent the group from going beyond the limits of his own pathology.

Although also a psychoanalyst trained in the individual tradition, Foulkes appears to have been less constrained than others by previous findings applicable to the individual, dyadic situation and, while maintaining a firm base in psychoanalytic ideas, has attempted to work them out afresh in relation to the complexity and potential of the group. His main contribution perhaps lies in his recognition of the inherent growth-facilitating possibilities of the group itself, and his view that the leader's main task is to facilitate these when necessary and indeed to remain open to correction by them himself. Transference to the leader is interpreted where this is dominant, and a here-and-now emphasis is maintained, but other types of contribution are recognized as equally relevant and communications are not forced into a theoretical mold. All communications and relationships are seen as part of a total *field* of interaction—the group matrix—but this awareness of the *whole* is not seen in any way as being inconsistent with an examination of intrapersonal dynamics, which will be a special case of the group theme, a *part* of the whole. This is in some ways not dissimilar to the approach of Ezriel, but in the group-analytic approach all group members take an active part in the total therapeutic process and the leader, though he may be active initially, will increasingly relinquish his pre-eminent position in order to encourage others to take responsibility.

Both Bion and Foulkes worked mainly with small groups of six to nine members (their followers have extended the principles to large groups and to different settings), but others, including T. Main (who was also at Northfield) and Maxwell Jones (who developed his concepts elsewhere in a similar military setting), later expanded awareness of the group dimension to the operation of mental hospitals and initiated the development of milieu and therapeutic community approaches.

In the United States a similar burgeoning of interest in groups took place in the war years, but this was conceptually less productive because two of the more influential leaders—A. Wolf and S. R. Slavson—clung more rigidly to individual psychoanalytic techniques and indeed condemned approaches that viewed the group as an entity in its own right. Group process studies were left to social psychologists, and until recently the two streams have been rather separate there; in Britain they have worked more productively together, as at the Tavistock Clinic and the Tavistock Institute of Human Relations.

As in individual psychoanalysis, concepts have tended at first to be developed in association with the treatment of educated, well-motivated, middle-class patients suffering from neurotic disorder. For this reason, those concerned with helping the socially deprived, ill-educated, poorly motivated or severely disturbed have often found it difficult to utilize the theories developed in the original small-group setting. In fact, borderline psychotics, deviants, sexual perverts, poorly motivated individuals or those lacking insight were at first seen as unsuitable for psychotherapy, but the need to provide psychotherapeutic help for a broader range of problems, particularly through the development of the National Health Service in Britain and of community health centers in the United States, has led to the development of different techniques applicable to a wider range of problems. Differences in techniques found to be necessary have included: 1. a greater degree of structure, such as centering the therapeutic activity around a task—for example, helping parents with their problems by avoiding direct reference to their own pathology, and getting them to talk about their children (Slavson), or helping children to form relationships while they cooperate in some enjoyable activity (Ginott, Slavson); 2. greater flexibility on the part of the therapist and willingness to undertake a more active, supportive and educational role, with a greater use of action methods and focus upon emotional exchange and learning by example and modeling rather than reliance upon verbal communication and insight alone; 3. a willingness to reach out to less motivated individuals, to see them in the community or school rather than to demand that they come to the helping service, and to win a positive relationship with them before attempting to promote change.

THE PLACE OF MAN IN THE UNIVERSE

Another change in basic philosophy concerning the principles effective in the treatment process has been the resurgence of religious ideas which see man as part of a greater, more meaningful pattern with which he must reconcile himself, after the long dominance of a materialistic, atheistic scientism which put man outside and on top of the rest of the universe, seeking to exploit and manipulate it. This religious understanding tends to view the era of scientism as an alienation of man from his true depth and potential, a dogmatic narrowing of experience which exalts intellect and denies a subtler intelligence and information provided by emotion and instinct, values external experience but disparages the inner world, prizes action and movement over stillness and contemplation, doing over being.

This reawakening of a more encompassing awareness has come about, of course, not so much through the influence of traditional Western religious influences, which have declined as they sought to adapt to the secular culture, as by a strange movement of Eastern mystical and contemplative practitioners to the West, often driven out from the fastnesses which protected them for millennia by the growth of coercive materialistic cultures originally copied from the West. One hears of Buddhist, Sufi, Hindu and other gurus teaching colleagues, neighbors, friends and patients; Tibetan monasteries appear in the Californian and Scottish countryside; and the practice of meditation is widespread, no longer a subject of amused curiosity but a regular topic of newspaper articles and television programs, even currently being utilized by the Pentagon.

The psychedelic drugs (mescaline and LSD) played an important part in the early stages, by their capacity to shatter defenses constricting inner and outer experience and bring about a more profound and integrated perception of reality. While at first widely used, and regarded as a short-cut to enlightenment, these "doors of perception" proved to be revolving ones which ejected the subject back onto the drab street of everyday observation after a brief vision of the promised land. An increasing awareness that the peace and relaxation of enlightenment required a long period of effort and struggle for greater self-discipline led many to turn from drugs to meditation, Yoga and other active methods of gaining contact with the "still center," but drugs opened the eyes of many to a possibility previously hidden from them. Similarly, I noticed in my first group, supervised by S. H. Foulkes, that patients apparently "got better" to the degree that they began to lose their burdensome egocentricity and consequent isolation, and to experience themselves instead as part of the human condition, part of the universe, "leaves on a tree."

ENCOUNTER METHODS

The encounter movement has been another area in which this interest in religious understanding (I refer to experience, of course, not to dogma of any sort) has reentered the broad field of mental health. At such centers as Esalen in California, individuals from widely differing backgrounds have brought together ideas and techniques from Zen Buddhism and other religious sources, from dynamic psychotherapy, from knowledge of group processes, with nonverbal modes of communication and techniques of the theater and drama. Alan Watts, an authority on Zen Buddhism and other Eastern practices, who worked at Esalen, has written with exceptional clarity on this integration of knowledge.

Though the encounter movement developed separately from more conventional psychotherapeutic endeavors, and indeed has had an anti-establishment, cultist flavor which until recently has deprived it of fruitful cross-fertilization with other fields, exchange is now beginning to occur as leading psychoanalysts seek encounter training and the encounter movement begins to allow a place for rational thought and objective scientific investigation. A recent book (Lieberman, *et al.*, see Appendix B), the first comprehensive scientific research into encounter techniques and results, is highly recommended.

SYSTEMS THEORY

Following close on the end of the Second World War, and no doubt stimulated by the development of weapons and other military hardware which utilized computers, guidance systems, automatic pilots, radar and other mechanical or electronic devices designed to take the place of a human intelligence, increasing interest was shown in the correspondence between the structure of these machines and of living organisms. Complex mathematical and logical systems were called upon to provide theories applicable to both, and this juxtaposition of machine and man led to strange and startling viewpoints and new concepts as each was seen from the standpoint of the other. The "games theory" of Von Neumann and Morgenstern (1947), the "information theory" of Shannon and Weaver (1949) and Weiner's "cybernetics" (1948) are some examples. General systems theory, which also had its origin at this period, represents an attempt to bring together in an integrated way the common principles underlying these new perspectives; in the words of the program of the Society for General Systems Research, set up in 1954, its aim was "to investigate the isomorphy of concepts, laws, and models in various fields and to help in useful transfers from one field to another" (1, p. 15).

Kuhn has pointed out that scientific revolutions are the consequence of a sudden "jump" to a new conceptual scheme or paradigm, not derivable from theories previously held, and thereby requiring a radical reorientation and discarding of previous habitual modes of thought. General systems theory represents such a conceptual leap, with all the resistance and incomprehension this involves. One might say of it that it is not so much a science, as a point of view, for essentially it is a way of looking at phenomena in their total relationships rather than in isolation from one another. In chemistry we tend to examine the combination of chemicals in a container without reference to what may be going on around. In psychology, as already noted, we have often studied the individual apart from his environment. Group psychotherapy or studies of the family have frequently looked at small groups without considering the impact upon them of the surrounding culture, and so on. In systems theory terms, science has tended to look at the world as a collection of closed systems, phenomena which can be studied in isolation from the totality. This approach works up to a point, and has made possible science as we know it. But as our knowledge expands we become increasingly aware that we cannot easily consider events apart from the context in which they appear, without distorting the truth and reaching misleading conclusions. The increasing interest in ecology, in pollution, in the accumulation of toxic agents in the food-chain is a manifestation of a broader point of view, a widening of our awareness; for me it is symbolized most meaningfully by the photographs of the earth taken by the astronauts from the moon, whereby we see even the globe in its context and can never again quite forget our total dependence on our tiny, beautiful, celestial island.

General systems theory is an expression of this more connected, encompassing attitude, which attempts to formulate basic principles which must apply to all systems, no matter what the size or level. Atoms, molecules, cells, tissues, individuals, groups, societies, and so on are all seen in terms of a hierarchy of *open* systems, like a succession of Chinese boxes one within another, in which the lesser systems have some independence from, yet are also influenced by and a part of larger systems. Ultimately the universe is seen, at least in principle, as a related whole. "There appear to exist general systems laws which apply to any system of a certain type, irrespective of the particular properties of the system and of the elements involved. These considerations lead to the postulate of a new scientific discipline which we call general systems theory. Its subject matter is formulation of principles that are valid for 'systems' in general, whatever the nature of their component elements and the relations or 'forces' between them" (1, p. 37).

Such concepts, and the change in orientation they represent, were influential in bringing together scientists from hitherto unrelated disciplines to study isomorphies between individuals, families and societies, and in showing that disturbed individuals could be "symptoms" of family tensions, or family disturbance in turn a reflection of social disorganization. The concepts of family homeostasis, of feedback, of the double-bind and of symptoms as nonverbal messages are well-known consequences of this new interest.

FAMILY THERAPY

All these developments in the understanding of human functioning and interaction and changes in our modes of perception and thought have contributed to the development of family and network therapy—techniques of working with and modifying natural systems and organizations rather than seeking to change their component parts piecemeal. As we have seen, the first four decades of the century were mainly concerned with intrapsychic functioning, while the forties saw a rapid development of interest in the dynamics and therapy of small and large artificial groups. Though some pioneering work like John Bowlby's took place earlier, the fifties witnessed the emergence of studies of family interaction in many centers, each team often at first ignorant of the work of others, and the decade ended with the publication of the first comprehensive book on the subject by Ackerman in 1958. During the sixties these early speculative theorizations were worked out in detail and subjected to more exacting study, while as the investigators came together to share ideas at conferences and seminars the different theoretical influences which underlay each approach became more integrated. The task of the seventies, already underway, is perhaps to apply this now well-established knowledge on a broader scale, to discover its limits and indications, so that it can find its place within the broad spectrum of our treatment armamentarium throughout the helping services.

I have suggested that the family is an interface where youth meets age and birth and death are juxtaposed, linking the inner with the outer world, the individual with the group. It should come as no surprise that these studies of the family, in the context of its wider social network and in relation to its component individuals, have proved to be a meeting ground and integrating factor for such a diversity of knowledge. Psychoanalysis and its derivatives have entered through Ackerman, Boszormenyi-Nagy, Framo, Friedman and others of the Eastern Pennsylvania Institute group, and lately in England from Byng-Hall and Cooklin. Communication and systems theory has entered particularly through the Palo Alto group of Bateson, Weakland, Jackson and Haley. Satir, earlier a member of this group, later became part of the Esalen team and has been particularly influential in introducing encounter methods and ideas.

From the field of social psychology and sociology, such authors as John

Spiegel, Helen Perlman, Otto Pollak and Frances Scherz have brought the integrative concept of role, seeking isomorphies between the individual, the family and wider social systems. Wynne, Bowen and Lidz have sought clarification of the relationship of individual to family dynamics, and the need for flexible treatment approaches that allow for a change in the individual through the system and vice versa. Minuchin and his colleagues in the United States, and the teams with which I have been associated in England, have extended the growing interest in the needs of the deprived and disadvantaged to the family field and, together with the Galveston team, have demonstrated the value with these social levels (but also with others) of a more educative, modeling approach, based on learning and identification processes.

The next link will no doubt be with the behavioral psychologists, who formerly have kept themselves isolated within their own language of "contingencies" and in their own journals; this integration is, happily, already underway and, for example, at the Institute of Psychiatry and the Maudsley Hospital many trainees study simultaneously under Dr. Isaac Marks and myself while at the Institute of Group Analysis leaders with a behavioral orientation from the Maudsley work harmoniously with psychoanalysts from the Tavistock Clinic and with group analysts from the Institute in the team teaching on the Family and Marital Courses. This integration has been further cemented by the formation of the Institute of Family Therapy (London) by the staff concerned with these Courses, to expand them and provide in addition a more extensive training or qualification; and by the formation of an Association for Family Therapy, as a broadly-based scientific society to facilitate exchange of information and experience, to stimulate research, and to improve training facilities generally.

B FURTHER RECOMMENDED READING

For those who wish at some point to follow up some aspect of the ideas discussed here, the following books are particularly recommended:

1. *General Outline*

THOMPSON, R. *Pelican History of Psychology* (Harmondsworth, Pelican, 1968). Good general survey.

2. *Psychoanalysis, Dynamic Psychology, The Unconscious*

ELLENBERGER, H. F. *The Discovery of the Unconscious* (New York, Harper & Row, 1969; London, Allen Lane, 1970). This is a major source-book relating the ideas of Freud, Jung, Adler and Janet, not only to each other, but also to historical, cultural and social factors. A large book, but well written, easy to understand, a superb and unique work of scholarship for which there is no substitute.

MUNROE, R. L. *Schools of Psychoanalytic Thought* (New York, Holt, Rinehart, Winston, 1955; London, Hutchinson, Medical Publications, 1957). Excellent account of concepts and different approaches.

BROWN, J. A. C. *Freud and the Post-Freudians* (New York, Penguin, 1961; Harmondsworth, Pelican, 1961). Good outline of Freudian concepts and later developments.

FORDHAM, F. *Introduction to Jung's Psychology* (New York, Penguin, 1953; Harmondsworth, Pelican, 1953). Good outline.

FREUD, S. At least the following should be read in the original: *The Ego and the Id* (New York, Norton, 1962; London, Hogarth, 1927); *Three Essays on the Theory of Sexuality* (New York, Avon, 1965; London, Hogarth, 1962).

JUNG, C. A feeling for the man and his ideas is perhaps conveyed most clearly in his autobiography: A. JAFFE (Ed.), *Memories, Dreams and Reflections* (New York, Pantheon, 1973; London, Routledge and Kegan Paul, 1963). The reader can choose which of Jung's other prolific writings may be of most interest, but *The Practice of Psychotherapy* (Vol. 16 of the *Collected Books*) (Princeton, N.J., Princeton University Press, 1966) is of special interest particularly in relation to problems of countertransference.

SEGAL, H. *Introduction to the Work of Melanie Klein* (New York, Basic Books, 1974; London, Heinemann, new ed. 1973). A brief and very clear account of the main Kleinian ideas. Essential reading.

THOMPSON, C. *Psychoanalysis: Evolution and Development* (London, Allen and Unwin, 1952). Good outline and comparison of Freudian and American neo-Freudian ideas.

385

SULLIVAN, H. S. *The Interpersonal Theory of Psychiatry* (New York, Norton, 1953).

ERIKSON, E. *Childhood and Society* (New York, Norton, 1964; Harmondsworth, Pelican, 1950). A seminal work attempting to integrate psychoanalytic and anthropological knowledge.

CAPLAN, G. *Principles of Preventive Psychiatry* (New York, Basic Books, 1964; London, Tavistock, 1964). Application of developmental-crisis principles to therapy and consultation.

WINNICOTT, D. W. *Therapeutic Consultations in Child Psychiatry* (New York, Basic Books, 1971; London, Hogarth, 1971). Application of psychoanalytic principles to short-term therapy.

3. *Learning Theory, etc.*

BORGER, R. and SEABORNE, E. E. M. *The Psychology of Learning* (New York, Penguin, 1967; London, Pelican, 1966).

HAMILTON, M. (Ed.) *Abnormal Psychology* (New York, Penguin, 1967; Harmondsworth, Penguin Modern Psychology, 1967). See particularly Part 3: Conditioning and behaviorism in relation to animal disturbances.

4. *Ethology and Non-verbal Communication*

HINDE, R. Non-Verbal Communication (Cambridge, Mass., Cambridge University Press, 1972).

5. *Group Psychotherapy*

SKYNNER, A. C. R. "Group Psychotherapy," in VARMA, V. P. (Ed.) *Psychotherapy Today* (London, Constable, 1974). Very brief summary of the field.

DURKIN, H. *The Group in Depth* (New York, International University Press, 1964). Outline of principles and schools of thought.

YALOM, I. W. *The Theory and Practice of Group Psychotherapy* (New York, Basic Books, 2nd Edition, 1975). Review of research in group psychotherapy.

FOULKES, S. H. and ANTHONY, E. J. *Group Psychotherapy: The Psychoanalytic Approach* (New York, Penguin, 1965). Outline of group-analytic principles.

GINNOTT, H. *Group Psychotherapy with Children* (New York, McGraw-Hill, 1961). The best introduction.

SLAVSON, S. R. *Child-centered Group Guidance of Parents* (New York, International University Press, 1958). Though focused on situations where the child is presented as the problem, Slavson's method of using an analytic *understanding* of the family dynamics without necessarily making this explicit is of wide relevance, especially with less educated and insightful families, and was an essential component in the techniques developed by the present author.

KREEGER, L. (Ed.) *The Large Group: Dynamics and Therapy* (London, Constable, 1975). A collection of original papers on the special advantages and problems found with large groups, including a chapter by the present author on The Large Group in Training.

6. *Relationship of Psychotherapy to Religion, Meditation, etc.*

WATTS, A. W. *Psychotherapy East and West* (New York, Pantheon Books, 1961; London, Cape, 1971).

NEEDLEMAN, J. *The New Religions* (New York, Doubleday, 1970; London, Allen Lane, 1972); (Ed.), *On the Way to Self-Knowledge: Sacred Tradition and Psychotherapy*. (In press.) Contains a chapter by the present author.

7. *Encounter Groups, New Therapies*

LISS, J. *Free to Feel; Finding Your Way Through the New Therapies* (New York, Praeger, 1974; London, Wildwood House, 1974). Good general survey.

ROGERS, C. R. *Encounter Groups* (New York, Harper & Row, 1970; Harmondsworth, Penguin, 1969). A simply written account by a distinguished enthusiast.

LIEBERMAN, M. A., YALOM, I. D., and MILES, M. B. *Encounter Groups: First Facts* (New York, Basic Books, 1973). An objective survey of present knowledge, embodying research findings.

8. *Systems Theory, etc.*

See Chapter I, Note 1. The paper by Miller and the paperback edited by Emery provide the best introductions.

C ARRANGING FAMILY APPOINTMENTS BY LETTER: SUGGESTED DRAFTS

The following letters have been used routinely for some years in arranging family interviews at the Woodberry Down Child Guidance Unit. Their simplicity is the outcome of much discussion and correction, in the light of misunderstandings by families of previous drafts, and they are reproduced here so that other professionals may benefit from our experience when composing their own.

The first letter (A) is sent when the referral is received by the clinic. Some delay between referral and the first appointment (usually two to three months for less urgent cases, decreasing with the level of urgency) has been inevitable in a unit where there is no restriction regarding referral source, and where the demand is greater than can be met even using family and group methods. The letter informs the family that the clinic is aware of the problem, offers earlier help if the family considers the problem serious enough to request this, and prepares them for the need for the father's attendance.

A. Dear Mr. and Mrs. ――――――――――

   We have heard from ―――――――― about the difficulties that ――――――――
is having and we have been asked to try to help.
   We should like to see you to hear more about this but unfortunately we have a waiting list and it may be about ―――――――― before we can arrange an appointment.
   We find it is very important for both parents to come for the main appointment if we are to understand the problem properly and find a way to help, and as we realize that it is not easy for fathers to get away from their work we will try to let you know in good time so that you can make the necessary arrangements.
   However, if in the meantime you are worried and will let us know, we will try to see you sooner.

Yours sincerely,
(Miss W. L. R――――――)
Psychiatric Social Worker

The second letter (B) offers the appointment and is sent out about three to four weeks in advance of it. This appointment is for a family consultation, in which a psychiatrist and psychiatric social worker usually participate though arrangements may be varied in the light of referral information.

B. Dear Mr. and Mrs. _____

You will remember that I wrote to you after we had heard of the difficulties that _____ is having and I promised to let you have an appointment here as soon as it could be arranged.

Could you both come along with _____ to see _____ on _____ at _____ ?

You may remember that in our clinic we have found that it is very important for both parents to come if we are to be useful to you. We have also found it helpful to get a picture of the whole family, and if you have other children and they can come to join in the discussion at least for a time, we may be able to make quicker progress.

We have many families who are waiting to see the doctor and we try to avoid wasting appointment times, so if both parents at least cannot come on this day, and will let me know, I can then offer this appointment to another family and will gladly arrange an alternative time for you. I am enclosing a stamped addressed postcard so that you can let me know about this. If I do not hear by _____ I shall assume you are not coming and offer the appointment to another family.

I am enclosing a map of the neighborhood which will help you to find us. If you come in at the main entrance the receptionist will direct you to the Child Guidance Unit.

Yours sincerely,
(Miss W. L. R._____)
Psychiatric Social Worker

Naturally, the letter is altered in the case of one-parent families. Also, if great difficulty is experienced in securing the father's attendance during the day, the possibility of an evening appointment is mentioned in the next letter, while explaining that such appointments are limited and will result in greater delay.

At the Queen Elizabeth Hospital for Children another method was used, whereby the PSW undertook a short interview with one parent in order to explain and set up the family interview at a later date. The person seen first was usually the mother, and this different method was probably used because pediatricians in this general children's hospital would often phone to request psychiatric consultation while the children concerned, with their mothers, were attending their outpatient clinics or on their wards. Our immediate response, even with a brief preliminary interview, was no doubt one reason for the extremely high rate of cooperation by families in subsequent arrangements and this is probably the best method where resources permit it.

The third example (C) may be found helpful in a private practice setting

when children are referred, where the psychiatrist does not have the support
of social workers. It seems usually to result in the most suitable form of
attendance on the first occasion. Occasionally, a parent will telephone first
to seek further clarification or reassurance that bringing the whole family is
desirable.

When children are referred for behavior or nervous problems, whether
these are seen as a problem wholly within the child itself, or as a reaction
to other family stresses, it has been found helpful in all cases to arrange
the first interview with the whole family, including the brothers and
sisters as well as both parents. Any other member of the family with
particular influence or information is also welcome if the parents think
this would be helpful.

I would be grateful, therefore, if families would attend in this way at
least in the first instance. Should separate interviews be necessary, these
will be arranged later. The first interview is directed mainly towards
clarification of the problem, its effect on the family as a whole, and
factors which improve or worsen it. No member is expected to divulge
information he regards as confidential or private in this joint session,
unless he wishes to do so.

With young people over the age of 16 or so it is often difficult to know
whether it is best for them to be invited to come alone, or with the family.
Generally speaking they should come alone if they are personally concerned about some problem of their own and wish to discuss it in private.
If, however, the concern about the problem is felt mainly by the parents
or other members of the family, rather than by the young person they
are concerned about, then attendance as a family is obviously necessary.

Where the main problem is felt to be in the marital relationship it is
very often helpful for the whole family to attend on the first occasion
if there are children who appear to be affected, but usually it is preferable
for the couple to attend on their own.

NOTES AND REFERENCES

INTRODUCTION

1. GLICK, I. and HALEY, J. *Family Therapy and Research: An Annotated Bibliography* (New York and London, Grune and Stratton, 1971).

2. STEIN, J. W. *The Family as a Unit of Study and Treatment*. Seattle Regional Rehabilitation Research Institute, University of Washington School of Social Work. Obtainable from Bookstall Services, London and Bristol.

3. BEELS, C. C. and FERBER, A. "Family Therapy: A View." *Family Process, 8,* 280, 1969. Reprinted as chapter in: FERBER, A., MENDELSOHN, M. and NAPIER, A. *The Book of Family Therapy* (New York, Jason Aronson Pub., 1972).

4. BLOCH, D. A. (Ed.). *Techniques of Family Therapy: A Primer* (New York, Grune and Stratton, 1973).

At the time of the final revision of the present volume another introductory book has become available. It is:

GLICK, I. D. and KESSLER, D. R. *Marital and Family Therapy* (New York and London, Grune & Stratton, 1974).

It gives an excellent outline of the field (though British contributions are largely omitted) and is in many ways complementary to the present work. It is most highly recommended for all levels of experience, and contains further extensive references.

1. SYSTEMS, ORDER, HIERARCHY

1. The following books and papers are relevant to the application of systems theory to psychological and social systems. The paper by Miller is a superb outline of basic concepts, and the book edited by Emery is also a good introduction.

BERTALANFFY, LUDWIG VON. *General System Theory* (Braziller, New York, 1968).

MILLER, J. G. "Living Systems: Basic Concepts," *Behavioural Science, 10,* 193, 1965.

BECKETT, J. A. "General Systems Theory, Psychiatry and Psychotherapy," *International Journal of Group Psychotherapy, 23,* 292, 1973.

DURKIN, H. "General Systems Theory and Group Therapy: An Introduction," *International Journal of Group Psychotherapy, 22,* 159, 1972.

PETERFREUND, E. and SCHWARZ, J. T. *Information, Systems and Psychoanalysis* (New York, International University Press, 1971).

APPLEBAUM, S. A. "An Application of General Systems Concepts to Psychoanalysis," *British Journal of Medical Psychology*, 46, 1973.

BRADT, J. O. and MOYNIHAN, O. J. *Systems Therapy—Selected Papers: Theory, Technique, Research* (Obtainable from: Groome Child Guidance Center, 5225 Loughbrough Rd. N.W., Washington, D.C. 20016, 1973).

WILDEN, A. *System and Structure* (New York, Harper & Row, 1972; London, Tavistock, 1973).

EMERY, F. E. (Ed.). *Systems Thinking: Selected Readings.* Modern Management Readings (New York, Penguin, 1970; Harmondsworth, Penguin, 1969).

JONES, MAXWELL. "Psychiatry, Systems Theory, Education and Change," *British Journal of Psychiatry*, 124, 75, 1974.

2. BOWEN, M. "The Use of Family Therapy in Clinical Practice," *Comprehensive Psychiatry*, 7, 345, 1966.

BOWEN, M. "Towards the Differentiation of a Self in One's Own Family," chapter in *Family Interaction.* FRAMO, J. L. (Ed.) (New York, Springer, 1972).

3. LIDZ, T. *The Family and Human Adaptation: Three Lectures* (New York, International University Press, 1963).

LIDZ, T., *et al.* *Schizophrenia and the Family* (New York, International University Press, 1966).

4. WYNNE, L., *et al.* "Pseudo-mutuality in the Family Relations of Schizophrenics," *Psychiatry*, 21, 205, 1958.

5. This case study and some other material in this chapter originally appeared in a paper by the author entitled "Boundaries," in *Social Work Today*, 5, 290, 1974. It is used again here by kind permission of the Editor.

6. The full account of the experiment appeared as a paper by the author entitled "An Experiment in Group Consultation with the Staff of a Comprehensive School," in *Group Process*, 6, 99, 1974. It is abstracted here by kind permission of the Editor.

7. At the time of this work with the school my knowledge of large group dynamics was very limited. Subsequent experience of large training groups at the Institute of Group Analysis and elsewhere has made it clear that large groups require more structure and active leadership in the early stages. This is discussed in a chapter by the author entitled "The Large Group in Training," in KREEGER, L., *The Large Group: Dynamics and Therapy* (London, Constable, 1975).

8. RICE, A. K. *The Enterprise and Its Environment* (New York, Harper & Row, 1971; London, Tavistock, 1963).

9. There is a particularly clear account of this concept in MILLER, J. G., *op. cit.* (1965).

10. This case summary, together with a transcript of the crucial session, appeared in a paper by the author entitled "A Group-Analytic Approach to Conjoint Family Therapy," in *Journal of Child Psychology & Psychiatry*, *10*, 81, 1969. It is reprinted by kind permission of the Editor.

11. SPECK, R. *et al. The New Families* (New York, Basic Books, 1972; London, Tavistock Social Science Paperback, 1974).

2. DEVELOPMENTAL SEQUENCES: CONCEPTS

1. For a concise review of the present situation, see EISENBERG, L., "Child Psychiatry: The Past Quarter Century," *American Journal of Orthopsychiatry*, *39*, 389, 1969.

2. See, for example:

   BOWLBY, J. *Child Care and the Growth of Love* (Baltimore, Pelican, 1965; Harmondsworth, Pelican, 2nd. Ed. 1965). AINSWORTH, M. D. *et al. Deprivation of Maternal Care: A Reassessment of Its Effects* (Geneva, World Health Organization, 1962).

   RUTTER, M. *Maternal Deprivation Reassessed* (Baltimore, Penguin, 1972, Harmondsworth, Penguin, 1972).

3. FREUD, S. *Three Essays on the Theory of Sexuality* (New York, Avon, 1971; London, Hogarth Press, 1962).

   ERIKSON, E. H. *Childhood and Society* (New York, Norton, 1950; Harmondsworth, Pelican, 1965).

   BION, W. *Experiences in Groups* (New York, Basic Books, 1961; London, Tavistock, 1961).

   BENNIS, W. G. and SHEPARD, H. "A Theory of Group Development," *Human Relations*, *9*, 415, 1956.

   SCHUTZ, W. *Firo: A Three-Dimensional Theory of Interpersonal Behavior* (New York, Rinehart, 1960). Reprinted in paperback as *The Interpersonal Underworld* (Palo Alto, Science and Behavior Books, 1966).

   FOULKES, S. H. and ANTHONY, E. J. *Group Psychotherapy: The Psychoanalytic Approach* (Baltimore, Penguin, 1965; Harmondsworth, Penguin, 1965).

   ANTHONY, E. J. "Reflections on 25 Years of Group Psychotherapy," *International Journal of Group Psychotherapy*, *18*, 277, 1968.

4. Kleinian theory sets the origins of the oedipal conflict much earlier.

5. RUTTER, M., *op. cit.* (1972).

6. WINNICOTT, D. W. "Primary Maternal Preoccupation," in *Collected Papers: Through Pediatrics to Psychoanalysis* (New York, Basic Books, 1975; London, Tavistock, 1958).

7. KLEIN, M. *The Psychoanalysis of Children* (New York, Delacorte Press, 1975; London, Hogarth, 1932).

KLEIN, M., *et al. New Directions in Psychoanalysis* (New York, Basic Books, 1956; London, Tavistock, 1955).

KLEIN, M. *Envy and Gratitude* (New York, Delacorte Press, 1975; London, Tavistock, 1957).

8. SEGAL, H. *Introduction to the Work of Melanie Klein* (New York, Basic Books, 1974; London, Hogarth, 1973).

9. SULLIVAN, H. S. *The Interpersonal Theory of Psychiatry* (New York, Norton, 1953).

10. ERIKSON, E. H., *op. cit.* (1950).

3. DEVELOPMENTAL SEQUENCES: EXAMPLES

1. This aspect of development, and the father's role generally, has suffered quite astonishing neglect as compared with the earlier developmental period and the role of the mother. The most interesting study I have found is: TRUN-NELL, T. L., "The Absent Father's Children's Emotional Disturbances," *Archives of General Psychiatry*, *19*, 180, 1968, which supports completely the views expressed in these chapters. See also:

ANDRY, R. G. "Paternal and Maternal Roles and Delinquency," in *Deprivation of Maternal Care: A Reassessment of Its Effects* (Geneva, World Health Organization, 1962).

HOAG, J. M. "The Encopretic Child and His Family," *Journal of the American Academy of Child Psychiatry*, *10*, 242, 1971.

BEMPORAD, J. R., *et al.* "Characteristics of Encopretic Patients and Their Families," *Journal of the American Academy of Child Psychiatry*, *10*, 272, 1971.

BOWEN, M. "The Role of the Father in Families with a Schizophrenic Patient," *American Journal of Psychiatry*, *115*, 1017, 1959.

LIDZ, T., *et al.* "The Intrafamilial Environment of the Schizophrenic Patient: 1. The Father," *Psychiatry*, *20*, 329, 1957.

CHEEK, F. E. "The Father of the Schizophrenic," *Archives of General Psychiatry*, *13*, 336, 1965.

ANDERSON, R. E. "Absence of the Father as a Cause of Delinquency," *Archives of General Psychiatry*, *18*, 641, 1968.

NEWMAN, G. "Felony and Paternal Deprivation: A Socio-Psychiatric View," *International Journal of Social Psychiatry*, *17*, 65, 1971.

LEVI, L. D., *et al.* "Fathers and Sons: The Interlocking Crises of Integrity and Identity," *Psychiatry*, *35*, 48, 1972.

FOREST, T. "Treatment of the Father in Family Therapy," *Family Process*, *8*, 106, 1969.

STOLLER, R. J. *Sex and Gender* (New York, Jason Aronson, 1974; London, Hogarth Press, 1969). See particularly Chapter 18 and pp. 216–217.

4. INNER AND OUTER WORLDS: MODELS

1. BANDURA, A. (Ed.). *Psychological Modeling: Conflicting Theories* (Chicago–New York, Aldine-Atherton, 1971); *Principles of Behavior Modification* (New York, Holt Rinehart, 1969; London, Holt Rinehart, 1970).

2. BOWLBY, J. "Self-Reliance and Some Conditions that Promote It," in GOSLING, R. (Ed.). *Support, Innovation and Autonomy: Tavistock Clinic Jubilee Papers* (New York, Harper & Row, 1973; London, Tavistock, 1973).

   BOWLBY, J. *Attachment and Loss: Vol. 1: Attachment and Vol. 2: Separation, Anxiety and Anger* (New York, Basic Books, 1969, 1973; London, Hogarth Press, 1969, 1973).

3. SEGAL, H. *Introduction to the Work of Melanie Klein* (New York, Basic Books, 1974; London, Hogarth, 2nd Edition, 1973).

4. FREUD, A. *The Ego and the Mechanisms of Defense* (New York, International University Press, 1967; London, Hogarth, 1937).

5. SULLIVAN, H. S. *The Interpersonal Theory of Psychiatry* (New York, Norton, 1953).

6. HENDERSON, E. and HYATT-WILLIAMS, A. "Transference in Family Therapy." Lecture to Tavistock Clinic Family Therapy Conference. 3 July 1973.

7. FREIDMAN, A. S., et al. *Psychotherapy for the Whole Family* (New York, Springer, 1965).

8. COOKLIN, A. "Family Preoccupation and Role in a Conjoint Therapy." Paper read to the Royal College of Psychiatrists, 12 June 1974.

5. CONSCIOUSNESS, COMMUNICATION AND CONTROL

1. BATESON, G., JACKSON, D., HALEY, J. and WEAKLAND, J. "Towards a Theory of Schizophrenia," *Behavioural Science*, 1, 251, 1956.

   This whole view has recently been called into question, and it has been suggested that mental disorder in general, and schizophrenia in particular, may be due more to a failure to meet the ambiguity, contradictions and general nastiness which make up much of human life, in a graded fashion and with adequate support—i.e., that the parents are not so much willfully malevolent as overtly "too nice," leading to an inappropriate "innocence" in the children also, with of course an inability to face and control the inner violence and malevolence which is therefore denied and projected outside. See for example:

   KAFKA, J. S. "Ambiguity for Individuation: A Critique and Reformulation of Double-Bind Theory," *Archives of General Psychiatry*, 25, 232, 1971.

   KURSH, C. O. "The Benefits of Poor Communication," *Psychoanalytic Review*, 58, 189, 1971.

The truth probably lies somewhere between the two extreme positions.

2. LAING, R. D., and ESTERSON, A. *Sanity, Madness and the Family* (New York, Basic Books, 1971; London, Tavistock, 1964).

COOPER, D. *The Death of the Family* (New York, Random House, 1970; London, Penguin, 1971).

3. FERRIERA, A. J. "Psychosis and Family Myth," *American Journal of Psychotherapy, 21*, 186, 1967, and "Family Myth and Homeostasis," *Archives of General Psychiatry, 9*, 457, 1963.

4. BYNG-HALL, J. "Family Myths Used as Defense in Conjoint Family Therapy," *British Journal of Medical Psychology, 46*, 239, 1973.

5. BELL, J. E. "Recent Advances in Family Group Therapy," *Journal of Child Psychology and Psychiatry, 3*, 1, 1962.

6. DARWIN, C. *The Expression of the Emotions in Man and Animals* (New York, Philosophical Library, 1955; London, John Murray, 1872).

7. SKYNNER, A. C. R. *The Relation of Muscle Tension to Awareness of Emotional State.* Dissertation submitted as part of the requirements for the Diploma in Psychological Medicine in The University of London, 1957.

8. See, for example: LORENZ, K. *On Aggression* (New York, Harcourt, Brace, 1966; London, Methuen, 1966).

TINBERGEN, N. *The Study of Instinct* (New York, Oxford University Press, 1969; London, Oxford University Press, 1951).

MORRIS, D. (Ed.). *Primate Ethology* (London, Weidenfeld and Nicholson, 1967).

MORRIS, D. *The Naked Ape* (New York, McGraw, 1967; London, Cape, 1967).

MORRIS, D. *The Human Zoo* (New York, McGraw, 1969; London, Cape, 1969).

ARDREY, R. *The Territorial Imperative* (London, Collins, 1967).

See also, for a profound and systematic attempt to relate ethological knowledge to some aspects of human behavior:

BOWLBY, J. *Attachment and Loss: Vols. 1 and 2* (New York, Basic Books, 1969, 1973; London, Hogarth, 1969, 1973).

9. BULL, N. *The Attitude Theory of Emotion* (New York, Nervous and Mental Disease Monograph #81, 1951).

10. One interesting approach to the recognition of such muscular preparatory sets, usually below the threshold of awareness, was developed by F. M. Alexander and used as the basis of a whole system of postural (and indirectly also of emotional) re-education. The system is described most clearly in:

BARLOW, W. *The Alexander Principle* (New York, Random House, 1973; London, Gollancz, 1973), and has been reported on by a distinguished ethologist both from the standpoint of his personal experience of the technique and its relation to ethological findings. See: TINBERGEN, N. "Ethology and Stress Diseases," *Science, 185,* 20, 1974. Certainly my own experience of this method of heightening awareness and control, under the guidance of the Barlows and their colleagues, has been of the greatest value in developing the increased sensitivity to the emotional significance of postural cues advocated in this chapter.

11. For a clear and concise summary of their position see:

  BEELS, C. C., and FERBER, A. "Family Therapy: A View," *Family Process, 8,* 280, 1969.

12. KORZYBSKI, A. *Science and Sanity* (Lancaster, Penn., Science Press, 1933; 2nd Ed., 1941).

13. WATZLAWICK, P., BEAVIN, J. and JACKSON, D. *Pragmatics of Human Communication* (New York, Norton, 1967).

14. WHITEHEAD, A. N. and RUSSELL, B. *Principia Mathematica* (Cambridge, Cambridge University Press, 1910).

15. BULL, N., *op. cit.* (1951).

16. SKYNNER, A. C. R., *op. cit.* (1957).

17. In trying to observe and organize the nonverbal component of interviews I have found the most helpful information contained in the following papers:

  GRANT, E. C. "An Ethological Description of Non-Verbal Behaviour During Interviews," *British Journal of Medical Psychology, 41,* 177, 1968; "Human Facial Expression," *Man, 4,* 525, 1969; and "Facial Expression and Gesture," *Journal of Psychosomatic Research, 15,* 391, 1971.

6. MARRIAGE: GENDER AND ROLE

1. HUTT, C. "Neuroendocrinological, Behavioural, and Intellectual Aspects of Sexual Differentiation in Human Development." In OUNSTED, C. and TAYLOR, D. C. (Eds.). *Gender Differences: Their Ontogeny and Significance* (New York, Longman, 1972; Edinburgh & London, Churchill Livingstone, 1972).

2. HUTT, C. *Males and Females* (Baltimore, Penguin, 1973; Harmondsworth, Penguin, 1972).

3. HUTT, C. in Ounsted and Taylor, *op. cit.* (1972).

4. WHITING, B. B. & WHITING, J. W. M. *Children of Six Cultures* (Cambridge, Mass., Harvard University Press, 1975).

5. MONEY, J. & EHRHARDT, A. A. *Man and Woman; Boy and Girl; the Differentiation and Dimorphism of Gender Identity from Conception to Maturity* (Baltimore and London, Johns Hopkins University Press, 1972).

6. STOLLER, R. J. *Sex and Gender* (New York, Jason Aronson, 1974; London, The Hogarth Press, 1969).

7. HUTT, C. As Note 2.

8. MONEY, J. & EHRHARDT, A. A. As Note 5.

9. GERSON, M. "Women in the Kibbutz," *American Journal of Orthopsychiatry*, *41*, 566, 1971. For a good study of the psychological factors underlying the Women's Liberation Movement and its benefits see also:

   CHERNISS, C. "Personality and Ideology: A Personological Study of Women's Liberation," *Psychiatry*, *35*, 109, 1972. The "Psychology" issue of *Shrew*, Vol. 4, No. 2, April 1972 is also extremely informative.

10. JOSLYN, W. D. "Androgen-induced Social Dominance in Infant Female Rhesus Monkeys," *Journal of Child Psychology and Psychiatry*, *14*, 137, 1973, p. 140. See also:

    YALOM, I. D., *et al.*, "Prenatal Exposure to Female Hormones; Effect on Psychosexual Development of Boys," *Archives of General Psychiatry*, *28*, 554, 1973. Here a corresponding effect was found, the boys affected becoming less aggressive and athletic than the control group.

11. MONEY, J. & EHRHARDT, A. A. As Note 5.

12. MONEY, J. & EHRHARDT, A. A. As Note 5.

13. DICKS, H. V. *Marital Tensions* (Boston and London, Routledge and Kegan Paul, 1967, p. 32–34).

14. BREEN, D. *The Birth of a First Child: Towards an Understanding of Femininity* (London, Tavistock, 1975). She concludes that:

    > ... those women who are most adjusted to childbearing are those who are less enslaved by the experience, have more differentiated, more open appraisals of themselves and other people, do not aspire to be the perfect selfless mother which they might have felt their own mother had not been but are able to call on a good mother image with which they can identify, and do not experience themselves as passive, the cultural stereotype of femininity.
    >
    > Amongst these well-adjusted women, there seem to be those who tend to be simply adjusted or resigned to a social definition of the new role and those who are more truly in harmony with themselves. ... It would be important and useful if change is to take place to look at the social situation and current life situation of these latter women. Particularly relevant would be an understanding of the husbands' images of womanhood and manhood, motherhood and fatherhood and their ability to reconsider these with the birth of their child and if necessary to free themselves from past images and cultural stereotypes (p. 193).

15. STEINMANN, A. "Cultural Values, Female Role Expectancies and Therapeutic Goals." In FRANKS, V. & BURTLE, V. (Eds.) *Women in Therapy* (New York, Brunner/Mazel, 1974).

    > ... the results were extraordinarily consistent. All over the world, the same pattern emerged, a pattern that showed little variation among different age groups, ethnic groups and educational groups. The pattern, simply stated, was that the vast majority of women

perceived themselves as more or less balanced between self and family orientations. Furthermore, when these same women were asked to describe their ideal woman, there was a similar consistency of response.... The basic quality of this ideal woman...was one of relative balance between the extremes of activity and passivity (as was the most common self-perception of the subjects), with a slight tilt towards family orientation (p 58).

The different results obtained with a group of women belonging to a feminist organization are also interesting, and suggest that the feminist movement, while it has benefited women generally, represents an extreme position that does not reflect the desires and interests of women in general:

> ...a major finding of this study was that whereas most women in previous samples presented self-concepts combining family and self-achieving orientations, the sample of professional feminist women tended to reject traditional roles associated with marriage and the family, and to emphasize instead the primary importance of self-realization and activities outside the home...the results of this study, compared with those of the national composite, suggest the depth of conflict and confusion in educated feminist women (p. 65–66).

16. KELLER, S. "The Female Role: Constants and Change." In: FRANKS, V. & BURTLE, V. (Eds.) *Women in Therapy* (New York, Brunner/Mazel, 1974).

17. CHARNY, I. W. "Marital Love and Hate," *Family Process*, 8, 1, 1969.

18. PITTMAN, F. S. "Treating the Doll's House Marriage," *Family Process*, 9, 143, 1970.

19. The greater control of conception now possible, together with the more permissive attitude towards sexual relationships other than traditional marriage, has given more options as to the degree of responsibility and involvement ultimately accepted, or the timing by which each successive challenge is faced. But I do not think that any of these social changes has altered the fundamental issues though there is danger that they may, by leading us to *imagine* that they change the fundamental issues, facilitate the avoidance of growth-enhancing but effortful experience. However, it will be evident that the "genital-level" relationship regarded here as a sign of emotional maturity resembles in many ways that advocated by such writers as N. and G. O'Neill in their *Open Marriage* (Philadelphia, J. B. Lippincott, 1972), rather than the closed, mutually possessive and demanding interaction that has often characterized descriptions of traditional marriage.

20. FREUD, S. *Three Essays on the Theory of Sexuality* (London, Hogarth Press, 1962).

21. KLEIN, M. *Our Adult World and Its Roots in Infancy* (New York, Basic Books, 1963; London, Heinemann, 1963).

22. See also, for example: MASLOW, A. H., RAND, H., and NEWMAN, S., "Some Parallels Between Sexual and Dominance Behavior of Infra Human Primates and the Fantasies of Patients in Psychotherapy, in MASLOW, A. H., *The Far-*

ther Reaches of Human Nature (New York, Viking, 1972; Harmondsworth, Penguin, 1973). Maslow and his colleagues put forward a similar view to that expressed here—that with increasing maturation towards genital sexuality in the Freudian sense, the power-oriented issue of dominance and submission in male-female relationships gives way to the broader and more love-oriented relationship of *responsibility* and *trust*, in which the roles also become increasingly reversible.

Unfortunately, the careful studies of marriages carried out by Kreitman and his colleagues, using more objective measures, control groups and statistical treatment of the results, have not yet reached a point where this issue can be decided more clearly. One main finding has been the lower degree of cooperation between spouses in the psychiatrically abnormal as opposed to the control group, the greater incidence of conflict being handled either by a more rigid segregation of roles, or by the wife submitting to domination by the husband. (COLLINS, J., KREITMAN, N., NELSON, B. and TROOP, J., "Neurosis and Marital Interaction: III. Family Roles and Functions," *British Journal of Psychiatry, 119,* 233, 1971). Kreitman has acknowledged (personal conversation) that the possibility of an optimum gender-leadership pattern within a *cooperative* marriage has not yet been adequately studied. However, it is certainly of great relevance to our present concern that, in the disturbed, uncooperative marriages, one of the principal areas of disagreement was the management of the children.

7. MARRIAGE: RELATIONSHIP AND SEXUALITY

1. DICKS, H. V. *Marital Tensions* (Boston and London, Routledge and Kegan Paul, 1967).

2. PINCUS, L. (Ed.). *Marriage: Studies in Emotional Conflict and Growth* (London, Methuen, 1960; Paperback, Institute of Marital Studies, 1973).

   BANNISTER, K. and PINCUS, L. *Shared Phantasy in Marital Problems: Therapy in a Four-Way Relationship* (Washington, D.C., National Association of Social Workers, 1971; London, Codicote, 1965).

   GUTHRIE, L. and MATTINSON, J. *Brief Casework with a Marital Problem* (Washington, D.C., National Association of Social Workers, 1971; London, Institute of Marital Studies, 1971).

   LYONS, L. "Therapeutic Intervention in Relation to the Institution of Marriage," Chapter in: *Support, Innovation and Autonomy*, GOSLING, R. (Ed.) (New York, Harper & Row, 1973; London, Tavistock, 1973).

3. BYNG-HALL, J. "Family Myths Used as Defence in Conjoint Family Therapy" *British Journal of Medical Psychology, 46,* 239, 1973.

4. TERUEL, G. "Considerations for a Diagnosis in Marital Psychotherapy" *British Journal of Medical Psychology, 39,* 231, 1966.

5. DICKS, H. V., *op. cit.*

6. DICKS, H. V., *ibid.*

7. DICKS, H. V., *ibid.*

8. Sexual *dysfunctions* are disorders affecting the physical "machinery" of sexuality—failure to achieve erection, premature ejaculation, inability to reach orgasm, etc. Sexual *deviations* (also called variations or perversions) do not necessarily involve any dysfunction, but the aim or object of the sexual drive is different from that generally accepted as normal in the community concerned—a person of the same sex, children, animals, the infliction of suffering, etc. The former are more likely to seek help in changing; the latter are less likely to wish to change, for their choice of sexuality is the most pleasurable of which they are capable; society may however pressure them to change.

9. STOLLER, R. J. *Sex and Gender* (New York, Jason Aronson, 1974; London, Hogarth, 1969).

> ... it is the style these days to blame women when weakness, passivity and effeminacy are found in men, to point especially to mothers as the agents who damage their sons' sense of identity. The above findings do nothing to dispel this impression. However,... another essential factor plays a part in the feminization of a man. It is the failure of his father to be an adequate model of masculinity with whom the child can identify when he needs to turn to a man, and, even earlier in the boy's existence, the failure of his father to act as a shield protecting his son against the urges to feminize him that his mother or sisters may have. As many workers have noted in cases of markedly feminized men, whether they were transsexuals, transvestites, or effeminate homosexuals, their fathers were either physically absent or practically nonexistent although living in the family (p. 217).

10. MASTERS, W. H. and JOHNSON, V. E. *Human Sexual Inadequacy* (Boston, Little, Brown, 1970; London, Churchill, 1970).

For a briefer, simplified account of their views and techniques, authorized and endorsed by Masters and Johnson, see:

BELLIVEAU, E. and RICHTER, L. *Understanding Human Sexual Inadequacy* (Boston, Little, Brown, 1970; London, Hodder Paperbacks, 1970).

11. See, for example: MAIN, T. F. "Mutual Projection in a Marriage," *Comprehensive Psychiatry*, 7, 432, 1966.

PASMORE, J. W. D. and PASMORE, H. S. "Premarital and Marital Problems," *Medical World*, *101*, 302 and 367 and 465 (3 parts), 1964.

COURTENAY, M. *Sexual Discord in Marriage* (Philadelphia, Lippincott, 1968; London, Mind and Medicine Monographs, Tavistock, 1968).

COURTENAY, M. "Troubles in Marriage: The General Practice Setting," *Proceedings of the Royal Society of Medicine*, 67, 776, 1974.

12. CROWE, M. J. "Conjoint Marital Therapy: Advice or Interpretation?", *Journal of Psychosomatic Medicine*, *17*, 309, 1973.

13. STUART, R. B. "Operant-Interpersonal Treatment for Marital Discord," *Journal of Consulting and Clinical Psychology*, *33*, 675, 1969.

14. LIBERMAN, R. "Behavioral Approaches in Family and Couple Therapy," *American Journal of Orthopsychiatry*, 40, 106, 1970.

15. GOLDSTEIN, M. K. and FRANCIS, B. "Behavior Modification of Husbands by Wives." Presented at the National Council for Family Relations, Washington (1969).

16. WEISS, R. L., HOPS, H. and PATTERSON, G. R. "A Framework for Conceptualising Marital Conflict, a Technology for Altering It, and Some Data for Evaluating It." Paper presented to *Fourth International Conference on Behaviour Modification*, Banff, Alberta (1972).

17. EISLER, R. M., HERSEN, M. and AGRAS, W. S. "Effects of Videotape and Instructional Feedback on Non-Verbal Marital Interaction," *Behavior Therapy*, 1973.

18. THOMAS, E. J., WALTER, C. L. and O'FLAHERTY, K. "Assessment and Modification of Marital Verbal Behavior Using a Computer Assisted Signal System (CASM)." Paper presented at the *Association for Advancement of Behavior Therapy*, New York, 1972.

19. TURNER, A. J. "Couple and Group Treatment of Marital Discord: An Experiment." Paper presented at the *Association for Advancement of Behavior Therapy*, New York, 1972.

20. KNOX, D. *Marriage Happiness: A Behavioral Approach to Counselling* (Champaign, Ill., Research Press, 1971).

21. MASTERS, W. H. and JOHNSON, V. E., *op. cit.*

22. CROWE, M. J. Problems and Solutions in Conjoint Marital Therapy. Unpublished Open Lecture at Institute of Psychiatry, London, November 6th, 1974.

23. KAPLAN, H. S. *The New Sex Therapy: Active Treatment of Sexual Dysfunctions* (New York, Brunner/Mazel; London, Baillière Tindall, 1974).

8. THE RELATIONSHIP BETWEEN MARITAL AND
FAMILY INTERACTION

1. This study was originally reported in the form of a paper—SKYNNER, A. C. R., "School Phobia: A Reappraisal," *British Journal of Medical Psychology*, 47, 1, 1974.

2. MACGREGOR, R., *et al. Multiple Impact Therapy with Families* (New York, McGraw-Hill, 1964).

3. POSTNER, R. S., *et al.* "Process and Outcome in Conjoint Family Therapy,"

Family Process, *10*, 451, 1971. However, it must be emphasized that what little *objective* evidence exists is both conflicting and methodologically unsatisfactory, so that the question can only be left open. One study (GASSNER, S. and MURRAY, E. J. "Dominance and Conflict in the Interactions Between Parents of Normal and Neurotic Children," *Journal of Abnormal Psychology*, *74*, 33, 1969) suggested that neurotic disturbance in the children was associated more with hostility and conflict between the parents (as common sense would suppose) than with a particular dominance pattern, though neurosis in general seemed more often associated with dominance by the parent of opposite sex to the children afflicted. Another study, of parental dominance patterns across several different ethnic groups in New York (ZWERLING, I. "Role Variations in Normal and Pathological Families." Paper read to American Psychiatric Association, Washington, May, 1971), found considerable differences in role assignment between male and female parents across the different cultures, and disorder in the children seemed associated less with particular dominance patterns (which were often opposite in different cultures) than with unclear roles and blurred boundaries between male and female parent, and between parents and children. See also the following paper where the different role of the father and mother are made particularly clear: MASLOW, A. H., and DIAS-GUERRERO, R., "Adolescence and Juvenile Delinquency in Two Different Cultures," in MASLOW, A. H., *The Farther Reaches of Human Nature* (New York, Viking Press, 1971; Harmondsworth, Penguin, 1973). See also Chapter 6, Note 13.

4. BARDWICK, J. M. "The Sex Hormones, the Central Nervous System and Affect Variability in Humans." In FRANKS, V. & BURTLE, V. (Eds.) *Women in Therapy* (New York, Brunner/Mazel, 1974).

In this chapter Judith Bardwick provides a concise summary of present knowledge of the relations between the level of circulating sex hormones, subjective experience and behavior. In the fragments quoted (pp. 39–40) she summarizes the conclusions of a paper by: BROVERMAN, D. M., KLAIBER, E. L., KOBAYASHI, Y. and VOGEL, W. "Roles of Activation and Inhibition in Sex Differences in Cognitive Abilities," *Psychological Review*, *75*, 23, 1968. The attributes of behavior which have been shown to be superior in *females* are summarized by the latter authors as:

1. The behaviors appear to be based mainly upon past experience or learning, as opposed to problem solving of novel or difficult tasks. Thus, color naming, talking, reading, etc., are based upon extensive previous experience.

2. As a result of extensive prior practice the behaviors appear to involve minimal mediation by higher cognitive processes. Sensory thresholds represent an extreme of this attribute; but other more obviously learned behaviors such as typing, color naming, or conditioning are termed skilled or well-acquired as they move towards reflexive automatic responses.

3. The behaviors typically involve fine coordinations of small muscles with perceptual and attentional processes, such as in typing or reading, rather than coordination of large muscle movements as in athletics.

4. Finally, the behaviors are evaluated in terms of the speed and accuracy of repetitive responses, as in color naming, rather than in terms of production of new responses or "insight," as in maze solutions (p. 28).

and those in which *males* are superior as:

1. The behaviors involve an inhibition or delay of initial response tendencies to obvious stimulus attributes in favor of responses to less obvious stimulus attributes . . .

2. The behaviors seem to involve extensive mediation of higher processes as opposed to automatic or reflexive stimulus response connections.

3. Finally, the behaviors are evaluated in terms of the production of solutions to novel tasks or situations, such as assembling parts of a puzzle or object, as opposed to speed or accuracy of repetitive responses (p. 28).

It has been possible to change the balance of these different types of ability, in animals, by reversing the balance of sex hormones.

5. Of interest here is a film made by the BBC for the television series "Developments in Social Work," which was shown on three occasions during 1974. It shows the author meeting with a large and poverty-stricken family, and can be hired or bought from the BBC by application to:

BBC Enterprises,
Non-Theatric Film Sales,
Villiers House
The Broadway,
London, W5 2PA.   OR

BBC Enterprises Film Hire Library,
25, The Burroughs,
Hendon,
London, NW4.

6. BOWLBY, J. *Attachment and Loss, Vols. 1 and 2* (New York, Basic Books; 1969, 1973; London, Hogarth, 1969, 1973).

7. COOKLIN, A. "Family Preoccupation and Role in Conjoint Therapy." Paper read to Royal College of Psychiatrists, 12 June 1974.

8. SCOTT, R. D. and ASHWORTH, P. L. "The Shadow of the Ancestor: A Historical Factor in the Transmission of Schizophrenia," *British Journal of Medical Psychology*, 42, 13, 1969.

9. STABENAU, J. R. "Schizophrenia: A Family's Projective Identification," *American Journal of Psychiatry*, 130, 19, 1973.

10. BYNG-HALL, J. "Family Myths Used as Defence in Conjoint Family Therapy," *British Journal of Medical Psychology*, 46, 239, 1973.

11. PAUL, N. and GROSSER, G. "Operational Mourning and Its Role in Conjoint Family Therapy," *Comm. Mental Health Journal*, 1, 339, 1965; PAUL, N. "The Role of Mourning and Empathy in Conjoint Marital Therapy," in ZUK, G., and BOSZORMENYI-NAGY, I. (Eds.) *Family Therapy and Disturbed Families* (Palo Alto, Science and Behavior Books, 1967).

9. THE ETHICS OF CHANGE

1. LAING, R. D. *The Politics of Experience and The Bird of Paradise* (New York, Random House, 1967; London, Penguin, 1967).

   For a very fair critique of Laing's position, by supporters as well as critics, see BOYERS, R. and ORRIL, R. *Laing and Anti-Psychiatry* (New York, Harper, 1971; Harmondsworth, Penguin, 1972).

2. COOPER, D. *The Death of the Family* (New York, Random House, 1971; London, Penguin, 1971).

3. SZASZ, T. *The Myth of Mental Illness* (New York, Harper & Row, 1961; London, Routledge, 1971); *The Ethics of Psychoanalysis* (New York, Harper, 1965; London, Routledge, 1974).

4. FREUD, S. *The Ego and the Id* (New York, Norton, 1962; London, Hogarth, 1942).

5. Several of the ideas presented here were first set out in a paper by the author entitled, "The Minimum Sufficient Network," in *Social Work Today*, 2/9, 3, 29 July 1971.

10. TECHNIQUES: GENERAL APPROACHES

1. See, for example, BOWEN, A. "A Family Concept of Schizophrenia," in JACKSON, D. (Ed.), *The Etiology of Schizophrenia* (New York, Basic Books, 1960); "Family Psychotherapy," *American Journal of Orthopsychiatry*, 30, 40, 1960; "Family Psychotherapy with Schizophrenia in the Hospital and Private Practice," in BOSZORMENYI-NAGY, I., and FRAMO, J. (Eds.) *Intensive Family Therapy* (New York, Harper & Row, 1965).

2. BOWEN, M. "The Use of Family Therapy in Clinical Practice," *Comprehensive Psychiatry*, 7, 345, 1966.

3. BOWEN, M. "Principles and Techniques of Multiple Family Therapy." In BRADT, J. O. and MOYNIHAN, O. J. (Eds.) *Systems Therapy—Selected Papers: Theory, Technique, Research*. Obtainable from Groome Child Guidance Center, 5225 Loughborough Road, N W., Washington, D.C. 20016.

4. LIDZ, T., *et al. Schizophrenia and the Family* (New York, International Universities Press, 1966). See also: FLECK, S. "Psychiatric Hospitalization as a Family Experience," *Acta Psychiatrica Scandinavica Supplement* 169; 39, 1, 1963.

5. WYNNE, L., *et al.* "Pseudomutuality in the Family Relations of Schizophrenics," *Psychiatry*, 21, 205, 1958.

6. BATESON, G., *et al.* "Towards a Theory of Schizophrenia," *Behavioural Science, 1, 251, 1956.*

   JACKSON, D. "The Question of Family Homeostasis," *Psychiatric Quarterly, Supp. 31,* 79, 1957; "Conjoint Family Therapy," *Psychiatry, 24* (Suppl.), S30, 1961.

7. LAING, R. D. and ESTERSON, A. *Sanity, Madness and the Family* (New York, Basic Books, 1971; London, Tavistock, 1964).

8. COOPER, D. *The Death of the Family* (New York, Random House, 1971; Harmondsworth, Penguin, 1971).

9. SATIR, V. *Conjoint Family Therapy* (Palo Alto, Science and Behavior Books, 1964).

10. LAING, R. D. *The Politics of Experience and The Bird of Paradise* (New York: Random House, 1967; Harmondsworth, Penguin, 1967).

11. See the references to the work of Minuchin and his colleagues in notes 11 and 12, Chapter 12. Also: MINUCHIN, S. *Families and Family Therapy* (Cambridge, Mass., Harvard University Press, 1974).

12. MACGREGOR, R., *et al. Multiple Impact Therapy with Families* (New York, McGraw-Hill, 1964).

13. SPIEGEL, J. P. "The Resolution of Role Conflict Within the Family," in BELL, N. W. and VOGEL, E. (Eds.) *A Modern Introduction to the Family* (Glencoe, Free Press, 1960).

14. POLLAK, O. "Issues in Family Diagnosis and Family Therapy," *Journal of Marriage and the Family, 26,* 270, 1964.

15. SCHERZ, F. "Multiple-Client Interviewing: Treatment Implications," *Social Casework, 43,* 209; "Exploring the Use of Family Interviews in Diagnosis," *Social Casework, 45,* 209, 1964; and "Theory and Practice of Family Therapy," in ROBERTS, R. W. and NEE, R. H. (Eds.), *Theories of Social Casework* (Chicago and London, University of Chicago Press, 1970).

16. See for example: LIBERMAN, R. L. "Behavioral Approaches to Family and Couple Therapy," *American Journal of Orthopsychiatry, 40,* 106, 1970.

   PATTERSON, B. R., *et al.* "Reprogramming the Social Environment," *Journal of Child Psychology and Psychiatry, 8,* 181, 1968.

   JOHNSON, S. M. and BROWN, S. M. "Producing Behavior Change in Parents of Disturbed Children," *Journal of Child Psychology and Psychiatry, 10,* 107, 1969; JOHNSON, C. A. and KATZ, R. C. "Using Parents as Change Agents for their Children: A Review, *Journal of Child Psychology and Psychiatry, 14,* 181, 1973. (Good recent bibliography).

17. FRAMO, J. L. "Rationale and Techniques of Intensive Family Therapy," in BOSZORMENYI-NAGY, I. and FRAMO, J. L. (Eds.) *Intensive Family Therapy* (New York, Harper & Row, 1965).

18. BOSZORMENYI-NAGY, I., "A Theory of Relationships: Experience and Transaction" and "Intensive Family Therapy as Process," in BOSZORMENYI-NAGY, I. and FRAMO, J. L. (Eds.) *op. cit.* (1965).

19. FRIEDMAN, A. S., BOSZORMENYI-NAGY, I., *et al. Psychotherapy for the Whole Family* (New York, Springer, 1965).

20. PAUL, N. "The Role of Mourning and Empathy in Conjoint Marital Therapy," in ZUK, G. and BOSZORMENYI-NAGY, I. (Eds.) *Family Therapy and Disturbed Families* (Palo Alto, Science and Behavior Books, 1967).

   PAUL, N. and GROSSER, G. "Operational Mourning and Its Role in Conjoint Family Therapy," *Community Mental Health Journal, 1,* 339, 1965.

21. DICKS, H. V. *Marital Tensions* (Boston and London, Routledge and Kegan Paul, 1967).

22. See Note 2, Chapter 7.

23. BYNG-HALL, J. "Family Myths Used as Defence in Conjoint Family Therapy," *British Journal of Medical Psychology, 46,* 239, 1973.

24. FERREIRA, A. J. "Family Myth and Homeostasis," *Archives of General Psychiatry, 9,* 457, 1963; "Psychosis and Family Myth," *American Journal of Psychotherapy, 21,* 186, 1967.

25. MACGREGOR, *et al., op cit.*

26. MINUCHIN, S., *op. cit.* (1974).

27. HOWELLS, J. "The Nuclear Family as the Functional Unit in Psychiatry," *Journal of Mental Science, 108,* 675, 1962; *Family Psychiatry* (London and Edinburgh, Oliver and Boyd, 1963); (Ed.), *Theory and Practice of Family Psychiatry* (New York, Brunner/Mazel, 1971; London and Edinburgh, Oliver and Boyd, 1968).

28. BELL, J. E. "Recent Advances in Family Group Therapy," *Journal of Child Psychology and Psychiatry, 3,* 1, 1962; *Family Group Therapy,* Public Health Monograph No. 64 (U.S. Dept. of Health, Education and Welfare, 1961; reprinted in England and available from Bookstall Services, 10, Etloe Road, Bristol JS6 7PA).

29. BEELS, C. C. and FERBER, A. "Family Therapy: A View," *Family Process, 9,* 280, 1969.

30. References have already been provided to the work of these individuals.

31. References have already been given to the work of most of the individuals classified under this category, but one member, whom many consider the most gifted clinician of all but who has not committed himself much to paper, needs to be added: WHITAKER, C. "Psychotherapy with Couples," *American Journal of Psychotherapy, 12,* 18, 1958; and with WARENTKIN, J. "Countertransference in the Family Treatment of Schizophrenia," in BOSZORMENYI-NAGY, I. and FRAMO, J. (Eds.), *op. cit.* (1965).

32. GRIMBLE, A. *A Pattern of Islands* (London, Murray, 1952).

33. References for Jackson and Haley have already been provided. See also: ZUK, G., "Family Therapy, Formulation of a Technique and its Theory," *International Journal of Group Psychotherapy, 18,* 42, 1968.

34. WATZLAWICK, P., BEAVIN, J. H. and JACKSON, D. D. *Pragmatics of Human Communication* (New York, Norton, 1967; London, Faber and Faber,

1968). Watzlawick, P., Weakland, J. and Fisch, R. *Change* (New York, Norton, 1974). The following two papers are of special interest in that they both seek to identify different patterns of family malfunctioning, from a "systems" viewpoint: Sorrells, J. M. and Ford, F. R. "Toward an Integrated Theory of Families and Family Therapy," *Psychotherapy*, 6, 150, 1969; Ford, F. R. and Herrick, J. "Family Rules: Family Life Styles," *American Journal of Orthopsychiatry*, 44, 61, 1974.

35. Beels, C. C. and Ferber, A., *op. cit.* (1969).

36. Stein, J. *The Family as a Unit of Study and Treatment* (Seattle, University of Washington School of Social Work: Regional Rehabilitation Research Institute. Copies obtainable in Britain from Bookstall Services, 10, Etloe Road, Bristol JS6 7PA).

37. Howells, J. *Theory and Practice of Family Psychiatry* (New York, Brunner/Mazel, 1971; London and Edinburgh, Oliver and Boyd, 1967).

38. Haley, J. (Ed.) *Changing Families: A Family Therapy Reader* (New York and London, Grune and Stratton, 1971).

39. Bell, J. E., *op. cit.* (1962, 1961).

40. Bowlby, J. "The Study and Reduction of Group Tensions in the Family," *Human Relations*, 2, 123, 1949.

41. Foulkes, S. H. *Introduction to Group-Analytic Psychotherapy* (London, Heinemann, 1948); *Therapeutic Group Analysis* (London, Allen and Unwin, 1964); and with Anthony, E. J. *Group Psychotherapy: The Psychoanalytic Approach* (Harmondsworth, Penguin Books, 1957; 2nd Ed. 1965); *Group Analytic Psychotherapy* (London, Ford and Breach, 1975).

42. Anthony, E. J. "Reflections on Twenty-Five Years of Group Psychotherapy," *International Journal of Group Psychotherapy*, 18, 277, 1968.

43. A "square search" is a method used to search for lost aircraft or ships, when their exact position is uncertain. Beginning from the position judged most likely, or from which the last distress signal was received, the search is carried out in the pattern of a widening spiral (though a "square" rather than a "circular" spiral because this is easier to steer). This method gives the best chance of finding the missing craft in a limited time.

44. Winnicott, D. W. *Therapeutic Consultations in Child Psychiatry* (New York, Basic Books, 1971; London, Hogarth, 1971).

45. Cooklin, A. "Family Preoccupation and Role in Conjoint Therapy." Paper read to the Royal College of Psychiatrists, 12 June 1974.

11. techniques: practical considerations

1. The Rorschach is the well-known "ink-blot" test while the TAT (Thematic Apperception Test) is used in a similar fashion but employs pictures of people in situations that can be interpreted in many different ways. The subject

is asked to give his associations to, or make up stories about, the pictures and it is assumed that what is produced will be influenced by, and so give evidence about, the subject's inner world of hidden attitudes and feelings.

2. BERNE, E. *Games People Play* (New York, Grove Press, 1964; London, Deutch, 1966).

3. SPECK, R. "Family Therapy in the Home," *Journal of Marriage and the Family*, 26, 72, 1964.

4. BELL, J. E. "Recent Advances in Family Group Therapy," *Journal of Child Psychology and Psychiatry*, 3, 1, 1962.

5. This case illustration is taken from a paper by the author entitled, "The Minimum Sufficient Network," in *Social Work Today*, 2/9, 3, 29 July 1971, and is reproduced by kind permission of the Editor.

12. INDICATIONS AND CONTRAINDICATIONS

1. BOWEN, M. "Family Therapy after Twenty Years," in *American Handbook of Psychiatry*, Vol. 5, S. Arieti (Ed.) (New York, Basic Books, 1975).

2. SKYNNER, A. C. R. "Indications and Contraindications for Conjoint Family Therapy," *International Journal of Social Psychiatry*, 15, 245, 1969, reprinted in *Social Work Today*, 2/7, 3, July 1, 1971.

   LYONS, A. "Therapeutic Intervention in Relation to the Institution of Marriage," in *Support, Innovation and Autonomy*, GOSLING, R. (Ed.) (New York, Harper & Row, 1973; London, Tavistock, 1973).

   See also, for a profoundly interesting study of this subject: SAGER, C. J., *et al.* "Selection and Engagement of Patients in Family Therapy," *American Journal of Orthopsychiatry*, 38, 715, 1968.

3. BYCHOWSKI, G. "Psychoanalytic Reflections on the Psychiatry of the Poor," *International Journal of Psychoanalysis*, 51, 503, 1970.

4. COBB, C. W. "Community Mental Health Services and the Lower Socio-Economic Classes: A Summary of Research Literature on Outpatient Treatment, 1963–1969," *American Journal of Orthopsychiatry*, 42, 404, 1972.

5. CHRISTMAS, J. J. and DAVIS, E. B. "Group Therapy Programs with the Socially Deprived in Community Psychiatry," *International Journal of Group Psychotherapy*, 15, 471, 1965.

6. BLOCH, H. S. "An Open-ended Crisis-oriented Group for the Poor who are Sick," *Archives of General Psychiatry*, 18, 178, 1968.

7. BECK, J. C., *et al.* "Learning to Treat the Poor: A Group Experience," *International Journal of Group Psychotherapy*, 18, 325, 1968.

8. WHITE, A. M., *et al.* "Evaluation of Silence in Initial Interviews with Psychiatric Clinic Patients," *Journal of Nervous and Mental Diseases*, 139, 550, 1964.

9. McKINNEY, G. E. "Adapting Family Therapy to Multideficit Families," *Social Casework, 51,* 327, 1970.

10. MINUCHIN, S. "The Study and Treatment of Families that Produce Multiple Acting-out Boys," *American Journal of Orthopsychiatry, 34,* 125, 1964; "Conflict-Resolution Family Therapy," *Psychiatry, 28,* 78, 1965; and with MONTALVO, B. "An Approach to Diagnosis of the Low Socio-Economic Family," in COHEN, I. (Ed.), *Family Structure, Dynamics and Therapy,* Psychiatric Research Reports, No. 4, American Psychiatric Association; and with MONTALVO, B. "Techniques for Working with Disorganized Low Socio-Economic Families," *American Journal of Orthopsychiatry, 37,* 880, 1967.

11. MINUCHIN, S., et al. *Families of the Slums* (New York and London, Basic Books, 1967).

12. MINUCHIN, S. et al., *op. cit.* (1967).

13. MINUCHIN, S. et al., *Ibid.*

14. MINUCHIN, S. *Families and Family Therapy* (Cambridge, Mass., Harvard University Press, 1974).

15. See, for example, the following papers by two colleagues who worked with me in deprived areas of London: ROBERTS, W. L., "Working with the Family Group in a Child Guidance Clinic," *British Journal of Psychiatric Social Work, 9,* 175, 1968; GORELL BARNES, G. "Working with the Family Group," *Social Work Today, 4,* 65, 1973; and the following booklet which includes a number of papers on this theme, including one by the present author. FINN, W. H. *Family Therapy in Social Work: Conference Papers, Sept. 1973* (London, Family Welfare Association).

16. SULLIVAN, H. S. *The Interpersonal Theory of Psychiatry* (New York, Norton, 1953).

17. BOWLBY, J. "The Nature of the Child's Tie to His Mother," *International Journal of Psychoanalysis, 39,* 350, 1958.

18. LIDZ, T., et al. *Schizophrenia and the Family* (New York: International Universities Press, 1966); "The Influence of Family Studies on the Treatment of Schizophrenia," *Psychiatry, 32,* 237, 1969.

19. FLECK, S. "Family Dynamics and the Origin of Schizophrenia," *Psychosomatic Medicine, 22,* 33, 1960.

20. BOWEN, M. "A Family Concept of Schizophrenia," in *Etiology of Schizophrenia,* JACKSON, D. D. (Ed.) (New York, Basic Books, 1960).

21. WYNNE, L. C. "Pseudo-Mutuality in the Family Relations of Schizophrenics," *Psychiatry, 21,* 205, 1958; and "Thought Disorder and Family Relations of Schizophrenics: 1. A research strategy and 2. A classification of forms of thinking," *Archives of General Psychiatry, 9,* 191 & 199, 1963.

22. BATESON, G., et al. "Towards a Theory of Schizophrenia," *Behavioural Science, 1,* 251, 1956; JACKSON, D. D. "The Question of Family Homeostasis," *Psychiatric Quarterly Supplement, 31,* 79, 1957; and "Conjoint Family Therapy," *Psychiatry, 24,* (Suppl.) S30, 1961.

23. FRIEDMAN, A. S., *et al. Psychotherapy for the Whole Family* (New York, Springer, 1965).

24. LANGSLEY, D. G. and KAPLAN, D. M. *The Treatment of Families in Crisis* (New York, Grune and Stratton, 1968).

25. SCOTT, R. D. and ASHWORTH, P. L. "The Shadow of the Ancestor: A Historical Factor in the Transmission of Schizophrenia," *British Journal of Medical Psychology*, 42, 13, 1969; SCOTT, R. D. "The Treatment Barrier: Parts 1 and 2," *British Journal of Medical Psychology*, 46, 45 & 57, 1973.

26. BOSZORMENYI-NAGY, I. and FRAMO, J. L. (Eds). *Intensive Family Therapy* (New York and London, Harper and Row, 1965).

27. STABENAU, J. R., *et al.* "A Comparative Study of Families of Schizophrenics, Delinquents and Normals," *Psychiatry*, 28, 45, 1965. Excerpts from this paper are reproduced by kind permission of the Editor.

13. MULTI-FAMILY AND COUPLES' GROUPS

1. BOWEN, M. "Principles and Techniques of Multiple Family Therapy," in BRADT, J. O. and MOYNIHAN, O. J. *Systems Therapy—Selected Papers: Theory, Technique and Research*, obtainable from Groome Child Guidance Center, 5225 Loughborough Rd., N.W., Washington, D.C. 20016.

2. FOULKES, S. H. See references under Note 41, Chapter 10.

3. SKYNNER, A. C. R. "Comment on Implications of Recent Work in Conjoint Family Therapy for Group-Analytic Theory," *Group Analysis*, 5, 95, 1962.

4. BLINDER, M. G., *et al.* "MCFT: Simultaneous Treatment of Several Families," *American Journal of Psychotherapy*, 19, 559, 1965.

   CURRY, A. E. "Therapeutic Management of Multiple Family Groups," *International Journal of Group Psychotherapy*, 15, 90, 1965.

   LEICHTER, E. and SCHULMAN, G. L. "Emerging Phenomena in Multi-Family Group Treatment," *International Journal of Group Psychotherapy*, 18, 59, 1968.

   DURRELL, V. G. "Adolescents in Multiple Family Group Therapy in a School Setting," *International Journal of Group Psychotherapy*, 19, 44, 1969.

   POWELL, M. B. and MONAHAN, J. "Reaching the Rejects through Multifamily Group Therapy," *International Journal of Group Psychotherapy*, 19, 35, 1969.

   PAUL, N. L. and BLOOM, J. D. "Multiple-Family Therapy: Secrets and Scapegoating in Family Crisis," *International Journal of Group Psychotherapy*, 20, 37, 1970.

   LURIE, A. and RON, H. "Multiple Family Group Counseling of Discharged Schizophrenic Young Adults and their Parents," *Social Psychiatry*, 6, 88, 1971.

LEICHTER, E. and SCHULMAN, G. L. "Interplay of Group and Family Treatment Techniques in Multifamily Group Therapy," *International Journal of Group Psychotherapy*, 22, 167, 1972.

LAQUEUR, H. P. "Multiple Family Therapy: Questions and Answers," in BLOCH, D. A. *Techniques of Family Therapy: A Primer* (New York, Grune and Stratton, 1974).

5. BOWEN, M. *op. cit.*

FRAMO, J. L. "Marriage Therapy in a Couples Group," in BLOCH, D. A. (Ed.), *Techniques of Family Therapy: A Primer* (New York, Grune and Stratton, 1974).

6. GURMAN, A. S. "Group Marital Therapy: Clinical and Empirical Implications for Outcome Research," *International Journal of Group Psychotherapy*, 21, 174, 1971.

For a good brief introduction to the technique see also: LINDEN, M. E., *et al.* "Group Psychotherapy of Couples in Marriage Counselling," *International Journal of Group Psychotherapy*, 18, 313, 1968.

14. CO-THERAPY, TEAMWORK, TRAINING

1. SAGER, C. J. "An Overview of Family Therapy," *International Journal of Group Psychotherapy*, 18, 302, 1968.

For a very clear exposition of the need for those concerned with training to be aware of the *model* they are providing through the form of training itself, and a deliberate use of this aspect, see also: WALROND-SKINNER, S. "Training for Family Therapy," *Social Work Today*, 5/5, 149, 30 May 1974.

2. ANDERSON, B. N., *et al.* "Resident Training in Cotherapy Groups," *International Journal of Group Psychotherapy*, 22, 192, 1972.

BENJAMIN, S. E. "Cotherapy: A Growth Experience for Therapists," *International Journal of Group Psychotherapy*, 22, 199, 1972.

DAVIS, F. B. and LOHR, N. E. "Special Problems with the Use of Cotherapists in Group Psychotherapy," *International Journal of Group Psychotherapy*, 21, 143, 1971.

MINTZ, E. E. "Male-Female Cotherapists: Some Values and Some Problems," *American Journal of Psychotherapy*, 19, 293, 1965.

MACLENNAN, B. W. "Cotherapy," *International Journal of Group Psychotherapy*, 15, 154, 1965.

MCGEE, T. F. and SCHUMAN, B. N. "The Nature of the Cotherapy Relationship," *International Journal of Group Psychotherapy*, 20, 25, 1970.

WOODY, R. H. "Conceptualizing the 'Shared Patient': Treatment Orientations of Multiple Therapists," *International Journal of Group Psychotherapy*, 22, 228, 1972.

3. BERNE, E. *Games People Play* (New York, Grove Press, 1964; London, Deutch, 1966).

4. BRODY, W., and HAYDEN, M. "Intra-Team Reactions: Their Relation to the Conflicts of the Family in Treatment," *American Journal of Orthopsychiatry*, 27, 349, 1957.

5. MAIN, T. F. "The Ailment," *British Journal of Medical Psychology*, 30, 129, 1957.

6. KAFKA, J. S. and McDONALD, J. W. "The Latent Family in the Intensive Treatment of the Hospitalized Schizophrenic Patient," *Current Psychiatric Therapies, Vol. 5* (New York, Grune and Stratton, 1965).

7. SKYNNER, A. C. R. "A Family of Family Casework Agencies," *International Journal of Group Psychotherapy*, 18, 352, 1968.

8. SONNE, J. C. and LINCOLN, G. L. "Heterosexual Co-therapy Team Experiences during Family Therapy," *Family Proces*, 4, 177, 1965; "The Importance of Heterosexual Co-therapy Relationship in the Construction of a Family Image," in COHN, I. (Ed.) *Family Structure, Dynamics and Therapy*: Psychiatric Research Reports No. 20, American Psychiatric Association.

9. FRIEDMAN, A. S. *et al.*, See note 19, Chapter 10.

10. MACGREGOR, R., *et al.*, See Note 2, Chapter 8.

11. SKYNNER, A. C. R. "The Large Group in Training," in KREEGER, L. (Ed.) *The Large Group: Dynamics and Therapy* (London, Constable, 1975).

12. SKYNNER, A. C. R. "Group-Analytic Themes in Training and Case-Discussion Groups," in *Selected Lectures: 6th International Congress of Psychotherapy* (New York, Basel & Karger, 1965); "A Family of Family Casework Agencies," *op. cit.*

13. The Department of Psychiatry at McMaster University, Hamilton, Ontario, Canada, under the leadership of Professor Nathan Epstein, has been particularly active in attempting to conceptualize family psychotherapy, to break down the process into its elements, and to find more effective methods of communicating these to students by combinations of conceptual instruction and simultaneous illustration of the principles using audio-visual aids.
See: EPSTEIN, N. B. "Training for Family Therapy within a Faculty of Medicine." Paper presented at the National Conference on Training in Family Therapy, Philadelphia, 1972; LEVIN, S. "Training Family Therapists by Setting Instructional Objectives." Videotape Learning Resources of the Department of Psychiatry, McMaster University, 1972; WALSH, W. "The Development of the McMaster Programme in Medical Education," *British Journal of Hospital Medicine*, December 1973, p. 722.

14. Those wishing to obtain information about the hire of these video-tapes or films should write to:
Film—Videotape Library
Philadelphia Child Guidance Clinic

15. DUHL, F. J., KANTOR, D. and DUHL, B. S. "Learning, Space and Action in Family Therapy: A Primer of Sculpture," in BLOCH, D. A. (Ed.) *Techniques of Family Therapy: A Primer* (New York, Grune & Stratton, 1974).

16. BOWEN, M. See note 1, Chapter 13.

17. PAUL, N. Unlike Bowen, Paul appears not to have written on this work. Our knowledge of his techniques is derived from Dr. Stuart Lieberman, an American psychiatrist who worked with Paul and is now Consultant Psychiatrist at St. George's Hospital, London, and a member of staff on the Institute of Group Analysis Family and Marital Group Work Course.

18. ANONYMOUS. "Towards a Differentiation of a Self in One's Own Family." In: FRAMO, J. L. *Family Interaction* (New York, Springer, 1972).

19. MORSE, S. J. "Perfecting the Parents: A Family Romance Resistance," *American Journal of Orthopsychiatry*, *3*, 410, 1973.

20. Tavistock Clinic/Nathan Ackerman Institute Conference on Family Therapy, held at the American School, London, July, 1974.

21. ROSENBERG, P. and CHILGREN, R. "Sex Education Discussion Groups in a Medical Setting," *International Journal of Group Psychotherapy*, *23*, 23, 1973.

22. Dr. Elizabeth Stanley, a British physician who has recently returned to Britain after some years in the United States studying these more active methods of sexual re-education and therapy, has begun to introduce the ideas to British medical schools and other professional organizations.

23. A number of films dealing with problems of interviewing where sexual problems need to be discussed are available from: Films Division, Ortho Pharmaceutical Ltd., Saunderton, High Wycombe, Bucks. HP14 4HJ. Particularly recommended is the Film Sexuality and Communication in which Dr. Avinoam Chernick and Dr. Beryl Chernick take turns in role-playing doctor and patient discussing sexual difficulties.

15. RESULTS, FREQUENCY OF MEETINGS

1. WELLS, R. A., DILKES, T. C. and TRIVELLI, N. "The Results of Family Therapy: A Critical Review of the Literature," *Family Process*, *11*, 189, 1972.

2. LANGSLEY, D. G., *et al.* "Family Crisis—Results and Implications," *Family Process*, 7, 145, 1968.

   LANGSLEY, D. G., *et al.* "Follow-up Evaluation of Family Crisis Therapy," *American Journal of Orthopsychiatry*, *39*, 753, 1969.

3. GURMAN, A. S. "The Effects ond Effectiveness of Marital Therapy: A Review of Outcome Research," *Family Process*, *12*, 145, 1973.

4. FRIEDMAN, A. S., *et al.* See note 19, Chapter 10.

5. BOWEN, M. "Family Psychotherapy," *American Journal of Orthopsychiatry*, *31*, 40, 1961.

6. MACGREGOR, R., *et al.* See note 12, Chapter 10.

7. RACHMAN, S. H. "The Effects of Psychotherapy," in EYSENCK, H. J. (Ed.), *The Handbook of Abnormal Psychology* (San Diego, Knapp, 1973; London, Pitman, 1960, 2nd Ed., 1973), p. 808. Eysenck still regards this formula as an acceptable estimate of the likelihood of "spontaneous" improvement (personal communication), though it is here extrapolated far beyond the periods of time concerned in material on which the formula was based. The extrapolated figures must therefore not be taken too seriously, but they suggest that *if* the results claimed for conjoint interventions were confirmed by comparison with proper control groups, the results might be very significant indeed.

8. SOLOMON, M. L. "Family Therapy Drop-outs: Resistance to Change," *Canadian Psychiatric Association Journal*, *14*, 21, 1969.

9. MALAN, D. H. "Therapeutic Factors in Analytically Oriented Brief Psychotherapy," in GOSLING, R. (Ed.), *Support, Innovation and Autonomy* (New York: Harper & Row, 1973; London, Tavistock, 1973).

10. BOWEN, M. "Principles and Techniques of Multiple Family Therapy," in BRADT, J. O. and MOYNIHAN, O. J. *Systems Therapy—Selected Papers*. See Chapter 13, Note 1.

    HATFIELD, F. E. S. "A System of Family Therapy Suitable for Use by Family Doctors in General Practice." This paper (unpublished, but copies obtainable from Dr. Hatfield at 212, High Street, Ongar, CM5 9JJ, Essex) describes short-term techniques based on Bowen's concepts, suitable for use within the bounds of an ordinary surgery consultation, as well as longer-term work.

11. HEARD, D. H. "Crisis Intervention Guided by Attachment Concepts—a Case Study," *Journal of the Association of Child Psychology and Psychiatry*, *15*, 111, 1974.

    See also: ARGLES, P. and MACKENZIE, M. "Crisis Intervention with a Multiproblem Family—a Case Study," *Journal of Child Psychology and Psychiatry*, *11*, 187, 1970.

12. CAPLAN, G. *Principles of Preventive Psychiatry* (New York, Basic Books, 1964; London, Tavistock, 1964).

13. CROWE, M. J. "Conjoint Marital Therapy: Advice or Interpretation," *Journal of Psychosomatic Research*, *17*, 309, 1973.

14. CROWE, M. J. "Problems and Solutions in Conjoint Marital Therapy," Open Lecture delivered at the Institute of Psychiatry, London, 6 November 1974 (unpublished).

15. CROWE, M. J., *op. cit.*

16. WEAKLAND, J. H., FISCH, R., WATZLAWICK, P. and BODIN, A. M. "Brief Therapy: Focussed Problem Resolution," *Family Process*, *13*, 141, 1974.

16. APPLICATION OF FAMILY TECHNIQUES TO THE STUDY
OF A SYNDROME: SCHOOL PHOBIA

1. JOHNSON, A. M., *et al.* "School Phobia," *American Journal of Orthopsychiatry,* *11,* 702, 1941.

2. WARREN, W. "Acute Neurotic Breakdown in Children with Refusal to Go to School," *Archives of Diseases of Childhood, 18,* 266, 1948.

3. HERSOV, L. A. "Persistent Non-Attendance at School," *Journal of Child Psychology and Psychiatry, 1,* 130, 1960.

4. COOLIDGE, J. C., HAHN, P. B. and PECK, A. L. "School Phobia: Neurotic Crisis or Way of Life," *American Journal of Orthopsychiatry,* 27, 296, 1957.

5. KAHN, J. H. and NURSTEN, J. P. "School Refusal: A Comprehensive View of School Phobia and Other Failures of School Attendance," *American Journal of Orthopsychiatry, 32,* 707, 1962.

6. DAVIDSON, S. "School Phobia as a Manifestation of Family Disturbance," *Journal of Child Psychology and Psychiatry, 1,* 270, 1961.

7. BOWLBY, J. *Attachment and Loss: Vol. 2* (New York, Basic Books, 1973; London, Hogarth, 1973). See Chapter 18 particularly.

8. MALMQUIST, C. P. "School Phobia: A Problem in Family Neurosis," *Journal of the American Academy of Child Psychiatry, 4,* 293, 1965.

9. WALDFOGEL, S., COOLIDGE, J. C., and HAHN, P. B. "The Development, Meaning and Management of School Phobia," *American Journal of Orthopsychiatry, 27,* 754, 1957.

10. LIPPMAN, H. S. "School Phobia Workshop: Discussion," *American Journal of Orthopsychiatry, 27,* 776, 1957.

11. COOLIDGE, J. C., *et al., op. cit.* (1957).

12. THOMPSON, J. "Children's Fears in Relation to School Attendance," *Bulletin of the National Association of School Social Workers,* Sept. 1948.

13. GOLDBERG, T. B. "Factors in the Development of School Phobia," *Smith College Studies in Social Work, 23,* 227, 1953.

14. HERSOV, L. A. "Refusal to Go to School," *Journal of Child Psychology and Psychiatry, 1,* 137, 1960.

15. WALDFOGEL, S., *et al., op. cit.* (1957).

16. HERSOV, L. A., see note 14.

17. KAHN, J. H. and NURSTEN, J. P., *op cit.* (1962).

18. COLM, H. C. "Phobias in Children," *Psychoanalysis and Psychoanalytic Review, 46,* 65, 1959.

19. LEVENSON, E. A. "The Treatment of School Phobia in the Young Adult," *American Journal of Psychotherapy, 15,* 539, 1961.

20. LEVENTHAL, T. "Self-image in School Phobia," *American Journal of Orthopsychiatry, 34,* 685, 1964.

21. RADIN, S. S. "Psychodynamic Aspects of School Phobia," *Comprehensive Psychiatry, 8,* 119, 1967.

22. WINNICOTT, D. W. "Primary Maternal Preoccupation" in *Collected Papers: Through Pediatrics to Psychoanalysis* (New York, Basic Books, 1975; London, Tavistock, 1958).

23. Bowlby, in the recent work already referred to (see Note 7) expresses a view that is very similar in some respects, though different in others. Using the word "attachment" in a strictly defined way, based on the ethological concept that immature members of many species, including man, have an inborn, survival-facilitating tendency to maintain proximity to adults caring for them (usually or especially the mother), he regards the commonest form of "school phobia" as a response to a parent who is "...intensely anxious about the availability of her own attachment figures and unconsciously...inverting the normal parent-child relationship by requiring the child to be the parent figure and adopting the role of child herself. Thus the child is expected to care for the parent and the parent seeks to be cared for and comforted by the child. As a rule the inversion is camouflaged. Mother claims that the person who is in special need of care and protection, and who is receiving it, is the child...." (pp. 265–266) Bowlby emphasizes the parental attachment, which in my experience is certainly true, but does not attach enough importance to the inversion which, through *projective identification,* leads to a double reversal. For a child to have to support a fearful, dependent parent is difficult enough, but in addition to this burden there is a demand that the situation be incorrectly perceived; the parent's dependency is not only alternately exhibited and *denied,* but also *attributed* to the child, producing pathology of a different order altogether. The child can scarcely wean himself from his own attachment when he has become totally confused as to where his attachment ends and that of others begins. Also, when he in turn becomes a parent, he will perpetuate the problem and be unable to help his child define, face and master the same challenge.

Bowlby also makes too much, in my view, of the role of real fears based on parental hints of illness and threats to desert or commit suicide in the genesis of such phobic states. Though these factors are important and have undoubtedly been neglected, such parental behavior is more meaningfully understood as part of the general pattern of manipulative control that characterizes all members of such families, which I have emphasized in this chapter. It is interesting that the main example Bowlby cites (pp. 274–6) in support of this aspect of his views (See ARGLES, P. and MACKENZIE, M. "Crisis intervention with a Multi-Problem Family: A Case Study," *Journal of Child Psychology and Psychiatry, 11,* 187, 1970) in fact supports my own just as clearly. The therapists took the step, which they make clear was an unusual one for them in such cases, of *setting a time limit* (three months) to the treatment, and making it plain from the beginning that the Local Authority would not be prevented from taking alternative action if school attendance had not by then been resumed. They thus introduced structure, control and limits into a chaotic situation, as in the successful cases described here, *in addition* to providing reliable support. This aspect of phobic disorders and their treatment is given little attention in Bowlby's ideas; the father is seen almost entirely as a substitute attachment figure rather than as a parent with a definite role which is quite different from, and complementary to, that of the mother.

24. KENNEDY, W. A. "School Phobia; Rapid Treatment of Fifty Cases," *Journal of Abnormal Psychology*, 70, 285, 1965.

25. FROMMER, E. A. "Treatment of Childhood Depression with Antidepressant Drugs," *British Medical Journal*, 1, 729, 1967.

26. I would like to thank those colleagues, education officers and education welfare officers who provided generous help with the follow-up, particularly Miss Moger and Mr. Terry of Area 4, Inner London Education Authority, from whose area most of the cases were referred. I would also like to acknowledge the help of my psychiatric social worker co-therapists, both in the treatment process and in discussions of the issues involved, particularly Mrs. P. Goldblatt, my co-therapist with "the exception that proved the rule," and the late Miss P. A. Brierley, with whom most of the subsequent work with school phobics was done. I am grateful also to the latter for permission to use some of her unpublished research material.

27. Follow-up of one boy, however, was limited to a year, after which the family moved away and has not been traced. During that year his attendance was regular.

28. RODRIGUEZ, A., RODRIGUEZ, M., and EISENBERG, L., "The Outcome of School Phobia; A Follow-up Study based on 41 Cases," *American Journal of Psychiatry*, 116, 540, 1959.

APPENDIX A

1. von Bertalanffy, L., *General Systems Theory*, New York: Braziller, 1948.

Index